PROSPECTING

PROSPECTING

From Reader Response to Literary Anthropology

Wolfgang Iser

The Johns Hopkins University Press
Baltimore and London

© 1989 The Johns Hopkins University Press
All rights reserved
Printed in the United States of America

The Johns Hopkins University Press
701 West 40th Street
Baltimore, Maryland 21211

The Johns Hopkins Press Ltd., London

The paper used in this publication meets the minimum requirements of American National Standard for Information Sciences—Permanence of Paper for Printed Library Materials, ANSI Z39.48-1984.

Library of Congress Cataloging-in-Publication Data

Iser, Wolfgang.
    Prospecting: from reader response to literary anthropology /
Wolfgang Iser.
        p.   cm.
    Bibliography: p.
    Includes index.
    ISBN 0-8018-3792-8 (alk. paper)
    1. Criticism.   I. Title.
PN83.I84   1989   88-46065
801'.95   CIP

Contents

Preface

The essays in this book cover a range of interests which, in spite of their apparent diversity, are closely connected. What links them is literary theory and its application to texts. Together they outline a stage of transition between reader response and literary anthropology.

What has come to be called reader-response criticism provides a framework for understanding text processing, revealing the way in which the reader's faculties are both acted upon and activated. By putting the response-inviting structures of a literary text under scrutiny, a theory of aesthetic response provides guidelines for elucidating the interaction between text and reader. In part 1, the essays pivot on my formulation of such a theory in *The Act of Reading*. They delineate the steps that led to it and cover some of the subsequent discussions it sparked off.

The paradigms of part 2 show how the framework focused on in part 1 is applied and, in the same process, modified. I have deliberately chosen areas of literature which are worlds apart in order to demonstrate the ability of reader-response criticism to resuscitate a genre like pastoralism, which seems to be buried in the past, and to shed light on the enigmatic side of modern literature.

The need for theory becomes paramount in the last of the interpretations, which deals with the stifled laugh in Beckett's theater. If a literary text does something to its readers, it also simultaneously reveals something about them. Thus literature turns into a divining rod, locating our dispositions, desires, inclinations, and eventually our overall makeup. The question arises as to why we need this particular medium. Questions of this kind point to a literary anthropology that is both an underpinning and an offshoot of reader-response criticism.

The essays of part 3 tentatively approach this area with a view to mapping it out. They are signposts to what literature may tell us about our anthropological makeup. The quest for understanding that makeup may do away with the old intrinsic-extrinsic dichotomy, as the special nature of literature will enable us to explore the human need for make-believe even when it is known to be what it is.

A great many of these essays were first drafted as lectures addressed to a variety of audiences; furthermore, they present a shift of interest over the years, arising out of what remained open ended in reader-response criticism. Consequently, they are written in different styles and proceed at varying levels of abstraction.

Two essays in part 3 make substantial reference to my essay "Feigning in Fiction," not included in this collection. I refrained from reprinting it here, since it will form a chapter in the book I am currently writing concerning the fictive and the imaginary. I intend to provide in that book a systematic view of what might be considered literary anthropology. I have, however, reproduced certain aspects of that essay in order to be able to develop implications necessary for the argument put forward in "Representation: A Performative Act" and "Toward a Literary Anthropology." I ask the reader's forgiveness for having reproduced two virtually identical sections in the essays mentioned; this seemed to me unavoidable as I use the argument for different inferences.

Acknowledgments

I thank the publishers and editors for permission to reprint the following essays: "Indeterminancy and the Reader's Response in Prose Fiction," in *Aspects of Narrative* (Selected Papers from the English Institute), ed. J. Hillis Miller. New York: Columbia University Press, 1971. "Interaction between Text and Reader," in Susan R. Suleiman and Inge Crosman, eds., *The Reader in the Text: Essays on Audience and Interpretation.* Copyright © 1980 by Princeton University Press. Reprinted with permission of Princeton University Press. "*Ulysses* and the Reader," in *James Joyce Broadsheet* 9 (1982). "The Pattern of Negativity in Beckett's Prose," in *The Georgia Review* (1975). "The Art of Failure: The Stifled Laugh in Beckett's Theater," in *Bucknell Review, Theories of Reading, Looking and Listening,* ed. Harry R. Garvin. Lewisburg, Pa., 1981. "Changing Functions of Literature," in *London German Studies III,* ed. J. P. Stern (Publications of the Institute of Germanic Studies 38), pp. 162–79. London: Institute of Germanic Studies, 1986. "Representation: A Performative Act," in *The Aims of Representation: Subject/ Text/History,* ed., Murray Krieger. New York: Columbia University Press, 1987. "The Play of the Text," in *Languages of the Unsayable,* ed. Sanford Budick and Wolfgang Iser. New York: Columbia University Press, 1989. "Toward a Literary Anthropology," in Ralph Cohen, *The Future of Literary Theory.* New York: Routledge, 1989.

PART I
READER RESPONSE IN PERSPECTIVE

ONE
INDETERMINACY AND THE READER'S RESPONSE IN PROSE FICTION

n place of a hermeneutics we need an erotics of art."[1] With this irony-edged demand Susan Sontag, in her essay "Against Interpretation," aimed at that form of textual interpretation which is concerned with finding out the meaning contained in literary texts. What was originally a useful activity—the process whereby damaged texts were made legible, or intelligible, by supplying meaning to the damaged parts—has, according to Sontag, mushroomed more and more into a distrust of the perceptible form of the text, whose so-called hidden meaning supposedly can only be revealed through interpretation.[2] That texts have contents, which in turn are carriers of meaning, was until the arrival of modern art an almost uncontested assumption. Therefore interpretation was always legitimate if it reduced the text to meaning. The advantage of this was that meanings could be generalized, that they represented established conventions, and that they brought out accepted or at least understandable values. Interpretation served the purpose of conveying meaning, in order that comprehension might be assured. Texts had to be seen in the context of what was already familiar or comprehensible to the reader. The zeal of critics for classification—their passion for pigeonholing, one might almost call it—only subsided when some special significance of the content had been discovered and its value ratified by means of what was already common knowledge. Referral of the text to some already existing frame of reference became an essential aim of this method of interpretation, by means of which the sharpness of a text was inevitably dulled.

But how shall we then describe the dynamic character of a text? Can one, in fact, assess the keen disturbance so often experienced in reading serious literature? Some texts certainly have stimulating moments that disturb, and even provoke a certain nervousness in the reader—a reaction that Susan Sontag might describe as having to do with the "erotics of art." If texts actually possessed only the meaning brought to light by interpretation, then there would remain very little else for the reader. He could only take it or leave it. The fundamental question is, however, what actually does take place between text and reader? Is it possible to look into that relationship at all, or is not the critic simply plunging into a private world where he can only make conjectures and speculations? It must be pointed out that a text can only come to life when it is read, and if it is to be examined, it must therefore be studied through the eyes of the reader. "Involvement of the reader or spectator as accomplices or collaborators is essential in the curious situation of artistic communication."[3] What, then, does the process of reading consist of?

Briefly, it might be described as the reader's transformation of signals sent out by the text. But if the act of reading is indeed the transformation of the author's signals, then one is bound to ask whether such a process can ever be described without recourse to the psychology of the reader. Then again, if one tries to draw a distinction between a text and the various possible forms of its transformation, one risks being accused of denying the identity of a text and of merely letting it dissolve into the arbitrariness of subjective perception. A text, the argument runs, must represent something, and the meaning of what is represented exists independently of every single reaction that such a meaning might arouse. To counter this, however, one might suggest that this "meaning," which is apparently independent of every realization of the text, is in itself nothing more than an individual reading experience that has now simply been identified with the text itself. Interpretations based on conveying meaning have always been along these lines, with a consequent dilution of the texts they dealt with. Fortunately, such interpretations have been contradicted from time to time, but for the most part only with the consequence that an equally restricted interpretation was ultimately set up in place of the one knocked down. The history of responses to literary works, which in turn is a history of variations, offers countless examples of this.

If it were really true—as the author of a certain well-known essay on "The Art of Interpretation" would have us believe—that the meaning is concealed within a text itself, one cannot help wondering why texts should play hide-and-seek with their interpreters; and even more puzzling, why the meaning, once it has been found, should then change again, even though the letters, words, and sentences of the text remain the same. Isn't it here that the meaning-grinder begins to obscure the text, thus canceling out his own avowed intent—to bring clarity and light to the text he is examining?

Shouldn't the interpreter in fact renounce his sanctified role of conveying meanings, if he wants to open up the possibilities of a text? His description of the text is, after all, nothing more than the experience of a cultured reader—in other words, it is only one of the possible realizations of a text. If this is the case, we could then maintain, at least tentatively, that meanings in literary texts are generated in the act of reading; they are the product of a complex interaction between text and reader, and not qualities that are hidden in the text and traced solely by that traditional kind of interpretation I have described. If the individual reader generates the meaning of a text, then it follows that these meanings will always appear individualistic.

There are many more questions one could ask of "The Art of Interpretation," but the nature of the problem is already tangible and can now be stated: If a literary text could really be reduced to one particular meaning, it would be the expression of something else—namely, of that meaning whose status is determined by the fact that it exists independently of the text. Put in extreme terms this means that the literary text would then be the illustration of this meaning existing outside itself. Thus the literary text would sometimes be read as evidence of the *zeitgeist*, sometimes as an expression of its author's neuroses, sometimes as a mirror reflection of social conditions, or what have you.

Of course, no one will deny that literary texts do contain a historical substratum; however, the manner in which literature takes it up and communicates it does not seem to be determined merely by historical circumstances, but by the specific aesthetic structure inherent in it. That is why we often have the feeling, when reading words of past ages, that we are actually transported back into those times and move in historical circumstances as if we belonged to them or as if the past were again the present. The preconditions for this experience are certainly provided by the text, but we as readers also play a part in the creation of this impression. It is we who bring the text to life. Obviously it must offer a certain amount of latitude, as far as its realization is concerned, for different readers at different times have always had differing apprehensions of such texts, even though the general impression may be the same—that the world revealed, however far back in the past it may lie, comes alive in the present.

At this point we can formulate our task in more precise terms: How can we describe the relationship between text and reader? We shall search for the answer in three stages. The first step will be to indicate the special qualities of a literary text that distinguish it from other kinds of discourse. The second step will be to name and analyze the basic elements that trigger the response to literary works. Here we shall pay special attention to different degrees of what I should like to call indeterminacy in a text and the various ways in which it is brought about. In the third step we must attempt to clarify the observable increase of indeterminacy in narrative literature since the eighteenth century. If one supposes that indeterminacy embodies an elementary condition for readers' reactions, then one must ask what its expansion, above all in modern literature, indicates. Without doubt it changes the relationship between text and reader. The more texts lose their determinacy, the more the reader is shifted into the full operation of their possible intentions. If indeterminacy exceeds the reader's limit of tolerance, he will feel overburdened. He can in that case reveal attitudes that might lead to a rather surprising insight into what usually determines his reactions. At this point, the question arises as to what insights literature can open up into the workings of the human mind.

LET US NOW take the first step. How can we describe the status of a literary text? This first point is that it differs from any text presenting an object that exists independently of the text. If a piece of writing describes an object that exists with equal determinacy outside it, then the text is simply an exposition of the object. In Austin's terms, it is a "constative utterance," as opposed to a "performative utterance,"[4] which actually creates its object. It goes without saying that literary texts belong to the second category. There is no concrete object corresponding to them in the external world, although of course they produce their objects out of elements to be found in the external world.

This rough distinction of texts as statement and performance must, however, be still further differentiated if we are to arrive at a preliminary definition of a literary text. For there are texts that constitute something without being literary. For instance, all texts that present claims, state aims, define purposes, and formulate rules likewise produce new objects, but these objects achieve their existence only through the determinacy brought about by the text. Legal texts are the most obvious examples of this form of language. They lay down principles that are binding for the behavior of human beings. A literary text, however, can never set out anything factual of this nature. It is not surprising, therefore, that we call such a text fictional.

But is literature wholly devoid of reality, or is it perhaps imbued with a reality of its own, which sets it off from the linguistics of expository texts as well as from those texts that constitute general norms of human behavior? A literary text neither portrays nor creates objects in the way we have described; at best we can say that it is the description of reactions to objects.[5] "All art originates," E. H. Gombrich once remarked, "in our reactions to the world rather than in the visible world itself."[6] This is why we recognize in literature so many elements that play a part in our own experience. They are simply put together in a different way—in other words, they constitute a familiar world reproduced in an unfamiliar form. Thus the intention of a literary text can never be completely identified with our experience. Instead, it presents reactions to and attitudes toward the world we live in, and it is these reactions and attitudes that constitute the reality of a literary text. If a literary text presents no real objects, it nevertheless establishes its reality by the reader's participation and by the reader's response. The reader, however, cannot refer to any definite object or independent facts in order to judge whether the text has presented its subject rightly or wrongly. This possibility of verification that all expository texts offer is, precisely, denied by the literary text. At this point there arises a certain amount of indeterminacy which is peculiar to all literary texts, for they permit no referral to any identical real-life situation.

When the reader has gone through the various perspectives offered him by the text, he is left with nothing but his own experience to judge what has been communicated to him. There are two extremes of reaction that can arise from the confrontation between one's own world and that of the literary work involved: either the literary world seems fantastic, because it contradicts our own experience, or it seems trivial, because it merely echoes our own. This shows clearly the significance of our own experience in the realization of a text, and here we have an initial insight into the specific nature of a literary text. First, it differs from other forms of writing in that it neither describes nor constitutes real objects; second, it diverges from the ordinary experiences of the reader in that it offers views and opens up perspectives in which the empirically known world of one's own personal experience appears changed. And so the literary text cannot be fully identified either with the objects of the external world or with the experiences of the reader.

This lack of identification produces a degree of indeterminacy which normally the reader will counterbalance through the act of reading. Here, too, there is scope for a wide variety of reactions on the part of the reader. The gaps of indeterminacy can be filled in by referring the text to external, verifiable factors, in such a way that it appears to be nothing more than a mirror reflection of these factors. In this case its literary quality fades into reflection. Alternatively, the indeterminacy of a text may be so resistant to counterbalancing that any identification with the world we live in is impossible. Then the world of the text establishes itself as being in competition with the familiar world, a competition that must inevitably have some repercussions on the familiar one. In this case, the text may tend to function as a criticism of life.

Indeterminacy can also be counterbalanced at any given time in terms of the individual experience of the reader. He can reduce a text to the level of his own experiences, provided that he projects his own standards onto the text in order to grasp a specific meaning. This, too, is a counterbalancing of indeterminacy which disappears when the subjective norms of the reader guide him through the text. On the other hand, a text may conceivably contradict our own preconceptions to such a degree that it calls forth drastic reactions, such as throwing a book away or, at the other extreme, being compelled to revise those preconceptions. This also constitutes a way of removing indeterminacy which always permits the possibility of connecting one's own experience with what the text wants to convey. Whenever this happens, indeterminacy tends to disappear, because communication has occurred.

Such basic reactions clarify the status of the literary text: Its main characteristic is its peculiar halfway position between the external world of objects and the reader's own world of experience. The act of reading is therefore a process of seeking to pin down the oscillating structure of the text to some specific meaning.

SO FAR, WE have only described the literary text from the outside. We must now, in a second step, mention certain important formal conditions that give rise to indeterminacy in the text itself. At once, we are confronted with the question: what really is the substance of such a text? for it has no counterpart in the world of empirical objects. The answer is that literary objects come into being through the unfolding of a variety of views that constitute the "object" in stages and at the same time give a concrete form for the reader to contemplate. We shall call them "schematized views,"[7] after a term coined by the Polish philosopher Roman Ingarden, because every one of them is designed to present the object not in an incidental or even accidental way but in a representative manner. How many of these views are necessary to give a clear idea of the literary object? Obviously, a large number, if one is to get a precise conception.

This raises a highly relevant problem: each single view will generally reveal only one representative aspect. It therefore determines

READER RESPONSE IN PERSPECTIVE

the literary object, and at the same time it raises the need for a new determination. This means that a literary object never reaches the end of its multifaceted determinacy. In other words, a literary object can never be given final definition. This is borne out, for example, by the endings of many novels which often seem artificially imposed simply because the book must come to an end. Indeterminacy is then counterbalanced by the author himself with an ideological or utopian solution. There are other novels, though, which articulate this inconclusiveness at the end.

If we assume that the "schematized views" form a basic characteristic of the literary text, we must ask how they link up with one another. When they touch, the degree of connection is usually not stated but has to be inferred. Sometimes the sequence of views has the appearance of being dissevered, resembling a cutting technique. The most frequent application of this device occurs where several plot threads run simultaneously but must be dealt with one after the other. The connections that develop among such views are, as a rule, not set out by the text itself, although the way in which they are related is important for the intention of the text. In other words, between the "schematized views" there is a no-man's-land of indeterminacy, which results precisely from the determinacy of each individual view in its sequence. Gaps are bound to open up, and they offer a free play in the interpretation of the specific ways in which the various views can be connected with one another. These gaps give the reader a chance to build his own bridges, relating the different aspects of the object which have thus far been revealed to him. It is quite impossible for the text itself to fill the gaps. In fact, the more a text tries to be precise (i.e., the more "schematized views" it offers), the greater will be the number of gaps between the views. Classic examples of this are the last novels of Joyce, *Ulysses* and *Finnegans Wake*, where the overprecision of the presentation gives rise to a proportionate increase in indeterminacy. We shall return to this point later.

The indeterminate sections, or gaps, of literary texts are in no way to be regarded as a defect; on the contrary, they are a basic element for the aesthetic response. Generally, the reader will not even be aware of them—at least so far as novels up to the end of the nineteenth century are concerned. Nevertheless, they influence his reading, for the "schematized views" are continually connected with each other by the reading process. This means that the reader fills in the remaining gaps. He removes them by a free play of meaning-projection and thus himself provides the unformulated connections between the particular views. This is borne out by the fact that a second reading of a piece of literature often produces a different impression from the first. The reasons for this may lie in the reader's own change of circumstances, but all the same, the text must be such as to permit this variation. On a second reading, one has considerably more knowledge of the text, especially if the first reading took place only a short time ago. This additional information will affect and condition the meaning-projection, so that now the gaps between the different segments as well as the spectrum of their possible connections can be applied in a different, or perhaps more intensive, way. The increased information that now overshadows the text provides possibilities of combination which were obscured in the first reading. Familiar occurrences now tend to appear in a new light and seem to be at times corrected, at times enriched. But for all that, nothing is formulated in the text itself; rather, the reader himself produces these innovative readings. This would, of course, be impossible if the text itself was not, to some degree, indeterminate, leaving room for the change of vision.[8]

In this way, every literary text invites some form of participation on the part of the reader. A text that lays things out before the reader in such a way that he can either accept or reject them will lessen the degree of participation, as it allows him nothing but a yes or no. Texts with such minimal indeterminacy tend to be tedious, for it is only when the reader is given the chance to participate actively that he will regard the text, whose intention he himself has helped to compose, as real. For we generally tend to regard things that we have made ourselves as being real. And so it can be said that indeterminacy is the fundamental precondition for reader participation.

We might illustrate this fact by observing one literary form that makes very special use of the technique of indeterminacy. This is the serial story, the text of which is delivered to the reader in carefully measured installments. When serialized novels appear in newspapers today—as is customary in Europe—advertising the serialization plays an important role in attracting an audience to the novel. In the nineteenth century this procedure was of paramount importance. The great realistic writers courted an audience for their novels by this manner of publication, and it was in this way that many of their finest works appeared.[9] Charles Dickens actually wrote his novels from week to week, and in between episodes he tried to find out as much as possible about the way in which his readers visualized the development of the story.[10]

The experience of the reading public of the nineteenth century is extremely revealing and highly relevant to our discussion: readers often preferred the novel read by installments to the identical text in book form.[11] The same thing can still be seen today, if one only *Soaps* has the patience to go through with the experiment, for most of the stories that appear in papers nowadays tend to belong to the genre we generally call "light literature," bordering on the trivial. The object is still, of course, to attract a large public. If we read such novels in installments, they may at least be bearable; if we read them in book form, generally they will finish us before we finish them.

Let us examine the circumstances underlying this difference. The serialized novel uses a cutting technique. It interrupts the action usually where a certain tension that has been built up demands to be resolved, or where one is anxious to learn the outcome of the events one has just read about. The dramatic interruption or prolongation of suspense is the vital factor that determines the cutting, and the effect is to make the reader try to imagine the continuation of the action. How is it going to go on? In asking this question, we automatically raise the degree of our own participation in the further progress of the action. Dickens was well aware of this fact, and that is why he considered his readers to be coauthors.[12]

One could draw up a whole list of such cutting techniques, which for the most part are more sophisticated than the primitive, though highly effective, method of suspense. Another way, for instance, of involving the reader in a greater degree of composition is the abrupt introduction of new characters or even new threads of the plot, so that the question arises as to the connections between the story revealed so far and the new, unforeseen situations. This is a matter of discovering links and working out how the narrative will bring the different elements together. In view of the temporary withholding of information, the suggestive effect produced by details will increase, thus again stimulating a welter of possible solutions. Such a technique arouses definite expectations that, if the novel is to have any real value, must never be completely fulfilled.

The serialized novel, then, results in a special kind of reading. The interruptions are more deliberate and calculated than those occasioned in the book-reader by random reasons. In the serialized novel they arise from a strategic purpose. The reader is forced by the pauses imposed on him to imagine more than he could have done if his reading were continuous, and so, if the text of a serialized novel makes a different impression from the text in book form, this is principally because it introduces additional gaps, or alternatively accentuates existing gaps by means of a break until the next installment. This does not mean that its quality is in any way higher. The pauses simply bring out a different kind of realization, in which the reader is compelled to take a more active part by filling in these additional gaps. If a novel *seems* to be better in this form, then this is clear evidence of the importance of indeterminacy in the text-reader relationship. Furthermore, it reveals the requisite degree of freedom which must be guaranteed to the reader in the act of communication, so that the message can be adequately received and processed.

At this point there arises another matter that we can only touch upon here. This is the question of the whole repertoire of structures that lead to indeterminacy in a text. Further, we should try to describe the elementary activities in the reading process, of which the reader may not be aware but which nevertheless do occur.

Of the many ways in which a reader's response may be guided, there is one that might serve as a brief illustration for the type of pattern whose function should be investigated. The example is the simplest of all, and therefore the most common one. We all notice in reading novels that the narrative is often interspersed with the author's comments on the events. These comments are frequently in the nature of an evaluation of what has happened. Obviously, the narrative contains elements that require such explanations. In view of our preceding discussion, we might say that here the author himself removes the gaps; for with his comments, he tries to create a specific conception of his narrative. So long as this remains the sole function of the commentary, the participation of the reader in the execution of the underlying narrative intention must diminish. The author himself tells the reader how his tale is to be understood. At best, the reader can only contradict the author's conception, if he thinks that he can extract different impressions from the work. However, there are many novels which do contain such comments and evaluations, and yet at the same time do not seek to interpret the story from one particular, consistent point of view, but vary considerably as far as perspectives and evaluations are concerned.

This device was already in use at the beginning of the eighteenth century and can be found in many novels whose historical basis is relatively uninteresting for us today. Our pleasure in reading such novels nevertheless does not suffer. In these novels, the author does not seem exclusively motivated to prescribe, by means of authorial intervention, the understanding of the narrative by the reader. The

READER RESPONSE IN PERSPECTIVE

great English novels of the eighteenth and nineteenth centuries, which today seem just as alive as when written, belong to this category. In these works one has the feeling that the author's remarks are made with a view not to interpreting the meaning of the events but to gaining a position outside them—to regarding them, as it were, from a distance. The comments, then, strike one as mere hypotheses, and they seem to imply other possibilities of evaluation than those that arise directly from the events described. This impression is borne out by the fact that the comments on different situations often reveal different standpoints of the author himself. Are we, then, to trust the author when he makes his comments?[13] Or are we not, rather, to test what he says for ourselves? Frequently the author's own comments seem to contradict what we have assumed from the events he has described, and if his comments are to make sense to us, we may feel we need further information. Has one perhaps read inattentively there? Or should one, solely on the ground of the reading, correct the comments of the author in order to find by oneself the evaluation of the events? Unexpectedly, then, the reader finds that he is dealing not only with the characters in the novel but also with an author who interposes himself as a mediator between the story and the reader. Now he demands the attention of the reader just as much as the story itself does.

The comments may provoke a variety of reactions. They can disconcert, arouse opposition, charm with contradiction, and frequently uncover many unexpected features of the narrative process, which without these clues one might not have noticed. And so such comments do not provide any definite assessments of the events; rather, they offer an assessment that contains different possibilities open to the reader's choice. Instead of offering the reader a single and consistent perspective, through which he is supposed to look on the events narrated, the author provides him with multiple viewpoints, the center of which is continuously shifting. These comments thus open a certain free play for evaluation and permit new gaps to arise in the text. The gaps now no longer lie in the recounted narrative, but between the narrative and the various ways of assessing it. They can only be removed, then, while or after judgment is passed on the existing process already described.

The comments provoke the faculty of judgment in two ways: while they exclude any unequivocal judgment of the events, they create gaps that in turn admit many differently shaded judgments; but these judgments are not completely arbitrary, because the author outlines by his comments the possible alternatives for the reader.

This particular structure therefore involves the reader in the evaluative process and yet, at the same time, it controls the reader's evaluation.

Let us briefly consider this reader manipulation, using an example that could be considered almost an embodiment of this process. Given that an author wants to phrase his comments in such a way as not just to limit the scope of his reader's response but actually to guide him along one specific path, what is he to do? If our observations so far have been correct, we cannot expect the comments to lay down hard-and-fast rules for the response desired from the reader. The reader would react to these prescriptions, but not in the context of the planned purpose.

Now the example. It is the well-known passage in Dickens's *Oliver Twist* where the hungry child is in the workhouse and with the courage of despair dares to ask for more gruel. The supervisors of the workhouse are appalled by this monstrous insolence.[14] What does the commenting narrator have to say? Not only does he support them, but he even gives his reasons for doing so.[15] The reaction of the reader is unequivocal, for the author has formulated his comment in such a way that the reader simply has to reject it. In this manner, the reader's participation in the fate of the child can be brought to the level of actual engagement. The reader is torn from his comfortable seat and plunged into the situation. This is no longer a matter of filling a gap by making a judgment; here the reader is forced to reverse completely a false judgment. If he is to be brought into the action and guided along a specific path, then the text, paradoxically, cannot mean what it says. In this respect Dickens's episode represents an interesting borderline case of indeterminacy. For the same criterion applies here as normally obtains for indeterminacy: what is stated must not exhaust the intention of the text.

Literature abounds in structures like this. Many of them are more complicated than the teamwork between commentator and reader indicated here. One might consider the fact that we as readers are constantly reacting to the characters in a novel, while they never react in any way to our attitudes. In life, obviously, things are very different. What use do we make of the freedom from other people's reactions granted us by the novel? What function has this form of indeterminacy, which elicits our response to the characters, and then seems to leave the rest to us?

At this point we ought to consider above all the technical requirements of language which are responsible for directing the reader's response. We should, in the first place, break down a literary text into its constituent elements, because for an analysis of its appeal it is necessary to spotlight the patterns of its construction. If such texts reveal for example, a cutting-montage or segmenting technique, it means that they permit relative freedom with respect to the concatenation of their textual patterns in the reading process. If, on the other hand, they are structured according to a principle of contrast or opposition, the linkup of the textual patterns is rigidly prescribed. In the one case, a relatively high degree of "performance" is asked of the reader in view of a smaller amount of authorial prescription; in the other case, the opposite is true.

Furthermore, it is important to specify on what textual level and how frequently the gaps occur. If they crop up more often in the narrative strategy and less often in the actions of the characters, there will be different consequences for the communication process. Moreover, they are bound to work out quite differently if they occur in the role assigned to the reader.

But the frequency of gaps can also be significant for another kind of classification of textual levels. They may predominate on the syntactic level of the text—that is, in the recognizable system of rules responsible for marshaling the textual patterns into a premeditated order. They may predominate on the pragmatic level of the text—that is, in the intention pursued by it. Or they may ultimately predominate on the semantic level of the text—that is, in the generating of meaning, which is the readers' foremost task. Whatever the distribution of gaps on each of the respective levels, they will have different consequences for the process of steering the reader, the direction of which is to a large extent dependent on the specific textual level at which the gaps predominate. This fact can, however, only be mentioned rather than fully discussed here.

Let us now turn to the third stage of our analysis: the striking historical fact that since the eighteenth century, indeterminacy in literature—or at least an awareness of it—has tended to increase. The implications of this fact can be illustrated briefly in three examples taken from eighteenth-, nineteenth-, and twentieth-century English literature. There is no doubt that the same phenomena can also be found in the applicable texts of other literatures. The three examples are Fielding's *Joseph Andrews* (1741–42), Thackeray's *Vanity Fair* (1848), and Joyce's *Ulysses* (1922).

Fielding's *Joseph Andrews* begins as a parody of Richardson's *Pamela*, in which human nature and conduct were for the most part rigidly fixed. Doubting the definability of human nature, and yet formulating a conception of it—this is the paradoxical starting point of Fielding's novel. The construction is as simple as can be. On the one side is Abraham Adams, the hero, fully equipped with all the virtues of the Enlightenment; on the other side is a reality that ceaselessly attacks these virtues. From the standpoint of the hero, the world seems very bad; from that of the world, the hero is pig-headed and narrow-minded. Now it cannot be the intention of this novel to present the representative of moral principles as a pigheaded individual. At the same time, the world depicted here is no longer set out in accordance with the principles of morality, let alone dominated by them. What is to be discerned is a continual inter-action between the two poles of virtue and world, which seems to imply a kind of reciprocal correction. But the nature of this cor-rection is not laid out in the text itself. There is nothing but an interplay of relationships that has long since lost the determinacy recognizable in the two basic positions of hero and reality. This reciprocal correction aims at balancing out, and not at victory or defeat for the one or the other of the parties. Again, the nature of the balance is not set out in the text, but it can be imagined by the reader. Indeed, it may well be that it can only be imagined because it is not set down in words. In acting upon each other, the two sides reveal not so much their actual situation as their potential.

First, the text offers the reader nothing but a collection of po-sitions which it presents in a variety of relationships, without ever formulating the focal point at which they converge. For this point lies in the reader's imagination, and in fact can only be created by his reading. The structure is very close to the reading experience that Northrop Frye has described as follows: "Whenever we read anything, we find our attention moving in two directions at once. One direction is outward and centrifugal, in which we keep going outside our reading, from the individual works to the things they mean, or, in practice, to our memory of the conventional association between them. The other direction is inward or centripetal, in which we try to develop from the words a sense of the larger verbal pattern they make."[16] This "hermeneutic operation" of reading intensifies itself to the degree that the novel renounces definition of its intention. However, the fact that the novel does not set forth its own intention does not mean that no intention exists. Where is it to be found? The answer must be that the reciprocal correction of the positions opens up a dimension that only comes into being through the act of reading. It is only in reading that there occurs an uninterrupted modification of the various positions involved. The hero keeps sal-lying forth into the sordid world of reality, and thus continually provokes changing judgments on the part of the reader. But at the same time, the reader looks through the hero's eyes at the world, so that it, too, is subject to changing judgments. Out of these continually interacting elements, the reader's imagination can build up the pattern of the text—a pattern that varies according to the imagination that is forming it. So the reading becomes an act of generating meaning.

Fielding himself seems to have been fully aware of this construction, for the part that he allocates to the reader is determined by one vital task: the reader is to discover.[17] This demand can be understood historically and structurally. Historically it means that the reader, in discovering that overall pattern for himself, is made to practice one basic principle of the Enlightenment. Structurally it means that the effect of the novel is heightened if it does not provide the focal point of its positions and patterns, but allows the reader himself to remove the inherent indeterminacy.

The author-reader relationship, as developed in the eighteenth-century novel, has been a constant factor in narrative prose and is still in evidence, even though the author seems to have disappeared and the reader to be deliberately excluded from comprehension. While Fielding, referring to his readers, offers them this reassurance: "I am, indeed, set over them for their own good only, and was created for their use and not they for mine,"[18] Joyce, at the other end of the scale, drops only the ironic information that the author has withdrawn behind his work, "paring his fingernails."[19] The reader of modern novels is deprived of the assistance that the eighteenth-century writer gave in a variety of devices, ranging from exhortation to satire and irony. Instead, today's reader is expected to strive for himself to unravel the mysteries of a sometimes strikingly enigmatic composition. This development reflects the transformation of the very idea of literature, which seems to have ceased to be a means of relaxation and even luxury, making demands now on the capacity for understanding because the world presented seems to have no bearing on what the reader is familiar with. This change did not happen suddenly. The stages of transition are clearly discernible in the nineteenth century, and one of them is virtually a halfway point in the development: the so-called realistic novel, of which Thackeray's *Vanity Fair* is an outstanding example. Here, the author-reader relationship is as different from the eighteenth-century "dialogue" as it is from the twentieth-century demand that the reader find for himself the key to a many-sided puzzle. There is, however, a noticeable increase in indeterminacy in Thackeray, although the author still provides his reader with unmistakable clues to guide him in his search. If indeterminacy regulates the gradual participation of the reader in the fulfillment of the text's intention, one wonders what an intensified participation can involve.

Vanity Fair consists partly of a story, in which are described the social ambitions of two girls in Victorian society, and partly of the commentary by a narrator who introduces himself as a theatrical producer, his productions being almost as extensive as the story itself. At the start of the novel, the "Manager of the Performance"[20] gives an outline of what the audience is to expect. The ideal visitor to "Vanity Fair" is described as a "man with a reflective turn of mind"(1:liv); this is an advance indication of what the reader has to accomplish, if he is to realize the meaning of the proceedings. But at the same time, the "Manager" offers something to everyone: "Some people consider Fairs immoral altogether, and eschew such, with their servants and families: very likely they are right. But persons who think otherwise, and are of a lazy, or a benevolent, or a sarcastic mood, may perhaps like to step in for half an hour, and look at the performances. There are scenes of all sorts: some dreadful combats, some grand and lofty horse-riding, some scenes of high life, and some of very middling indeed; some love-making for the sentimental, and some light comic business" (1:liv). In this way the "Manager" tries to entice different types of visitors to enter his fair—bearing in mind the fact that such a visit will also have its repercussions. After the reader has been following the narrator for quite some time, he is informed: "This, dear friends and companions, is my amiable object—to walk with you through the Fair, to examine the shops and shows there; and that we should all come home after the flare, and the noise, and the gaity, and be perfectly miserable in private" (1:225). But the reader will only feel miserable after walking through the fair if, unexpectedly, he has come upon himself in some of the situations, thereby having his attention drawn to his own behavior, which has shone out at him from the mirror of possibilities. The narrator is only pretending to help the reader; in reality he is goading him.

His reliability is already reduced by the fact that he is continually donning new masks: at one moment he is an observer of the fair, like the reader (1:236, 2:431); then he is suddenly blessed with extraordinary knowledge, though he can explain ironically that "novelists have the privilege of knowing everything" (1:29); and then, toward the end, he announces that the whole story was not his own at all, but that he overheard it in a conversation (2:344,

404). Thus at the beginning of the novel the narrator is presented as the "Manager of the Performance," and at the end he presents himself as the reporter of a story that fell into his hands purely by chance. The further away he stands from the social reality depicted, the clearer becomes the outline of the part he is meant to play. But the reader can only view the social panorama in the constantly shifting perspectives that are opened up for him by this protean narrator. Although he cannot help following the views and interpretations of the narrator, it is essential for him to understand the motivations behind this constant changing of viewpoints, because only the discovery of the motivations can lead to the comprehension of what is intended. Thus the narrator regulates the distance between reader and events, and in doing so brings about the aesthetic effect of the story. The reader is given only as much information as will keep him oriented and interested; the narrator deliberately leaves open the inferences that are to be drawn from this information. Consequently, empty spaces are bound to occur, spurring the reader's imagination to detect the assumption that might have motivated the narrator's attitude. In this way, the reader gets involved because he reacts to the viewpoints advanced by the narrator.

When the "Manager of the Performance" introduces his characters at the beginning of the novel, he says of Becky: "The famous little Becky Puppet has been pronounced to be uncommonly flexible in the joints, and lively on the wire" (1:lv). That the characters are "puppets" is brought home to the reader throughout the novel by the fact that the narrator lets them act on a level of consciousness far below his own. This almost overwhelming superiority of the narrator over his characters—he often depicts them in the light of a knowledge that at best could only have been arrived at by anticipating future events—also puts the reader in a privileged position, though he is never allowed to forget that he should draw his own conclusions from the extra knowledge imparted to him by the narrator. There is even an allegory of the reader's task in the novel, when Becky is basking in the splendor of a grand social evening:

> The man who brought her refreshment and stood behind her chair, had talked her character over with the large gentleman in motley-coloured clothes at his side. Bon Dieu! it is awful, that servants' inquisition! You see a woman in a great party in a splendid saloon, surrounded by faithful admirers, distributing sparkling glances, dressed to perfection, curled, rouged, smiling and happy:—Discovery walks respectfully up to her, in the shape of a huge powdered man with large calves and a tray of ices—

with Calumny (which is as fatal as truth)—behind him, in the shape of the hulking fellow carrying the wafer-biscuits. Madam, your secret will be talked over by those men at their club at the public-house to-night. . . . Some people ought to have mutes for servants in Vanity Fair—mutes who could not write. If you are guilty, tremble. That fellow behind your chair may be a Janissary with a bow-string in his plush breeches pocket. If you are not guilty, have a care of appearances: which are as ruinous as guilt. (2:112)

This little scene contains a change of standpoints typical of the way in which the reader's observations are conditioned throughout this novel. The servants are suddenly transformed into allegorical figures in order to uncover what lies hidden beneath the façades of their masters. But the discovery will only turn into calumny from the standpoint of the person affected. The narrator compares the destructive effect of calumny with that of truth, and advises his readers to employ mutes, or better still illiterate mutes, as servants, in order to protect themselves against discovery. Then he brings the reader's view even more sharply into focus, finally leaving him to himself with an indissoluble ambiguity: if the reader feels guilty because he pretends to be something he is not, then he must fear those around him as if they were an army of Janissaries. If he has nothing to hide, then the social circle merely demands that he keep up appearances; but since this is just as ruinous as deliberate hypocrisy, it follows that life in society imposes rules on all concerned, reducing human behavior to the level of playacting. All the characters in the novel are caught up in this play, as is expressly shown by the narrator's own stage metaphor at the beginning and at the end. The key word for the reader is "discover," and the narrator prods him along the road to discovery, laying a trail of clues for him to follow.

The aesthetic effect of Vanity Fair depends on activating the reader's critical faculties so that he may recognize the social reality of the novel as a confusing array of sham attitudes, and experience the exposure of this sham as the true reality. Instead of being expressly stated, the criteria for such judgments have to be inferred. They are the blanks that the reader is supposed to fill in, thus bringing his own criticism to bear.

W. J. Harvey describes the reading situation for the novel in similar terms as one involving "conditional freedom."

A novel . . . can allow for a much fuller expression of this sensed penumbra of unrealized possibilities, of all the what-might-have-beens of our lives. It is because of this that the novel permits a much greater liberty of such speculation on the part of the reader than does the play. ... The character moves in the full depth of his conditional freedom; he is what he is but he might have been otherwise. Indeed the novel does not merely *allow* for this liberty of speculation; sometimes it *encourages* it to the extent that our sense of conditional freedom ... becomes one of the ordering structural principles of the entire work.[21]

The "Manager of the Performance" opens up a whole panorama of views on the reality described, which can be seen from practically every social and human standpoint. The reader is offered a host of different perspectives, and so he is almost continually confronted with the problem of how to make them consistent. This is all the more complicated as it is not just a matter of viewing the social world described, but of doing so in face of a rich variety of perspectives offered by the commentator. There can be no doubt that the author wants to induce his reader to assume a critical attitude toward the social reality portrayed, but at the same time he gives him the alternative of adopting one of the views offered him, or of developing one of his own. This choice is not without a certain amount of risk. If the reader adopts one of the attitudes suggested by the author, he must automatically exclude the others. If this happens, the impression arises, in this particular novel, that one is looking more at oneself than at the event described. There is an unmistakable narrowness in every standpoint, and in this respect the reflection the reader will see of himself will be anything but complimentary. But if the reader then changes his viewpoint, in order to avoid this narrowness, he will undergo the additional experience of finding that his behavior is very like that of the two girls who are constantly adapting themselves in order to rise up the social scale. All the same, his criticism of the girls appears to be valid. Is it not a reasonable conclusion then, that the novel was constructed as a means of turning the reader's criticism of social opportunism back upon himself? This is not mentioned specifically in the text, but it happens all the time. Thus, the reader finds himself instead of society to be the object of criticism.

Thackeray once mentioned casually: "I have said somewhere it is the unwritten part of books that would be the most interesting."[22] It is in the unwritten part of the book that the reader has his place— hovering between the world of the characters and the guiding sovereignty of the "Manager of the Performance." If he comes too close to the characters, he learns the truth of what the narrator told him at the beginning: "The world is a looking-glass, and gives back to every man the reflection of his own face" (1:12). If he stands back with the narrator to look at things from a distance, he sees through all the activities of the characters. Through the variableness of his own position, the reader experiences the meaning of *Vanity Fair*. As this basic fabric of the novel is not set out in words, the written text would then be nothing more than the shadow thrown by this unformulated base. This would mean, in turn, that the text is constructed in such a way that it provokes the reader constantly to supplement what he is reading. This act of completion, however, is not concerned merely with secondary aspects of the work, but with the central intention of the text itself. Whenever this occurs, it is clear that the author is not mobilizing his reader because he himself cannot finish off the work he has started; his motive is to bring about an intensified participation that will compel the reader to be that much more aware of the intention of the text.

If the reader of *Vanity Fair* connects the many positions offered him in the text, he will not find the ideal critical stance from which everything will become clear; he will, rather, find himself frequently placed in the very society that he is to criticize.

The reader of the Fielding novel had to coordinate or reconcile respectively two contrary positions and was expected ultimately to find the right balance. The multiplicity of gaps in *Vanity Fair*, however, makes it inevitable that the reader should reveal a great deal of himself if he makes use of the scope of comprehension offered him. Against the background of *Vanity Fair*, the indeterminacy of *Ulysses* seems out of control. And yet this novel only attempts to portray a single ordinary day. The subject, then, is considerably reduced when one thinks of the fact that Thackeray wanted to paint a picture of Victorian society, and Fielding, one of human nature itself. Clearly, the amount of indeterminacy does not depend on the size of the theme. Moreover, *Ulysses* contains nearly every device of description and narration that the novel has developed in the course of its relatively short history—and all this for the simple purpose of depicting complete ordinariness? Is it, perhaps, not so much a question of describing everyday reality as conveying the conditions under which it is experienced?[23]

If this is so, then the theme is only the initial impulse, and it is the attempts to deal with the theme that are all-important; for everyday reality does not, in this book, reflect some hidden meaning. In *Ulysses* there are no longer any ideals underlying the world portrayed. Instead, there is an unprecedented wealth of viewpoints and textual patterns which the reader at first finds confusing.

READER RESPONSE IN PERSPECTIVE

The "Aeolus" chapter is a striking example of the point in question. Bloom's visit to the newspaper office provides the framework for a curiously patterned form of narration. Two separate levels of the text are highlighted, which one might call, for the sake of convenience, the micro- and the macrostructure of the chapter. The microstructural level consists of a large number of allusions which basically can be divided into three different groups: (1) those dealing with the immediate situation, Bloom's effort to place an advertisement at the newspaper office and the events connected with it; (2) those referring to completely different episodes outside the chapter itself, sometimes relating to incidents already described, and sometimes anticipating them; and (3) those passages that seem to slide into obscurity when one tries to work out exactly where they might be heading. However, as these allusions are not distinctly separated but are in fact woven into an intricate pattern, each one of them tends to entice the reader to follow it. Thus the allusions themselves turn into microperspectives that, because of their very density, simply cannot be followed through to the end. They form abbreviated extracts from reality which inevitably compel the reader to a process of selection.

This is also true of the other stylistic pattern to be discerned within the microstructural stratum. Just as with the allusions, there is throughout an abrupt alternation between dialogue, direct and indirect speech, authorial report, first-person narrative, and interior monologue. Although such techniques do impose a certain order on the abundance of allusions, they also invest them with differing importance. An allusion by the author himself certainly has a function for the context different from one that is made in direct speech by one of the characters. Thus extracts from reality and individual events are not contracted merely into allusions, but, through the different patterns of style, emerge in forms that endow them with a varied range of relevance. At the same time, the unconnected allusions and the abrupt alterations of stylistic devices disclose a large number of empty spaces.

All this gives rise to the stimulating quality of the text. On the one hand, the density of allusions and the continual segmentation of style involve an incessant changing of perspectives, which seem to go out of control whenever the reader tries to pin them down; on the other hand, the empty spaces resulting from cuts and abbreviations tempt the reader to fill them in. He will try to group things, because this is the only way in which he can recognize situations or understand characters in the novel.

The macrostructure of the chapter lends itself to this need for "grouping," though in a peculiar way. Heading and "newspaper column" form the schema that incorporates the allusions and stylistic changes. The heading is an instruction as to what to expect. But the text that follows the caption reveals the composition above, and so in most cases does not fulfill the expectation raised by the heading. As the newspaper headlines refer to various incidents in the city of Dublin, the situation of Ireland, and so forth, they would seem to be concerned with everyday events, the reality of which is beyond question. But the column that follows frustrates this expectation, not only by leading commonplace realities off in unforeseeable directions, thus destroying the grouping effect of the headline, but also by fragmenting facts and occurrences in such a way that to comprehend the commonplace becomes a real effort. While the heading appears to gratify our basic need for grouping, this need is predominantly subverted by the text that follows.

In this chapter, the reader not only learns something about the events in Dublin on 16 June 1904, but he also experiences the difficulties inherent in the comprehension of the barest outline of events. It is precisely because the heading suggests a way of grouping from a particular viewpoint that the text itself seems so thoroughly to contradict our expectations of perception. It appears to defy transcription of the circumstances indicated and instead offers the reader nothing but attitudes or possibilities of perception relating to these circumstances. In exploiting these possibilities, the reader is stimulated to a form of activity that B. Ritchie, in another context, has described as follows:

> The solution to this paradox is to find some ground for a distinction between "surprise" and "frustration." Roughly, the distinction can be made in terms of the effects which the two kinds of experiences have upon us. Frustration blocks or checks activity. It necessitates new orientation for our activity, if we are to escape the *cul de sac*. Consequently, we abandon the frustrating object and return to blind impulsive activity. On the other hand, surprise merely causes a temporary cessation of the exploratory phase of the experience, and a recourse to intense contemplation and scrutiny. In the latter phase the surprising elements are seen in their connection with what has gone before, with the whole drift to the experience, and the enjoyment of these values is then extremely intense. . . . [A]ny aesthetic experience tends to exhibit a continuous interplay between "deductive" and "inductive" operations.[24]

Now it does sometimes occur in this chapter that the expectations aroused by the headings are fulfilled. At such moments, the text seems banal,[25] for when the reader has adjusted himself to the nonfulfillment of his expectations, he will view things differently when they *are* fulfilled. The reason for this is easy to grasp. If the text of the column does not connect with the heading, the reader must supply the missing links. His participation in the intention of the text is thus enhanced. If the text does fulfill the expectations aroused by the heading, no removing of gaps is required of the reader and he feels the "letdown" of banality. In this way, the textual pattern in this chapter arouses continual conflicts with the reader's own modes of perception, and as the author has completely withdrawn from this montage of possibilities, the reader is given no guidance as to how to resolve the conflicts. But it is through these very conflicts, and the confrontation with the array of different possibilities, that the reader of such a text is given the impression that something does happen to him.

The innumerable facets of this everyday reality have the effect of seeming as if they were merely suggested to the reader for observation. The various perspectives as provided by the other chapters of the novel abruptly join up, overlap, are segmented, even clash, and through their very density they begin to overtax the reader's vision. The density of the presentational screen, the confusing montage and its interplay of perspectives, the invitation to the reader to look at identical incidents from many conflicting points of view — all this makes it extremely difficult for the reader to find his way. The novel refuses to divulge any principle for binding together this interplay of perspectives, and so the reader is forced to provide his own liaison. Then, inevitably, reading becomes a process of selection, with the reader's own imagination providing the criteria for the selection. For the text of *Ulysses* only offers the conditions that make it possible to conceive of this everyday world—conditions that each reader will exploit in his own way. Whenever this happens, "consistent reading suggests itself and illusion takes over."[26]

Yet it is difficult to sustain this illusion in the reading process, for all the eighteen chapters of the novel are written in continually changing styles, so that the view conveyed by each particular style can only be regarded as a suggestion for observation. In what, then, does the achievement of the various modes of presentation consist? First, one can say that they bring to bear a form of observation which underlies the very structure of perception. For we "have the experience of a world, not understood as a system of relations which wholly determine each event, but as an open totality the synthesis of which is inexhaustible. . . . From the moment that experience—that is, the opening on to our de facto world—is recognized as the beginning of knowledge, there is no longer any way of distinguishing a level of a priori truths and one of factual ones, what the world must necessarily be and what it actually is."[27] Through their countless offshoots, the different styles of *Ulysses* preclude any meaning directed toward integration, but they also fall into a pattern of observation that contains within itself the possibility of a continual extension. It is the very abundance of perspectives which conveys the abundance of the world under observation.

The effect of this continual change is dynamic, as it proves to be unbounded by any recognizable teleology. From one chapter to the next the "horizon" of everyday life is altered and constantly shifted from one area to another through the links that the reader tries to establish between the chapter styles. Each chapter prepares the "horizon" for the next, and it is the process of reading that provides the continual overlapping and interweaving of the views presented. The reader is stimulated into filling the "empty spaces" between the chapters in order to group them into a coherent whole. This process, however, has the following results: the conceptions of everyday life which the reader forms undergo constant modifications in the reading process. Each chapter provides a certain amount of expectation concerning the next. The gaps of indeterminacy which open up between the chapters, however, tend to diminish the importance of these expectations as a means of orienting the reader. As the process continues, a "feedback" effect is bound to develop, arising from the new chapter and reacting upon the preceding, which under this new and somewhat unexpected impression is subjected to modifications in the reader's mind. The more frequently the reader experiences this effect, the more cautious and the more differentiated will be his expectations as they arise through his realization of the text. Thus, what has just been read modifies what was read before, so that the reader himself operates the "fusion of the horizons," with the result that he produces an experience of reality which is real insofar as it happens. Reality, then, is a process of realization necessitating the reader's involvement, because only the reader can bring it about. This is why the chapters are not arranged in any sequence of situations that might be complementary to one another; in fact, the unforeseen difference of style seems to make each chapter into a turning point as opposed to a continuation. And as the whole novel consists of such turning points, the connections between the chapters appear as indeterminate gaps that in turn do not permit of any clear-cut link, so that the process of reading unfolds itself as a continual modification of all previous conceptions.

The novel opposes the desire for consistency which we constantly reveal when we are reading. Here we are confronted with a gamut of possible reactions. We may be annoyed by all these gaps, which arise in fact through the overprecision of presentation, but this would be like a confession on our part, for it would mean that we prefer to be pinned down by texts, foregoing our own judgment. In this case, we obviously expect literature to present us with a world that has been cleared of contradictions.[28] If we try to break down the areas of indeterminacy in the text, the picture that we draw for ourselves will then be, to a large extent, illusory, precisely because it is so determinate. The illusion arises from a desire for harmony, and it is solely the product of the reader.

This marks an important development. The realistic novel of the nineteenth century set out to give its reader an illusion of reality; in *Ulysses*, the high degree of indeterminacy has the effect of rendering illusory any meaning ascribed to everyday reality. The indeterminacy of the text sends the reader off on a search for meaning. In order to find it, he has to mobilize all the forces of his imagination. And in doing this, he has the chance of becoming a discriminating reader through the realization that his projected meanings can never fully cover the possibilities of the text. By exposing the limitations inherent in any meaning, modern literature offers the discriminating reader a chance to come to grips with his own ideas.

In some modern texts, this fact can be studied under almost experimental conditions. The works of Beckett are among those whose indeterminacy content is so high that they are often equated with a massive allegorization. The tendency to regard them as allegories is in itself a kind of exasperated form of meaning projection. What causes this exasperation, which can clearly only be pacified by imposing some meaning on the text? Beckett's works, with their extreme indeterminacy, cause a total mobilization of the reader's imagination; the effect of this, however, is that the totally mobilized world of imagination finds itself to be powerless when called upon to explain. And yet this impotence on the part of one's own imagination seems to be necessary if one is to accept Beckett's work at all, for the individuality of his text only becomes apparent when the world of our imagination is left behind. It is not surprising, therefore, that one's first reaction is to mount a massive operation of meaning-projection in order to haul the texts back within the limits of normal thinking.

If fiction stubbornly refuses to reveal the sought-after meaning, then the reader will decide what it has to mean. But then one realizes that by imposing an allegorical or unequivocal meaning onto the text, one's approach tends to be superficial or even trivial. Should not this allegorization be seen as an indication of the nature of our current conceptions and preconceptions rather than as a means of explaining the text? If so, then such texts will show us the fundamental lack of freedom resulting from our self-imposed confinement within the world of our own ideas. In making his reader experience the embarrassing predicament of the failure of his understanding, Beckett opens up a road to freedom which can be embarked on whenever we are prepared to shed the preconceived notions that so far have dominated our outlook.

The works of Beckett provoke a desire for understanding which can only be satisfied if we apply our own ideas to the text, to have them duly rejected as redundant. It is precisely this process that both stimulates and exasperates us, for who likes to learn that his own ideas have to be subjected to a fundamental revision if they are to grasp phenomena that seem to lie beyond their scope?[29]

AT THIS POINT, we are on the verge of leaving our historical perspective of indeterminacy, which so far has revealed that an increase in degree results in a proportionally enhanced involvement of the reader, which in turn can range from bringing out the author's own premeditated yet unformulated intention of the text to a gradual entanglement of the reader with himself, whenever the removal of indeterminacy gives rise to the generation of meaning. Let us therefore, by way of conclusion, examine the consequences of the facts we have outlined. First of all, we can say that the indeterminate elements of literary prose—perhaps even of all literature—represent a vital link between text and reader. They are the switch that activates the reader into using his own ideas in order to fulfill the intention of the text. This means that they are the basis for a textual structure in which the reader's part is already incorporated.

In this respect, literary texts differ from those that formulate a concrete meaning or truth. Texts of the latter kind are, by their very nature, independent of the individual reader, for the meaning or truth that they express exists independently of any reader's participation. But when a vital element of a text is reader participation, it is forced to rely on the individual reader for the realization of a possible meaning or truth. The meaning is conditioned by the text itself, but only in a form that allows the reader himself to bring it out.

An important sentence in semiotics runs: within a system, the lack of one element is important in itself. If one applies this to literature, one will observe that the literary text is characterized by the fact that it does not state its intention, and therefore the most important of its elements is missing. If this is so, how is the intention to be fulfilled? The answer is: by the guided projections of the reader's imagination. Even though the literary text has its reality not in the world of objects but in the imagination of its reader, it wins a certain precedence over texts that seek to make a statement concerning meaning or truth; in short, over those that claim or have an apophantic character. Meanings and truths are, by nature, influenced by their historical position and cannot in principle be set apart from history. The same applies to literature, but since the reality of a literary text comes to life within the reader's imagination, it must, again by nature, have a far greater chance of outlasting its historical genesis. From this arises the suspicion that literary texts are resistant to the course of time, not because they represent eternal values that are supposedly independent of time, but because their structure continually allows the reader to place himself within the world of fiction.

What is it that makes the reader want to share in the adventures of literature? This question is perhaps more for the anthropologist than for the literary critic, but the fact is clear that people have always tended to enjoy taking part in the fictitious dangers of the literary world; they like to leave their own security and enter into realms of thought and behavior which are by no means always elevating. Literature simulates life, not in order to portray it, but in order to allow the reader to share in it. He can step out of his own world and enter another, where he can experience extremes of pleasure and pain without being involved in any consequences whatsoever. It is this lack of consequence that enables him to experience things that would otherwise be inaccessible owing to the pressing demands of everyday reality. And precisely because the literary text makes no objectively real demand on its readers, it opens up a freedom that everyone can interpret in his own way. Thus, with every text we learn not only about what we are reading but also about ourselves, and this process is all the more effective if what we are supposed to experience is not explicitly stated but has to be inferred. A piece of literature wishing to exercise an impact and laying claim to some value has to comply with the basic requirement that Sir Philip Sidney tersely summed up in his *Defence of Poesie*: "the Poet . . . never affirmeth."[30] It is largely because of this fact that literary texts are so constructed as to confirm none of the meanings we ascribe to them, although by means of their structure they continually lead us to such projections of meaning. Thus it is perhaps one of the chief values of literature that by its very indeterminacy it is able to transcend the restrictions of time and the written word and to give to people of all ages and backgrounds the chance to enter other worlds and so enrich their own lives.

A Retrospective Note (1988)

This reprinting of "Indeterminacy and the Reader's Response in Prose Fiction" includes some minor changes in phrasing for the sake of improving the essay's clarity but no changes that alter substantially the character of the original. In particular, I decided it would be unmanageable to change phrases that emphasize subjective response and textual "intention." These phrases misled some critics about the directions I was setting in the essay by creating some erroneous impressions. The formulations were part of the first statements of a problem that I deal with again at much greater length in the discussion of meaning assembly in *The Act of Reading*, a book that grew out of the essay. Toward the end of the essay, the impression is conveyed that meaning projection might be left entirely to the discretion of individual reader. The descriptions and comments that create that impression were not meant as a plea for subjectivism. I provide a more detailed description of how meaning is to be brought alive in the interview that follows in this volume, making it clear that the reader's response is neither subjective only nor prestructured only, but the result of a guided interaction.

The suggestion that the intention of the text is not stated might be equally misleading. The phrasing was not meant to claim that the text itself produces its own intention, which—though authorial in origin—can only be ascertained by the inroads made into extratextual systems, by the way in which the encapsuled material is arranged within the text. This form of intentionality is traceable in the text, though not set out in words. I provide a more detailed analysis in my essay "Feigning in Fiction," in *Identity of the Literary Text*, ed. Mario J. Valdés and Owen Miller (Toronto, 1985), pp. 204–28.

TWO

INTERACTION BETWEEN
TEXT AND READER

entral to the reading of every literary work is the interaction between its structure and its recipient. Therefore an exclusive concentration on either the author's techniques or the reader's psychology will tell us little about the reading process itself. This is not to deny the vital importance of each of the two poles, yet separate analysis would only be conclusive if the relationship were that of transmitter and receiver, for this would presuppose a common code, ensuring accurate communication since the message would only be traveling one way. In literary works, however, the message is transmitted in two ways, in that the reader "receives" it by composing it. There is no common code; at best one could say that a common code may arise in the course of the process. Starting out from this assumption, we must search for structures that will enable us to describe basic conditions of interaction, for only then shall we be able to gain some insight into the potential effects inherent in the work.

It is difficult to describe this interaction, not least because literary criticism has very little to go on in the way of guidelines, and, of course, the two partners in the communication process, namely, the text[1] and the reader, are far easier to analyze than is the event that takes place between them. However, there are discernible conditions that govern interaction generally, and some of these will certainly apply to the special text-reader relationship. The differences and similarities may become clear if we briefly examine types of interaction which have emerged from psychoanalytic research into the structure of communication. The findings of the Tavistock School will serve as a model in order to move the problem into focus.[2]

In assessing interpersonal relationships R. D. Laing writes: "I may not actually be able to see myself as others see me, but I am constantly supposing them to be seeing me in particular ways, and I am constantly acting in the light of the actual or supposed attitudes, opinions, needs, and so on the other has in respect of me."[3] Now, the views that others have of me cannot be called "pure" perception; they are the result of interpretation. And this need for interpretation arises from the structure of interpersonal experience. We have experience of one another insofar as we know one another's conduct;

but we have no experience of how others experience us.

In his book *The Politics of Experience* Laing pursues this line of thought by saying: "*[Y]our experience of me is invisible to me and my experience of you is invisible to you.* I cannot experience your experience. You cannot experience my experience. We are both invisible men. All men are invisible to one another. Experience is man's invisibility to man."[4] It is this invisibility, however, that forms the basis of interpersonal relations—a basis that Laing calls "no-thing."[5] "That which is really 'between' cannot be named by any things that come between. The between is itself no-thing."[6] In all our interpersonal relations we build upon this "no-thing," for we react as if we knew how our partners experienced us; we continually form views of their views, and then act as if our views of their views were realities. Contact therefore depends upon our continually filling in a central gap in our experience. Thus, dyadic and dynamic interaction comes about only because we are unable to experience how we experience one another, which in turn proves to be a propellant to interaction. Out of this fact arises the basic need for interpretation, which regulates the whole process of interaction. As we cannot perceive without preconception, each percept, in turn, only makes sense to us if it is processed, for pure perception is quite impossible. Hence dyadic interaction is not given by nature but arises out of an interpretative activity, which will contain a view of others and, unavoidably, an image of ourselves.

An obvious and major difference between reading and all forms of social interaction is the fact that with reading there is no face-to-face-situation.[7] A text cannot adapt itself to each reader it comes into contact with. The partners in dyadic interaction can ask each other questions in order to ascertain how far their images have bridged the gap of the inexperienceability of one another's experiences. The reader, however, can never learn from the text how accurate or inaccurate his views of it are. Furthermore, dyadic interaction serves specific purposes, so that the interaction always has a regulative context, which often serves as a *tertium comparationis*. There is no such frame of reference governing the text-reader relationship; on the contrary, the codes that might regulate this interaction are fragmented in the text, and must first be reassembled or, in most cases, restructured before any frame of reference *can* be established. Here, then, in conditions and intention, we find two basic differences between the text-reader relationship and the dyadic interaction between social partners.

Now, it is the very lack of ascertainability and defined intention

READER RESPONSE IN PERSPECTIVE

that brings about the text-reader interaction, and here there is a vital link with dyadic interaction. Social communication, as we have seen, arises out of the fact that people cannot experience how others experience them, and not out of the common situation or out of the conventions that join both partners together. The situations and conventions regulate the manner in which gaps are filled, but the gaps in turn arise out of the inexperienceability and, consequently, function as a basic inducement to communication. Similarly, it is the gaps, the fundamental asymmetry between text and reader, that give rise to communication in the reading process; the lack of a common situation and a common frame of reference corresponds to the "no-thing," which brings about the interaction between persons. Asymmetry and the "no-thing" are all different forms of an indeterminate, constitutive blank which underlies all processes of interaction. With dyadic interaction, the imbalance is removed by the establishment of pragmatic connections resulting in an action, which is why the preconditions are always clearly defined in relation to situations and common frames of reference. The imbalance between text and reader, however, is undefined, and it is this very indeterminacy that increases the variety of communication possible.

Now, if communication between text and reader is to be successful, clearly the reader's activity must also be controlled in some way by the text. The control cannot be as specific as in a face-to-face-situation; equally, it cannot be as determinate as a social code, which regulates social interaction. However, the guiding devices operative in the reading process have to initiate communication and to control it. This control cannot be understood as a tangible entity occurring independently of the process of communication. Although exercised *by* the text, it is not *in* the text. This is well illustrated by a comment Virginia Woolf made on the novels of Jane Austen:

> Jane Austen is thus a mistress of much deeper emotion than appears upon the surface. She stimulates us to supply what is not there. What she offers is, apparently, a trifle, yet is composed of something that expands in the reader's mind and endows with the most enduring form of life scenes which are outwardly trivial. Always the stress is laid upon character. . . . The turns and twists of the dialogue keep us on the tenterhooks of suspense. Our attention is half upon the present moment, half upon the future. . . . Here, indeed, in this unfinished and in the main inferior story, are all the elements of Jane Austen's greatness.[8]

What is missing from the apparently trivial scenes, the gaps arising out of the dialogue—this is what stimulates the reader into filling the blanks with projections. He is drawn into the events and made to supply what is meant from what is not said. What is said only appears to take on significance as a reference to what is not said; it is the implications and not the statements that give shape and weight to the meaning. But as the unsaid comes to life in the reader's imagination, so the said "expands" to take on greater significance than might have been supposed: even trivial scenes can seem surprisingly profound. The "enduring form of life" which Virginia Woolf speaks of is not manifested on the printed page; it is a product arising out of the interaction between text and reader.

Communication in literature, then, is a process set in motion and regulated not by a given code but by a mutually restrictive and magnifying interaction between the explicit and the implicit, between revelation and concealment. What is concealed spurs the reader into action, but this action is also controlled by what is revealed; the explicit in its turn is transformed when the implicit has been brought to light. Whenever the reader bridges the gaps, communication begins. The gaps function as a kind of pivot on which the whole text-reader relationship revolves. Hence, the structured blanks of the text stimulate the process of ideation to be performed by the reader on terms set by the text. There is, however, another place in the textual system where text and reader converge, and that is marked by the various types of negation which arise in the course of the reading. Blanks and negations both control the process of communication in their own different ways: The blanks leave open the connection between textual perspectives, and so spur the reader into coordinating these perspectives and patterns—in other words, they induce the reader to perform basic operations *within* the text. The various types of negation invoke familiar and determinate elements or knowledge only to cancel them out. What is canceled, however, remains in view, and thus brings about modifications in the reader's attitude toward what is familiar or determinate—that is, he is guided to adopt a position *in relation* to the text.

In order to spotlight the communication process we shall confine our consideration to how the blanks trigger and simultaneously control the reader's activity. Blanks indicate that the different segments and patterns of the text are to be connected even though the text itself does not say so. They are the unseen joints of the text, and as they mark off schemata and textual perspectives from one another, they simultaneously prompt acts of ideation on the reader's part. Consequently, when the schemata and perspectives have been linked together, the blanks "disappear."

If we are to grasp the unseen structure that regulates but does not formulate the connection or even the meaning, we must bear in mind the various forms in which the textual segments are presented to the reader's viewpoint in the reading process. Their most elementary form is to be seen on the level of the story. The threads of the plot are suddenly broken off, or continued in unexpected directions. One narrative section centers on a particular character and is then continued by the abrupt introduction of new characters. These sudden changes are often denoted by new chapters and so are clearly distinguished; the object of this distinction, however, is not separation so much as a tacit invitation to find the missing link. Furthermore, in each articulated reading moment only segments of textual perspectives are present within the reader's wandering viewpoint.

In order to become fully aware of the implication, we must bear in mind that a narrative text, for instance, is composed of a variety of perspectives, which outline the author's view and also provide access to what the reader is meant to visualize. As a rule, there are four main perspectives in narration—those of the narrator, the characters, the plot, and the fictitious reader. Although these may differ in order of importance, none of them on its own is identical with the meaning of the text, which is to be brought about by their constant intertwining through the reader in the reading process. An increase in the number of blanks is bound to occur through the frequent subdivisions of each of the textual perspectives; thus the narrator's perspective is often split into that of the implied author's set against that of the author as narrator. The hero's perspective may be set against that of the minor characters. The fictitious reader's perspective may be divided between the explicit position ascribed to him and the implicit attitude he must adopt toward that position.

As the reader's wandering viewpoint travels between all these segments, its constant switching during the time flow of reading intertwines them, thus bringing forth a network of perspectives, within which each perspective opens a view not only of others but also of the intended imaginary object. Hence no single textual perspective can be equated with this imaginary object, of which it forms only one aspect. The object itself is a product of interconnection, the structuring of which is to a great extent regulated and controlled by blanks.

In order to explain this operation, we shall first give a schematic description of how the blanks function, and then we shall try to illustrate this function with an example. In the time flow of reading, segments of the various perspectives move into focus and are set off against preceding segments. Thus the segments of narrator, characters, plot, and fictitious reader perspectives are not only marshaled into a graduated sequence but are also transformed into reciprocal reflectors. The blank as an empty space between segments enables them to be joined together, thus constituting a field of vision for the wandering viewpoint. A referential field is always formed when there are at least two positions related to and influencing one another; it is the minimal organizational unit in all processes of comprehension,[9] and it is also the basic organizational unit of the wandering viewpoint.

The first structural quality of the blank, then, is that it makes possible the organization of a referential field of interacting textual segments projecting themselves one upon another. Now, the segments present in the field are structurally of equal value, and the fact that they are brought together highlights their affinities and their differences. This relationship gives rise to a tension that has to be resolved, for, as Arnheim has observed in a more general context: "It is one of the functions of the third dimension to come to the rescue when things get uncomfortable in the second."[10] The third dimension comes about when the segments of the referential field are given a common framework, which allows the reader to relate affinities and differences and so to grasp the patterns underlying the connections. But this framework is also a blank, which requires an act of ideation in order to be filled. It is as if the blank in the field of the reader's viewpoint has changed its position. It began as the empty space between perspective segments, indicating their connectability, and so organizing them into projections of reciprocal influence. But with the establishment of this connectability, the blank, as the unformulated framework of these interacting segments, now enables the reader to produce a determinate relationship between them. We may infer already from this change in position that the blank exercises significant control over all the operations that occur within the referential field of the wandering viewpoint.

Now we come to the third and most decisive function of the blank. Once the segments have been connected and a determinate relationship has been established, a referential field is formed which constitutes a particular reading moment and which in turn has a

READER RESPONSE IN PERSPECTIVE

discernible structure. The grouping of segments within the referential field comes about, as we have seen, by making the viewpoint switch between the perspective segments. The segment on which the viewpoint focuses in each particular moment becomes the theme. The theme of one moment becomes the background against which the next segment takes on its actuality, and so on. Whenever a segment becomes a theme, the previous one must lose its thematic relevance[11] and be turned into a marginal, thematically vacant position, which can be and usually is occupied by the reader so that he may focus on the new thematic segment.

In this connection it might be more appropriate to designate the marginal or horizontal position as a vacancy and not as a blank; blanks refer to suspended connectability in the text, while vacancies refer to nonthematic segments within the referential field of the wandering viewpoint. Vacancies, then, are important guiding devices for building up the aesthetic object, because they condition the reader's view of the new theme, which in turn conditions his view of previous themes. These modifications, however, are not formulated in the text; they are to be implemented by the reader's ideational activity. And so these vacancies enable the reader to combine segments into a field by reciprocal modification, to form positions from those fields, and then to adapt each position to its successor and predecessors in a progress that ultimately transforms the textual perspectives, through a whole range of alternating themes and background relationships, into the aesthetic object of the text.

Let us turn now to an example in order to illustrate the operations sparked off and governed by the vacancies in the referential field of the wandering viewpoint. We shall have a brief look at Fielding's *Tom Jones* and again, in particular, at the characters' perspectives — that of the hero and that of the minor characters. Fielding's aim of depicting human nature is fulfilled by way of a repertoire that incorporates the prevailing norms of eighteenth-century thought systems and social systems and represents them as governing the conduct of the most important characters. In general, these norms are arranged in more or less explicitly contrasting patterns; Allworthy (*benevolence*) is set against Squire Western (*ruling passion*); the same applies to the two pedagogues, Square (*the eternal fitness of things*) and Thwackum (*the human mind as a sink of iniquity*), who in turn are also contrasted with Allworthy and so forth.

Thus, in the individual situation, the hero is linked with the norms of latitudinarian morality, orthodox theology, deistic philosophy, eighteenth-century anthropology, and eighteenth-century aristocracy. Contrasts and discrepancies within the perspective of the characters give rise to the missing links, which enable the hero and the norms to shed light upon one another, and through which the individual situations may combine into a referential field. The hero's conduct cannot be subsumed under the norms, and through the sequence of situations the norms shrink to a reified manifestation of human nature. This, however, is an observation that the reader must make for himself, because such syntheses are rarely given in the text, even though they are prefigured in the theme-and-background structure. The discrepancies continually arising between the perspectives of hero and minor characters bring about a series of changing positions, with each theme losing its relevance but remaining in the background to influence and condition its successor. Whenever the hero violates the norms—as he does most of the time—the resultant situation may be judged in one of two different ways: either the norm appears as a drastic reduction of human nature, in which case we view the theme from the standpoint of the hero, or the violation shows the imperfections of human nature, in which case it is the norm that conditions our view.

In both cases, we have the same structure of interacting positions being transformed into a determinate meaning. For those characters who represent a norm—in particular, Allworthy, Squire Western, Square, and Thwackum—human nature is defined in terms of one principle, so that all those possibilities that are not in harmony with the principle are given a negative slant. But when the negated possibilities exert their influence upon the course of events, and so show up the limitation of the principle concerned, the norms begin to appear in a different light. The apparently negative aspects of human nature fight back, as it were, against the principle itself and cast doubt upon it in proportion to its limitations.

In this way, the negation of other possibilities by the norm in question gives rise to a virtual diversification of human nature, which takes on a definite form to the extent that the norm is revealed as a restriction on human nature. The reader's attention is now fixed, not upon what the norms represent, but upon what their representation excludes, and so the aesthetic object—which is the whole spectrum of human nature—begins to arise out of what is adumbrated by the negated possibilities. In this way, the function of the norms themselves have changed: they no longer represent the social regulators prevalent in the thought systems of the eighteenth century, but instead they indicate the amount of human experience which they suppress because, as rigid principles, they cannot tolerate any modifications.

Transformations of this kind take place whenever the norms are the foregrounded theme and the perspective of the hero remains the background conditioning the reader's viewpoint. But whenever the hero becomes the theme, and the norms of the minor characters shape the viewpoint, his well-intentioned spontaneity turns into the depravity of an impulsive nature. Thus the position of the hero is also transformed, for it is no longer the standpoint from which we are to judge the norms; instead we see that even the best of intentions may come to nought if they are not guided by *circumspection*, and spontaneity must be controlled by *prudence*[12] if it is to allow a possibility of self-preservation.

The transformations brought about by the theme-and-background interaction are closely connected with the changing position of the vacancy within the referential field. Once a theme has been grasped, conditioned by the marginal position of the preceding segment, a feedback is bound to occur, thus retroactively modifying the shaping influence of the reader's viewpoint. This reciprocal transformation is hermeneutic by nature, even though we may not be aware of the processes of interpretation resulting from the switching and reciprocal conditioning of our viewpoints. In this sense, the vacancy transforms the referential field of the moving viewpoint into a self-regulating structure, which proves to be one of the most important links in the interaction between text and reader, and which prevents the reciprocal transformation of textual segments from being arbitrary.

To sum up, then, the blank in the fictional text induces and guides the reader's constitutive activity. As a suspension of connectability between textual perspective and perspective segments, it marks the need for an equivalence, thus transforming the segments into reciprocal projections, which in turn organize the reader's wandering viewpoint as a referential field. The tension that occurs within the field between heterogeneous perspective segments is resolved by the theme-and-background structure, which makes the viewpoint focus on one segment as the theme, to be grasped from the thematically vacant position now occupied by the reader as his standpoint. Thematically vacant positions remain present in the background against which new themes occur; they condition and influence those themes and are also retroactively influenced by them, for as each theme recedes into the background of its successor, the vacancy shifts, allowing a reciprocal transformation to take place. As the vacancy is structured by the sequence of positions in the time flow of reading, the reader's viewpoint cannot proceed arbitrarily; the thematically vacant position always acts as the angle from which a selective interpretation is to be made.

Two points need to be emphasized: (1) we have described the structure of the blank in an abstract, somewhat idealized way in order to explain the pivot on which the interaction between text and reader turns; and (2) the blank has different structural qualities, which appear to dovetail. The reader fills in the blank in the text, thereby bringing about a referential field; the blank arising in turn out of the referential field is filled in by way of the theme-and-background structure; and the vacancy arising from juxtaposed themes and backgrounds is occupied by the reader's standpoint, from which the various reciprocal transformations lead to the emergence of the aesthetic object. The structural qualities outlined make the blank shift, so that the changing positions of the empty space mark out a definite need for determination, which the constitutive activity of the reader is to fulfill. In this sense, the shifting blank maps out the path along which the wandering viewpoint is to travel, guided by the self-regulatory sequence in which the structural qualities of the blank interlock.

Now we are in a position to qualify more precisely what is actually meant by reader participation in the text. If the blank is largely responsible for the activities described, then participation means that the reader is not simply called upon to "internalize" the positions given in the text, but he is induced to make them act upon and so transform each other, as a result of which the aesthetic object begins to emerge. The structure of the blank organizes this participation, revealing simultaneously the intimate connection between this structure and the reading subject. This interconnection completely conforms to a remark made by Piaget: "In a word, the subject is there and alive, because the basic quality of each structure is the structuring process itself."[13] The blank in the fictional text appears to be a paradigmatic structure; its function consists in initiating structured operations in the reader, the execution of which transmits the reciprocal interaction of textual positions into consciousness. The shifting blank is responsible for a sequence of colliding images, which condition each other in the time flow of reading. The discarded image imprints itself on its successor, even though the latter is meant to resolve the deficiencies of the former. In this respect the images hang together in a sequence, and it is by this sequence that the meaning of the text comes alive in the reader's imagination.

THREE
INTERVIEW

Introduction

My aim in organizing this written interview was to encourage an exchange between reader-oriented theories developed in the United States and at Constance. The publication of Iser's own translation of *Der Akt des Lesens* provides the occasion. Initially, I sought our questions from three sources. I asked Norman Holland to take part in this interview since his empirical investigations of reader responses seem to be in sharp contrast to Iser's abstract theory, and since Iser rather extensively criticizes the psychoanalytic model of *The Dynamics of Literary Response*. Wayne Booth's *The Rhetoric of Fiction* has been a central text for Iser, whose earlier notion of the "implied reader" can be regarded as a development of Booth's concept of the "implied author." Moreover, the concerns Wayne Booth articulates in his recent *Critical Understanding* seemed sure to yield incisive questions about *The Act of Reading*. Stanley Fish's earlier affiliation with the "Constance School," set off against the independent and provocative position on the reader's relationship to the literary text that he has subsequently developed, suggested a critical standpoint on Fish's part that would lead to a significant exchange.

Each of the three interviewers was asked to formulate three central questions and, so as to avoid misunderstandings, to specify the context in which the questions were to be taken. Once all the questions were in, I checked them to make sure there was no duplication and sent them to Iser, who sent back his answers. I then furnished the interviewers a complete copy of all the questions and answers, offering them the opportunity to ask follow-up questions, but none felt that this was necessary. However, Stanley Fish, who had complied with my original request for concise, pointed questions, was dissatisfied with the form that the interview—with the extended questions elaborated by Holland and Booth—had taken; he indicated that he would prefer to withdraw. But Iser, having written replies to Fish's "Counterstatements," and having conceived of them as part of the overall statement he sought to convey through the text of the interview, was reluctant to withdraw them. Faced with the need for some kind of compromise, Iser took it upon himself to specify the general concerns articulated in Fish's statements; he then converted his answers into comments on these central issues that he—Iser—had gleaned from Fish's questions and stated in his own—Iser's—terms.

—Rudolf E. Kuenzli

Norman N. Holland Given a chance to ask Wolfgang Iser three questions, I feel like a hero in a fairy tale who has been granted three wishes: my first should be for many more. But three questions have I been granted and three it shall be.

(1) My first, indeed each of my questions, grows out of my experience with actual readers, myself as the test case in *The Dynamics of Literary Response*,[1] other people in *Poems in Persons*,[2] *5 Readers Reading*,[3] and later articles. I and others working at our Center for the Psychological Study of the Arts in Buffalo have been able to collect the varying responses of readers and explicate them in terms of the identities of the different readers.

In *The Act of Reading*,[4] you, just as I, wish "an analysis of what actually happens when one is reading a text" (p. 19). You find it "imperative that these seemingly 'private' processes should be investigated" (p. 24). In *The Act of Reading*, however, there is not one reference to an actual reader actually reading (unless "the" reader or "we" stands for your own readings). Instead, you arrive at your model of reading by building on Husserl, Ingarden, and other philosophical (as opposed to empirical) evidence.

You draw a sharp distinction between a *Rezeptionstheorie*, a theory dealing with actual readers' responses (which you limit to *Urteilen*, judgments (p. 28), by readers in past ages) and a *Wirkungstheorie* of response by an implied reader understood by analyzing the text. I have trouble with this distinction, because I think one can only arrive at a theory of response by induction from actual responses. While that may be difficult for past eras, we have readers aplenty in our own day who are quite willing to tell us (at length!) about a given literary experience. We can actually analyze what they say instead of relying on inference from a text. To insist on the latter seems to me like trying to decide whether the sun is shining by pulling down the shades and consulting an almanac.

Interestingly, in *The Act of Reading*, you dismiss outright the possibility of working with the "contemporary reader," because he "is difficult to mould to the form of a generalization" (p. 27). Yes, it is difficult, yet that, I submit, is precisely what we at this Center have done: provide a general explanation of the readings of contemporary readers. More exactly, we have provided a way of inquiring into the experiences of actual readers that can yield intellectually satisfying answers.

I realize, however, that in calling your attention to empirical results, I am accenting the American (and, to some extent, English) separation of psychology from philosophy. William James is probably the last American whom one could consider both philosopher and psychologist, while in the Continental tradition one could instance Husserl, Merleau-Ponty, Sartre, and many others on whom you rely.

It is this divergence in what we accept as psychological evidence that underlies the deepest difference between your approach and mine, which is also the most tempting to try to bridge through these questions and answers. Hence, my first question to you is: What evidence about the experience of literature can carry weight in both your and my psychological traditions?

(2) Most literary people believe that readers' readings, or (to use a general term) literents' experiences of literature, so overlap that we can safely assume a certain determinate core of shared "meaning." The text defines or limits something all literents share, although individual literents compare or vary that central experience in their individual ways. In literary circles, it seems as obvious and undebatable that texts limit response as that the sky is blue.

On the other hand, our analyses have shown over and over again no such overlap as would allow us to assume the text limits response in any significant way. If we leave readers on their own, as one might read a novel or a book of poems in an armchair at home, we find little or no commonality in what literents report about their responses to literature. To be sure, if we insist on a certain way of reading, as by a final examination in a course, a critical journal's requirements, or psychologist's questionnaire, we do find similar phrasings in responses, but then, obviously, the similarities stem not from the text but from the reader's consenting to the constraints we added. Left to their own desires, literents have such variable experiences, it seems futile to think in terms of a core of limit to response set by the text.

For example, with ten readers reading a short poem by Denise Levertov about her feelings on picking up a green snake, there was not one element common to all ten sets of free associations. The nearest items were the signifier "snake"—but not the animal—and the speaker's being a woman—and that was not stated in the text.[5] We find, for example, that women read gothic novels and men don't—but not all women and not all men.[6] Similarly, there seem to be male-female differences in responses to the death of Cordelia, but the differences among individual men and individual women are just as essential.[7] We find, however, we can account for these differences in response in a systematic, rigorous way, through psychoanalytic identity theory.

It may seem obvious that the sky is blue, but if we explore that perception, we find a complicated refraction of many colors besides blue interacting with an equally complex arithmetic summing of energies through "edge-reading" integrations by our visual cells. Similarly, if we look more closely at the supposed commonalities in literary experiences, we find a complex interaction of shared expectations individually held and individually applied to a shared but individually constituted text. Our analyses of actual readers reading show that commonality comes from expectations in relation to the text rather than a textual determinism. At the very least, I think we have shifted the burden of proof. It is incumbent on those who claim that texts limit response to demonstrate that commonality in specific readings.

In broad outline, Professor Iser, your model in *The Implied Reader*[8] and in *The Act of Reading* posits a text that prestructures a certain role for the reader. The literent is then compelled to fulfill that role, but in tension with his individual "disposition" (I would say "identity"). "Textual repertoires and strategies simply offer a frame within which the reader must construct for himself the aesthetic object" (p. 107). "The relation between text and reader . . . is a moving viewpoint which travels along *inside* that which it has to apprehend" (p. 109). Thus the "concretization" of a literary work—our actual experience of it—comes about as a sequence of schemata in the text stimulates us "to constitute the totality of which the schemata are aspects" (p. 227).

I call this a "bi-active" model. That is, the text actively defines part of the literary experience, and the literent actively fills in the rest. My own model in *Dynamics* was also, more or less, a bi-active model: the text embodies a psychological process, the transformation of fantasy through form (analogous to ego defenses) and the press toward theme (analogous to sublimation). The reader took this process into himself, passing his personal analogies through it. The *Dynamics* model thus comes rather close to yours. It too treats the text as providing "conditions of actualization" (*Aktualisie-*

rungsbedingungen) or "response-inviting structures" *(Wirkungs-strukturen)*, although it does not treat the text as inducing, impelling, or compelling the reader to commit himself to them.[9]

"For our present analysis," you write, "it is the sameness of the process and not the differences in realization that we are concerned with" (p. 143). I could have written the same in 1968. As a result of working with actual readers, however, I have found the differences in literary responses to a given text far more essential than the similarities. Hence, I believe, bi-active models of the literary experience need to be recast within the larger framework of a transactive model.[10]

In a transactive model, the literent begins and creates the response. The text changes the consequences of what the literent brings to it. The literent creates meaning and feeling in one continuous and indivisible transformation of unconscious fantasy through defenses toward theme (the transformation of *Dynamics*, not "in" the text, but created as the reader adapts the text to her needs). One cannot separate, as in a bi-active theory, one part of response coming from the text and another part coming from the literent. Rather, the literent builds a personal response by a personal use of the several elements of the text, a response that the text may or may not reinforce. In a transactive model, I am engaged in a feedback loop (or, to be less technical, a dialogue) with the text. I bring schemata to bear on the text, and the text either does or does not reward them. The schemata I bring to bear may be literary, cultural, biological, or the results of economic class (as with your "real" reader), but it is I who bring them to bear as I understand and use them through my unique identity. It is I who start the dialogue with the text and I who sustain it. It is I who ask questions of the text and I who hear and interpret the answers in the idiom of my personal identity. And we can explore the relation of such a response to the reader's personality in great detail, unfolding terms like "subjective" or "intersubjective" so they need no longer serve to end discussion.

Interestingly, Professor Iser, you also discuss your model as a feedback loop, but with a fundamental difference. "Each text constitutes its own reader" (p. 157). "The reader's communication with the text is a dynamic process of self-correction, as he formulates signifieds which he must then continually modify" (p. 67). He "must" because of new information the text feeds him, he being inside its frame. In other words, the determinism in the loop comes from the text.

Can this text-active assumption explain the very large differences

READER RESPONSE IN PERSPECTIVE

in readers' responses to any one text? They can be accounted for by a feedback loop if the determinism comes from a reader who begins, shapes, and ends his relation to the text in his own idiom by his own choices (which we can understand as functions of his identity). Can they be accounted for by a determinism from the text? The differences in response are thus a crucial element between us and the basis for my second question: If—and that "if" echoes my first question about evidence—if differences in responses to literature are very substantial relative to the similarities, can you use a bi-active model to provide a comprehensive account of the literary transaction?

(3) My third question searches two assumptions in *The Act of Reading*. First, you have a very specific notion of what makes up reading. "Consistency-building is the indispensable basis for all acts of comprehension" (p. 125), leading, presumably, to "the production of the aesthetic object (i.e., the meaning of the text)" (p. 96). "The perception of deformed [i.e., unrealistic?] aspects can only be completed by producing the virtual cause of the deformations" (p. 228). Reading, in other words, consists of building some consistent, explanatory totality. Now, while I feel sure many readings, particularly by critics, answer to this description, I feel equally sure that other relations to literary texts are possible.

One might simply laugh at *Tristram Shandy* instead of "constituting meaning" for it in the special uniting of perspectives you describe. One might analogize one's own history to key events or words. One might identify with a Hamlet or a Mrs. Ramsey. One could just enjoy the sensuous beauty of a line in a narrative like "Azure saints mid silver rays." One might freely associate to a text, as in my experiments with readers. In seminars at our Center, we have learned to convert such free associations to a richer response by a process called "poem opening": one passes an association, even if very remote, back through the text to see what new features and themes the association leads one to highlight.[11] In short, I think "reading" can include many kinds of literary experience besides constituting meaning. And of course, one can hear a poem recited or see a play performed as well as "read" literature—I use the term "literent" to include and remind us of these possibilities.

A second assumption: although your title and preface promise a theory of reading in general, in practice you limit your model to fiction. Indeed your reliance on the four perspectives of narrator, character, plot, and the fictitious reader and your discussion of blanks and negation seem to confine your theory intrinsically to a more or less realistic fiction, more if Fielding, less if Beckett, but mimetic always. Now any definition of "mimetic" fiction is bound to get blurry round the edges. Does not that blur get carried over to the model of reading you propose?

If you limit your theory to fiction, then I think you are making essential to the fundamental processes by which we perceive and know literature the iffy and ephemeral distinctions among our definitions of literary genres, say, among fiction and closet or epic drama or among fiction, narrative poetry, or dramatic monologue. Indeed, if the limitation of your model to reading mimetic fiction is essential, ruling out the seeing or hearing of literature, you may have narrowed your theory of reading so it will not distinguish the seeing of *The Comedy of Errors* from reading the *Cliff's Notes* summary of its plot.

You also suggest that your bi-active, filling-the-limits model for apprehending an object (an Other) "is unique to literature" (p. 109), although I suppose I must read "fiction" for "literature"—indeed your German is *fiktionale Texte*. In a way, this limitation is flattering to us literary people: you make fiction something quite special. Intellectually, however, it is awkward to suppose that we suddenly reverse our entire cognitive system when we shift from fact to fiction, from, say, the real *Fanal de Rouen* to Flaubert's fictional imitations of such a provincial newspaper.

You seem to imply that the status of the text, fiction or nonfiction, determines our reading of it. So far as I can find out, however, the direction of causality is the other way round. Eighty years of experimental psychology testify with extraordinary unanimity that, in perception, cognition, and memory, we actively construct the world which then does or does not reward our constructions according to whether they are adaptive or not. My beliefs about fiction determine, not "fictionality."

Again, we encounter Wiener's seminal concept of the feedback loop. A bi-active model of reading or any model in which the text on its own initiative, so to speak, controls a part of response reverses the feedback loop that this long line of psychological research has so firmly established. By contrast, a transactive model of literary response puts the literent or reader in the driver's seat (to continue Wiener's metaphor of the *cybernos* or steersman) and matches the psychological tradition. We read literature as we perceive reality, by bringing schemata to bear on a chunk of reality, the text, that may or may not gratify them.

Further, many of these psychologists have pointed out that one needs a "top-level" concept of human nature to account for our active, indeed controlling, role in perception and cognition.[12] The identity theory by which we explain characteristic styles of interpreting and experiencing literature provides just such a top-level theory of motivation, so that a transactive theory of reading meshes precisely with contemporary psycholinguistics and cognitive and perceptual psychology.[13]

My third question, then, asks if your bi-active theory can do the same. Can you open your bi-active model toward other relations to a text besides the constituting of meaning, other kinds of texts besides fiction, other modes of seeing or hearing literature besides reading, and other non-literary acts of perception and cognition?

Wolfgang Iser. My answer to Professor Holland's first question may appear somewhat circumstantial, but I hope it will bring out the basic difference between his approach and my own. If there is no reference in my book "to an actual reader actually reading," this is because my aim was to construct a heuristic model of the activities basic to text-processing. I freely admit that this approach is indicative of my "Continental tradition," but I must stress the fact that I have constructed this model not for its own sake but in order to provide a *framework* that would permit assessment and evaluation of actual readers' responses to a literary text.

I believe Professor Holland would agree that one needs certain presuppositions if one is to investigate what happens in the reader while he reads. If one had no heuristic assumptions, it would be difficult to learn anything from an actual reader's response, and so our prime requirement is a frame of reference to which we can relate our findings. I take it that Professor Holland would not dispute this procedure, since he himself started out with definite assumptions in his *Dynamics of Literary Response.* However, instead of committing myself to a clear-cut theory like psychoanalysis, I have tried to establish my idealized model of text-processing along phenomenological lines. I have done so mainly for two reasons: (1) a phenomenological description allows us to focus on processes of constitution that occur not only in reading but also in our basic relations to the world in general; and (2) an idealized model that allows description of constitutive processes bears within itself a hermeneutic implication. Idealization entails abstraction. An abstraction, in turn, requires modification through empirical findings. Thus there is two-way traffic between an idealized model and the data that it is meant to assess, so that certain data must inevitably call for differentiation of the model. If I had committed myself in advance to a specific psychological concept, I might have eliminated this hermeneutic interaction, since the idealized model would then have been unable to accommodate contradictory findings. But it is precisely this interaction that seems to me indispensable if the critic wishes to help chart the human imagination by ways of its responses to literature. The hermeneutic feedback is blocked or even obliterated if one sets out with an established theory for which one seeks support in literature. The literary work is then downgraded to the status of an illustration for the theory in question. There have been tremendous changes in psychoanalytic theory since it was first formulated by Freud, and these prove that a hermeneutic process has been operative here too, reorienting if not recasting the initial framework.

I believe that this basic hermeneutic procedure can bridge the gap between Professor Holland and myself. If he intends to build a theory out of his mass of data, he will have to differentiate his initial psychoanalytic orthodoxy; I for my part will have to differentiate the patterns and features of my construct in view of the results that assessments of actual reader responses by a descriptive model are bound to yield.

One remark of Professor Holland's highlights the difference between our angles of approach. My distinction between *Rezeptionstheorie* and *Wirkungstheorie* strikes him as problematic, because "one can only arrive at a theory of response by induction from actual responses," but I maintain that a framework must precede this induction if one is to draw any inferences from the responses. Therefore, what I call reception is a product that is initiated in the reader by the text, but is molded by the norms and values that govern the reader's outlook. Reception is therefore an indication of preferences and predilections that reveal the reader's disposition as well as the social conditions that have shaped his attitudes. If I wish to assess such a product, I must examine the response-inviting structures of the text, so that I can see how much the actual reader has selected from the potential inherent in the text. This potential is discernible through the history of reception, which enables us to understand why certain aspects of the response-inviting structures have remained unactivated in certain periods while others were given preference. Obviously the textual organization allows for these different actualizations, and so reception (and interpretation, for that matter) may therefore be considered as important evidence for (1)

READER RESPONSE IN PERSPECTIVE

a historically conditioned unfolding of the text's potential; (2) the indispensable constitution of the text in the reader's mind, which brings it to life; and (3) the observable shift in backgrounding and foregrounding of textual features that occur in every actual response. There thus emerges an intricate hermeneutic interrelation between *Wirkung*, as a response-inviting structure, and reception, as the result of a selective operation carried out by the actual reader.

At this point, we come to various options arising out of Professor Holland's first question. One could focus on the historically conditioned selective operations underlying documented reader responses, with a view to explaining why particular attitudes have been elicited by a text. Or one could equally well focus on the network of interrelations between textual features and the patterns into which they have been combined. In the one instance, my concern is with the results produced by a text when a reader has been affected by it; in the other, I am interested in the patterning of the text, which I would regard as aesthetic since it both initiates and pre-structures the actual response. In the final analysis, one must keep both ends of the spectrum in view, but in my book I have concentrated on describing the network of textual relationships as a basic prerequisite for the production of the aesthetic effect.

Professor Holland's second question arises from a fundamental agreement between the blueprints of our respective theories. I am particularly grateful to him for crediting my model—at least up to a point—with what he calls the feedback loop, implying that an initially bi-active model is thereby transformed into a transactive one. It was indeed my intention to grapple with the text-reader interaction—an event considerably less easy to define than the two positions individually. On the basis of this shared understanding Professor Holland takes exception to the prominence I appear to give the text in this "literary transaction." If my dialogue-model does indeed give the impression that I emphasize a "determinism in the loop" coming solely from the text, I can only say that this was quite unintentional. What I meant to say was as follows: textual schemata function basically in two ways—they impart information to the reader, but equally they invoke knowledge from his own highly individualized store of experience. In this sense, the schemata restrict the scope of the material from which the overall textual pattern is to be built; at the same time they prefigure what the reader is given to ideate.

I emphasize the difference between ideation and perception because when one reads a text, there are no given objects to be perceived; instead objects must be built up from the knowledge invoked or the information provided. It is this operation—common to every reader—that lifts the reader out of the situation he was in prior to reading. Perhaps it even "teases him out of thought." This temporary removal from everyday life is evident when, for instance, we are immersed in a book, someone enters the room, and we need a few moments to adapt ourselves to the new and actual situation. In this respect—taking the reader away from actuality—I would say that the text does constitute its reader, because it gives him certain instructions that he has to fulfill; but it is, of course, beyond question that the chain of images produced in the continual process of ideation is colored and permeated by highly individual associations. In this sense, the text triggers the ideational activities intended and, up to a point, guided by the sequence of its schemata. There is no doubt that the content of these schemata is pictured according to the disposition of the individual reader. However, I would not go as far as Professor Holland does, in saying that the determinism in the feedback loop "comes from a reader who begins, shapes, and ends his relation to the text in his own idiom by his own choices (which we can understand as functions of his identity)." There are two main reasons why it is hard for me to go along with this kind of statement, and these may perhaps help to make my position clear. First, I feel that the identity of a reader is not so clear-cut as the statement seems to assume. Reading sparks off an ideational activity in the course of which each individual reader will have to discard and replace the ideas formed through information provided and knowledge invoked; it seems to me that this process, always active as the reader travels inside the text and executes the instructions given to him, actually gives shape to his identity. If that is the case— and following the lines of gestalt psychology, I would plead most emphatically that it is—then the actual reader's so-called identity may, in the final analysis, be brought to light and articulated by the very activities to which he has been subjected in following the instructions laid down by the text.

Second, divergent responses need not necessarily be an indication that the determinism of the feedback loop comes from the reader. The divergencies could simply indicate the way each reader translates the text-induced experience into his own frame of reference, which Professor Holland calls his identity. The "determinism" would then imply not that the reader merely projects his own existing identity onto the text but that his identity—which assumes its shape through the text-guided ideational activities—is a means of taking over into his own store of experience something that had so far been alien to him. Identity would then, of course, have a completely different function from that which Professor Holland attributes to it.

Divergent responses would be an interesting basis for investigation into the proliferative effect resulting whenever a literary text is to be incorporated into the individual reader's store of experience. A new area of research would open up, relating to the degree in which (1) fictionality activates human faculties in a way not called upon during our everyday lives, and (2) we are able to understand a literary experience that as an actual experience has never been our own.

Finally, I am not very happy with the word *determinism* as applied to a transactive model. If Professor Holland and I agree that our models should be, and perhaps are, conceived in terms of a text-reader dialogue, then the term *determinism* seems to me inappropriate, for it transmutes the two-way traffic between text and reader into a one-way system, either from text to reader or from reader to text. Should Professor Holland really commit himself to some form of determinism, then I fear his own transactive model will relapse into a bi-active one.

Professor Holland's final question seems drastically to constrict the range of my key term *consistency-building*, which I consider to be basic to text-processing and hence to grasping a text. First of all, consistency-building has nothing to do with explanation. It is a passive synthesis occurring below the threshold of our consciousness while we read. Consistency-building establishes "good continuation" between textual segments in the time-flow of reading, and is thus an indispensable prerequisite for assembling an overall pattern. This pattern is what I have called the aesthetic object of the text: it is an object, insofar as it assumes a gestalt during the process of consistency-building; it is aesthetic insofar as it is produced by the reader following the instructions—at least up to a point—laid down by the text. The aesthetic object is a product of ideation, and so cannot be matched with any other object in the empirical world. It may have a whole range of qualities. It might simply be an experience—which of course initially it always will be—or it may assume a degree of precision which could then be considered meaning. And although the latter is very frequently the case, I should certainly not want to identify the aesthetic object solely with meaning; had I wished to do so, I should scarcely have bothered to use two different terms.

Now all the different reactions that Professor Holland describes, such as identifying with Hamlet, analogizing one's own history to key events in the story, and so forth, are no doubt possible. However, all such reactions must be preceded by the process of consistency-building, which arises from the suspended connectability of segments—I must build up an image of Hamlet before I can identify with him. Let me stress again that, although consistency-building is indispensable to the act of constituting meaning, it is not confined to that act. Professor Holland's list of reactions do not depend on meanings being constituted, but they are all related to consecutive operations through which we absorb into ourselves that which the text has given us to do. This holds equally true of our laughter at certain passages in *Tristram Shandy*, where the laugh is a physical reaction to the apparent incompatibility of textual perspectives. I do not laugh all the time while I am reading *Tristram Shandy*, but when I do, it is often because the perspectives refuse to be united; this "refusal" can only come about if I am engaged in an effort to establish "good continuation"—and this, after all, is only the psychological term for the phenomenological concept of consistency-building.

If we are to find a term to cover Professor Holland's other "kinds of literary experience," we might perhaps use 'significance' in Hirsch's sense. I would consider 'meaning' to be the referential totality implied by the different segments of the text, and 'significance' to be the reader's absorption of the meaning or experience into his own existence.

Professor Holland's next point also harps on limitations inherent in the model proposed. It is certainly true that I have used mainly fiction to illustrate my argument. I have done so because narrative texts provide the greatest variety of facets pertinent to an analysis of the act of reading. It is not true, however, that I have drawn all my examples from and based my findings on mimetic fiction. I have dealt extensively with modern nonmimetic fiction from Joyce to Beckett—a fact that, in turn, has given rise to another charge occasionally leveled against me: that *The Act of Reading* is basically a modernistic aesthetics. In fact I could just as easily have illustrated my arguments through poetry or drama, and indeed these 'genres' might well have made it easier for me to expound, for instance, the function of blanks and negations. The basic idea of theme and horizon can be strikingly illuminated by poems, where the reading of the second stanza occurs against the background or horizon of the first and is conditioned by it. The empty space between stanza

1 and stanza 2 is an invitation to link both together, and thus the reading of stanza 2 is indisputably shaped by what has been read before. Take Keats's "Ode on a Grecian Urn," for example: Stanza 4 appears to contrast with and even to negate much of what we have read before, and this negation is conditioned by the snowballing consistency-building through which the previous stanzas have become interlinked. But as the negation appears against this background, there is not only a link but also a retroactive effect on what has gone before, with a consequent reshaping of the images built up in the reader's mind. Thus the conditioning view and the conditioned view are constantly interacting, and my basic idea of switching perspectives as the particular mode through which consistency-building occurs is clearly characterized by a feedback loop and not by a mechanical, one-way process through which either text or reader determines what is going on.

This reciprocal conditioning that occurs in the time-flow of reading is also influenced, of course, by the 'genre.' The genre is a code element that invokes certain expectations in the reader, given his familiarity with the code. In this respect, I would regard the genre as part of the repertoire, though there is no doubt that the many elements of the repertoire encapsulated in each text will not be equally well known to every reader of the text. Nevertheless, the basic differences between genres will precondition different attitudes toward the text, and this applies equally to the distinction between fiction and nonfiction.

In fiction, the aesthetic object is something that has to be assembled and ideated in the reader's mind and has no exact match in the empirically given world; different readers will evolve different attitudes toward what they are made to produce, simply because each one is personally (and so differently) involved in the production. The aesthetic object ideated in the reader's mind simultaneously emerges from him and absorbs him.

With nonfiction—a newspaper report, for instance—we are also given something to ideate. However, the facts themselves exist independently of our activity of picturing them. The object and the image are two different things, and the object would certainly look different if I were to perceive it—as Gilbert Ryle has explained at some length. If we have to ideate an existing, though absent, object, we produce certain views of it, but we do not produce the object itself. In reading fiction, we produce both the views and the object. Consequently, we are transposed into an imaginary existence—we live, as Henry James once said, at least temporarily another life.

Clearly the reading of fiction and nonfiction results in a different molding of our existence, and yet both types of writing—representing extreme positions on the scale—require consistency-building as a basic prerequisite if the reader is to relate subsequently either to that which is given (factual object) or to that which he has produced (aesthetic object).

Finally, Professor Holland's concluding remark seems to me to underline what is perhaps the basic difference between us. He maintains that one needs a top-level concept of human nature in order to account for all the active processes of perception and cognition that occur in reading. I would argue the other way round. As literary critics, we deal with a medium that is not only different from other media, but that stimulates perceptional, ideational, and cognitive activities in a way that offers a special access to the workings of the human imagination. Instead of *starting out* with a top-level concept of human nature, I should prefer to arrive at such a concept *after* having charted the various modes through which literature acts upon, utilizes, and molds human faculties. If this brings out our difference, it strikes me as strange that Professor Holland, having been raised in the Anglo-American intellectual tradition, is pleading for a deductive operation, whereas I myself, being conditioned by the Continental tradition, am advocating an inductive one. Of course each inductive move presupposes certain models in order to map out a path along which investigations may be conducted, but such models are only heuristic instruments; the path would be blocked if any model achieved sufficient success to become reified.

Wayne Booth It is not hard to predict some of the unhelpful responses that your splendid inquiry into "the 'dialogue' between text and reader" will produce. Some will think that you are not *really* a "reader-critic," because you betray much too strong a reliance on the reality of the text; again and again you show that for you different texts require different reading behavior, and you clearly imply that you do not accept all readings as equally valid. Others will think that you have sold out to subjectivism (despite your own clear demurrers), because you show too *little* respect for the text's authority; you consistently defend the legitimacy of many different responses to any one text, and you never provide the kind of full formal analysis of a complete work that would have been typical of some American new critics, or of my own mentors, "The Chicago School." There may even be some who will defend this or that rear or advance guard by deploring your neglect of talk about the *real* author, or the real writer of the text, language.

Such continuations of ancient debates about the primacy of author, text, or reader (speaker, speech, audience) are pointless, I think, but I fear that you may unintentionally invite them by the way in which you set up your case for "the reader-oriented" perspective. I hope I am wrong, and in any case the strength of your method in no way depends on proving the invalidity of possible similar inquiries about how *real* authors, say, create *implied* authors and thus mold implied readers; about how joining an implied reader may have ethical effects on readers; or about how texts reflect both the intentions of authors and the norms of cultures.

Rather than pursue any of those questions that would be extrinsic to your enterprise, I'd like to try out two related questions that might be prefaced with some such query as: "Do you see the possibility for a further chapter on . . . ?"

(1) What I would miss most, if I took your book as an effort to describe everything important that happens to me when I read a fictional text, is an account of my irresistible impulse to deal with the text as a person, or, if you prefer, as the act of a person, the implied author. You do, of course, talk occasionally about the implied author, but you consistently avoid personifying *the text* as implied author, or as a reader and author dramatized in a joint action together.

In most of my reading of fiction and poetry, and in much of my reading and viewing of drama, I find prominent in both thought and emotion not only the interest of the reconstructive steps you describe but also my sense of a person addressing me as his prospective friend, crony, co-conspirator, fellow victim, prospective convert, or what not, and I thus find that my responses are often best put not in your terms of seeking a *meaning* or becoming "entangled in the text" (p. 130), but rather in the terms of love or hate, admiration or detestation, good or bad fellowship, domination or seduction, and so on.

Here, then, is my first question: Do you see any use, building from what you have done, in exploring the ways in which authors imply and often achieve such personal, powerfully dramatic bondings? Would a consideration, say, of Kenneth Burke's "dramatic" vocabulary, describing texts not only as interesting bodies of meaning but as dramatic personal encounters accomplishing many different ends, be a possible addition to what you have done? Burke is fond of making wonderful long lists of the great miscellany of literary purposes that contrast sharply with our usual reductions to one grand purpose, or at most two: mimetic/didactic; pleasure/ instruction; dulce/utile. In "Literature as Equipment for Living,"[14] for example, he describes literary works as helping us to select enemies and allies, to socialize our losses, to ward off the evil eye, to purify or desanctify our worlds, to propitiate our gods; as consoling and admonishing and exhorting us; as foretelling, instructing, charting, and praying.

Could one add such talk to what you have done? Or do you see it as in conflict because it is so obviously not "aesthetic"? In short, is your relatively emotion-free account of encounters with *texts* in conflict with Burke's (or any other) language of dramatic encounter with authors, or could it serve as a basis for extending into such matters?

In thinking about this question I have found myself wondering why you were in general so chary of affective responses to the text. You seldom talk about the text arousing any desire except for our interest in its "meaning." The "tenterhooks of suspense," for example, that Virginia Woolf mentions in her reading of Austen (p. 168) play no significant role in your own analysis; the stimulation of "desires," described in your quotation from W. D. Harding (p. 158), is also not given much attention—except, of course, the desire to discover a meaning. I don't want to suggest that you never touch on such matters, only that they play no strong functional role in an analysis that quite rightly insists on talking about functions.

One might view my trouble here as simply a variant of the first question: Is what I see as a neglect of matters like laughter, tears, fear, horror, disgust, joy, and celebration inherent to your analysis or simply something that requires a supplemental account, "another chapter"?

(2) I am not at all sure that I have figured out what you mean by the "implied reader." At times you talk as if you would restrict the term to something like "the totality of tasks of interpretation *required* by a given text." At other times you seem to extend it to include "the totality of inferences *allowed by* a given text." Sometimes the implied reader spreads over the whole of what is allowed and at other times he becomes sharply distinguished from either the "fictitious reader" dramatized in the text, or the flesh-and-blood reader who exists independently of the text, or the ideal reader.

Perhaps a re-reading of your book will clear this up for me, but meanwhile I hope that the following question can be answered within the scope allowed for your reply here:

Would your conception of the implied reader be underlined, or destroyed, or enriched, by saying that the reader-in-the-text, at least when the text is what we call fictional, is *always* a double figure? He is *both* a credulous or "pretending" person, and a doubter. The first could be said to accept all the moves required including fantastic steps, like turning young men into beetles, and incredible beliefs, such as "people can live happily forever after." The second is a more sophisticated ambassador from the "real world," one who is able to permit or even encourage the credulous activity of his twin but who knows all the while that some parts of what is embraced during the reading do not accord with his beliefs back in the "real world."

I have slowly discovered that my own discussion of the implied author in *The Rhetoric of Fiction* was too simple in this respect, as you suggest in chapter 2. It seemed at times to say that the author we find implied in the text has cut all of his moorings with the "real world," and it thus led some readers into awkward ways of talking about how we in fact do make valid inferences from implied authors to real authors. But both the author and the reader in the text are not simple, single, credulous folk who believe in all the norms of the work, including beetle-metamorphoses: they are complex folk who can pretend to believe and yet remember that they are pretending. They are thus like those sophisticated spectators Samuel Johnson talks about when he refutes the importance of unity of place; they are never troubled by being transported from Egypt to Rome between scenes, because they had never fully believed themselves anywhere but in the theater. Like those spectators, the implied reader must be able to carry out both demands simultaneously; if he misplays either role, the fiction will be destroyed. And both roles are implied in the text.

You often imply this inescapable double effect, but when you *talk* about it (e.g., on p. 37), you seem to see the *implied* reader as only the credulous reader in the text, while the resisting, criticizing, modifying, remembering of the real world is all done somehow by the "real reader" as *not* implied in the text. Do I misread you? If not, would you see any way to deal with what seems to me inescapable, that the text does absolutely imply, indeed demand, a reader who can perform both of the described roles? Surely it could not succeed, as fiction, if it did not.

Another way of putting this question would be to ask what moves, taken by the "real reader" after the reading experience, would distress the implied author of a given work. (You see how

I sneak in my language of personification! Does it seem unreasonable to talk of an implied author being distressed? It does not to me, since I carry with me a picture of the author after the reading is over—that is, I go on "reading" a work, in a sense, long after I have put down the physical object, and I can surely distress or please the implied author—whom I have after all made for myself in re-constructing the text—by violating his beliefs and desires.) It seems to me self-evident that the implied author of any *didactic* work, at least, whether we define such works as simple and blatant, like Aesop's fables, or subtle and complex, like Milton's epics, would be distressed if, after I put down the work, I said to myself, "Well, now I can go back to my previous beliefs about overweening pride or about how the ways of God are to be justified." But is it not equally true that some of the norms of even the most fully purified *non-didactic* works are clearly seen by the implied author as not simply taken up for the duration and then dropped (for me the question of what the real writer felt about them is entirely separate, though not beyond speculation).

In short, some beliefs and norms are for the implied author fixed, and some are not; he implies that some not only can be applied in the real world but should be (e.g., in *Ulysses*, sensitivity to delicate distinctions of verbal tone is important, and that sensitivity is not to be shucked off when we stop reading); and some are merely provisional for the duration (e.g., again in *Ulysses*, Stephen Dedalus is a real person with a theory about *Hamlet*—a belief that *is* to be shucked off after reading).

I've chosen here extreme and easy examples to illustrate the double nature of the persons implied, but obviously the chief interest to criticism, and particularly to evaluative criticism (which of course is not your immediate concern) would lie in the range of discrim-inations such doubling would allow in our descriptions of the im-plied readers we are to become. Such interest will be greatest pre-cisely at those points at which the discrimination between fixed and unfixed norms is hardest to make. A whole new kind of "ethical criticism" might become possible if we learned how to distinguish books that invite us to embrace fixed norms that are not, on cool reflection after the reading experience, supportable, from those whose implied authors survive intact, in all their complexity, after our most rigorous criticism.

If this does not seem to you a promising direction for some kind of criticism of ethical effects on real readers, effects that result from the implied readers they have joined (or become), what is *your* way of dealing with the fact—and surely it is a fact—that who we are in "real life" is in large part a result of the friendships we have made with various implied authors?

Wolfgang Iser It may well be, as Professor Booth has suggested, that my exposition of the dialogue between text and reader gives rise to a host of charges along the lines of the old questions and old answers that have beset and plagued literary criticism in our time. Up to a point I may even have asked for it by leveling criticism at entrenched positions. However, I could not agree more with Professor Booth in that "continuations of ancient debates about the primacy of author, text and reader . . . are pointless," and that the various unhelpful responses that have sprung to his mind might in the final analysis be extrinsic to what I had intended to do.

The event that takes place between text and reader is a peculiarly difficult region to chart. Literary criticism has so far been very hesitant in coming to grips with the intangible processes operative between text and reader. This may be one reason why it lags behind the social sciences, which have devised different frameworks to encompass these seemingly ungraspable operations of dyadic interaction. Devising a framework for literary communication would imply exploring the basic asymmetry between a literary text and its potential reader; one would have to describe this asymmetry in terms of why and how it triggers, stimulates, and even controls the developing communication between text and reader. Focusing on this area implies rearranging the traditional set of questions and answers in literary criticism, and a rearrangement of this kind will—as Professor Booth has suggested—invite all kinds of critical reservations from those who not only have well-established opinions on what text, author, reader, subjectivism, and objectivism are, but who also know for sure that what they know is true. If text-processing is a covered process, then an explanation of how literature communicates requires a heuristic model in order to spotlight the basic features of this transaction.

This brings me to Professor Booth's first question. Basically I would admit that there is "the possibility of a further chapter on . . ." As to the one that Professor Booth proposes, I should like to emphasize a distinction that I consider to be important. If a reader's reading gives prominence to "dramatic bondings" with the author, who may emerge as "friend, crony, co-conspirator, fellow-victim, prospective convert," such a relationship can only arise from an operation carried out by the reader. The image of the author gradually gaining shape in the mind's eye of the reader presupposes consistency-building, without which no image, even of an author, could be entertained in one's imagination. Consistency-building in turn is governed, of course, by the reader's preferences, predilections, codes, and also his unconscious disposition. Consequently this very process is bound to be selective, and its outcome indicates both the implications of the text and the preferences of the reader. The reader's relationship with the author therefore results from a sequence of imaginings, in the course of which he ideates the author as crony or as prospective friend, and he can only experience such a "bonding" because he has been caught up in the very ideas that the text has stimulated him into producing. Thus the encounter with the author may be all the more powerful as we have not encountered him in person but in a text-guided, though self-produced, image; the subsequent affective reaction to something we have produced ourselves may then account for the laughter, tears, fear, horror, and so forth that Professor Booth has mentioned.

Now if there were a further chapter to my book on readers' reactions to "dramatic bondings" with an author, I would show that these indicate certain preferences in the reader concerned— preferences that manifest themselves in the very selections the reader has made within the network of possible connections between textual segments.

Furthermore, I do not—as Professor Booth quite rightly assumes—consider these 'products' as aesthetic; I would, however, maintain that they issue forth from an aesthetic effect indicated, developed, and carried out in text-processing. It may be in the nature of an aesthetic effect that it eventually results in something non-aesthetic, that is, practical, and in this respect I would subscribe to all those suggestions that Professor Booth has quoted from Kenneth Burke's "Literature as Equipment for Living." I would even go so far as to say that the very importance of these practical or (as Professor Booth suggests toward the end of his statement) ethical results necessitates a much more detailed inspection of the processes that enable an aesthetic effect to arise and transmute itself into something nonaesthetic. I have focused on these hidden processes, and have tried to devise a framework in order to come to grips with them; such a framework may enable us not only to spotlight the transmutation, but also to assess the results at which each individual reader may arrive, thereby revealing his governing codes and habitual orientations.

If I had to tack on another chapter to my book concerning the reader's particular image of the implied author, I would continue to follow my initial line and emphasize not so much the personification of the text, but the particular type of "conversation" to which the implied author invites his potential reader. There is always a game going on between author and reader, and I am not sure to what extent one could separate the image of an implied author from the part that each plays in that game. The two are clearly tied together, and so the image of the implied author appears less a self-sufficient entity than a function of seducing, tempting, exasperating, affirming, and pleasing the reader—thereby indicating that the very image is a constitutive feature for the cooperative enterprise that is a basic condition of the literary text.

As to the second question regarding my concept of the "implied reader," I also meant to stress the double figure of the reader-in-the-text, although perhaps not exactly along the lines Professor Booth has developed. We are in agreement that the implied reader designates the reader's role and is not identical with the dramatized fictitious reader (which I consider to be a textual strategy and thus an integral *feature* of the reader's role). As a rule we readers slip into the role mapped out by the text. The split that then occurs, and that is responsible for the double figure, is due to the fact that on the one hand we are prepared to assume the role, and yet on the other we cannot completely cut ourselves off from what we are—not least as we have to understand what we are given to perform. Thus, the double figure—at least to my mind—is not inscribed into the reader-in-the-text, but comes about whenever we perform the role assigned to us by placing ourselves at the disposal of someone else's thoughts, thereby relegating our own beliefs, norms, and values to the background. This also holds true in the instances Professor Booth has enumerated, when the reader's role itself becomes more complicated. I would not deny that in certain texts this role is itself marked by a split, in the sense that the reader is cast both as a credulous person and as a doubter of his own credulity; Joyce may be a case in point. Nevertheless, a role marked by this dichotomy is still related to the disposition of the real reader, as its function is to draw him into the text and thus separate him, at least temporarily, from his habitual orientation. So there may be a double figure inscribed into the very role the reader is given to perform, but this does not affect the basic split that always occurs between role and habitual orientation.

Now, this situation gives rise to two consequences. There is definitely a graded range of relationships between the real reader and his role. Even if he is absorbed in the role, his preferences, dispositions, and attitudes will still govern his relationship to what the role offers him. Scott's *Waverley Novels* are a striking example in this respect. The role provided by them has been differently actualized by nineteenth-century readers, children, and twentieth-century readers. Obviously the role itself is not only subject to selective realizations, but will also be differently actualized according to prevailing codes. Still I would maintain that in all instances the basic split between the role assumed and the habitual orientation of the reader is bound to occur.

This ties in with the second consequence to be drawn. Whenever the split occurs—I have suggested that it results in a "contrapuntally structured personality" in reading—the resultant tension calls for resolution. The resolution, however, cannot come about simply by restoring habitual orientation to the self which had been temporarily relegated to the background. Playing the role involves incorporating the new experience. Consequently, the reader is affected by the very role he has been given to play, and his being affected does not reinvoke his habitual orientation but mobilizes the spontaneity of the self. The type of mobilized spontaneity will depend, though, on the nature of the text to which we have made ourselves present in playing the role. It will cast the released spontaneity into a certain shape and thus begin to mold what it has called forth. As the nature and the extent of released spontaneity are governed by the individuality of the text, a layer of the reader's personality is brought to light which had hitherto remained hidden in the shadows. In this sense something is formulated in the reader under conditions that are not set by himself and that thus enable the experience to penetrate into his consciousness. This marks the point where the split between habitual orientation and role may result in what Professor Booth calls "criticism of ethical effects on real readers." I attach as much importance to this as does Professor Booth, and it was my endeavor to give a phenomenologically oriented account of the way in which a literary text begins to claw its way into us. The reader-in-the-text, or what I have called the implied reader, is meant as a heuristic concept that will help us to focus on the split and thus establish a framework for assessing the variegated types of realization that occur whenever we read.

There are two minor points to which I should like to address myself briefly. If I have given the impression that I seem obsessed by "seeking a meaning" this is due to the fact that I should like to move the discussion of meaning onto a different plane: not what the meaning is, but how it is produced. This seems to me to require investigation in view of the fact that we take something for granted of which we have so little knowledge. My basic concern, however, is not with meaning-assembly as such but with what I have termed the aesthetic object, which has to be created in the act of reading by following the instructions given in the text. Analysis of production is important for two closely related reasons: (1) the aesthetic object the reader is given to build involves him in an experience that he himself has to bring about, and (2) as the aesthetic object emerges from the aspects and schemata given in the text, it provides a vantage point for assessing and evaluating these very aspects or schemata, which in themselves represent extratextual realities. Thus, the aesthetic object—text-guided though reader-produced—makes the reader react to the world represented in the text. In this respect it has both an experiential and a cognitive consequence, and as these are virtually inseparable, their impact is all the more powerful. This impact is important for exactly those reasons with which Professor Booth concludes his argument, and so I would maintain that the production of the aesthetic object requires the closest possible analysis.

The second point relates to "the discrimination between fixed and unfixed norms" in texts set up by the implied author. I agree with Professor Booth that this discrimination is very hard to make, and I am basically skeptical whether we ever shall arrive at a clear-cut decision as to which is which. My skepticism is nourished by the history of interpretation, which indicates clearly that what one generation used to regard as fixed norms in an author have been either downgraded or made taboo by the next, in consequence of which the qualification of fixed and unfixed has been shifted. Still, there seems to be a hermeneutic process discernible in that history. Late nineteenth-century Shakespearean criticism, for instance, focused on organic unity of character, whereas early in the twentieth century, the historically and sociologically oriented school considered the very breaks in Shakespearean characters to be the fixed norms, as they provide the audience with information necessary for its understanding of what the character is meant to convey. This complete reversal from organic unity to discrepancy as the fixed norms in Shakespeare's character-building testifies to an important hermeneutic relationship in the history of interpretation. What had been emphasized by the Bradley 'school' now became a closed door for the Stoll and Schücking 'school', which nevertheless was conditioned, though negatively, by what had been the seemingly un-shakable findings of the previous generation of Shakespearean schol-ars. Consequently, the findings of one generation imprint themselves on those of the next by blocking certain roads and thereby con-ditioning the opening up of opposed, deviating, and contrasting lines of thought.

If we want to assess fixed or unfixed norms in an author, we must not only reflect on our own position, but also on the kind of reshuffling which has taken place in the history of interpretation. This means that we must take into account far more factors than have hitherto been considered when norms have been declared fixed or unfixed. Any such declarations must be accompanied by a re-flective reason that, in turn, will also say something about ourselves. This again ties in with the kind of ethical criticism for which Pro-fessor Booth makes such a strong plea and to which I too would be prepared to subscribe, for the study of literature may not only result in ethical consequences but, through these very consequences, should reveal something of the specific makeup of ourselves and our faculties, which are activated and acted upon by literature.

Concluding Statement

Professor Stanley Fish of the Johns Hopkins University submitted three counterstatements in criticism of my thesis. On reading my replies, Professor Fish insisted on withdrawing his statements. As my replies may help to clarify important aspects of my thesis I consider it necessary to publish them here.

Professor Fish complains, first, that my method bypasses the chance to consider the world itself (as well as the literary work) as a text. The world as a literary text, however, is a metaphor that had already lost its validity as long ago as when Fielding made his Abraham Adams throw his Aeschylus onto the open fire. Thus, one should not confuse reality with interpretation of reality. My inter-pretation of the world may well be as much a product of linguistic acts as my interpretation of a literary text, but I maintain that there are substantial differences between the things being interpreted. First, the real world is perceivable through the senses, whereas the literary text is only perceivable through the imagination—unless one believes that reading the words sunset, music, silk, wine, and scent is the same as seeing, hearing, touching, tasting, and smelling the real things. Second, all known experience suggests that the real world (uninterpreted) lives and functions independently of the individual observer, whereas the literary text does not. Third, our contact with the real world has immediate physical or social consequences, whereas our contact with the literary text need not, and indeed rarely does have any such consequences. It is precisely these restrictions of the literary text that make it an unsuitable metaphor for reality.

Professor Fish's second objection argues against my determinacy/indeterminacy distinction, while the third objection (another form of the second) sees this distinction as just another version of the subjectivism/objectivism distinction, deploring it as "hopelessly conservative," indeed "reactionary." The objection seems to me to be based on the false assumption that my key terms *determinacy* and *indeterminacy* represent something given. They do not. What is given is textual segments; the links and motivations of these segments are indeterminate, but take on an ever increasing degree of determinacy (at least in traditional forms of literature) through the process of interpretation. The relation between indeterminacy and determinacy is basic to all kinds of interaction and interpretation. In the Thackeray example (which Professor Fish refers to for substantiating his objection), we have the given textual segments of chapter heading and chapter. The link is indeterminate (i.e., it is to be supplied by the reader). Once the reader supplies the link—in this case irony, but the same process applies even with a nonironic interpretation—it becomes determinate (i.e., formulated by the reader—not "what is there"). But what has become determinate must then be related to further textual segments that bring about further places of indeterminacy, and so on. As everybody seems to acknowledge that texts are interpreted, why should we then resist seeing the distinction between a significance that is *to be* supplied and a significance that *has* been supplied?

Now as to the charge of being "reactionary," I wish to make an equally sweeping statement expounding my basic intention. What I say about the text as process and reading as processing, I consider to be a starting point for charting and thematizing the intangible interaction between text and reader. Therefore I could not just reiterate the old timeworn dichotomy of subjectivism/objectivism; instead, I have tried to pinpoint the intersubjective structures underlying this interaction. In giving an exposition of these structures, I thought I had already "begun to see that neither the text nor the reader stand independently of one another," as I testified in the final chapter of my book analyzing the interrelation between the two.

The elucidation of intersubjectivity entails a twofold operation:

(1) devising modes by which subjective responses can by objectified in order to turn them into objects for introspection, the results of which can be intersubjectively shared; and (2) tracing patterns in the covert process between text and reader which is common to all readers irrespective of subjective preferences, inclinations, and beliefs. In order to establish these intersubjective patterns, I may not have taken account of all "sets of institutional assumptions." However, I *have* tried to establish institutional assumptions, so called, by bringing four frames of reference to bear: (1) Gestalt Psychology, in order to pinpoint grouping of signs, and *good continuation* of textual patterns as intersubjective structures; (2) Social Psychology, in order to pinpoint structured contingency occurring and produced in dyadic interaction as an intersubjective propellant triggering and controlling communication. This process is corroborated by Psychoanalytic Communication Theory, which stresses asymmetry between partners and blanks in the ability to experience each other as intersubjectively operative structures, the resolution of which asymmetry brings about understanding; (3) General Systems Theory, which allows us to spotlight intersubjectively verifiable transcodings between dominant, neutral/virtual, and negated elements that make up a system, and that become re-evaluated whenever a literary text makes inroads into the systems of its context, either upgrading what has been negated or neutralized or downgrading what has been dominant. Consequently, the text itself has the structure of a system, which allows us to pinpoint its relationship to its context; and (4) Phenomenology, in order to set up the wandering viewpoint, the perceptual *noema* that is the correlate of the text in the reader's mind, the passive syntheses, and the structures of ideation as intersubjective patterns *always* occurring in covert processes. Now, if the various frames of reference which function in my book as a "set of institutional assumptions" put me in a reactionary camp, then at least I find myself in good company.

Having invited all these criticisms, I should perhaps finally restate what I was after. In devising a model of interaction between text and reader I have tried to conceptualize—in the idealized manner that is fundamental to model-building—basic acts of communication, whose structure is intersubjective by nature. Consequently I have had to focus on areas that—at least theoretically speaking—have been more or less eclipsed in current literary criticism. The reason is obvious: these areas are very hard to chart. There is, on the one hand, the relation between the text and the extratextual systems that form its context and to which it relates, and on the other the cooperation, occurring in the time-flow of reading, between what the reader is given on the page and his habitual orientations. Consequently, I could not fall back on a given definition of the text or a given definition of the reader; I had to build up constructs of the text in terms of function and of the reader in terms of operations to be performed.

Thus, the model seeks to chart areas into which we should like to obtain insight. The findings we are going to get will have to be fed back into the model, resulting in its differentiation and modification. Consequently, theory and practice become closely interlinked in a hermeneutic operation that, in its reciprocity, turns the whole process into an instrument of cognition. There is no doubt that cognition can proceed along the lines of taste and beliefs prevalent in each critic. What I have endeavored to do, however, is to suspend my own tastes and my own beliefs—at least up to a point—in order to focus on the fact that all our beliefs have theoretical presuppositions, in consequence of which theoretical reasoning should enable us not only to refine our tastes and differentiate our beliefs, but also to change the questions and answers of literary criticism.

PART II
PARADIGMS

FOUR

SPENSER'S ARCADIA: THE INTERRELATION BETWEEN FICTION AND HISTORY

or twentieth-century man, Arcadia seems like a world that has long since vanished into the mists of time. Those shepherds who have managed to survive in literature since the eighteenth century have done so merely as nostalgic clichés.[1] Arcadia, like every other paradise, has faded away, despite its amazingly long life of some two thousand years. But this very longevity is proof that the concept of Arcadia must have contained elements that far transcended the needs of one single epoch, and so the question arises: What was it that placed Arcadia beyond the pale of history, and why has this apparent immunity to time now itself become historical? This question takes us back to the origins of Arcadia and to the function that was associated with pastoral poetry.

Out of all the concepts of paradise, Arcadia is unique in that it originates neither from myth nor from the Bible, but from literature itself. Arcadia is a product of art, generated by the pastoral poetry of Virgil.[2] It is true that in the course of its long history this bucolic world has absorbed many features drawn from the myth of the Golden Age and from the Christian *hortus conclusus*, but the historical manifestations of Arcadia have never been identical with these forms of paradise. The Golden Age was not acquainted with decay; nor was it marred by conflict, let alone by the fickleness of Fortuna. But the Golden Age was always in the past, for it could only be invoked by a present that fell short of such total perfection and therefore could only dream of it. Arcadia, however, is traditionally full of conflicts. Against the background of the Golden Age, it seems like an eternal present. Nor is Arcadia to be confused with a Christian Paradise, for the *hortus conclusus*—as a typological correspondence to the garden of Eden—owes its perfection to the fact that it is cut off from the world. Should the world obtrude upon its borders, then thanks to the total self-containment of the garden, it is the world that will seem excluded and unreal.

In contrast, Arcadia, at least since Virgil, has always been linked to the world. Contemporary history extends deep into the eclogues, and the bucolic world therefore brackets poetry and politics together. Bruno Snell describes this fusion in Virgil's work as follows:

The fact that one shepherd must leave his homeland is like the curse of a confused age; the fact that another can begin a new and comfortable life in his old age seems like the act of a redeeming god, who has appeared to him in the great city of Rome and has brought to an end the misery and confusion of existence. . . . These dreams of the poet give to history a meaning that corresponded to many expectations of that time: after the terrible upheavals of the civil wars, it was above all the leading lights of the age who had an overwhelming desire for peace. In this respect there is something genuinely political and topical in Virgil's poetry, and it is significant that when Augustus first began to change the history of Rome, Virgil was already expressing the longing for peace that Augustus was to fulfill. Thus, to a large extent Virgil determined the political ideology of the Augustan era, and his eclogues had a significant political and historical effect.[3]

Here we have a basic feature of the Arcadian tradition: as a product of art, Arcadia offers solutions to the conflicts of the political and historical world. It is this link to reality that underlies the achievement of Arcadian fiction. Although Arcadia is directly related to political history, pastoral poetry is not a representation of political events. This apparent paradox is already to be found in Virgil, who transplanted Theocritus's shepherds from Sicily to Arcadia. As Snell remarks, he needed "another land for his shepherds that lay further away from a reality that had grown ugly; and as pastoral poetry for him was, from the outset, not the same as it was for Theocritus, he looked for a land that would melt into the golden haze of distance."[4] The intentional removal of Arcadia from the setting of the familiar world, without actually cutting it off from that world, constitutes a basic condition of all literature — a condition that was summed up two thousand years after Virgil by Daniel Defoe. In "Serious Reflections" on his *Robinson Crusoe*, Defoe wrote: "Facts that are formed to touch the mind must be done a great way off."[5]

Throughout its history, Arcadian fiction has always preserved this distance; the love-play of the shepherds, their songs, their care of their flocks, their rustic daily work, all this endows the Arcadian world with a sense of otherness, and this is necessary if it is to remain detached from the political present whose problems it attempts to solve. For Virgil, the indispensable remoteness of Arcadia could still be articulated in terms of geography, as Sicily had become a Roman province and the shepherds of Syracuse, who loomed large in Theocritian poetry, were now serving new masters.[6] Thus, they had to be transplanted in order to serve their poetic function. But for the Arcadian tradition, the basic commonplaces of pastoral poetry sufficed to evoke the distance of a world that was to reflect the present. However, such a reflection can never be a mirror of political and historical reality; the reflection is, rather, of that which is hidden in the present, of solutions that cannot as yet be seen in the current conflict. This fact is already an indication of certain vital functions that pastoral poetry was able to fulfill during the Renaissance.

No CENTURY BROUGHT forth so much pastoral poetry as that which marked the beginning of the modern world. When at the turn of the fifteenth century Sannazaro announced in the epilogue to his *Arcadia* that he was the first to reawaken the slumbering forests and to teach the shepherds to sing again their old and half-forgotten songs, he started a wave of pastoral poetry that was to sweep over Europe. At that time, there must have been a fundamental need for revitalizing Arcadian fiction. Shepherds made their way into virtually every literary "genre." Classical literature had confined them to the eclogues—a lesser genre—but now they burst their literary bonds, and indeed themselves became the subject of a new form of epic prose that extends from Sannazaro to Montemayor, and from him again to Sidney. This massive incursion of shepherds into the literature of the Renaissance cannot be explained simply by a humanistic predilection for a rediscovered antiquity—though this certainly played its part; of far greater significance is the fact that Arcadian fiction offered a highly efficient means of presenting contemporary problems in the reflection of their possible solutions.

This being so, pastoral poetry had to undergo certain changes, despite the continual stress on its links with the past, for the historical conditions of the sixteenth century with which it was attempting to deal were not the same as those of Augustan Rome. Although the Virgilian link between Arcadia and contemporary situations was carried over into the pastoral literature of the Renaissance, it was different in kind, and this difference was to influence both the form and the function of Arcadian fiction. If we wish to observe the changes and to evaluate their effects, we cannot do better than to direct our attention to Spenser's concept of Arcadia, for this was a major event, not only for the Arcadian tradition, but also for Renaissance literature generally and English literature in particular.[7] There are, in fact, many different reasons for studying Arcadian fiction by way of Spenser's Arcadia.

At first it may appear that Spenser merely follows in Virgil's footsteps: for the twelve eclogues of his *Shepheardes Calender*, he chooses the old form of pastoral poetry, and there are many other features reminiscent of Virgil, including the fact that as a young poet he has to begin by trying his hand at bucolics before he embarks on writing an epic—in this case *The Faerie Queene*. This link with tradition becomes even clearer when Spenser goes beyond the limitations of classical forms. In this respect, we are fortunate to have detailed knowledge of the political situation to which the *Shepheardes Calender* is a response. Of course, this situation was not on the same scale as the Virgilian longing for, and promise of, peace after the turbulence of the civil war. But it was of considerable importance to the England of the day. The situation Spenser responds to is the marriage, at least briefly considered in 1579, between Elizabeth and the Duc d'Alençon.[8] Politically this alliance was a potential bombshell, and to understand why, we must first sketch in the historical background.

Protestantism had triumphed politically with Elizabeth's accession to the throne in 1558, but its victory was by no means secure. By 1579 the number of Catholics in England far exceeded the number of Protestants, but with the Protestant Elizabeth on the throne, the Catholics at first had no political center. However, since 1574 more and more Catholic priests had been pouring into the country, not only organizing the spiritual life of their communities, but also strengthening ties with Mary Stuart. If Elizabeth had married the Duc d'Alençon, the large Catholic majority would suddenly have gained a political focal point, and for the Protestants, this very idea was rather alarming.[9] The intense emotional and indeed political reaction to this danger can be gauged from the considerable number of pamphlets that sought to influence the queen; indeed these proliferated to such a degree that Elizabeth abruptly issued an edict forbidding all discussion of her marriage to the Duc. Three important examples illustrate the nature of this situation. The Puritan Stubbs wrote a book entitled *The Gaping Gulf*, in which he said the marriage was so monstrous that it would arouse the wrath of God. Stubbs had his right hand chopped off for his pains. Sir Philip Sidney wrote the queen a letter warning her of the incalculable consequences of such a marriage. For this he earned her disfavor. Spenser wrote his *Shepheardes Calender*, using Arcadian fiction in order to point out the danger and the solution. Spenser remained unscathed. This very briefly is the historical background.

Thus the *Shepheardes Calender* is a particularly good vehicle by which to approach the subject of Arcadia, as its historical references

PARADIGMS

are so well documented and are politically so clear. However, it cannot be said that Spenser's eclogues are only readable so long as we keep that political situation in mind. The eclogues themselves are not completely determined by the political problems to which they respond, although much of their formal patterning is conditioned by the historical circumstances. The Arcadian fiction far transcends the historical event that was its starting point, and herein lies something basic to the nature of fiction in general. This is what we are about to study, and we shall be following three particular directions: first we shall observe the macrostructure underlying the sequence of the eclogues; then we shall trace the changes in pastoral poetry that come about through the particular problems and situations dealt with; and finally we shall try to define the achievement of Arcadian fiction and the reasons for its eventual decline.

LET US BEGIN with the macrostructure to be discerned in the sequence of eclogues. England in the sixteenth century was obsessed by a particular fear: that of mutability.[10] The reasons for the lack of stability in an increasingly expanding world were many and varied and are too multifarious to be enumerated here in detail.[11] One need only mention the conflicts of doctrine and religious conscience brought about by state-imposed changes in the ecclesiastical structure of society at that time. Henry VIII broke away from Rome and, for political reasons, established his own church. His successor, Edward VI, was a child and left church reform to his bishops, who together with many other Protestants came to a sticky end under Bloody Mary. During the first five years of her reign, the Reformation backpedaled, only to continue afresh under Elizabeth. There were times in which many congregations had to suffer months or even years of moratoria as to religious rites and liturgy, because agreement could not be reached on what types of prayer book and ritual were to be used.[12] It is hardly surprising that, when Elizabeth died and the Catholic Stuarts came to power, the situation became ripe for the Puritan revolution. *Mutability* meant not only the dangerous instability of the age but also, and especially, fear of cosmic anarchy. This obsession is strikingly expressed in the "Mutabilitie Cantos" at the end of Spenser's incomplete *Faerie Queene*, as well as in many images of chaos that are to be found in Shakespeare's plays.

Thus, literature found itself confronted by the problem of the inevitable changing of all things. For Spenser, the origin of mutability was the combination of earth and chaos; it operated by opposing the order laid down by the gods.[13] At the very beginning of the cantos, we read

> Ne shee the lawes of Nature onely brake,
> But eke of Iustice, and of Policie;[14]

and when at the end *Mutability* has to justify itself to *Natura*, it demonstrates its power by parading the months of the year, summer and winter, day and night and life and death before the court to show that everything in this world is caught in the spell of its own instability. It is interesting to note the solution that Spenser put forward at the end through the pronouncement of *Natura*. At first sight it seems conventional and is comparable to that with which Boethius canceled out the power of *Fortuna*:

> I well consider all that ye haue sayd,
> And find that all things stedfastnes doe hate
> And changed be: yet being rightly wayd
> They are not changed from their first estate;
> But by their change their being doe dilate:
> And turning to themselues at length againe,
> Doe worke their owne perfection so by fate:
> Then ouer them Change doth not rule and raigne;
> But they raigne ouer change, and do their states
> maintaine.[15]

Taking change as a necessary transitional stage on the road to perfection makes it possible once more to reconcile the Platonic concept of the immutability of "things" with the no longer disputable power of time. But the fact that things need the uncertainty of change in order to reach perfection shows clearly that originally they are not the same as that which time ultimately reveals them to be. Thus the real, observable world—the old Platonic realm of shadows—begins to take on a scale that rivals the Platonic realm of Ideas. Here tradition and experience clash head-on.

Against this background, *mutability* was bound to arouse fear, though this fear itself appears now to be a necessary agent in bringing about perfection. It is therefore hardly surprising that poets at that time kept harking back to Arcadia, which seemed to vouchsafe the immutability of Nature and to offer a solid alternative to the changes of the historical world. And yet this alternative is itself characterized in Spenser's eclogues—written about thirty years before the "Mutabilitie Cantos"—by change. Peaceful Arcadia has become joyless and indeed is on the verge of self-destruction. The shepherds break their flutes, for they know how ineffective their songs are, and even the stability of Nature has ceased to be a consolation; instead it mirrors the very change lamented by the shepherds. It is here that Spenser's Arcadia and the symbolically charged repertoire of pastoral poetry take on a new function that can no longer be grasped in terms of the old tradition.

When the dangers of this world begin to intrude on and distort even its traditional counterpart, the eclogues turn into alarm signals. But for these to be properly perceived, the bucolic world and the real world must be linked together accurately. This is achieved through a massive allegorization of the bucolic. In this context, Spenser was able to rely on a commonly shared and widespread understanding prevailing throughout the sixteenth century as to what pastoral poetry was meant to be and to achieve. In his *Arte of English Poesie*, Puttenham wrote:

> The Poet deuised the Eglogue . . . not of purpose to counterfait or represent the rusticall manner of loues and communication: but vnder the vaile of homely persons, and in rude speeches to insinuate and glaunce at greater matters, and such as perchance had not bene safe to haue beene disclosed in any other sort, which may be perceived by the Eglogues of Virgill, in which are treated by figure matters of greater importance than the loues of Titirus and Corydon. These Eglogues came after to containe and enforme morall discipline, for the amendment of mans behauiour, as be those of Mantuan and other modern Poets.[16]

In this respect, the pastoral poet was faced with a fundamental problem that Spenser himself took up in all its implications. If the trappings of pastoral poetry are used to glance at greater matters than those of rustic life, and if those greater matters stem from the world of human experience and not from that of Platonic Ideas or of Christian ethics, then the mode of allegory must undergo considerable changes in order to set out, with the clarity desired, the situation with which it is concerned. Instead of allegorizing ideas, or the Christian code of vices and virtues, it must now juggle its pastoral commonplaces in such a way that it can present an empirical conflict in the light of its inherent solution.

The allegorization of empirical conflicts may have one of two basic consequences: either the individuality of the situation will be lost in the generality of its presentation, or the pastoral repertoire— for all the simplicity of its components—must be exploited on different levels and must fulfill a variety of functions. This latter category gives rise to a form of allegory which operates on several often changing semantic levels and can, therefore, no longer be equated with the old allegorical mode of *significatio* and *personificatio*. This is precisely the case with Spenser's eclogues. The shepherd Colin Clout is sometimes the poet, sometimes Spenser himself, sometimes just a shepherd, and sometimes the English people as a whole.[17] The same is true of the shepherdess Eliza, who at different times represents a loved one, Elizabeth, and the mourning Dido.[18] The figure of Pan undergoes some curious variations: he is the god of the shepherds, then Jesus, and even Henry VIII.[19] The pastoral masks appear on a wide variety of levels. They all serve a multiple sense that may be literal, personal, romantic, moral, religious, political, or any combination of these, so that whichever sense is uppermost at one particular moment, it can never fully eclipse the other senses. Thus, every situation within this rustic world is adumbrated by a multiple sense that makes it capable of differentiated references.

Thanks to this structure, the pastoral situations always contain several different potential senses, and at the same time they offer a wide latitude as to how they can be related one to the other. But because Spenser's eclogues are aimed at a concrete political event, this means that they offer alternative judgments of the given situation and at the same time allow different bases for the choice of one or other of those alternatives. Here we have a first important gain for Arcadian fiction, which we may sum up in the words of Richard Cody: "The trick of seeing into pastoralism, one may conclude, is not to allow any of its details, such as the shepherd's life, to limit the view, but to look for meaning and value in perspectives of one's own choosing."[20] Furthermore, we can now see how the Arcadian fiction transcends the political situation it refers to: instead of mirroring it, the fiction organizes attitudes toward it. This is brought about in the first place by the compositional features of Spenser's sequence of eclogues.

The *Shepheardes Calender* may well be the first text in Renaissance literature to have been published with a commentary. If at that time any secular literature did appear with commentaries, it would only have been that of epoch-making authors such as Dante and Petrarch.[21] The idea of a young author, in his debut, providing his own commentaries on his own verse must have been quite extraordinary. As far as can be ascertained, it seems highly probable that Spenser himself did indeed create the commentator of the *Shepheardes Calender*. But even if the cryptic E.K. was in fact someone other than Spenser,[22] the fact remains that the commentary is an integral part of the text. E.K. is intimately acquainted with all the poet's intentions; he writes an introduction to the whole work and comments on each individual eclogue, appending his glosses directly to the text. He tells us who Colin Clout, Eliza, Pan, and all the other rustic characters are. He also makes it clear to us that the author's intention is to "vnfold great matter of argument couertly, then professing it . . . touching the generall dryft and purpose of his Aeglogues, I mind not to say much, him selfe labouring to conceale it. . . . I was made priuie to his counsell and secret meaning in them" (pp. 10f.).[23] Concealing the purpose and keeping the meaning secret involves saying nothing explicit about the political situation—with the intention, however, of thus steering the reader's attention in a premeditated direction. The eclogues conceal their raison d'être; they do not represent the situation, but they transpose it in such a way that a variety of interpretative stances begin to emerge. This, in fact, is typical of fiction in general: it is at one and the same time both more and less than the reality it refers to; it is less because it is not real, and it is more because it makes reality accessible.

One final important aspect of the external layout of the *Shepheardes Calender* is the parallel between the twelve eclogues and the months of the year. This points to a complicated network of correspondences. The eclogues are linked to the months of the year, the year is linked to life, and life, to the astrological constellation of the firmament. This multifarious interdependence was set out in calendars and almanacs that, in the popular literature of the time, took on the status of prophecy.[24] Pastoral poetry and the calendar seem to have been linked together very early on, for in the world of the shepherds one could expect the ideal realization of the commandments and prophecies inherent in the Christian year. Thus, the commentary to Spenser's eclogues informs us that the poet called his cycle *Shepheardes Calender* "applying an olde name to a new worke" (p. 10). This can only mean that he intended to preserve the traditional calendar element of prophecy. But prophecy here no longer applies to the human race in general; it concerns the future of one particular situation. If the work could succeed in showing the possible consequences of Elizabeth's marriage, then through the reflection of these consequences, it might even succeed in preventing such an occurrence.

Prophecy, then, assumes a practical character: it seeks to influence events by anticipating their dangerous consequences.[25] But to do this, it must offer indications of the correct behavior, for the declared intention of pastoral poetry was, in Puttenham's words, the "amendment of mans behauiour." In this sense, the *Shepheardes Calender* prognosticates attitudes and modes of conduct that would enable a dangerous situation to be brought under control. Thus, the prophetic element of the old calendar now takes on a new function: forebodings are combined with orientation of behavior; the two together give promise of a radical change in the situation. The latter is not explicitly formulated; it only assumes its definitive form by way of the selection of attitudes toward it. If the right attitude is chosen, the situation loses its sting; with the wrong choice, it runs out of control. Herein lies the first major modification that the traditional form of pastoral literature undergoes in Spenser. Prophecy becomes largely dependent on the decisions that people must make with regard to their conflict-ridden situation. Such prophecy is concerned not with the inevitability of what is to come but with the possibility of influencing human action in view of imminent events that call for a decision.

WE NOW COME to the second stage in our study of the changes Spenser made in traditional forms and, above all, of the consequences those changes brought about. In addition to the above-mentioned commentary, the eclogues have their own particular appendages. In most editions, they are preceded by a picture, usually taken from the zodiac, and they all end with what Spenser calls an "emblem," which sums up what has gone before and is thus distinct from the eclogue proper. Many of these emblems are proverbs, often taken from classical literature, but it is not their origin so much as their ambiguity that is revealing. Generally the shepherds draw their own conclusions from their discussions, and these range from contrast to contradiction. Even when there is no split between the emblems, the emblem features—with very few exceptions—a contrast to the situation unfolded in the shepherds' song. What is presented by the initial picture in each eclogue has by the end split up into alternatives that even the commentator can no longer reconcile. By calling these solutions emblems, Spenser indicates that his shepherd's world is characterized not by its blitheness but by its division into alternatives. However, if this pastoral fiction constantly breaks up into alternative solutions, then clearly the addressee of the fiction is implicitly invited to choose and decide for himself.

In order to observe this process more closely and to see what

PARADIGMS

consequences it has for pastoral poetry itself, let us look at one of the eclogues in more detail. The "February Eclogue" contains an interesting combination of traditional forms. First, we have the contest between two singers—a typical feature of the eclogue. However, this generic feature is reduced to a bare outline; instead of trying to outdo each other in singing the praises of a beautiful lady, we now have youth and old age disputing with each other. But such a dispute belongs to the *altercatio* or medieval debate rather than to the eclogue.[26] In the tradition of the *altercatio*, a third party is usually appointed to pronounce judgment. But even here the medieval theme or confrontation between old age and youth has been significantly transformed. The disputation starts out from traditional correspondences: age corresponds to winter and experience, and youth, to spring and immaturity. However, these representative aspects are relegated further and further into the background, giving way to particular motives that each disputant believes to be the driving force behind the other. Thus, the true theme of the disputation emerges, as each character exposes what the other is trying to hide by that which he represents. But as a result, the positions themselves become ambiguous, and it is this fact that, surprisingly, links them together.

Now the appointed judge ought to make the final decision, but at this juncture a different literary genre makes its way into the eclogue. Thenot relates a fable that takes the place of the expected decision: A brier accuses an old withered oak of tyranny and selfishness, although in fact the oak offers protection to the rose. The complaint is addressed to man himself, who is equipped with all the attributes that correspond to his position in the chain of being; it appears that the judge has been found. But man is misled by the rhetoric of the brier, which knows how to arouse his passions; he cuts down the oak and destroys the balance of Nature, so that when winter comes, the brier, too, is destroyed. Now just as Thenot is about to tell the moral of his fable, Cuddie stops him. The expected conclusion is therefore missing. Instead, the eclogue ends with a dual emblem, which the commentator proceeds to interpret in his gloss. He implies that men do not regard cosmic order and the attributes of their position as an expression of their own situation within the world, but that they tend rather to use such correspondences to validate their own partly private but always human motives of conduct.

Given the substance of the eclogue, how are we to evaluate it, and what conclusions can be drawn from this strange combination of different generic features? The form is certainly complicated, thanks to the intermingling of song contest, medieval debate, and fable. What is strange about this telescoping of the genres is that an essential element of each one is omitted: there is no victor in the song contest, no decision in the *altercatio*, and no moral to the fable. Because of the intermingling, each genre undergoes substantial modification, as its intention is either suppressed or deliberately cut out. In such combinations—which are frequently found in the *Shepheardes Calender*—the individual genres are reduced to the status of perspectives whose prime function is to bring out the different facets of the dispute rather than to offer specific solutions. The implied addressee of the text is left to find these for himself. Thus, the telescoped genres serve first and foremost to fulfill the communicatory intention of the text, for through the omission of their respective dominant features the reader's attention is focused on the search for possible solutions. Clearly the old solutions are no longer applicable in the present situation. The situation itself, however, can only become clear if one starts out from traditional concepts that are now cast in a surprising pattern, so that they may emit the appropriate signals.

The orientation of human behavior is the message underlying these signals. And if this is the task that falls to literature, it is clear that human behavior can no longer be grasped only in terms of Christian values and commands or those of a syncretistic world order. The *Shepheardes Calender* does not seek to remind us of what man should be: it seeks to influence a political situation by unfolding a whole range of possible modes of conduct through the discussions of the shepherds. This intention also explains the changes we have observed in the traditional genres drawn upon by the eclogues. If a political event is now uppermost and has to be focused upon, the consequences envisaged can only be assessed properly if the event is understood as more than just another example of the accepted order. Now the signs, symbols, and genres made available by tradition must be separated from their original functions, so that the individuality of the empirical event may be brought to the fore. A genre such as the eclogue is obviously unable to achieve this effect, since its basic generic feature is such that it absorbs and blots out the individuality of a given case, instead of adapting itself and thus representing the special nature of the case in question. Hence the telescoping of genres,[27] for now the aim is to bring out attitudes toward the concrete event so that it may be seen in the light of the problem it creates.

One striking aspect of the interwoven genres is the fact that they only represent negative situations; they give no indication of how to get over the gap that is left when — as in the "February Eclogue" — the disputants don the old representative masks of youth and age in order to cover up their human motives. Nor do they tell us how man is to behave if he is to avoid the wrong decision taken in the fable. Solutions are prevented by the interference of one genre with another, and so it is clear that, although the problem underlying the eclogue demands a solution, a paradigmatic answer appears to be deliberately omitted. Instead, the traditional schemata must be modified so that the intention of the eclogue may be brought out. But these modifications themselves are not verbalized; it becomes the task of the reader to extrapolate correct conduct from the negative situation with which he is faced. If literature wishes to respond to history without itself becoming reductively partisan, rather than parading its intentions it presents them in such a way that the reader can uncover them for himself. The negative situation is, therefore, not an illustration of the depravity of man but a response-inviting structure that will stimulate the reader into working out the suggested solution for himself.

This stimulation is most evident in those eclogues where the different genres are telescoped together. Apart from the "February Eclogue," this applies particularly to the "May Eclogue," which radicalizes the problem of behavior insofar as the two shepherds are now guardians of the parish as well as the flock: Catholic and Protestant doctrines here confront one another. Once more the song contest becomes a debate, and once more the themes of Catholicism and Protestantism give place to a two-way warning against what each disputant believes to be the hidden motive behind the other's conduct. And finally we once more have a fable that is meant to offer guidance as to the right decision. This fable is approximately the same length as the debate, so that the genres appear to be symmetrically balanced in this eclogue, turning it into a *genus mixtum*. The manner in which the text guides the reader is marked by two revealing features that are to be discerned through the given assessment of the conclusion and also through a remark made by the commentator.

The fable is told by the Protestant shepherd. It concerns an old goat who vainly warns her kid against the treachery of the fox. When the fox has finally caught the kid, Piers concludes:

Such end had the Kidde, for he nould warned be
Of craft, coloured with simplicitie:
And such end perdie does all hem remayne,
That of such falsers freendship bene fayne.

(p. 54)

Palinode, the Catholic shepherd, rejoins:

Truly *Piers,* thou art beside thy wit,
Furthest fro the marke, weening it to hit.

(p. 54)

Palinode not only disputes Piers's explicit conclusions, but he also claims that this fable applies very well to those stupid village pastors who never know what they should say in their Sunday sermons (p. 55). Palinode would actually like to borrow this fable to pass it on to his village priest. If the moral to be drawn from the negative example of the fable is stated explicitly, it can only be for the benefit of fools, for only fools need to be told what not to do. Thus, what would appear to be a clear account of correct behavior tends to become eclipsed, not because the conduct itself is wrong, but because its unequivocalness should not be prescribed in the text; it is meant to take its effect through the decision of the reader.

This tendency is underlined by another feature of the eclogue. When the goat gives her kid advice about how to behave, the commentator observes that this is all *Fictio,* a rhetorical figure "which useth to attribute reasonable actions and speaches to vnreasonable creatures" (p. 57). The advice as such will remain ineffective so long as the preconditions for its effectiveness are absent from the addressee. It follows that the rules of conduct can only gain validity through corresponding deeds, and without these they must remain nothing but a fiction. This brings out an important historical implication: the mere knowledge of behavioral norms has now ceased to be an adequate and reliable guarantee for correct conduct. Logically, therefore, all the unequivocal statements in this eclogue appear in a negative light. The moral of the fable is only good for fools or at least for those with no ideas of their own; and the warnings are fictions as long as the addressee has no inclination to follow them. Thus, here as elsewhere, the negative situation reveals the gulf that yawns between knowledge and action and that can only be bridged by means of correct behavior.

The extent to which this tendency permeates the *Shepheardes Calender* may be gauged from the fact that very few of the eclogues are traditional in form. Even where there is no mixture of genres, there are different perspectives brought about by eclogues within eclogues or by other forms of song within the framework of the eclogue. This changing of perspective is an indication that the subject matter of the text can only come to light by way of its different facets seen from different standpoints. Occasionally even the poet himself intervenes, adding his own verses to those of the shepherds and, by putting them in parentheses, identifying them as his own point of view, thus setting the shepherds' songs in a new and often contradictory context.

Throughout the *Shepheardes Calender* there is a wealth of perspectives that is quite astonishing for pastoral literature. These perspectives act upon and so restrict one another, thus bringing out the motives that govern the respective viewpoints. Clearly, no single motive can determine the attitude toward the political event that constitutes the *secret meaning* of the eclogue—since each motive is subject to the modifications of others—and so careful consideration is required if the reader is to work out the attitude most suited to the occasion. For this is not just a matter of assessing an ordinary situation; if it were, then examples from the past would probably suffice. The aim here is to influence events in order that a danger may be averted. The fact that the various attitudes are in the nature of perspectives prevents them from taking on the character of an overriding solution. But it is this very hindrance that creates the driving need for the decision that alone can change the situation. Thus, the perspectives that emerge from the individual eclogues offer the necessary guidelines for the all-important action.

The tendency described above is reinforced persistently by another reversal of traditional elements of the eclogue: in the Arcadian world, it is normal that the shepherds should live in blissful harmony with Nature. In the *Shepheardes Calender,* this harmony is almost continuously disturbed, if not shattered. In the very first eclogue, the link between shepherd and Nature and between flock and Nature is given a striking slant. The despair of the shepherd corresponds to the wastefulness of winter, and this in turn mirrors the condition of the starving sheep (p. 16). It is true that here we have a correspondence, but this is very far from being harmonious. In the "April Eclogue," the only joyful concord is between the shepherd and his imagination (pp. 38–41),[28] while the "June Eclogue" inverts the whole concept of correspondence. The perfection of Nature at the zenith of the year appears as a reverse image of the forsakenness of the shepherd (pp. 60f., 65).

FOR THE READER of that time, who was familiar with the old type of pastoral literature, these incursions on the traditionally well-balanced harmony between rustic life and the rhythms of Nature would have had an impact that could hardly be ignored. The skeleton of the old correspondences was still recognizable, but its function had now changed. It no longer served to present and animate the guaranteed order of the world; instead it signalized the extent to which the old certainties had disappeared. The symbolic language of the syncretistic Platonizing concept of the cosmos had now to detach itself from its original meaning, because only then could the familiar terms be used to describe the dangers of the new situation.

It is not without significance for this description that, even though the correspondences have changed their function, the familiar harmony between shepherd and Nature does still survive. The "June Eclogue" provides an excellent example. While Colin Clout sees this zenith of the year as the nadir of his despair, his friend Hobbinoll lives in happy harmony with all the splendors of Nature; he has rediscovered the Paradise that Adam lost.[29] For Colin Clout, the bliss of the *locus amoenus* now seems like a past that is lost beyond recall: the perfect correspondences of the old cosmos seem like history. Thus, the symbolic language of the time conveys to the reader the weight of the changes it highlights.

In some eclogues, Spenser differentiates this language with still more nuances. Now, if Colin Clout's situation and what it is meant to reveal, is indicated through the inversion of a familiar concept, this very inversion assumes a different function in the "May Eclogue," where readers are to be alerted to lurking dangers. For here the carefree self-identification with Nature awakening in the spring—described by the Catholic shepherd—is a departure from the right way (pp. 46f.). Piers condemns Palinode's harmony with Nature as pagan, so that the old correspondence now stands for incorrect behavior. Undoubtedly, this correction is conditioned by the denominational theme of the eclogues and by the moral intention explicitly stated in the *General Argument* (p. 12); however, the argument as to why the concord between shepherds and Nature is so dangerous is not based on theological reasons alone. While Palinode finds happiness in merging with his environment, Piers regards such harmony as a fatal trap, for being caught up in the present can only result in defenselessness against the unpredictable events of the future. Thus, "natural" behavior for him is folly, because responsible living requires discernment and understanding (pp. 50f., 58). Here too, then, the pastoral correspondence between shepherd and Nature is challenged in order that attention may be drawn to abilities that will point to the right way. The rupturing of the old concept of links represents an opportunity to find the correct form of behavior.

The "July Eclogue" is a particularly noteworthy example of the variations on the use of old correspondences. Here the correspondences are not natural—as in the other eclogues discussed—but typological, with each shepherd finding links between his person and his geographical position. Thomalin and Morrell graze their flocks in a valley and on a hill, respectively. Height and depth become typological points of reference for their interpretations of their own positions. According to their situation in the pastoral landscape, they attribute all the vices to each other and all the virtues to themselves. In the course of their discussions, they use different kinds of argument. When Thomalin extols the virtues of the valley, his arguments are mainly theological and moral: poverty and humility correspond typologically to the lowly plain (pp. 67, 69), whereas pride and ambition are associated with the hills (pp. 66, 69). Morrell's defense of the heights is mainly theological and cosmological: the hill is a bridge to heaven, a place of the saints and of the stars (pp. 67, 68) and also the place from which man falls (p. 66). The eclogue abounds with correspondences of this kind, all of which make it clear that interpretation is a matter of standpoint, and each standpoint can employ the same typological sense to justify itself and to discredit another. Thus, the typological exegesis itself can be manipulated to suit the argument. *Figura* and *complementum* can no longer embrace the God-given order as annunciation and fulfillment. Instead, they pale into metaphors, used to highlight both a growing freedom of choice and the ensuing perspectival assessment of a world and of human behavior. Employing the typological mode of exegesis for this purpose makes a newly discovered human situation translatable and endows it with a certain degree of validity.

The *Shepheardes Calender* is permeated by such transcodings, all of which indicate that the traditional commonplaces of pastoral poetry and of cosmology are only of significance now through the transformation or even reversal of their original values. Together they form a whole series of signals that direct attention to the situation they all refer to. It is this function that enables them to fit in with the perspective construction of the eclogues. On the one hand, they undermine the reliability of old codes to show that the order itself will change if Eliza ignores Colin Clout (i.e., if Elizabeth ignores the wishes of the English people); on the other hand, the different perspectives offer alternatives that show that the political problem can only be solved by means of suitable action within the framework of the choices offered. It can no longer be solved through recourse to a framework of orientation already laid down by tradition.

The question now arises as to whether the intention of the eclogues did not place too great a burden on the transcoded symbols of the old cosmology and the transformed elements of the old pastoral literature. Was there any prospect of art successfully intervening in a political crisis as it was meant to do? The difficulty of this task was obviously clear to Spenser himself, as no less than three of the eclogues are devoted to a discussion of the efficacy and function of art. Since Virgil, Arcadia—a realm created by art—had been regarded as the resolution of conflicts in the political and historical world; in the *Shepheardes Calender*, however, it comes to the verge of self-destruction. But the very threat of obliteration is itself highly significant, as can be discerned in the eclogues of April, June, and October.

"The Argument" of the "April Eclogue" states that it is "intended to the honor and prayse of our most gracious souereigne, Queene Elizabeth" (p. 36). In his song, Colin Clout draws on the whole pastoral repertoire, which is related by both typological and cosmological correspondences to the queen, the royal family, the court, and political actions (p. 38).[30] From Colin's song of praise there emerges the model of a perfect order: Elizabeth is the goddess of the Arcadian flower garden; she corresponds to the Sun—as is laid down in the hierarchical chain of being—and she is also queen of peace, because thanks to her the conflicts of the Wars of the Roses have now been stilled (p. 43).[31] But this ideal perfection exists only in the imagination, because Colin Clout is not granted a hearing, "whereby his mynd was alienate and with drawen . . . from all former delightes and studies, aswell in pleasaunt pyping, as conning ryming and singing, and other his laudable exercises" (p. 36). Thus Colin Clout's ideal is seen against the background of his real situation, as we learn from the two shepherds Thenot and Hobbinoll, who bemoan the absent Colin's fate (p. 37). The image of perfection remains overshadowed by an inescapable sense of futility, and the ideal condition becomes an illusion. But if the perfection depicted by art is only illusory, its significance can be interpreted in one of two ways: either it will seem useless, because it is unreal, or it can be taken to indicate how the political situation is to be evaluated when it begins to make an illusion out of perfection. Whichever view is taken, there is no escaping the conclusion that the ideal condition evoked by art is only meaningful if it takes effect in the addressee. And it can only do this if influence or even change is brought to bear on the situation to which the work of art refers.

The problem is heightened in the "June Eclogue." Once again there is a visible declivity from art to reality. Hobbinoll praises Colin Clout's art inordinately, claiming that it reduces even the Muses to silence:

> They drewe abacke, as half with shame confound,
> Shepheard to see, them in theyr art outgoe.
>
> (p. 61)

Colin, however, rejects this view of his verses, for they have been inspired not by competition with the Muses but by the pressure of his own unrest (pp. 61f). And they do not seek only to express this disquiet, but still more to soften the heart of his scornful love:

> Then should my plaints, causd of discurtesee,
> As messengers of all my painfull plight,
> Flye to my loue, where euer that she bee,
> And pierce her heart with poynt of worthy wight:
> As shee deserues, that wrought so deadly spight.
> And thou *Menalcas*, that by trecheree
> Didst vnderfong my lasse, to wexe so light,
> Shouldest well be knowne for such thy villanee.
>
> (p. 62)[32]

Only if art can effect the necessary change in the loved one and can unmask the treachery of the cunning suitor, will it regain its importance; in the *Shepheardes Calender* this importance resides not in the glorification of the harmonious shepherd's world or in the mere depiction of passion, but simply and solely in its effectiveness. Should it prove ineffective, then art will have lost its meaning. The effect intended is not made explicit: we only know that the loved one's heart is to be pierced, and the suitor's treachery is to be unmasked; the consequences are left unstated. And herein lies both the fragility and the potency of art: if nothing happens, then art is senseless; but if it takes root, then, paradoxically, the inherent intention is easier to imagine if it is not set out in words.[33]

This is the viewpoint that dominates the shepherds' discussion in the "October Eclogue." Here it is Cuddie and not Colin Clout who is introduced as the "perfecte paterne of a Poete" (p. 95). This change of shepherd makes it possible for the function of art to be discussed independently of the pangs of passion. Piers, who admires Cuddie, unfolds a whole catalogue of commonplaces by which art had been defined in the tradition of poetics (pp. 96f.). Cuddie has to be reminded of these because he no longer expects to derive any benefit from his own art. Glorification, instruction, praise, and advice—these all seem to him equally obsolete, just as the art of Virgil, which once heralded the way to virtue and to greatness for Augustan society, can never be resuscitated (pp. 97f.).

O pierlessee Poesye, where is then thy place?

(p. 98)

The central elements of art have ceased to have any influence on the present; they belong to the past. Does this mean that there is no longer such a thing as art? At the end of the eclogue, Cuddie merely indicates how art is to come into being: as "thondring words of threate" (p.99) it requires a Bacchian rapture of the poet if his verse is to blossom forth. This blossoming is spoken of only in theatrical metaphors, so that a definition of the new function of art, as viewed against the now historically superseded definitions, remains unformulated. But the emblem indicates the direction in which this function is to be found: art is meant to move (p. 99), and in the context of the *Shepheardes Calender* this can only mean movement to change the existing situation.

In view of the functions of art as a response to given historical situations, it is interesting to note that the hoped-for impact of art can only be elucidated against the background of those definitions that have been valid in the past and that now no longer apply. As glorification, knowledge, and immortalization of fame and greatness, art was first and foremost a representation of the extraordinary; its past-ness serves here to reveal the new function brought about by transgressing all these time-honored definitions. In this respect, the three eclogues developed to the exposition of art have an unmistakable degree of common ground. The "April Eclogue" depicts a state of perfection but presents it in a negative light: in respect of the real situation, the ideal is an illusion. In the "June Eclogue," art is only meaningful if it unmasks deceit and brings about changes of attitude. And in the "October Eclogue," art is seen as a force of "moving" (*movere*) which takes on a definite form to the extent that it divorces itself from what it had previously been. If one seeks to combine all three variants under a single banner, one might say that art emerges as a force running counter to existing situations. Here we are touching upon a general function of art which has a wider range of application than the attempt in the present case to directly avert the danger of Elizabeth's marriage. If impact is basic to art, it will constantly be overshadowed by the possibility of failure. Spenser seems to have used this unavoidable threat to serve his own communicatory intention. Not only in anticipating a possible misfiring but also in permeating his portrayal of art with fear of total failure, Spenser succeeds in signalizing the degree of danger, which in turn should strike home as an appeal for a decision to change course.

Each eclogue in the *Shepheardes Calender* details the alternatives that constitute the spectrum of choices, out of which the apt decision for orienting human conduct should be selected. The aim is to demonstrate the many-sidedness of all human situations in order to stress that correct behavior is a middle road between an abstract ideality and blind spontaneity. Man's position is halfway between experience and faith, and all conduct depends on standpoints that ultimately can only be endorsed by the right action. As the *Shepheardes Calender* is literature, it does not verbalize this action. It simply points out what will happen if nothing is done, and through this negative presentation heightens the impression that the action is now urgently required. From one eclogue to the next, it offers examples to orient the action concerned, and each example challenges the reader to uncover the basic principle underlying it: in the present case, this is the *secret meaning*[34] that the poet has hidden within the interplay of pastoral elements. For the addressee of the *Shepheardes Calender* to be induced to conduct this search, it is essential that the object of the search should not be formulated. "The fascination of pastoral language is the difficulty of coming to a just appreciation of what the poet does not say."[35] This appreciation is left to the reader to accomplish. What is prefigured by the eclogues can only be realized by the addressee, who must naturally be already "initiated" into the symbolic language of pastoral literature. And precisely for this reason, the changes in the pastoral repertoire will become for him unmistakable signs that can be transformed against the familiar traditional background into a new meaning related to a specific situation. Thus, the addressee himself can structure the hidden meaning and so exploit the freedom granted him by the text—a freedom that enables him to assemble the meaning and thereby relate it to a concrete situation.

WE NOW COME to the third and final point, which is the decline of Arcadian fiction. The intermingling of genres within individual eclogues and the transcoding of commonplaces endow the old shepherd's song with a highly complicated texture. The question is whether the eclogue as a genre is not overstrained, in view of the task it now has to perform. The pastoral world represented here is no longer conceived of merely as a detached counterimage through the gradually unfolded array of behavioral possibilities that it offers as solutions to particular problems. If these solutions are to be validated, the dominant features of the genre must be shifted, broadened, or even abandoned. Thus, the eclogues of the *Shepheardes Calender* develop into minidramas with open endings. They accentuate the conflict and so overburden the dramatic element of the genre.[36] But in that case, might not the drama and the novel be incomparably better media to convey the problems of conduct to be developed from the situations of conflict?

Pastoral romances not only shade in the details of the Arcadian world, but they also give a made-up picture of the political reality to which the increasingly complicated patterns of conduct relate. If there are any shepherd's songs in these romances, their function is to loosen the ties between Arcadia and political reality, so that the bliss of an ideal situation can cast its light over the conflicts of the shepherds. They offer a ready-made solution, for they guarantee the return to the original concept of Arcadia, namely what Snell calls a *jenseitiges Diesseits*—an earthly paradise.[37] They reveal none of that heavy burden with which Spenser loads his eclogues, for in these romances the prose ensures that the conflicts will be sufficiently particularized to elicit a differentiated attitude toward what they entail.

The need for orienting human action was even more comprehensively met by English Renaissance drama. Assessment of incorrect conduct and demonstration of its consequences form a recurrent theme of plays of that era. In view of the historical situation to which the Spenserian eclogue responded, the genre itself was subjected to a degree of complication that heralded its exhaustion: it was required to resolve an actual situation by using a traditionally fixed repertoire to signpost the right course of conduct.

For the functional history of literature, the *Shepheardes Calender* is an interesting example of how forms and genres increase in complexity when the language of traditional *genera* is to be used in dealing with new historical situations. This degree of complexity shows that the historical situation becomes a vital factor in the constitution of the work. It also shows that, faced by the requirement to cope with new situations, genres can lose their efficacy.

The fact that an old genre had reached its limits did not, however, mean that Arcadian fiction had to come to an end. What it could still achieve was demonstrated very clearly by the *Shepheardes Calender*, precisely through its complications. Spenser's Arcadia excludes nothing that is connected with man's historical reality: even Death stalks these Elysian fields. This proximity to the empirical world prevents Arcadia from becoming a mere escape from a deteriorating reality. Of course, Arcadia does provide relief as well; Spenser himself classified his eclogues as "Moral," "Plaintiue," and "recreatiue" (p. 12). But this relief does not mean that whatever makes reality so doleful is to be—even temporarily—forgotten. Thus, there is a remarkable split to be observed in Arcadian fiction: the pressing problems of historical reality recur, and yet they exist side by side with the sense of comfort. This always intriguing feature of the Arcadian realm is also clearly discernible in Spenser's eclogues. The conflicts are ever present, but they are never threateningly actual. Their distance is brought about not so much by transferring historical problems into a nonhistorical setting as by eclipsing the consequences of the shepherds' actions. This gives rise to the impression that it is all a game and that Arcadian actions are nothing but trial runs that are capable of innumerable variations. Such a *serio ludere* allows all preconditions for possible actions to be acted out before they become real and earnest.

Arcadia is inseparably linked to the political reality it refers to because only through this link do all the playfully projected situations obtain both their significance and relevance. At the same time, the Arcadian game is detached from direct conflicts—a detachment that allows contemplation of the correct course of action. The Spenserian eclogue unfolds a whole catalogue of possible courses, for if there were no choice there could be no detachment, and without detachment there would be the danger that the addressee might miss what was offered to him. Arcadian fiction seeks to lead him out of the darkness without actually presenting him with the new order that is to replace the existing political confusion. As fiction, Arcadia depends on historical reality; at the same time, it presents reality with one feature that reality itself lacks: it repeats real situations that, through repetition, are relieved of the necessity for action that is inescapable in reality itself. In this way, it becomes possible for new attitudes toward reality to be molded. Arcadia restores choice by relieving action of its consequences and by stopping, or even reversing, the course of real events, so that we may focus upon those facets of a situation which are normally thrust into the background by the real-life need for action. It is not surprising, therefore, that for all the disturbances to be found in it, Arcadia seems like a paradise and, despite the pangs of despised love, awakens the impression of unending happiness. Being relieved of consequences, stopping the world so that one may review the situation and thereby obtain an insight that will allow a change of course—how else could such a state be described except in terms of an earthly paradise? Thus, Arcadia provides a plethora of possible solutions that can be fed back into the historical situations to which Arcadia is tied. In this sense, it embodies a true model of what literature is or, rather, is able to achieve.

Why, then, did it fade away? We may find the germ of an answer in *Don Quixote*. In the Marcela episode, Cervantes makes Arcadia into a place where freedom of action is without limitation. But this freedom comes into direct conflict with the right to love and to be loved. Marcela cites her right to freedom in refusing Grisóstomo's demand to be listened to:

> The Arcadian concept of the loved one's right to be loved becomes an unbearable burden for the one who is greatly loved because of his or her beauty. In the figures of Grisóstomo and Marcela there is the final split between love and freedom—a split which became more and more apparent as Arcadia moved away from the Golden Age and toward historical reality.[38]

It is at this moment that there are consequences: the rejected shepherd Grisóstomo hangs himself. But it was the very lack of consequences that had made Arcadia so important in resolving the conflicts of reality. The more Arcadia became equated with historical reality, thus losing its old function of offering attitudes to it, the less meaningful Arcadian fiction turned out to be. As a mere mirror image of conflicts, it gradually faded away.

But Cervantes' still completely bucolic treatment of the disintegration of Arcadia does not yet fully explain its final demise. This can be attributed to a change in the nature of fiction itself. Since the end of the eighteenth century, when the last of the now highly sentimentalized shepherds disappeared from literature, fiction has ceased to restrict itself to the preconditioning of attitudes and actions. Fiction takes its characteristic features from its interaction with the given reality within which it is produced, and so fiction itself is bound to change in relation to the context to which it responds. The fact that Arcadia, as a model fiction, was able to survive so long is a clear indication of the importance fiction once enjoyed as a means of orienting behavior. Today, however, when literature subverts its own fictiveness, the shepherds of Arcadian fiction seem like painted figures in a painted paradisiacal landscape.

FIVE
THE DRAMATIZATION OF DOUBLE MEANING IN SHAKESPEARE'S *AS YOU LIKE IT*

s *You Like It* is a dramatic adaptation of a well-known pastoral romance, and as such it testifies to the irresistible wave of shepherds that engulfed the literary scene of the Renaissance.[1] The pastoral world embraced all genres of the age, and it changed the system of genres by introducing a new one in the shape of the pastoral romance, which broke down the boundaries within which the eclogue had been confined. But even the traditional form of the eclogue had not used its shepherds merely to depict rustic life; they always served to designate something other than themselves. In the pastoral romance, this purpose was fulfilled by the representation of two different worlds: Arcadia would either reflect the social and political world, or be confronted by it. And as Arcadia was, from the very beginning, a product of art—with its origins in Virgil's *Eclogues*—the romance also made it possible for the reader to observe the relation of art to reality as well as the effects brought about by this relation. Furthermore, Renaissance pastoral was considered to be a product of the feigning process through which reality could be repeated as a game, allowing a sort of replay of those courses of action excluded by the real actions of the social and political worlds. Thus the pastoral world remained tied to one outside itself, and by linking the two the pastoral romance took on its generic pattern.

Now despite the interrelation of these two worlds, they in fact embody two very different semiotic systems, with a clearly marked boundary running between them. The far-reaching importance of this dividing line can be gauged from the fact that the central characters who cross from the sociopolitical into the pastoral world are split into two persons, and thus by doubling themselves are able to act out the difference between what they have been and what they have now become. Playing a double role reflects the duality of the two worlds represented by the characters themselves, and in speaking with two voices, they are able to exceed the limitations of each of those worlds.

Though Shakespeare took the plot of his comedy from Lodge's *Rosalynde*, his adaptation did not focus so much on action as on the *"double-voiced discourse"* given dramatic expression by the dialogue.[2] And as the different speeches are spoken in different worlds, they have to incorporate the distinction between these worlds; thus the political "voice" has to be different from the pastoral—what is hidden by the one will be revealed by the other.

One might say that the whole comedy is based on the principle of doubling. At the beginning the political world itself appears on two different, though parallel, levels: Oliver has his double in his brother Orlando, who also has a claim to his father's inheritance, and Duke Frederick has his in his brother, the old duke, whose position he has usurped. In both cases the presence of the double is regarded as a threat that can be removed only by means of separation; the old duke is driven away, and Orlando is robbed of his rights. This separation, however, can be achieved only by breaking the code upon which the usurper depends for the stability of his own position: for Frederick it is government, for Oliver it is the family. Their protection of themselves through the very system they have violated entails the constant potential presence of their doubles, and herein lies the basic pattern of the political world.

The theme is made evident right from the start, through the eyes of Orlando, the rejected double. He is depressed by the miserable situation in which he is kept by his brother Oliver:

My brother Jaques he keeps at school, and report speaks goldenly of his profit: for my part, he keeps me rustically at home, or, to speak more properly, stays me here at home unkept; for call you that keeping for a gentleman of my birth, that differs not from the stalling of an ox? His horses are bred better; for besides that they are fair with their feeding, they are taught their manage, and to that end riders dearly hired: but I, his brother, gain nothing under him but growth, for the which his animals on his dunghills are as much bound to him as I. Besides this nothing that he so plentifully gives me, the something that nature gave me his countenance seems to take from me. (1. 1. 5–18)

The wordplay on "keeps" and "unkept" lights up connotations that, in each case, are swiftly snuffed out. The individual meanings of the word must clash if Orlando's "sadness" (1. 1.4) is to find expression. Since he receives so much of the nothing, and since Oliver continually takes away the something nature (their common stock) gave him, the key words of Orlando's statement can only be understood by way of their opposites (e.g., "keep" means unkeep, and "give" means take away). Thus the speech incorporates another speech that is not articulated because it lies outside the words spoken, but is nevertheless present through the distortion of meanings.

"Nothing" and "something" here are dialogic words that yoke together meaning and contradiction in such a way that each cancels out the other. Obviously, this brings out the unnaturalness of the brother's behavior, but the opening of the play contains more than just this piece of exposition. It also introduces the theme that is to be orchestrated throughout the comedy. Orlando's speech is what Bakhtin calls a "dialogized hybrid," for it is "precisely the fusion of *two* utterances into one," in which the speaker is present to the extent that he is there only to be displaced by a voice that is not speaking.[3] Thus the words incorporate the conflict between two voices, the dramatic point being that the silent voice prevails over that which is speaking.

The probability that Oliver will fail to suppress his double is already clear from the first dialogue between the brothers. After a short exchange, it leads very swiftly to violence, for Orlando continually doubles Oliver's words with their unsuspected implications, thus imposing on him the very double that he wishes to be rid of. The climax of this dialogue comes not with the actual violence but with a play on words. As the two of them scuffle, Oliver calls Orlando a "villain" (1. 1.55), whereupon Orlando answers:

> I am no villain. I am the youngest son of Sir Rowland de Boys: he was my father, and he is thrice a villain that says such a father begot villains. Wert thou not my brother, I would not take this hand from thy throat till this other had pulled out thy tongue for saying so. Thou hast railed on thyself. (1. 1. 56–62)

Thus if Orlando is a villain—because he is fighting Oliver—then Oliver is not only insulting their father, whose blood is doubled in the two sons, but also himself, because he is Orlando's double. Oliver may well have been unconscious of this implication at the moment of speaking, and he would most certainly not have intended it. But the implication is by no means an arbitrary one, for it links the utterance to a code that is valid for both characters, thereby endowing it with a meaning that must either thwart Oliver's intention or show it to be a violation of the code. Oliver remains unaware of this duality, for it is a feature of the language of usurpation that it is monologic; it always seeks to equate language and reality, thereby expunging those connotations that even a denotative use of language cannot help evoking.

The implications, however, which remain unconscious in such pragmatic speech, may have their repercussions if only through the fact that the listener must interpret his partner's words in order to understand them. There can never be an automatic transfer of intentions from one partner to the other; meaning is not integral to an utterance, but has to be ascribed to it by the listener, which entails a process of interpretation. This in turn depends upon the implications contained within the utterance, and these cannot always be fully controlled by the intention of the speaker. Thus the verbalization of the unspoken can lead to all sorts of surprises.

The dialogic character of language is thus evident from the very first lines of the very first scene: Oliver's injustice emerges through Orlando's irony, and Oliver's intentions fail through the implications of his utterances. This bracketing together of meanings that run counter to each other dramatizes the dialogic nature of the words.

For Oliver the best solution is a deliberately monologic use of words, and this is what he practices in the ensuing scene with Charles. Charles is a wrestler prepared to take on all challengers, but with the warning that the outcome of any match will be fatal. Charles is worried that Orlando wants to fight him and may therefore suffer a fate that Charles would rather not impose. Oliver, however, sees his chance to be rid of Orlando, and so he tells Charles about his brother's "villainous" nature and evil plots. Thus the two finally come to an understanding, but it is an understanding in which what is said (Orlando's alleged plotting) conceals what is meant.

The examples we have quoted from the beginning of the play reveal a conspicuous doubleness of the language, and although this varies in its nature, in all cases it is marked by the distinction between the manifest and the latent. The more the language negates itself, as in Orlando's speech, the more apparent is the latent meaning; the more exclusive the manifest seeks to be, the more illusory becomes the utterance. Orlando's speech appears to be negated as alien meanings insinuate themselves into what he says; although they are silent, they dominate the utterance. Orlando, then, is present in what he is not. Oliver's speech appears to be illusory, as he eradicates the interconnection between what is said and what is implied. Oliver, then, experiences this obliteration as a thwarting of his intentions. The difference that marks off the latent from the manifest may vary in degree, thereby requiring us to change our sense of the patterns of their relationship, but—whatever the relation—the difference can never be eradicated even if it is supposed to be. When difference is emphasized, negations abound; when it is wiped out, the utterance becomes illusive. Whichever is the case, difference makes itself felt in one form or another, and consequently all language use is inevitably marked by it. Regardless of which element is dominant, the latent comes to the fore both in negation and illusiveness, spotlighting what has not been coped with in the respective instances.

The dialogue arises out of what needs to be mastered, and it is doubtful whether it can ever take on a finality other than the pragmatic; for it would seem that the latent can never be fully integrated into the manifest, in consequence of which the dialogue can only unfold varying relationships between the two. This at any rate is the situation of the dialogue in the political world at the start of the play.

If the very first dialogue in the comedy fails, this is because words for Orlando are dialogic and for Oliver monologic; for the former the spoken is doubled by the unspoken, which endows it with its meaning, while for the latter the spoken aims at an equation of language and object, with all implications being suppressed. For Orlando, however, the dialogic word is merely a weapon with which to strike Oliver, and so ultimately it is subjected to pragmatic ends; the monologic word, on the other hand, is an expression of power which—because it imposes univocal meanings—inevitably results in a split between utterance and intention. In the first instance the double meaning is pragmatized, and in the second it has to be suppressed, and so it becomes a negative foil to the array of possibilities that are unfolded in the Forest of Arden.

There is one further sense in which the language of the dialogue acts as a reflection of the political world. The latter is characterized by the theme of usurpation—Oliver in the context of family, Duke Frederick in that of government. Usurpation depends on the suppression of the double, and this is why the monologic words of the usurper are always calculated to establish the univocal meaning he desires. But this very requirement betrays the fact that behind his utterances lurks a 'latent' that cannot be banished if the cherished purpose is to be fulfilled. Thus the monologic word is also caught up by the inherent structure of language itself. The spoken is always impregnated with associations that cannot be dispensed with, and every object to which the spoken refers is one that has already been described in countless ways, so that whatever is said about it can only be a selection from the possibilities, thus defining itself by what it excludes. The dialogue in the political world of this comedy shows the extent to which the unspoken is always present alongside the spoken. In the example we discussed earlier, what is unspoken in the quarrel between Oliver and Orlando is the breaking of the code that is equally valid for both—though here the unspoken establishes its presence by an utterance that undoes its own intention. The dialogue brings home to us the continual presence of something that is absent, and this applies even when hypocrisy—at least to the spectator's eyes—makes the spoken appear to be the suppression of the true intention. Through the doubling process of the overt and the covert, language brings about a constant switch between the present and the absent, and in this way it runs counter to the pragmatic actions of the political protagonists.

Thus we have Duke Frederick banishing Rosalind from his court and telling his daughter Celia, who has pleaded on Rosalind's behalf:

> She is too subtle for thee, and her smoothness,
> Her very silence, and her patience
> Speak to the people and they pity her.
> Thou art a fool; she robs thee of thy name,
> And thou wilt show more bright and seem more virtuous
> When she is gone.
>
> (1. 3. 73–78)

Here the Duke projects his own fear onto the situation of his daughter, whom he sees as being threatened by her double in such a way that along with the loss of her name she might herself be obliterated. This may well have been the reason for his removing his own double. Yet what is spoken appears to be unreal the moment Celia reveals what has so far been concealed, namely that she and Rosalind are two in one ("thou and I am one" [1. 3. 93]). This is why they now flee together to the Forest of Arden, although the whole point of the Duke's banishing Rosalind was to remove this "identity."

Thus failed speech-acts highlight the situation of the usurpers in the political world. They may be able to get rid of their doubles, but they cannot escape the doubleness of language. This endows the language of power with a touch of comedy, as the usurpers' removal of their respective doubles is imposed on language itself by eradicating its interplay between the manifest and the latent. Language, then, seems almost to defend itself against this manner of its use, reestablishing the doubleness between revealing and concealing by making the excluded strike back at the excluder. What has been suppressed now wrecks the plans that underlie the spoken, and this process turns language itself into a comic paradigm as it both undercuts the position of power and promises a resolution of the conflict. The pattern of restitution necessary for such an outcome is provided by the doubling of worlds that Shakespeare took over from the pastoral romance.

THE FOREST OF Arden, to which the main characters run away, is a northern Arcadia. Although the shepherds themselves become peripheral figures through the intrusion of the refugees from the political world, this does not affect their sign value, which invokes the traditional function of the pastoral world. This remains a creation of art which does not designate itself or exist in its own right, but refers to another world to which it is tied. No matter how different the rustic world may be from the political, this difference is never taken so far that the pastoral world can establish itself as a counter to the real one. If it did, it would have to carry its own definition with it, thus losing its true function: to mirror what is concealed in the world to which it is linked.

Although the usurpers force their doubles to take refuge in the Forest of Arden, this is conceived neither as a haven for the banished nor as a realm of escape. On the contrary, it is a place of freedom, as Celia points out when they are crossing the boundaries between the two worlds: "Now we go in content / To liberty, and not to banishment" (1. 3. 133–34). Thus the relation of rustic to political is one of the counterimage rather than the counterreality. Whatever may be the nature of the individual images, the rustic world as an image clearly represents something other than itself. Normally this 'other' is the political world, and so the conflicts and quarrels of this world constantly recur in the pastoral, but the image embodies, as Gadamer has put it, "an increase in being" of that which it pictures, and this is bound to result in a change of what is represented.[4]

Since the image changes the nature of the reality it depicts, clearly the change will be all the more fundamental in the case of the counterimage. This, like all images, takes an extract from reality, but turns it upside down, so that whatever may be the realities of the political world, in the pastoral they take on the character of a game. The old duke talks of them in terms of "the scene / Wherein we play in" (2. 7. 138–39). Whatever the actual events, life in the Forest of Arden is put in brackets, thus providing an opportunity for the characters to bring out into the open what the code of the political world has denied them. The substance of the ensuing game is a repeat of the lives of the characters who, being released from the encroachments of reality, indulge in playing themselves. Turning themselves into actors allows them to stage their own other selves.

The masks they have donned appear to be a mirror reflecting the reverse side of what they are, thereby making them aware of their own rear view, as it were. Thus they rehearse their actions as a test of reality in order, ultimately, to revolutionize the political world to which they will eventually return.

Furthermore, this constant staging and rehearsing of realities indicates that whatever is termed a world only reflects a state of affairs; it is one among many possibilities, and no single possibility can ever be equated with *the* world. Thus, the world mirrored in the counterimage is bound to undergo a change, simply because the state of affairs portrayed reveals itself as a particular form of world, highlighted by the fact that the pastoral counterimage has put the represented world in brackets. But since form is indispensable for the presentation of the world, only play allows for a depiction of the world as if it were such, thus avoiding the identification of the world with its form.

The game not only spotlights an aspect different from the world put in brackets, but it also represents the very conditions according to which a world may be assembled. This, however, is something that in the pragmatic world of political and social realities is always eclipsed, so that only the reality staged in the counterimage provides a glimpse into the circumstances that give rise to the organization of worlds. And this, in turn, can only be acted out in play, as any other means of objectifying would be tantamount to an explanation of origins, which play is forever subverting.

The distinction between the two worlds has certain repercussions on the language that may be seen on two widely differing levels. The first concerns the two extremes marked by Jaques and the fool, and the second is to be found in the characters who are disguised. The participation of Jaques and Touchstone in the two worlds is unbalanced in that Jaques only lives in the forest, whereas Touchtone lives in both worlds. Jaques and Touchstone also differ from the main characters in that they are not disguised and thus do not enter the play in the form of a counterimage.

Jaques's language is conspicuous through a feature that, in the political world, is only to be observed in Orlando's speeches. In the dialogue with Oliver, Orlando brought out the hidden implications in order to reverse the manifest meaning by uncovering the latent. In Jaques this tendency becomes virtually an obsession. Even before he comes on stage, we hear that:

Thus most invectively he pierceth through
The body of country, city, court,
Yea, and of this our life, swearing that we
Are mere usupers, tyrants, and what's worse,
To fright the animals and to kill them up
In their assign'd and native dwelling-place.

(2. 1. 58–63)

Jaques views all conventions as social disguises. They are for him fictions in which people wrap themselves in order to conceal the motives behind the behavior. This is why he regards himself as an outsider, living on the fringes of society. As conventions are merely a disguise, he continually pulls the rug from underneath all utterances in order to bring the speaker's overt behavior crashing down. In the political world, only Orlando unmasked the latent behind the manifest, but in the Forest of Arden this linguistic self-defense heads off in a slightly different direction. In principle, Jaques does the same as Orlando, but within the counterimage the same can never be the same, for while the real world *is*, the image world reflects. Exposing the hidden aspects of utterances in order to show them up as disguises must in turn entail a hidden code that regulates all links between the manifest and the latent in terms of a determinate relationship. Jaques sees this code as being integral to language itself, and so for him double meaning simply reflects concealment: it is a semiotics of duplicity. But this brings him into difficulties with his melancholy which he takes to be the only genuine reality that he has gained from experience — experience of which Rosalind remarks: "Then to have seen much and to have nothing is to have rich eyes and poor hands" (4. 1. 22–23). If the manifest is only a disguise of the latent, then one cannot help suspecting that Jaques's identification of himself with melancholy can itself only be a disguise. Indeed, it could even be the expression of a hidden desire to belong to the very society that he appears to despise. If this were so, the double meaning that Jaques purports to have seen through might well rebound on him, for the code he keeps unmasking would also apply to himself. Excepting oneself from an otherwise universal law is indicative of a blindness that in turn may raise the possibility that the link between manifest and latent is *not* as automatically coded as Jaques's unmasking technique would seem to imply. But if it is not, then either there must be alternative structures of double meaning, or Jaques is guilty of double standards.

The political world makes double meaning appear to be a matter only of disguise and unmasking, but this is not due to the structure of double meaning so much as to the prevailing pragmatic pressures. Jaques does identify the relation between the manifest and the latent with these pressures, for he invokes as evidence the lessons of his experience. But that which orients the political world does not govern behavior in the Forest of Arden, for this is not a world of experience: it is a reflection of the world to which it is linked for the purpose of divulging what has hitherto been concealed in that world.

Now, to what extent does Jaques reflect the reverse side of what became obvious in the dialogue between Orlando and Oliver? In the latter, double meaning indicated that which escaped mastery, whereas for Jaques double meaning is reduced to a trope for universal duplicity. Through him, the underlying structure of dialogue pervading the political world is repeated in the pastoral world, reifying, however, one aspect of the relation between manifest and latent, and thereby blacking out the whole range of possibilities inherent in this relationship. And this makes him into an outsider not only in the society in which he finds himself, but also in the pastoral play world. Whoever is in the game, but cannot take part in it, will be overcome by melancholy.

This is why Jaques cannot stand the game, for to him it is not different from reality; on the contrary, "All the world's a stage" (2. 7. 139), as he says at the beginning of the famous speech with which he equates the pastoral and political worlds. By canceling out the semiotic difference between game and reality, Jaques only causes this difference to emerge again as a sort of split in his own behavior. What he takes to be the code of double meaning appears to be nothing but an oppositional relationship between showing and concealing which merely points toward the pragmatic function double meaning is meant to serve, at the same time indirectly drawing attention to its other potential functions. What Jaques regards as his identity is as deceptive an appearance as the masks of the other characters, for he does not recognize that the melancholy by which he defines himself is as much a definition by convention as that which he applies to them. Ultimately his speech-acts, which he regards as acts of unmasking, always fall on stony ground because the play world brackets off that very reality within which the disclosure of hidden implications takes on its pragmatic significance. If Jaques takes one particular mode of double meaning to be its nature, then the nature of double meaning emerges from the fact that what he takes to be insight is actually blindness. Nowhere is the difference between game and reality, which Jaques suppresses, more evident than in the language of Orlando which Jaques reflects; in the political world, Orlando's language was self-defense, and by mirroring this speech-act under the changed conditions of the Forest of Arden, Jaques's language turns out to be a defense against other possible forms of double meaning. What led in the first instance to revelation, here in the second becomes concealment of all the other potential structures inherent in the relation of manifest to latent. In the pastoral counterimage, then, Jaques's utterances serve to show—though involuntarily—not only that there is multifarious interplay between the manifest and the latent, but also that the form of this relationship changes according to context. If the hidden can be drawn forth from dialogue, this implies that every utterance is doubled by what remains unspoken, the articulation of which makes the utterance transparent. But this, in turn, requires a standpoint that is able to bring forth the unspoken, thereby itself being doubled by an unspoken that does not become transparent in that particular speech-act. And so on, ad infinitum.

This prevents Jaques from becoming a fool, though he would like to be one (2. 7. 42). He has great admiration for the fool, but in fact he misunderstands him because he thinks that what is said and what is meant coincide in the fool's language, thereby eliminating double meaning (see especially 2. 7. 14–34). This implies, however, that in such cases Jaques cannot help presuming that the eradication of difference between saying and meaning in the fool's speech arises out of an as yet unfathomed meaning. If that were so, the much admired speech of the fool would not just highlight the obliterated interplay between the manifest and the latent, which Jaques assumes to be the case, but would turn the fool's speech into a manifest meaning pointing to an undisclosed latent one. Thus Jaques falls prey to the structure of double meaning which—though he recognizes it—he has reduced to double-tongued duplicity. His failure to see what he already knows—that is, the double meaning of language—is due to the fact that he thinks transparency removes double meaning. Although he shows an awareness that the characters from the political world lack, he nevertheless falls victim to this very awareness by making it the be-all and end-all and so failing to grasp that which gives rise to awareness. When he meets the fool, Jaques's failure to discern the difference between manifest and latent results in an admiration that amazes even himself; when he meets the other characters his awareness of the difference is all too strong, so that his idea of double meaning is itself a univocal meaning. Consequently, his unmasking activity seems futile because in the play world the context for such speech-acts has changed, and therefore double meaning as he sees it appears to be distorted and thus serves to show up his own lack of awareness. Double meaning has, so to speak, caught Jaques out because he can only conceive of the pragmatic conditions pertaining to the political world. If Jaques were not acting in a play world, he would be a figure of fun because his own consciousness dupes him. But in the play world, the man who thinks he knows everything becomes melancholic, because his certainty stops him from grasping the other possibilities that the game might add to those he already knows.

Unlike Jaques, Touchstone belongs to both worlds, though at the same time he remains an outsider in both. From the very start he has a double role that he can unite in his single person, in contrast with the other characters. In the political world, the protagonists suppress their doubles, and in the pastoral world they double themselves through their disguises. The Fool, however, is always his own double without ever having to disguise himself. The Fool is traditionally a doubling figure, usually functioning as an inverted mirror image of his master—the classic example being the Fool in *King Lear*. Touchstone also functions as a double, both in the world where the double is suppressed and in that where the characters provide their own doubles.

In Touchstone's first conversation with Celia and Rosalind, he swears by his honor that he is not a messenger from Duke Frederick. The dialogue continues as follows:

Celia: Where learned you that oath, fool?

Touchstone: Of a certain knight, that swore by his honour they were good pancakes, and swore by his honor the mustard was naught. Now I'll stand to it, the pancakes were naught and the mustard was good, and yet was not the knight forsworn.

Celia: How prove you that in the great heap of your knowledge?

Rosalind: Ay marry, now unmuzzle your wisdom.

Touchstone: Stand you both forth now: stroke your chins, and swear by your beards that I am a knave.

Celia: By our beards, if we had them, thou art.

Touchstone: By my knavery, if I had it, then I were. But if you swear by that that is not, you are not forsworn. No more was this knight, swearing by his honour, for he never had any; or if he had, he had sworn it away before ever he saw those pancakes or that mustard.

Celia: Prithee, who is't that thou mean'st?

Touchstone: One that old Frederick your father loves.

(1. 2. 58–76)

The logical proposition, the stringency of argumentation, and the linguistic precision are meant to substantiate the so-called honor that Touchstone has sworn by. Now honor is the highest value in courtly society and is therefore the prevailing convention in the political world of Duke Frederick. The argument itself is two-edged, for the social value is implicity downgraded by being linked to culinary matters in order to provide a seemingly unmistakable reference that will consolidate its validity. Built into this logical argument is a sort of toppling effect that, while leaving the argument itself intact, nevertheless sets it against a background that totally trivializes the point it seeks to make. This foreshadows the basic fabric of double meaning which can now emerge from the dialogue in so many different guises.

In this example, honor is trivialized because the knight in question has none. In this respect, the trivialization does not entail a devaluation of the social norm. But the knight happens to be a trusted follower of Duke Frederick's, and so if a man whom the duke loves has no honor, then the social system that the duke represents is unmasked as dishonorable. Conversely, if the knight does have honor, then the fool must be a knave. But since the ladies swear by their beards that he is a knave, thus basing their oath on something that does not exist, it follows that the fool is not a knave, and so the manifested social values of the political world are indeed shown to be disguises. Furthermore, the fool endows his speech with a high degree of precision, but this precision is based on something that does not exist. In this way the fool's language reflects the monologic speech of the usurpers, who not only make reality conform to what they say but also invent states of affairs, in order to posit them as realities.

The fool's language explodes into multiple senses, each of which coexists with the others and is controllable by the lexical meaning of the words, allowing for the comprehension of each of the individual significations. This multiplicity arises out of the fact that his utterances are always voiced in given situations that are themselves conditioned in many different ways. As the fool refrains from adopting any one permanent standpoint, he is in a position to bring out the many potential meanings inherent in a situation. He is therefore often misunderstood by his partners because they tend to extract a single sense from his utterances—a sense that may well have been intended but nevertheless is a misrepresentation insofar as this sense is only one among several and therefore takes its relevance more from its relation to other senses than from an understanding of the situation. The fact that his language is marked by multiple senses but is interpreted as if it were unequivocal points to the paradoxical structure of meaning itself. The multiplicity of senses is caused by the fact that every situation, brought about by interdependent actions and intersecting viewpoints, contains a plurality of voices. If this plurivocity is to be verbalized, the distinctions and differences of the various senses pertaining to and inherent in the situation have to be strictly observed. In order to accomplish this, the fool cannot have a personal language of his own, but must be able to speak all the "languages" of the situation without ever opting for just one, for if he did, he would then identify himself with that one and so exclude all the others. It is only because he has no language of his own that he can speak all these "foreign" languages. His partners, however, are bewildered by the apparent instability of his speeches, because what he says seems to be constantly switching over to other possible senses. And so when they misunderstand him or regard his utterances as nonsensical or opt for just one of the possible senses, they ought to realize that meaning only becomes meaning by way of the attitude adopted toward what has been said. But this attitude is of a pragmatic and not a semantic nature; it reveals the use that is made of meaning, as well as the degree to which this practical function blots out the range of other possibilities. Thus the pragmatic meaning is doubled by that which it excludes; it becomes meaning because of its preciseness, and this depends on those elements that the language does not articulate.

The dialogues between the fool and the other characters continually illustrate this principle. Thus, unlike Jaques, the fool does not pull out the double meaning of every utterance in order to expose its disguised motivations, but he twists every situation in such a way that its multifariousness reveals the extent to which meaning fulfills its pragmatic function by consolidating itself to the exclusion of other meanings.

Since the fool refrains from adopting any stance toward his own language, each of the emerging senses is made to topple over into another, and as this happens to all of them, they begin to parody one another. "Linguistic consciousness—parodying the direct word . . . its absurd sides . . . constituted itself *outside* this direct word and outside all its graphic and expressive means of representation. A new mode developed for working creatively with language: the creating artist began to look at language from the outside, with another's eyes, from the point of view of a potentially different language and style. . . . The creating consciousness stands, as it were, on the boundary line between languages and styles. This is, for the creating consciousness, a highly peculiar position to find itself in with regard to language."[5] The fool has this creative mind insofar as he always stands on the boundaries of possible senses, toppling what has been hidden by one out into the openness of the others. There are always several languages intersecting in his speeches, and the point of their intersection is a kind of semantic blank that denotes that meaning is not to be deduced from meaning but from a source that is not in itself semantic. In the fool's language, difference itself is made visible as the generative matrix out of which the multiplicity of senses arises, and as they mutually encroach upon each other, they point to an origin that is nonsemantic in nature.

The fool does not have to alter his linguistic behavior when he accompanies Rosalind and Celia to the Forest of Arden. As he is, so to speak, extraterritorial in relation to both worlds, his basic mode of speaking remains the same, though differently orchestrated in relation to the prevailing circumstances. If the mutual toppling of the multiple senses reveals what each one of them has excluded, then difference gives rise to a semiotic interplay between the overt and the covert. As the political world is dominated by pragmatic pressures of various kinds, this semiotic interplay is virtually endless; it reflects the never-ending exclusions brought about by the pressing demands pervading the political actions—demands that are counteracted by the plurivocity of the fool's speech. In the Forest of Arden everything turns into a game, allowing the fool to play with the toppling effect of his own plurivocal speech. In the political world, his language refers mainly to the norms of courtly society, whereas in the Forest of Arden its main concern is the game of love, but since the pastoral world is already a mirror of relationships as they existed in the political world, the fool's speeches go one better than this mirroring effect by bringing out the reverse side of the love-play, that is, they reflect what even play tends to eclipse. This is clearly to be seen in the conversation between Touchstone and Audrey, the shepherdess he is wooing:

> *Touchstone*: When a man's verses cannot be understood, nor a man's
> good wit seconded with the forward child, understanding, it strikes
> a man more dead than a great reckoning in a little room. Truly, I
> would the gods had made thee poetical.

Audrey: I do not know what "poetical" is. Is it honest in deed and word? Is it a true thing?

Touchstone: No truly; for the truest poetry is the most feigning, and lovers are given to poetry; and what they swear in poetry may be said as lovers they do feign.

Audrey: Do you wish then that the gods had made me poetical?

Touchstone: I do truly. For thou swear'st to me thou art honest. Now if thou wert a poet, I might have some hope thou didst feign.

(3. 3. 9–23)

At best, Touchstone's speech seems to Audrey to be loaded with countersense, and in any case, what he tells her overtaxes her intellect. Audrey swears she is honest, and thus implicitly invokes a love code through which society has brought man's basically antisocial passion under control. Now, if the desire for love can find its expression in terms of a prevailing code, then clearly it has already been tamed by social convention. Despite this adverse effect, the code is necessary if passion is to be fulfilled within the desired context. That which appears to be mutually exclusive can only be brought together by poetry, for only poetry can give uninhibited expression to the desire for love. Whenever expression is verbalized, this very act is permeated by a basic ambivalence. "Expression in language, . . . like all codes, has a double status: it is both the necessary systematization of experience and a reification of that experience."[6] Consequently, an awareness of fictionalizing is to be inscribed into the very language that is designed to express the complexity of the passion, thus avoiding its reduction to the level of convention or killing off the desire altogether. Only through feigning—an act that crosses all the boundaries—can the boundlessness of passion find its expression.

At this point there occurs a new turn in the toppling effect, introduced by Audrey's question: "Would you not have me honest?" (3. 3. 24). In his speech the fool had endowed feigning with a positive status, but Audrey interprets it according to the prevailing code as something dishonest which cannot therefore express her own passion. As she tries to clarify the fool's speech, the utterance takes on a double meaning she does not suspect. She is right to interpret feigning as lying, but her being right is the result of a selective interpretation of the fool's words; she has unwittingly closed off those possible meanings that he brought into play and that now have their own repercussions on Audrey's words by making her correct interpretation appear trivial or even ridiculous. The exclusion of possible senses may have a stabilizing effect within the political world, but in the pastoral counterimage they show up the comic limitation of whatever meaning has been formed.

We have not yet by any means exhausted the range of possible senses connected with Touchstone's language. When he describes poetry as feigning, he uses a superlative—"the truest poetry is the most feigning"—thereby opening up a new perspective on the poor verses that Orlando wrote for Rosalind in the preceding scene. The verses are bad because they follow the Petrarchan code and so attempt to equate desire with its linguistic expression. They lack the feigning force that crosses all boundaries and alone is able to picture unrestrained desire. Instead, Orlando subjugates his passion to censorship practiced by the Petrarchan love code, with the result that in trying to describe his wings of passion he finally clips them.

Once again another sense emerges: Against the background of such bad poetry, "true" poetry shows that passion must be something feigned. As a basic human impulse it can only achieve expression by way of existing conventions that govern human relations; but imposing a form on desire deprives it of its very nature. Consequently, only through distortion of forms can it burst out into the open, and such manifestations work best when desire discloses itself within the realm of conventions as something utterly fictional, mingling existing realities with that which they have negated. Passion cloaked in the trappings of pure invention is the adequate counterimage to the realities of existing conventions. The true lover must therefore always poeticize this passion, signalizing that whatever is said is meant to be outstripped. Only when he clothes his passion in the language of lies, according to existing conventions, can this passion be satisfactorily characterized through the distortion of the prevailing code. True poetry has absorbed the taint of untruth, because only in this way can expression be given to the truth of passion against the background of convention. It is therefore no accident that Jaques, who overhears the fool's conversation, is filled with admiration, for the fool succeeds in showing the falsity of poetry to be truthful, thereby achieving a balance that Jaques has sought in vain while penetrating the linguistic disguises of his fellow creatures.

What marks the fool off from all the other characters is the fact that his language differs from theirs. He does not identify himself with any one language, nor does he speak any one language that might be compared with the others. This is mainly because differentiation is a continually effective force within his own speech, turning it into a rhetoric of double meaning. It certainly cannot be seen as a rhetoric of emphasis, for it does not set out to bring about whatever is said through it. Thus it differs from the rhetoric of persuasion that tries to obtain explicit agreement.[7] This is why the fool is frequently misunderstood by the other characters, for they do not understand his rhetoric but only that which is said *through* the rhetoric. This, of course, complies with normal expectations of dialogue. The fool's rhetoric renounces emphatic persuasion because for him the utterance is merely a medium to ensure the return of elements suppressed by what has been said. This deconstruction of conventional emphatic rhetoric makes it possible to penetrate through the pragmatic and semantic functions of the utterance in order to show that such functions are the reason for exclusion taking place in all speech. The rhetoric of double meaning brings the utterance and that which it has excluded into co-presence, thereby making the displaced rebound on what is said. This "carnivalization" of rhetoric, according to Bakhtin, parades all definite meanings produced by language—provisional, restricted, and illusory as they are.[8] Hence the continual overturning of senses that ensue from the fool's speech.

This is evident in the dialogue about honor as well as in that about love. Each sense that emerges from the dialogue acquires its substance by excluding something equally pertinent, which in turn invalidates the first sense when it takes its own place in the foreground of the conversation. The one does not, however, establish ascendancy over the other; the process is rather one of reciprocal exclusion according to whatever elements have given rise to the respective sense. Carnivalization of rhetoric leads to a continual overturning of definitive meanings, and this spotlights the basic structure of meaning as a doubling of the overt by the covert.[9] Each definitive meaning, obtaining its position from pragmatic circumstances, is a resolution of the difference between the overt and the covert, but the fool's parade of topsy-turvy meanings continually reinscribes difference into meanings, and the resultant deconstruction of them lays bare the conditions that give rise to meaning.

By toppling all the senses of his speech, the fool stresses difference as the mainspring of sense, and he is able to afford this "game" because double meaning as thematized by his utterances is not tied to pragmatic applications. On the contrary, he banishes all practical usages from meaning in order to show that double meaning is the precondition for any definitive meaning. In this respect he contrasts with all the other characters in the play and, consequently, provides the necessary counterimage for each of the two worlds. It is through this incessant mirroring of the proceedings that the dialogue of the characters takes on its dramatic dimension, for the difference that he continually reinscribes into definitive meanings is bridged by many speeches made by those characters whose pragmatic intentions require unequivocalness.

If the game of double meaning is canceled for reasons of political power (Oliver and Duke Frederick), there is a corresponding increase in the degree of suppression, with the double meaning present as the displaced element. If the game is pragmatized, the revelation of implications serves to defend the disadvantaged party (Orlando), with double meaning present as a strategem (Orlando), or as the failure of intended speech-acts (Oliver). And if the game is seen as being regulated by a code of concealment inherent in language itself (Jaques), then double meaning is present in the guise of self-deception. However the difference may be bridged, double meaning cannot be obliterated, even though every pragmatic application of language has such obliteration as its aim.

This situation highlights an important consequence, which will be discussed at the end of the essay. Each character assumes his or her own individuality through the way in which difference is overcome in the respective speech-acts. Thus, bridging of difference turns out to be a basic condition for the act of representation which varies according to the individual mode in which difference is resolved. But from the standpoint of the fool, all the other characters' speech-acts appear merely as possibilities contained within the semiotic game of double meaning. This game is dramatic in that either one must act and therefore inevitably lose, or cancel out all actions, as does the master of the game, the fool himself.

This gap is always evident in the dialogues involving the fool. As a result, his partners find his speeches paradoxical, because he adapts himself to their expectations of dialogue only to elucidate double meaning on the semantic level, thereby undermining the vital precondition for the success of any linguistic interchange. On the surface he may appear to be making a concession to his partners, but, in fact, on the semantic level double meaning takes on the appearance of a failed speech-act, because at one moment the utterance is shown to be the suppression of something concealed, and the next what is concealed is shown to be the distortion of the utterance. The rhetoric of double meaning practiced by the fool can only be conveyed through the disintegration of semantics, which explodes into comedy. His language is comic because the utterance always has an annulling effect on what it says, while the replies to his speeches also appear comic because they try to reduce his words to an unequivocal meaning, the annulment of which gave rise to his speech in the first place. But this very process makes it possible for us to become aware of the losses and distortions that are the price of semantic clarity. Hence the dialogues involving the fool often result in failure, though the comedy of this failure holds out the promise of restitution, amounting here to a reconciliation of what appears to be irreconcilable: the pragmatic purpose of a speech-act and the structure of double meaning. The pattern of restitution is unfolded by the protagonists in the Forest of Arden.

Rosalind and Celia disguise themselves when they cross over from the political world to the pastoral. Celia becomes Aliena, and Rosalind becomes Ganymede. Just as the pastoral world is the counterimage to the political, these two characters assume roles opposite to themselves. The very name Aliena is a clear indication of Celia's self-alienation, and Rosalind alienates herself from her own sex, thus doubling herself in two mutually exclusive ways. There are two basic effects here: first, the radical split between appearance and reality, and, second, the character's own awareness of the split in her person. This in turn is a doubling of the structure of the two different worlds. Consequently, Rosalind will not only speak with two voices, but she will also use both registers of this double-voiced language simultaneously. Whenever this happens, disguise and real character function as reciprocal reflections. However, if the real self is reflected in the disguised character, the original Rosalind cannot remain unchanged, as the mask—being Rosalind's own otherness—adds something to what she has been so far.

Now disguise is a fiction, and in Elizabethan eyes it constitutes an illusory concealment of the reality hidden behind it. Therefore the disguise endowed that which was hidden with a higher status of reality than that represented by the disguise.[10] This process is a counterimage of the situation in the political world. Duke Frederick and Oliver were not in disguise, but their conduct *was* a disguise, concealing the reality that motivated their actions and with which they identified themselves. With Rosalind and Celia, the process is turned upside down in that the disguise is seen right from the start as something alienating—either through the name (Aliena) or through the change of sex—so that the character can direct herself as someone split apart from herself, thus enacting a play between the mutually exclusive selves.

When Rosalind speaks as Ganymede, Ganymede must constantly refer back to Rosalind because the disguise cannot be a true representation of herself. And so Rosalind always speaks through Ganymede as if she were someone else, and Ganymede, when he speaks, can only elucidate what Rosalind is. If Rosalind is the hidden reality behind Ganymede, Ganymede is a sort of guinea pig through whom Rosalind can adapt to reality. Originally Rosalind and Celia assumed their disguises in order to protect themselves on the way to the forest, but the fiction of the disguise changes once they have entered the pastoral haven. Initially Rosalind became a man to defend her womanhood, but now in the guise of Ganymede she wishes to play the role of the reluctant lady, so that she can test Orlando's love. Thus the character again doubles herself behind the mask by playing the role of the cynic—a role in accordance with the highly elaborate Petrarchan love code.

When Rosalind discovers Orlando's verses on the trees, her reaction is split. At first she speaks ironically of the low standard of this conventional poetry, without thinking of the author. But when she learns that Orlando wrote the verses, and must therefore be in the neighborhood, her attitude changes. She is suddenly shocked by the vast difference between what she is and what she appears to be. She asks Celia: "Good my complexion! Dost thou think though I am caparisoned like a man I have a doublet and hose in my disposition? One inch of delay more is a South Sea of discovery" (3. 2. 191–94). She is afraid that as a woman playing the role of a man she will not have sufficient control over her own emotions: "Do you not know I am a woman? When I think, I must speak. Sweet, say on" (3. 2. 245–46). Here a conflict of language begins to emerge within the conflict of roles, for as a man Rosalind cannot say what she feels, even though it demands immediate expression. How can that be said which must not be said although such a mind must needs say it?

Ganymede begins the conversation with Orlando by making ironic comments on the bad verses that evidently he has placed on the trees. Orlando acknowledges that the verses are his, whereupon Ganymede feigns astonishment at the fact that Orlando has none of the classic symptoms of a lovesick poet:

A lean cheek, which you have not; a blue eye and sunken, which you have not; an unquestionable spirit, which you have not; a beard neglected, which you have not . . . Then your hose should be ungartered, your bonnet unbanded, your sleeve unbuttoned, your shoe untied, and everything about you demonstrating a careless desolation.

(3. 2. 363–71)

Ganymede criticizes Orlando because his appearance has so little in common with the code of convention that underlies his poetry. But through Ganymede's criticism we can discover Rosalind's own desire to provoke Orlando so that she can hear more about his love. For Ganymede's critique of the Petrarchan clichés in Orlando's verses expresses Rosalind's own dissatisfaction with a love that clearly regards the Petrarchan code as an adequate means of describing itself. The reproach that Orlando does not look like a Petrarchan lover turns into an appeal to make Orlando reveal the true nature of his love, and evidently this can only be done if the conventional code is now abandoned.

The dialogue in this scene is typical of the conversations between the lovers. The silent voice of Rosalind is always speaking through the utterances of Ganymede. This entails a switch from one language function to the other, but frequently they are present at the same time. What Ganymede says always represents something else, and this something may be Rosalind's expression of her love, or it may be an appeal to Orlando to reveal his innermost feelings; and when Ganymede's speech represents the Petrarchan code of love, the language of representation is meant to give presence to both expression and appeal simultaneously. What is said serves to say something else without actually having to say it, and thus the character communicates the unsayable. In accordance with the progress or regress of the dialogue, the language function that is dominant at each respective moment will either topple into or adumbrate another one, but as already stated they are frequently present at the same time, and it is the simultaneity that gives to Ganymede's speech its double meaning. The completed utterance does not exclusively point to what is intended, but at the same time reveals what is eclipsed by it, so that Ganymede's language "means one thing, at the same time means *another*, and yet at the same time does not cease to mean the first thing."[11]

If double meaning entails an alternating dominance of one language function over the other, this must of necessity have certain effects on the relation between character and disguise. Although representation, expression, and appeal constantly shade into each other, and so appear to be simultaneously present, each nevertheless dominates at a given moment, and therefore all bring out varying identities of Rosalind. Sometimes she is Rosalind herself, sometimes she is Rosalind pretending to be Ganymede, and sometimes her double role of Rosalind/Ganymede serves to fictionalize Rosalind. And so whenever the expression of, or an appeal for, love takes over, the mask represents that which it is actually meant to conceal, but represents it without making it overt. When Rosalind, disguised as Ganymede, fictionalizes herself, she is at one and the same time herself and outside herself. At such moments she herself is almost pure difference, which manifests itself in a rapid change of roles, bringing about a co-presence of the three different language functions. Thus once again the unspoken speaks through what is said and indeed depends on the spoken for its presence. Even if every sentence has a definite reference, this always vanishes in order that the sentence may bear a different reference. And so when representation is uppermost, it ceases to portray the Petrarchan love code, the fading of which turns the sentence into a carrier for expression or appeal.[12]

We have here two languages that continually interweave, establishing and obliterating differences. So long as Rosalind/Ganymede tries to sound out Orlando about his love, using the Petrarchan code, her own desire can only be articulated through the fictionalization of this code. For only when this ceases to be able to represent love can her love take on expression. If expression is made possible by the fictionalization of the code, then the code itself must be outstripped by something that in turn does not have a form specific to any code. Outstripping the code testifies to the overpowering desire that breaks up the differentiation inherent in the code, whose distortion is proportionate to the genuineness of the passion to be communicated.

This transgression of the code is different from that which is to be found in the political world. There the code was violated so that the suppressed could remain hidden; here it is violated so that the hidden may be expressed. Thus each language function in Rosalind's speech brings out another function, which in turn changes into another, in consequence of which there is a constant interplay between differentiation and dedifferentiation. As this process is synchronic, the meaning of her utterance is decentered, so that meaning may be traced to a source that is other than semantic. Double meaning arises out of the difference that permeates the language functions, annuls their standpoints, and makes them coalesce. Thus the descriptive function of representative speech is annulled so that this can become the medium for a hidden desire, appearing either as unarticulated expression or as a wordless appeal to the lover. The manifest function is made to disappear in order to ensure the manifestation of the latent, though the suppressed function leaves behind its own traces in that it is the bearer of the now manifested unspoken. This is almost a direct reversal of the relation we discussed earlier between the manifest and the latent: here the covert becomes present by transforming the overt into the latent.

Despite its density, Rosalind's language does not itself have multiple meanings, even though what is said continually refers to something hidden, and every utterance is part of a disguise. The shifts and disguises do not spring from the wish to hide something, but signify that in the synchronic application of the different language functions, the dynamism of her passion is urging expression in the language of semantics. This is the reason why all the operations of the mask—to be conceived of as a structured focusing on existing challenges—are doubled by an operation of dedifferentiation carried out by the character underneath, reversing what the mask articulates. Each operation is doubled by a counteroperation, and the two operations in their simultaneity result in a depiction of change, catching it at the very moment of its happening. One might call this recurrent change the signified that, though ungraspable, burrows its way through the synchronic process of structured focusing (mask) and latent dedifferentiation (character underneath).

How is this process of constant change to be communicated? Rosalind/Ganymede seeks to produce in Orlando the same change of being that she has produced in herself. She wishes to cure him of his Petrarchism and so to penetrate below the surface of the code and bring forth the truer level that her love hopes to find. Therefore she arranges a game in which the male Ganymede plays the female role in the make-believe Petrarchan courtship. And as Ganymede knows that Orlando would do anything for love of Rosalind, he/she forces him to play the game:

> He was to imagine me his love, his mistress; and I set him every day to woo me. At which time would I, being but a moonish youth, grieve, be effeminate, changeable, longing and liking, proud, fantastical, apish, shallow, inconstant, full of tears, full of smiles, for every passion something and for no passion truly anything. (3. 2. 395–402)

As Ganymede, Rosalind plays the mistress's role and involves Orlando in a game that, had it taken place in the courtly world of Duke Frederick, would have been taken for reality, being in keeping with the prevailing conventions of courtly society. But what remains unconscious in the court is immediately observable in the Forest of Arden. Ganymede and Orlando are not playing roles that are accidentally thrust upon them by prevailing social conventions; they deliberately play what they are not or what they do not want to be. And so Orlando, being conscious of the fiction, can hint that Ganymede's acting is no true substitute for the real Rosalind. But while they are both playing their roles, they are also acting themselves. Rosalind is enacting her passion in order to test Orlando, and Orlando is enacting his and thereby leaving the Petrarchan code (as embodied by Ganymede) far behind. While Rosalind and Orlando each act their parts and at the same time play themselves, the game becomes a means of mastering that which is absent. Orlando enacts the fulfillment of his passion—and only the game makes it possible for him to express what is otherwise denied to him—and Rosalind experiences the love of Orlando, which assumes the desired form through the disintegration of the Petrarchan code that Ganymede represents.

Thus it turns out that only the game can be an adequate vehicle for double meaning, for it is understood within the play that whatsoever is enacted must be taken as if it were real. Consequently, the game mirrors the latent that is hidden behind the manifest. By mastering the absent, the game sets in motion a process of change, for it provides a form in which difference is simultaneously present and constantly bridged. Difference emerges as the constitutive matrix of play not least through the basic play movement of back and forth which is a constant effort to overcome difference, but it results only in an endlessly varied patterning of play structures. Obviously the dialogue achieves its ideality when speech loses its finality. But this is possible only in play, which alone can stage that which remains excluded from our everyday reality.

THE VARIATIONS WE have observed so far in the relationship between manifest and latent all arise from and are conditioned by dialogue. This seems only natural as dialogue is *the* medium of drama, and is moreover governed by the basic rule of linguistic interaction: the interplay between the overt and the covert. This rule enables language to function and appears to be a property of language existing independently of the context and code that further condition it. Each dialogue attempts to achieve a purpose, and it is this final goal that regulates the interplay of the overt and covert both in everyday conversation and in drama. A reason why Bakhtin views drama as a monologic form of speech may be that the purpose to be accomplished by dramatic interchange impedes the unfolding of the "dialogic word," conspicuous for its multifarious allusions and references.[13] The prevailing pragmatics that govern the interplay between the overt and the covert are thematized in Shakespeare's comedy; consequently the pragmatic intentions permeating the dialogue are bracketed off in order to dramatize the basic rule of language use itself. Each purpose that arises in dialogue is only to be taken as if it were one—a fact borne out by the pastoral mode in which the whole interchange is cast. Instead of dialogues we have staged dialogues; and it is a distinctive feature of pastoral literature that it mirrors fundamental aspects of human life. In this particular instance, the aspect is the basic rule of language use itself.

If the interplay between the spoken and the unspoken is to be foregrounded or thematized, the purpose that normally regulates the relationship in question must fail, because otherwise our attention would focus on the purpose rather than on the relationship. But at the same time, if dialogue is to disclose its basic rule, clearly the disclosure cannot be separated from the dialogue, and this in turn has repercussions on the interplay itself. Even the rule governing dialogue requires language for its depiction, and since all speech is intentional, the presentation of the rule will never escape the pragmatics of dialogue. The rule cannot be presented by itself, and so the pragmatic intentions of dialogue will shape the interplay between the overt and the covert, in consequence of which none of the forms it takes will ever encompass all the possibilities inherent in it. Instead, it will be disclosed only in variations according to what the dialogue is designed to achieve, so that its many manifestations may, more often than not, be in direct conflict with one another.

Now, when the speech-acts of the usurpers fail, their attitudes reflect either an unawareness of the interplay between overt and covert, or—if they are aware—a perception of it as a pair of opposites to be manipulated according to the purpose pursued. Their use of language prevents them from controlling the implications of their words, because they fail to see how the unspoken can rebound on the spoken. They are usurpers not only because they have suppressed their doubles, but also because they believe the manifest to be the successful suppression of the latent.

The interplay, however, is most vividly illuminated only when it is reflected in the mirror of the pastoral world. Jaques regards the interrelation between manifest and latent as one of dissimulation, thereby revealing its negative side as practiced in the political world. But if the interplay is unmasked as one of disguise only, then it is reduced to a univocal allegorization that brings the semiotic interplay between the spoken and the unspoken to a grinding halt.

The deficiency of this univocal allegorization is shown up by the multiple senses of the fool's language; its plurivocity opens up what Jaques's reduction eclipses. He wrecks all frames of reference essential for Jaques in order to expose the conditions on which they hinge. Thus the simultaneity of overt and covert within the fool's speech brings about a sort of explosion of meanings.

What is split asunder by the multiple senses of the fool's speeches is drawn together in Rosalind's synchronic use of language functions. The intentions underlying her words must be covered up in order that her wordless passion may be given linguistic expression.

All these variations within the relationship between the spoken and the unspoken are nothing but paradigms of double meaning, and indeed double meaning can only emerge through paradigms, since by itself it cannot be grasped. The paradigms, in turn, are conditioned by the ineradicable pragmatic intentions prevailing in each dialogue, and that holds true not least for an elucidation of the actual rule that underlies dialogue. Even in the pastoral world, where the interrelation between overt and covert becomes the topic of a multifaceted play, it is nevertheless tied to dialogue, with the resultant paradox that elucidation of the rule of dialogue can never be fully achieved because elucidation is itself a pragmatic function.

Thus, whatever the manner of elucidation, something is always going to be excluded. In the dialogue of the political world, it is the interplay between manifest and latent that is excluded, with the result that this world is marked by usurpation and failed speech-acts. In the pastoral dialogues, the interplay becomes the theme, but when conceived in terms of a univocal allegorization (Jaques), it excludes the multiple senses inherent in it, whereas when multiple senses are to be spotlighted (Touchstone), then there can be no telescoping of the overt and the covert. And even when the unspoken articulates itself through the spoken (Rosalind), there is still an exclusion, this time relating to the pragmatic function of dialogue itself. We have to keep in mind that dialogue in the pastoral world is already a staged dialogue, which is now turned into the subject of a game between Rosalind and Orlando, thus deliberately bracketing off the pragmatic function of what is spoken, in order for the unspoken to make its appearance through what is said. It is only the mutually agreed inconsequence of the Rosalind/Orlando dialogue that allows for the instantaneous presence of three different language functions: representation, expression, and appeal—all undoing each other and using each other for what each of them intends but does not verbalize. If the pastoral world is a mirror image revealing the reverse side of the political world, the staging of a play within this make-believe world constitutes a last chance of elucidating that which defies linguistic presentation. The play within the play is a form eminently suited to this process, for, as a heightened illusion, it gives presence—albeit in the form of a fleeting semblance—to that which by its nature can never assume even the shape of a given.

The paradigms discerned gain their individuality from the way in which the overt and the covert interrelate. Yet whatever the relationship may be like, something is excluded in every instance. As the excluded rebounds, the effect of the absent on the present emerges as a rich source of comedy. What has been cut off by the intentional speech-act reappears, and the resultant simultaneity of the mutually exclusive turns comedy into a potent medium for the dramatization of double meaning. But while the individual speech-acts become comic paradigms, their sequence also leads to another basic feature of comedy, which is the pattern of restitution. This, however, can only follow upon failure, and so the question arises, What exactly is it that fails here?

We have seen that double meaning takes on different forms according to the pragmatic function behind the dialogue. These forms are not double meaning itself, but are its representatives, whose difference denotes that double meaning can never be presented as itself. The moment it takes on a form through the finality of the dialogue, it establishes its presence through the fact that whatever is excluded from that form will strike back at it, subverting its claim to be truly representative. Consequently, the various representations of double meaning suffer the same fate as that which Freud attributed to the representation of drives—representations meant to make something present which they themselves are not and which hence cannot be equated with the drives. However, the continual formulation and failure of these representatives is necessary if one is to formulate a concept of that which can never be delineated.

Language, then, becomes the medium for comedy—not because it is comic in itself but because the interplay between manifest and latent can only be conveyed through a form that seeks to represent something that cannot be conveyed through any form. Comedy as a string of failed actions indicates that the structure of double meaning itself can never be cast in any form, since it is the generative matrix of language which defies translation into the symbolic order of language.

Comedy is an ideal setting for the elucidation of this process, because every failed action bears with it the promise of restitution. This interdependence highlights double meaning as an ineradicable structure inscribed into language itself which gains visibility through the dramatization of its failed representations, the inexhaustible variety of which assures a resolution to every conflict arising. There is always an alternative to failure, and consequently double meaning itself cannot finally fail, thus testifying to the fact that it is an inalienable part of our anthropological makeup.

The spoken is constantly toppled by the unspoken, and this toppling movement is further differentiated by the switch that keeps taking place between the comedy of the characters and that of their use of language. The less the characters know about how language functions, the more they are caught up in comedy that makes their unconscious language use rebound on them. Unlike most of the other characters, the fool is not subject to this type of comedy which, however, enhances the comedy of his linguistic manipulations. For him everything spoken becomes a springboard for everything unspoken, so that he produces a form of language which wrecks the pragmatic finality of the dialogue. And finally, Rosalind's play within a play is the complete carnivalization of all utterances, which so accelerates the toppling movement that double meaning appears as a process of transformation. This is without doubt the most comprehensive (though, of course, still not all-encompassing) form of its representation.[14]

OUR ARGUMENT SO far yields another completely different aspect of double meaning which also pertains to its dramatization, though it is not restricted to comedy. Whenever the manifest and the latent shade into each other and coexist, their relation is one of double meaning, as a prevailing difference marks them off from one another; without difference, there could be no double meaning. The difference, however, is a continual propellant for its own removal, and this leads to the creation of a gestalt. All the paradigms discussed arose out of an attempt to bridge difference, and their very differentness indicated the variety of possibilities inherent in difference as the constitutive matrix of double meaning. Removal of difference is therefore the impulse that gives rise to representation. This applies above all to the individuality of the characters, which establishes itself in accordance with the way they interweave the spoken and the unspoken. What they say is overshadowed either by what remains hidden or by what has been displaced through the utterance; this, in turn, reinscribes itself into what is spoken, thus delineating the individual contours of the characters. Each attempt at bridging difference has a unique feature, and so both the acknowledgment of difference and its removal turn out to be the origin of representation in literature.

If representation arises out of bridging difference, it can no longer be conceived of in terms of mimesis, but must be construed in terms of performance, for each act of difference-removal is a form of production, not of imitation. Furthermore, the fact that performance is a means of bringing something about suggests a process of staging, and this endows it with an intangible quality.

There is yet another even more comprehensive sense in which representation springs from the bridging of difference. Our individual paradigms showed that double meaning was revealed in ever-changing forms, culminating in Rosalind's play within the play turning transformation itself into a representative of double meaning. Now this constant switching, which becomes visible on all levels, thus emerges as the represented subject of the comedy. But this cannot possibly be mimetic; its performative starting point lies in the removal of difference—a process that continually alters the positions that it has marked out.

Difference, then, inspires the attempt to remove it, and it is this attempt that leads to representation as performance. Yet difference inscribes itself into representation by revoking the assumed authenticity of representation with regard to that which it makes present, and in so doing it turns representation into aesthetic semblance. Thus difference, though the origin of representation, is presented as deferral of knowing what origins are. Representation, therefore, has no original substance of its own, but is the imaginary capture of something that cannot be captured. Its transformation into aesthetic semblance is the price that representation must pay if it is to be successful. The compensation for such a price, however, is the ineluctable variety of depictions of something whose very nature prevents it from ever being conceived in terms of an object: in Shakespeare's comedy, this is transformation itself.

THE DRAMATIZATION OF double meaning reveals to what extent the semantics of language is left behind, though double meaning is still semantic to the extent that it has a form. But this serves primarily to focus on the processes whereby meaning is formed and to elucidate the fact that meaning cannot be its own origin. The question therefore arises as to how far this dramatization conditions its own reception. It is clear from the epilogue that it is meant to do so. The epilogue is delivered by Rosalind, who steps out of all her disguises to confront the audience as an actress—or, in Shakespeare's day, as a boy actor. What Rosalind has shown in the play is now to take effect on the audience. But how is she to address them? She decides: "My way is to conjure you" (5. 4. 208). "Conjure" has a striking double meaning—to charge, as she puts it a moment later, but also to produce through magic. Now by retreating to the pastoral world, Rosalind alienated herself into her own otherness, and through her disguise she underwent a transformation of what she had been. By the same means, she also worked a similar transformation in the other characters who had fled to the forest, and now that they have been transformed they may themselves produce equally magic changes in the political world. Thus the actor or actress ends the play by "conjuring" the audience, or charging them with a responsibility toward the play—that is, to like as much of it as pleases them and as perhaps their experience will allow ("for the love you bear to men, . . . women")—the implication being that the magic of the play might make them even capable of changing that experience; she asks them to make a decision about their response to the play.

Dramatized double meaning will give the audience the impetus for change through the problems its members will have in registering this double meaning. These problems begin when the plurality of senses is interwoven in the form of mutual dissimulation or is condensed by telescoping; they continue whenever the utterance becomes merely the medium for the recurrence of what it has displaced; and finally, they occur when a particular sense says something definite in order to mean something else. Such a presentation of double meaning either scatters the audience's attention or demands its multiple attention.[15] But the latter is contrary to the normal mode of perception. It is true that perception is also marked by a form of doubling, since it bisects each field of perception into figure and ground, but this doubleness is always hierarchically organized, whereas double meaning is distinguished by the absence of any such hierarchy. Hence double meaning brackets off the basic structure underlying perception—its pragmatic orientation—and in doing so, it makes us aware of the schemata that guide perception. Multiple attention is even more provocative to our acts of comprehension, for whenever phenomena have to be linked with each other, either a predicative or a passive synthesis is required. Double meaning, however, runs counter to any such dialectical solution, and so just as it delimits pragmatic semantics in relation to perception, so it delimits predicative semantics in relation to acts of comprehension.

All this becomes a dramatic experience when the spectator takes on the role of third party, being the only person in a position to perceive the presence of the absent in the present. Although it is the characters that produce this simultaneity, they are blinded to it by the pragmatic aims of their dialogue. But to this rule there are two exceptions: with the fool, the pragmatic element is wrecked, and with Rosalind it is put in brackets. These two exceptions sharpen our awareness that everything spoken is doubled by an unspoken. And once the spectator, as the third party, allows the dialogue to function as the bearer of double meaning, he or she may sense something of the nature of double meaning through the very exclusion of those principles that otherwise stabilize perception and comprehension.

Such an experience demands multiple attention, for the spectator has to grasp something that can emerge only through the suspension of established patterns of comprehension. And yet this demand is related to nothing in the least extraordinary, for the interplay of the overt and the covert is a basic principle of ordinary language. What happens here is simply that something is brought to the surface which normally remains hidden. But when double meaning translates itself into the production of multiple attention, it does run contrary to our everyday acts of perception and comprehension. Consequently the spectator must either transmute his multiple attention into acts of selective comprehension—thus reacting like those characters in the play who always foreshorten the double meaning—or he must maintain an awareness that will keep up with what is happening to him. Making someone aware of what had previously been closed to him entails conditioning him for a change. This is why Rosalind "conjures" the members of the audience to link their experience of the play with their own experience.

Since multiple attention cannot be maintained indefinitely, it triggers the demand for a semantic ordering of what has been given to experience. The meaning arrived at, both in the reception of the text and in its subsequent interpretation, turns out to be a semantic appropriation of an imaginary experience that in itself cannot be semantic, because the result cannot be its own origin. The imaginary, however, can only become an experience when molded by something other than itself which allows it to assume a tangible form. Thus double meaning may be regarded as the medium of the imaginary. When multiple attention releases an activity of semantic ordering, the spectator bridges differences and thereby repeats the very act out of which representation as performance has arisen in the text. The direction such processings will take depends on whether the spectator's existing codes remain dominant or are suspended by the imaginary experience. Multiple attention opens up a path for an unfamiliar experience to travel along by delimiting both the division between figure and ground, which is basic to perception, and the relations operative in predicative judgments, which are basic to comprehension. Such a decentering lays the spectator open to the imaginary experience, which establishes itself against the background of that which it has suspended.

SIX
ULYSSES AND THE READER

iterary theory in the modern sense dates back to the Romantic era. It marks a break with the Aristotelian tradition of prescriptive poetics; instead of laying down the rules according to which literature had to be produced, it set out to explore what literature was able to achieve. In the resultant correlation between literature and critical discourse, poets and critics extrapolated from contemporary writings those criteria from which guidelines could be formed that, in turn, were indispensable to the understanding of literature. The poets themselves (especially the Romantics, who ushered in this revolution) often wrote their own poetics, which they regarded as an exposition of the quintessence of art—something that could not be derived from observation of the traditional canon, whose legislative function prevented true insight into the nature of literature. As the critics came to take an ever greater role in this discussion about the substance of art, the links between critical discourse and contemporary writing became ever stronger, so that theory may be said to have grown out of the literature that it sought to understand. Modern literary theory began its career as a poetics of the quintessence of art, and as such it succeeded in supplanting the poetics of rules.

The premises, methods, and techniques brought to bear by a rapidly growing theoretical reflection on literature gained an overriding influence during the nineteenth century, but it was not until the early twentieth century that their full implications came to light. When this happened the poetics of quintessence came under fire, and only then did it become apparent to what extent the seemingly axiomatic norms of judgment had simply grown out of a literature that was now itself undergoing a revolution.

From our vantage point, there is no doubt that James Joyce's *Ulysses* was at the forefront of this revolution. Against this key work the interpretative modes developed by the nineteenth-century poetics, which retained and even extended their importance far into the twentieth-century, found themselves virtually helpless. Critical approaches that searched for the author's intention, for the message or meaning of the work, for its aesthetic value, and for the final reconciliation of its ambiguities, its diversity of tropes and figures, as well as for the harmonious balance between its layers, proved inadequate, and more often than not led to a condemnation of the novel.

Intention had always been held in high esteem, because it embodied one last vestige of the Romantic view of the artist as creator. The message remained essential, because, in the nineteenth century, art and literature were promoted to the status of a secular religion that occupied a leading position in bourgeois society, where all kinds of religious, scientific, political, and social thought systems were competing with each other for dominance. As for the classical concept of harmony, this derived its dignity from the fact that the reconciliation of opposites in art was believed to be the one and only form of the appearance of truth. But in the face of modern literature, these frameworks either collapsed or proved ineffectual for assessing works of art. In *Ulysses*, the intention, message, and harmony either remain in the dark or are destroyed; if one tries to hold on to such frameworks, the work will appear chaotic, or a sort of hoax, or at the very best a labyrinth for the reader to lose himself in. Judgments of this kind are not so much a reflection of the work itself as of the mode of perception used in trying to understand it. So long as the observer clings to the inherited norms of interpretation, not only *Ulysses* but also the whole range of modern art typified by *Ulysses* will seem no more than a gallery of abstruse images whose designation as art is difficult to account for. Obviously, modern literature is inaccessible by way of such norms, and those questions that in the past seemed natural to ask of literature now reveal themselves as an offshoot of a historically conditioned approach to art.

It is, however, a basic feature of the history of interpretation that the questions once asked are not without influence when new ones are framed: they have not simply disappeared from view, but turn into signs of a now blocked path of interpretation. The growing difficulties produced by the old questions give rise to new ones, so that the old questions themselves serve as pointers to new directions. Thus the classical preoccupation with the author's intention has led to our concern with the reader's response to a text. The old semantic search for the message has given rise to the analysis of the means of assembling the aesthetic object. The resolution of opposites, which was always bound up with the aesthetic value of work, has led to the question of how human faculties are stimulated and acted upon by the work. Historically one can trace the gradual emergence of a hermeneutic problem: the now invalid criteria of interpretation have given way to the questions that they did *not* pose, but these questions could not have arisen had it not been for the old answers that they replaced. The old answers, then, are not dead and buried but live on as a sort of negative fountainhead for new questions. Thus the author's intention, the work's message, and the value manifested in harmony all constitute a background to the theory of aesthetic response, and so they take on a hitherto unsuspected function that is fulfilled, above all, through the frustration of the reader's expectations as regards traditional norms of interpretation. In this sense the old questions condition a new focus, which could not have arisen from the old norms.

IF TRADITIONAL MODES of interpretation are rendered helpless by *Ulysses*, this is because the novel dispenses with a basic concept that was virtually taken for granted throughout the history of interpretation: namely, that the work of art should represent reality. In spectacular fashion, *Ulysses* puts an end to representation and hence to the expectations produced by the typical nineteenth-century novel with its illusion of reality. Any attempt to read *Ulysses* as an illusion of reality can only lead to bewilderment, because the reader is never given the chance to establish any overall perspective or an easily observable everyday pattern such as was always offered—in no matter what form—by the nineteenth-century novel. The latter always mimicked the central perspective of human perception in order to represent reality under the same conditions as it is perceived in the outside world. Representation, however, presupposes the time-honored, yet no longer tenable, belief that the world can be contained by a book, whereas *Ulysses* revives the old incompatibility between book and world, even if it is forever seeking to undermine the real world's refusal to be portrayed.

Ulysses resorts to nearly every mode of representation that the novel has developed during its comparatively short history. Its references, however, are peculiar in that these traditional modes are often exploited for the purpose of shattering expectations. They occur as "minus functions,"[1] because they draw attention to the absence of the expected orientation that the various techniques reliably produced in the past—techniques such as a coherent point of view, or a story line to give overall structure to the plot. In *Ulysses*, however, the various modes run counter to each other and the story is dispersed, so that expectations are constantly aroused only to be frustrated. This frustration reveals two things: first, that the world eludes portrayal, and, second, that the reader's activity is heightened when the orientation expected from the genre is withheld. *Ulysses* is a vast network of expectations, simultaneously evoked and made empty, which is all the more challenging as the gigantic mass of information is deprived of all coherence. In this form it seems like the ruins of the whole idea of representation, because what is depicted appears to distort everything that the novel was always expected to achieve. Feeling overtaxed or shut out, the reader makes projections onto the work in order to restore those dimensions that it seems to have lost. In doing so the reader cannot escape the experience that these projections themselves keep falling short; they fail to establish the expected context, and so ultimately they reveal their true nature as attempts to salvage an evidently lost meaning. Through these failed projections, the demise of representation makes itself present to the reader.

Now it cannot be the purpose of a novel to withhold meaning on the understanding that the reader must find it independently by piecing together a picture of represented reality from the jigsaw of fragmented patterns. But many critics still insisted that this must *be* the purpose, and so every effort was made to devise some network of coordinates which would enable all the scattered fragments of representation to be pieced together into a coherent whole. Thus they seized on the Homeric archetypes, on human organs, and on the many other ingeniously concocted correspondences traced by Stuart Gilbert in his commentary[2]—all of them characterized by the desire to bring 'order' to 'chaos'. Under such headings, the novel sinks to the level of a puzzle—a riddle for which the interpreter must find the one and only answer. How is such an answer to be found? Certainly not through the author's intention, the work's message, or the resolution of ambiguities. Even the criteria formulated by New Criticism proved to be inadequate for the task. For *Ulysses* is an open work: it resists all demands for closure and denies all attempts to reduce it to the clear-cut dimensions of a self-referential object. It constantly extends beyond the margins of the printed page. And yet, in spite of all these apparent violations of critical norms, *Ulysses* has long been accepted as a literary masterpiece and as a revolutionary landmark, although the guidelines operative in a great many of its interpretations have shown that it virtually marks the end of representation—even if this fact is not acknowledged explicitly by all the novel's admirers.

SUCH PARADOXES LED to a change of paradigm in literary theory. Even those critics who clung to traditional paradigms were clearly unable to resist the lure of *Ulysses*, though the very nature of their interpretations should have aroused doubts concerning their fidelity to the impression given by the novel. Simply working out the many allusions in *Ulysses* should have been enough to create the suspicion that such an overelaboration of representation could not serve to produce a faithful image of reality. Anyone taking the welter of unstructured details as a means of authenticating or lending verisimilitude to represented reality is liable to find that this reality is so overdeterminate that it simply leads him into new areas of indeterminacy. At the same time this indefatigable quest for an underlying organizational schema makes it evident that in *Ulysses* we are confronted with the processing of reality rather than with its representation. If the interpreters—who are, after all, readers first and foremost—feel themselves drawn into such a pursuit, then clearly the reader's involvement in the text is a matter of the utmost importance. Through this process, the novel itself brings about the necessary shift in the perspective of interpretation. It is therefore the act of response that we must focus on, because it is this act that sheds light on what is produced by a novel whose driving force is the thwarting of its reader's expectations. *Ulysses* is not to be seen as a copy of the world, or as a representation of the world's refusal to be portrayed—as Broch saw it[3]—but as a means of thematizing access to the world. This access does not have the character of an object, in the sense in which the world is an object, and so *Ulysses* cannot be a copy of such an access; it can only offer the opportunity for such an access to be constituted. It follows that the reader cannot help being drawn into a process of communication, and at the same time he is jerked out of an attitude of passive contemplation demanded of readers by all those works that encourage the grasping of a represented object. This radical switch engendered by *Ulysses* also necessitated a change of interpretative paradigm that would enable the critic to capture the experience undergone in *Ulysses*.

In this respect, literary theory continues to base itself on what happens in contemporary literature. Text-processing as an act of communication became possible, if not actually inevitable, with the failure of the belief that the world could be contained and represented in a book. This belief always cloaks the distinction between book and world, but Joyce's work tears the two asunder and radicalizes the difference so that the book can only explore paths of access, whose variability becomes an object of communication with the reader.

Ulysses destroys an illusion to which the realistic novel of the nineteenth century had accustomed its readers. This shattering of hallowed expectations points to the fact that the strategies of the novel are less concerned with depicting a given reality than with undermining attitudes of the reader established by tradition. This is why *Ulysses* was initially considered scandalous, for it clearly ran counter to those norms hitherto regarded as essential to a work of art. The undercutting of norms, however, will inevitably bring them above the threshold of consciousness and thus exhibit them for inspection. They are then shifted into a new perspective that is not part of them and that consequently brings to light that which remained hidden so long as their validity remained unquestioned. Literature cannot *be* literature unless it is accorded this status by prevailing standards of what is expected of art. The discovery of this fact is due in no small measure to *Ulysses*, as a key work of modern art.

If the shattering of expectation causes a scandal, this is symptomatic of deeply entrenched conventions that can only be deconstructed by exposing the need out of which they have arisen. In *Ulysses* this deconstruction marks the switch from representation to effect. If the novel is first and foremost a structure for eliciting responses and thereby engaging its readers, then a theory that is applicable to such literature must incorporate this change: it must replace the author-oriented perspective by one that is reader-oriented.

WHAT IS TO be gained by such a change of perspective? In asking this question one needs, above all, to bear in mind the fact that the subject of this novel is an ordinary day in Dublin. What could be the significance of this ordinary day? So long as one clings to the expectation that the novel should be a portrayal of the real world, this meaning will seem to be nothing more or less than the futility of such a transitory day, and indeed this notion permeates many interpretations of *Ulysses*. However, to conceive of this novel as reproducing an ordinary day entails a straightforward endorsement of the Marxist mirror-reflection theory to which, ironically, even that type of bourgeois criticism that believed itself to be worlds apart from such Marxist ideas has fallen victim. Why should the futility of everyday life be reproduced in a novel, and why should we be fascinated by the reproduction of our drabness and misery? Even if futility were the keynote of everyday life, the novel—to be comprehensible—would have to make that senselessness experienceable. And openness to experience is the vital dimension, preceding all evaluations of everyday life, that is made available in *Ulysses*. A reader-oriented analysis is therefore free from the task of telling the reader what Joyce might have meant. Instead, it serves to elucidate the processes by means of which everyday life is made accessible to experience.

The eighteen different chapter-styles, anchored in different perspectives, therefore assume a very special representational function. As the viewpoint changes with each successive style, so the ordinary day takes on an ever-changing appearance. When, for instance, in the "Nausicaa" chapter, everyday life is depicted both in the form of a sentimental novel and in that of a realistic interior monologue, the two contrasting, yet interrelated, modes of portrayal turn into parodies of each other, thereby revealing themselves not as representations of everyday life but as limited schemata by means of which a situation is organized within an otherwise shapeless ordinariness. These limitations apply equally to the patterning of that ordinary day produced by each of the chapter styles and to the narrative devices contained in each of them.

In the "Proteus" chapter, this process becomes graspable, and in "Oxen of the Sun" it becomes a theme in itself. In "Proteus" the world is only present for Stephen because it resists integration through perception. The continual effort to separate the patterns of one's perception from the things perceived, thus taking them out of their organizational context, adumbrates the multifariousness and openness of the real world. "Oxen of the Sun" is laid out in such a way that right from the start the reader is placed in a position of detachment from the different styles through which the process of birth is to be conveyed. The successive dominance of each period style of English literature encourages and enables the reader to adopt an interpretative attitude similar to that of the characters, who are presented in a bewildering variety of styles. In this way the reader becomes increasingly aware of the limitations imposed on the presentation by each style. Each trend has to be corrected by the subsequent one so that the limitations of each style can be brought out—limitations caused by the fact that each mode of representation is highly indeterminate. Thus all the modes are robbed of their representative importance and are transformed into means of organizing ordinariness into articulated situations. The continual clash of the styles and of the representational modes that they incorporate prevents this ordinary day from ever taking on representational significance; instead, through the rapid switching of vantage points, it makes itself felt as an event.

Reality therefore ceases to have any particular meaning—not because it is of itself meaningless, but because it is conveyed here as an experienceable event. If one is to 'interpret' *Ulysses*, one must seek to define the nature of this 'experienceability' that is thematized in the novel. All its modes of representation give rise to different views of the ordinary world, and through their individual limitations these views reveal themselves not as symbolic representations of this ordinary day but as effective irritants, disturbing conventional attitudes in such a way that everyday life cannot be equated with any of those attitudes.

This process brings to light the artificiality of all concepts employed to pattern the ordinary day. At any time one can stop observing the everyday experiences of the characters and switch one's attention to the modes and techniques out of which the text arises. This switching is inherent in the form of presentation developed in *Ulysses*—a form that is indeed so artificial that initially it seems anything but everyday. But it is this very artificiality that makes us conscious of the need—constantly elicited by the layout of the text—to link the disjointed segments in order to establish situational contexts. Thus the blueprint of the text forces the reader into a reading process that is structurally similar to the process by which everyday life in the novel itself is constituted. Consequently the reader simultaneously experiences a process and observes it taking place in the characters who articulate a situation by means of their view. The patterns established by the reader equally contain only situational arrangements but never merge into an overriding scheme, and so the reader is constantly oscillating between observation of the characters and experience of what is being observed. The reader stands in two places at once: outside the characters and between that external position and the characters. The awareness created in this involvement makes the experience an aesthetic one that is not itself represented but that happens to the reader as an effect of the novel.

The basis of such an effect is the Joycean discovery that everyday life is a kaleidoscopic changing of situations which arises from the organizational activities of those who live that life. Consequently the structures of the daily world are also those of consciousness, so that the characters' mastery of the everyday world is always accompanied by and parallel to the reader's mastery of the text. As there is an implicit denial of any hierarchy among the vantage points set out in *Ulysses*, the reading process is a ceaseless variety of attempts to mediate between discontinuous situations. The variety entails that new attempts at mediation should be made under new conditions, and through this constant change the experience of everyday life is transposed into the reader's mind: reality *is*, while and because it happens.

The uncovering of such processes will lead ultimately to an analysis of aesthetic function, for the discernible structures of the text only take on their particular quality through the function that they serve. This means that the old poetics of quintessence of art must be supplanted by a poetics of aesthetic function—a function that takes on solid form through the impact caused by the text. Joyce's *Ulysses* necessitated a shift of direction in literary criticism, for the work itself embodies the possibilities of its own disclosure, and these must be traced if the work is to be made accessible to discussion. Every important work will have repercussions on the existing cultural code, and as literary theory is part of that code it is bound to change its approach if the aesthetic experience conveyed by the revolutionary work is to be translated into discourse, thus making it available for the purpose of analyzing contemporary consciousness.

SEVEN

THE PATTERN OF NEGATIVITY IN BECKETT'S PROSE

egativity and construction—this is Sartre's definition of the principle underlying literature.[1] He uses this definition in order to try to establish the function of literature in the context of human society. Negativity is to be regarded as one aspect of freedom, because it is not, as Sartre says in *What Is Literature?*, a matter merely of "the abstract ability to say no, but of a concrete negativity that retains for itself that which it rejects, and is completely colored by it."[2] As such, it gives a degree of free play to the reader of the literary text it colors, for his task is to discover that which the work suppresses. One might say, in this respect, that negativity transforms the work into a kind of suction effect: because the reader seems to be relentlessly drawn into the world, the text opens up for him.

This particular effect distinguishes negativity from simple negation for, as Kenneth Burke[3] has shown, negation contains the imperative demand to seek the positive elsewhere than in what is negated, and this demand is nearly always accompanied by a number of signposts to point the way: what the reader has to find can be taken to be the opposite of what has been negated, and so contrasts and contradistinctions form a frame of reference within which the intention of the negation can be discovered. In this way negations enable literary texts to stimulate specific attitudes to specific social situations. However, when such frames of reference are dismantled or even deliberately suppressed, negation changes into negativity, and instead of a demand we have what I have called a suction effect.

Negativity is the hallmark of the typical Beckett text. It is produced by a relentless process of negation, which in the novels applies even on the level of the individual sentences themselves, which follow one another as a ceaseless rejection and denial of what has just been said.[4] The negation may relate either to a statement or to something preceding that statement. If a statement is negated, this does not mean that nothing is left of it. A poster stamped "performance canceled" is still a poster, and is all the more striking if, as in this case, there are no other posters to tell you what *is* on. The fewer orientations there are, the more oppressive will be the cancellation of what we *have* been given. The Beckett reader is continually being confronted by statements that are no longer valid.

But as the negated statements remain present in his mind, so the indeterminacy of the text increases, thus increasing the pressure on the reader to find out what is being withheld from him. At the same time the cancellation of statements teaches him that he is not to be given any specific orientation, and this evokes in him an even greater need to find out what the negated orientation actually drives at. Thus negativity turns out to be a basic constituent of communication. If we look at the process of negativity in this light, we will see that Beckett's work is by no means so negative or destructive as many critics would have us believe—especially those who, like Lukács, feel obliged to view his writings as the "most profound pathological debasement of man."[5] Indeed negativity can be regarded here as a structure of bringing forth—at least potentially— infinite possibilities. This becomes clearer if we take a closer look at the other type of negation, the one that is related to what precedes a statement. If a negation can no longer be viewed in terms of any given frame of reference, it explodes into a multiplicity of possibilities. This process is as old as human society. The Ten Commandments contain a typical example: "Thou shalt not make thee *any* graven image, *or* any likeness *of any thing* that *is* in heaven above, or that *is* in the earth beneath, or that *is* in the waters beneath the earth" (Deut. 5:8). The history of Christian art shows the extent to which this negative commandment has "exploded" into an endless variety of graven images and likenesses. The same applies to Beckett. The continual negation of the ideas evoked by the texts— the self and its history, the end and its ending, the demand (in *Imagination Dead Imagine*) that imagination itself be negated as the origin of such images—constitutes the massively productive force that releases all these possibilities, a force to which the very existence of Beckett's own works bears eloquent testimony.

Negativity brings into being an endless potentiality, and it is this potentiality that forms the infrastructure of Beckett's writings. By negativity we mean the hidden motive for the many negations and deformations that condition the characters we meet in these works. It stimulates communicative and constitutive activities within us by showing us that something is being withheld and by challenging us to discover what it is. If we take the term *negativity* to cover the deformations of Beckett's characters and also their own negative aspects, which in turn lead to so many negativized situations, we may begin to understand what is actually conveyed by negativity. Merleau-Ponty has said, with reference to pictorial art, that "it is peculiar to the visible . . . that it is duplicated by something invisible which is, to a certain extent, absent and which the visible makes present."[6] If we apply this to Beckett's works, we will find that our own imaginations are concerned not with concretizing the deformations of the characters or their constant failures so much as with the duplication of the "invisible," for the concretizing of deformations and failures can only come about if we can discover their cause, and this is never given to us. We are compelled to try to fulfill a hidden potential, as we seek to conceive the conditions that alone can lead us to the sense of what we are reading. Thus negativity mediates between presentation and reception: it initiates those processes of imagination which are necessary to bring out the virtuality of those conditions, which—though linguistically not stated—are responsible for all the deformations of the characters and their constant failures. It is an important agent of the interaction between text and reader, and at the same time it constitutes the point at which Beckett's texts sink their roots into life itself.

Tavistock School's psychoanalytic research into communication takes as its starting point the fact that negativity is the basic regulator of human communication. As R. D. Laing remarks, it is characteristic of human relations that we have no real knowledge of how we experience one another.[7] This fundamental gap in our knowledge leads us first to a productive process through which we build up our own conceptions of how our partner experiences us; we base our reactions upon these projections. Our imaginary picture, then, is a product that enables us to cover the unbridgeable gap in human relations. However, we then find that this product is only the image of a reality that certainly exists—for our partner must experience us in some way or other—but that we can never know. Consequently such images can also distort human relations and even destroy them, as they tend to become reified, that is, come to be taken for realities in themselves and not just as substitutes that we need in order to bridge the gaps of the unknowable in interpersonal relations. Herein lies the ambivalence of negativity: the interaction might be a triumph of social creativity in which each is enriched by the other, or it might be a spiraling debacle of increasing mutual hostility from which neither benefits.[8]

In Beckett's dramas there is an almost total breakdown in communication. Perhaps this is because the characters spring from a consciousness of the extent to which communication can only take place by way of projected ideas, and from an awareness of the fact that these can only be revealed as projections if they are constantly made to disappear in the dialogue of the characters. Therefore these characters appear to be constantly on their guard to prevent a communicative interaction from happening. Built into their behavior is the knowledge that dialogue as a means of partners "tuning in" to each other can only produce projections; these may provide the bridge between people, but at the same time they undermine that bridge, because they are subjective ideas that can slide all too easily into psychopathologic conditions. Beckett's art of negativity consists in the fact that this situation, which prevails throughout human society, is not simply conveyed to us as such; instead we are made to feel the impact of this situation for ourselves by the deliberate omission of the basic features of dialogue in the conversation of these characters.

This impression is all the more remarkable in that the titles of the plays always open up horizons of human endings — *Waiting for Godot, Endgame, Happy Days, All That Fall* — as a background against which we are to see the characters. We expect them to come to some kind of understanding in the face of such situations. However, as we are deprived of their projections, we begin to project ourselves, only to realize again and again that our conceptions fall short or lead nowhere — that they *are* projections. And yet in our everyday lives we are always guided by the conviction that our conceptions can grasp realities; we are not aware that they may represent mere fictions formulated because we find ourselves confronted by realities of whose existence we are conscious but which we can never actually know. In our human relationships we act as if we knew what our partner was experiencing from our presence. But in Beckett's drama, we can only provide motives for the continual negation of the dialogue by realizing that our explanatory conceptions are in fact nothing more than fictions. This realization, however, does not help us in any way to solve the social or historical problems we are faced with. On the contrary, the fact that we have seen through our fictions brings forth a new and almost insoluble dilemma: we know that they are false, but at the same time we know that they are useful. They seem to provide us with knowledge wherever we are temporarily or permanently ignorant. Now if we know that, as Vaihinger puts it, they are "deliberately false,"[9] do we sacrifice their usefulness? Or do we hold onto them precisely because they are useful, and so close our eyes to what we know about them? It is this problem that we must now consider in more detail, with reference to Beckett's trilogy *Molloy, Malone Dies,* and *The Unnamable.*[10]

IN ORDER TO gain access to this trilogy, we must first elaborate a little on the definition of negativity. So far we have described it as a structure of bringing forth infinite possibilities, in the sense that it is a formal but at the same time central condition of communication. In Beckett, however, this structure is related not just to individual situations but to basic features of human existence whose reality is indisputable, although we cannot *know* what this reality consists in. We have already mentioned one such feature: interpersonal communication, which arises from what we shall have to call the inexperienceability of other people's experiences. The other features are the self and the end. In the first case we have an unknowable reality, and in the second, an inexperienceable one.

Communication, the self, and the end are not subjects chosen at random. They are central preoccupations of contemporary thought. But in dealing with these basic themes, Beckett discloses something that is not brought out by the current interpretations attached to these themes by present-day thought and value systems; perhaps it is not meant to be brought out, as it would otherwise cancel the validity of the explanations offered by the systems concerned. Herein lies the structural relevance and function of Beckett's negativity. It does not lead to other explanations that will vie with those already in existence, but it draws attention to those factors that condition existing explanations of self and end.

From *Murphy* right through to the end of the trilogy the dominant theme is the identity of the self; the characters are obsessed with the desire to know themselves.[11] Murphy tries to bring himself back to an identifiable point, to what "makes him tick," by a constant withdrawal from his social environment, from his body, and finally from the recognizable forms of his spiritual activities. He strives for the absolute contact of the ego with itself, releasing himself from all worldly ties in order to get to the point where, in his attitude toward himself, he can finally coincide with himself. What happens in this process has been made explicit by Merleau-Ponty in a different context:

> My absolute contact with myself, the identity of being and appearance cannot be posited, but only lived as anterior to any affirmation. In both cases, therefore, we have the same silence and the same void. The experience of absurdity and that of absolute self-evidence are mutually implicatory, and even indistinguishable. The world appears absurd, only if a demand for absolute consciousness ceaselessly dissociates from each other the meanings with which it swarms, and conversely this demand is motivated by the conflict between those meanings. Absolute self-

PARADIGMS

evidence and the absurd are equivalent, not merely as philosophical affirmations, but also as experiences.[12]

If the identity of the self has, at best, the character of self-evidence, identity can only exist as experience and never as knowledge. Self-evidence and knowing exclude one another—or in other words, the certainty of self-evidence does not lend itself to be questioned. It is characteristic of Beckett's texts that from the very beginning they are concerned with those experiences of which we can never know anything. This does not satisfy Beckett's characters; on the contrary, they demonstrate what it means to have no knowledge of what is self-evident and of what consequently can only be experienced, thus setting off a process that clearly goes against the modern theme of subjectivity which has constantly defined identity in terms of historically motivated norms. But they do not stop at undermining the historical manifestations of such norms; instead they show the problematic but utterly indispensable necessity of these norms.

"Live and invent"[13] is Malone's summary of the situation. "I'm tired of being matter, matter, pawed and pummelled endlessly in vain,"[14] says the Unnamable. Here we have a basic dilemma of life itself: though we are alive, we do not know what it is to be alive. If we try to know what it is to be alive, we are constrained to search for the meaning of something we can, in the last analysis, know nothing about. And so the constant invention of images and the immediate rejection of their claim to elucidation or to truth constitutes the only possible product of this dilemma. Malone and the Unnamable are not taken in by their own inventions, but they are able, at least to a certain degree, to satisfy their urge to know something about which there can be no knowledge. Malone goes on writing, because by nullifying what he has written he can ensure that he is not inventing himself; he knows that everything he writes is a lie, because any conception of himself can only be a fiction.[15]

This awareness is built into the Unnamable. He not only defends himself against being invented by the conceptions that he himself has formulated and that now have merged into "gestalts" whom he calls vice-existers; he also knows the conditions that have led to these self-engendering fictions continually usurping him in order to tell him what and who he is:[16] "I don't believe in the eye . . . there's nothing . . . to see with . . . when you think what it would be, a world without spectator. . . . No spectator then, and better still, no spectacle, good riddance."[17] The Unnamable knows the restrictedness of vision that conditions all our knowledge and in its turn is merely an indication that we are inescapably caught up in the ever-changing situations of life. Our efforts to raise ourselves above this being in the midst of ever-changing situations, while we still remain trapped within the limitations of human vision, must inevitably lead to fictions, but we hold onto these fictions because they satisfy our need for knowledge. We are like Beckett's characters to the extent that we are not content merely with the fact of being alive; but we lag behind them because we are not willing to see our conceptions of the experienceable but unknowable, or of the inexperienceable, relegated to the level of mere fiction.

BECKETT'S MODE OF communication makes it impossible for us to escape from this situation, and this is the reason why we often feel oppressed by his work. From *Molloy* to the *Unnamable* there is continual narration, but in this narrative process we experience an increasing erosion of what we expect from a narration: the unfolding of a story. This expectation is actually encouraged by the many fragments of stories, but these serve only to show up the narrative process as one of continual emptying out. Furthermore, the whole trilogy is littered with the empty husks of traditional literary conventions. We normally take it for granted that a story is told because of its exemplary value, so that the facts of the plot—which we can generally summarize ourselves—only take on their real function when they begin to interact with one another, thus adumbrating the meaning that is to be communicated. However, if statements are made and then instantly rejected, as happens all the time in this trilogy, then we can have nothing more than the beginnings and the re-beginnings of a plot. As a result of all this fragmentation, meaning becomes impossible to grasp, and instead there arises a massive blank—partially structured, it is true, by the rudiments of plot—and the reader finds himself almost compelled to produce a filling for this blank. A further stimulus to the reader's imagination is the fact that the first-person narrators[18]—just like Hamm and Clov in *Endgame*[19]—are all afraid that what they say or do might mean something; their fear is that some representative value might be extracted out of what they have said and might be taken for the meaning of the whole.

The reader is continually tempted to try to fill the blank with his own projections, simply because he longs to find a plausible explanation for a narrative process that frustrates all his expectations by denying him access to any specific meaning. If any of his explanations did cover the meaning of Beckett's novels, then we should have to regard these as mere picture puzzles that one need only gaze at with a certain amount of application in order to uncover the secret message. But the structure of these novels is such that the reader himself is forced to reject all the explanations provoked by the "plot" if he is to keep up with the observations of the characters, who know all too well the value, or lack of value, of their own explanations. Of course, the reader need not follow the dictates of the structure; he may be unwilling to give up the explanation provoked by the "plot," because his one concern is to endow the story with the consistency essential for comprehension; in this case, though, he will find that the meaning he has produced and ascribed to the novels themselves is almost impossibly abstruse. The complaint is not an unfamiliar one in Beckett criticism. But if the reader does follow the dictates of the structure, in order to gain access to the conscious minds of the characters, then he will be forced to take the continual obsolescence of his own meaning-projections — which basically are conditioned by his own particular world of ideas — as the meaning of Beckett's novels.

This process can perhaps be best understood with reference to Beckett's use of language. To a high degree, Beckett has stripped language of implications: it means what it says, and nothing more. It looks as if it were pure denotation, at pains to exclude connotation. In Stanley Cavell's words, Beckett "shares with positivism its wish to escape connotation, rhetoric, the noncognitive, the irrationality and awkward memories of ordinary language in favor of the directly verifiable, the isolated and perfected present."[20] But Beckett writes novels. Literary texts do not denote any given, empirical world, and so they ought to use the denotative function of language in order to build up instructions about how meaning is to be produced. Beckett, however, constantly takes language at its word, and as words always tend to mean more than they say, all statements must be qualified or even canceled. By turning language against itself, Beckett shows clearly how language actually functions. But as language is used here to prevent the formation of connotations, without fulfilling its alternative function of denoting an empirically existing object, inevitably the reader will find himself trying to supply those connotations denied him by the text. He has to take over the responsibility for building up a meaning, and so the language — reduced to mere utterance by the eradication of its implications — becomes conspicuously operative in the mind of the reader: he must experience the continual invalidation of the meanings he is continually formulating. This is the cause of the profound discomfort most Beckett readers have to endure; it also enables us to understand what Beckett may have meant when he spoke of the power of texts that claw their way into us.[21] Furthermore, the way in which the reader is induced to reject the meanings he himself has formulated brings to the fore an expectation all of us have about the meaning of works of art: meaning should bring the resolution of all the disturbances and conflicts that the work has brought into being. Both classical and psychological aesthetics have been united in their demand for the relief of tensions as the basic feature of meaning and intention of literary works.[22] However, this view of meaning constitutes a historical but by no means normative expectation, and Beckett for one is clearly concerned with a very different sort of meaning.

BECKETT'S NOVELS TURN upon two basic elements of human existence: the identity of the self, and the end. We have not discussed the "end" in any detail here,[23] but suffice it to say that these are two topics one of which can only be experienced by means of self-evidence, while the other, a reality that affects us all, cannot be experienced (except, of course, in a way that is incommunicable). This "inexperienceability" and "unknowability" is profoundly disturbing for us. The extent of the disturbance can be gauged from the plethora of pictures and images produced by it, ranging from the apocalypse to the new political millennium.[24]

Now as such pictures constitute our response to "inexperienceability" and "unknowability," they are by their very nature fictional. And yet their lack of reality does not disturb us, because they give us the illusion of access to those areas of life that are inaccessible. Beckett's novel certainly shows us that fiction acts as a compensation for what our mental processes and physical actions cannot supply, but the process does not stop at revealing to us why we stand in need of fiction. Although we become aware of it, this insight does not make us act on what we know. Thus Beckett's first-person narrators go on. Even though they cancel out the possible meanings of their utterances with every succeeding sentence, they still go on, so that they are clearly fascinated by the process of cancellation itself and cannot tear themselves away from it. If the unmasking of fiction as deliberate falsehood were the sole object of these novels, the time and energy spent on the unmasking would be out of all proportion. The same purpose would have been more convincingly served by a pointed satire. The fact that these narrators cannot stop is an indication of the degree to which they are caught up in the process of fiction-building and -destroying. This may seem like an end in itself, but it is in fact conditioned by a self-generating structure that *cannot* be halted. The characters know that all access to the world and to themselves is subject to the restrictions of their perspective. Perspective, however, is as Merleau-Ponty says, "the invention of a controlled world, which one possesses totally in a momentary synthesis."[25] The characters are continually frowning upon such syntheses as pragmatically oriented fictions. But as they are inescapably caught up in the midst of ever-changing situations, this mode of comprehension is the only one possible, even though real comprehension is *not* possible. Their knowledge of this fact can only retain its validity through a ceaseless production and rejection of perspective-oriented meanings.

Such an unremitting process of rejection might be expected to bore both character and reader to death, but this is not the case because the rejections never remain static. A perspective can only come into being through a situation, and the fiction can only be useful in terms of a situation. The fiction takes on its form through its reference to concrete problems that it has to solve, and that is why there can be no such thing as an abstract fiction, for without this concrete function, it would really be nothing. And so Beckett's characters reject ever-changing fictional "gestalts," each of which they have themselves invented in order to solve ever-changing, concrete problems.

Every cancellation involves a negation, but negations take longer to work out than affirmations, and as this process again can only take place through the mode of perspectives, the characters find themselves with more and more to do. As we have already observed, the negations cancel out previous fictional "gestalts," but these are not removed from the scene altogether; they remain as canceled "gestalts," and so inevitably give rise to conjectures as to the cause and motivation of the cancellation. Thus negation leads to an unending and ever-increasing activity on the part of the characters.

This activity is by no means welcome, for it constitutes the growing compulsion to get away from something to which they are in fact permanently fixed. The perpetual effort to retract what has been stated has its counterpart in their physical existence as well: it is to be seen in the paradoxical cheerfulness that overcomes them in their increasing deformity and paralysis. For the body is the first and last hold that man has on the world; reliance on the body means recognition of an irrevocable factor to which we owe our presence in the world. And so as the body (like the language) progressively loses its function, Beckett's characters formulate new hopes. Stanley Cavell, with reference to *Endgame*, gives the following description of these hopes:

> Salvation lies in the ending of endgames, the final renunciation of all final solutions. The greatest endgame is Eschatology, the idea that the last things of earth will have an order and a justification, a sense. That is what we hoped for, against hope, that was what salvation would look like. Now we are to know that salvation lies in reversing the story, in ending the story of the end, dismantling Eschatology, ending this world of order in order to reverse the curse of the world laid on it in its Judeo-Christian end. Only a life without hope, meaning, justification, waiting, solution—as we have been shaped for these things—is free from the curse of God.[26]

A rejection of hope, meaning, justification, and a simultaneous repudiation of our being caught up in the ever-changing situations of life leaves us, in fact, like nowhere men in a nowhere land. And this is precisely the position of Beckett's characters, who have rejected all the alternatives and so leave themselves without alternatives, thus revealing the insurmountable finiteness of man to be an endless or in-finite going on. They know that all connections and relations are fictional in that these are the means by which we delude ourselves that we have brought order into chaos. The only escape from this naiveté is to reject fiction, but such a rejection can then be as meaningful (and so as suspect) as the meaning we gain from establishing connections, and so on. Any meaning, any interpretation, automatically carries with it the seeds of its own invalidity, for it must exclude everything that runs counter to it. Beckett's characters know this, and so with every interpretation they present the weakness of that interpretation, thereby invalidating it. This process is extremely ambivalent: on the one hand it shows that the indeterminacy of human existence cannot be resolved by pragmatic definitions; on the other, it does away with the coagulating demand for validity posed by all forms of interpretation.

Fiction, then, is both a symptom and a product of man's finiteness. It permits those pragmatic extensions necessitated by his entanglement in an indeterminate and undefinable life. The rejection of fiction, however, prevents us from arbitrarily following our inclinations to reify what we should so like to regard as realities—those explanations that clarify the inexplicable. But the rejection of fiction does not lead to a Utopian enlightenment of man, for what would be the use of merely fixing ourselves in the knowledge of our unknowability? What Beckett's rejection of fiction reveals is the nature of man's inescapable limitations: it is an infinite retention of the self within this insurmountable finiteness. Herein lies the true significance of Beckett's negativity, for finiteness means being without alternatives, and this intolerable condition explodes into an endless productivity, of which both the origin and the product are fictions. The game with fictions can never stop, and it is this fact that endows man's finiteness with its infinitude. Such a situation can only be conveyed through the rejection of fiction if finiteness is to be seen as itself and not as the expression of something else. The perpetuity of the progress springs from the fact that a denial must be preceded by a statement, but in turn the denial itself becomes a statement, and this brings forth the next denial, and so on ad infinitum. Thus the rejection of fiction becomes a structure of communication; it conveys the ceaseless activity of man as the irremovability of his finiteness.

If finiteness is to be experienced as itself, it must be without meaning, because otherwise it would be experienced in terms of a frame of reference greater than itself from which it would receive its meaning. Beckett's novels are an attempt to show up all references as pragmatic fictions, so that ultimately we may see finiteness as the basic condition of our productivity. But the novels themselves are fiction. And herein lies both the fascination and the oppressiveness of Beckett's work, for this fiction does not help us to forget our finiteness by virtue of orderly myths and explanations; it makes us *feel* what we are inescapably caught up in. We can no longer retreat to a safe distance through such explanations, because the experience communicated here continually brings us back to their pragmatic conditionality, which in turn invalidates them. Explanations are not possible; the most we can do is experience the unknowable, and herein lies the greatness of Beckett's achievement. He has fulfilled to the letter a saying attributed to him "that art, an arrangement of the inexplicable, never explains."[27]

EIGHT

THE ART OF FAILURE: THE STIFLED LAUGH IN BECKETT'S THEATER

ur insight in the essence and scope of the aesthetic dimension can only gain from being oriented by human behavior—a territory that has been hitherto much discussed and yet has remained virtually undiscovered. Until today, the study of human behavior has always stood in the shadow of classical philosophy and has received its guidelines from the normative disciplines."[1] To Plessner's words one may add that the study of literature has stood equally long in this very same shadow, and through its preoccupation with the meaning and essence of the literary work has been unable to focus upon such vital questions as its function and its experiential nature. These questions, however, offer a much more fertile approach to the "scope of the aesthetic dimension"; for literature in particular this approach entails studying the work's response to its given contexts, the mode of its impact upon these contexts, its unique way of being experienced, its demands on human faculties, the processes and processing brought about by its fictions, and the resultant differentiations in attitudes and shifts in opinion. If the literary text is regarded as an incursion upon historical situations and upon the social norms and anthropological framework of its recipients, then there must be a relationship of mutual influence between its structures and the acts of human behavior molded by those structures. This relationship is hermeneutic in the sense that the literary work opens up human conduct for exploration, while the molding of human conduct in turn is the presupposition made in order to uncover the function and structure of the literary work.

Beckett's theater is a striking paradigm of this interlinkage, which allows us not only to estimate the range of the aesthetic dimension, but also to judge how art is to be experienced in the modern world. In order to elucidate this tangled issue, we may begin with the following observation: it has been frequently noted, during performances of such plays as *Waiting for Godot, Endgame,* and *Happy Days,* that there are sudden bursts of laughter from the audience which end as abruptly as they began.[2] Evidently the laughter cannot be enjoyed to the full, but is cut off, so to speak, in mid-guffaw. Even if one cannot say with certainty that the individual spectator is shocked at his own laughter, what is clear is that the laughter has lost its contagious nature. It cannot set off a chain reaction in Beckett's theater; it is the stifled laugh of the individual, and not the liberating communal laugh[3] by means of which members of an audience confirm one another's reactions. The feeling behind it is one of impropriety rather than confirmation.[4] This has been particularly noticeable in Beckett's own productions of his plays, though there was a considerable decline in the frequency of outbursts from *Waiting for Godot* to *Happy Days*.[5] However, even during the performances of *Waiting for Godot* there was no communal laughter, and when *Happy Days* was performed during the Beckett colloquium at the Berlin Academy the occasional laugh from an audience of Beckett specialists virtually died on the lips of the individual laugher.

The rare comments Beckett himself has made when directing his own plays show clearly that he aims to make his audience laugh. During the London production of *Endgame* in 1964, he said to the actor playing Hamm: "Let's get as many laughs as we can out of this horrible mess."[6] For the Berlin production of the same play, he based all directions on the line: "Nothing is funnier than unhappiness."[7] It is evident that, although the plays are not comedies as such, they must contain a substantial comic element, which Beckett himself has stressed in his productions and which is evidenced by the audience's laughter, even if this is accompanied by an unprecedented degree of discomfort that finally stifles the laugh. This constitutes a comparatively well documented example of the mutual influence of literary work and human behavior, and from it we may already deduce the thesis that is to form the basis of the essay that follows. The mutual influence is at its most effective when the work releases modes of conduct which are not required or are suppressed by our everyday needs, but which—when they *are* released—clearly bring out the aesthetic function on the work: namely, to make present those elements of life which were lost or buried and to merge them with that which is already present, thus changing the actual makeup of our present.

BEFORE WE DELVE into Beckett's comedy, it will be helpful to make a few observations on the nature of comedy and laughter in general. No one will dispute that the two are interdependent, or that laughter is the natural outcome of comedy. But *how* does the latter give rise to the former (and this question is important, as laughter is the answer of spectators or readers to a given comic situation)? Historically, comedy has usually been defined in terms of oppositions.

The contrast between imagination and reality, the clash or violation of norms, the nullifying of current values, and the sudden and unexpected upgrading of the null or the leveling-out of the multivalent, or even more far-reaching formulas such as refocusing on aspects excluded by the prevailing norm, thereby creating a polysemantic effect—these are all examples of the many definitions of comedy deduced from the basic element of contradiction. Without doubt, contradiction is central to comedy, but such definitions do not seem to cover the phenomenon in its entirety, and this is so mainly for two reasons: (1) contradictions entail an opposition of one kind or another, and the structure of opposition is a highly stable one. But an essential ingredient of comedy is precisely the instability of its relationships; and (2) contrasts, violations, deviations, clashes, and even refocusing on excluded aspects imply a reference that permeates such definitions and so creates an impression that every given position is to be related to it. The question then, of course, is why people laugh at such contrasts and contradictions instead of concerning themselves with the newly discovered reference.

An explanation of comedy in terms of contrast gives absolute priority to semantics. But perhaps comedy simply cannot be pinned down by any semantic definition. Today comedy has so many meanings that it would seem clear that all of them merely reflect historically conditioned manifestations of a structure whose main function is pragmatic. The semantics of comedy would therefore denote nothing but the pragmatic, historical realizations of this structure, not least because the semantic approach concerns itself first and foremost with the juxtaposed positions out of which a comic relationship arises. These positions are inevitably historical in character, and should their actual opposition really be the mainspring of comedy, the relationship itself will also be historical, so that one is then bound to ask why we can still laugh when these historical positions and interrelationships have long since become a thing of the past. It would therefore seem advisable to think of comedy less in terms of its positions than in terms of an *event* that these interrelated positions bring about. The question "What is comedy?" is therefore replaced by the question "What is the function of comedy?"—for the latter question would seem to offer far richer grounds for observation and generalization.

If we proceed from the fact that the positions negate or at least undermine one another, it is clear that their relation will be mutually destructive: each upsets the other. Herein lies the instability of comic situations, for the collapse of one position does not necessarily lead to the victory of another, but, on the contrary, will frequently draw it into a chain reaction of continual upsets. At first sight it may seem as if the negated position is overturned into its contrary—which is why we speak of the unmasking effect of comedy—but at the same time the negating position often loses its contrastive validity and itself begins to topple. In such cases of mutual negation, we no longer have one defeated position and one position triumphant; instead, we have a toppled position, which, by being changed, actually allows us to see hitherto hidden faces of the "conquering" position, which in turn begins to topple.

IT IS SCARCELY surprising that the first reaction to such a development is bewilderment. Bewilderment, however, is not a component of comedy but an effect set off in the spectator. This momentary perplexity indicates the breakdown of an apparently contrastive situation together with the perspectives inherent in it, for the mutual upsetting of the positions cancels out the secure base provided by their opposition. In this way the spectator is drawn into the comic proceedings, and the peculiar effect of mutually toppling positions throws light on the extraordinary process of interaction between positions as well as on the communication between the comic situation and its spectator.

If we understand comedy as a process of mutually toppling positions, it will be clear that such a description will far transcend historical contents as well as the general definition in terms of contrast. It can incorporate any number of different contents, for its concern is with the operations upon which these contents depend. Whenever positions upset each other, their relationship tends to become more complicated, as their mutual undermining destroys the definitive motive underlying the negating act. The collapse of a mutually contrasted relationship is bound to have repercussions on our means of comprehending what is going on. The spectator comes under a surprise attack and cannot help being involved because the mutual upsetting of positions deprives him not only of a clear pattern but also—above all—of distance, a necessary prerequisite for understanding. His loss of all points of reference gives him a momentary feeling of overstrain, which leads to bewilderment and finally to laughter.

The fact that laughter is the natural reaction to comedy brings out one central quality of the toppling effect. The mutual negation of collapsing positions is such that these can no longer be grasped by the cognitive or emotive faculties of the spectator; consequently, he can neither detach himself from them nor gain control over them. For laughter, in Plessner's words, is a crisis response by the body when the cognitive or emotive faculties prove incapable of mastering a situation.[8] Here the toppling structure of comedy actually extends into the attitude of the spectator, for it not only presents him with the collapse of positions but also upsets and renders ineffective his own cognitive or emotive capabilities for dealing with a situation. The fact that these faculties have been incapacitated is revealed by the laugh insofar as this physical reaction is no longer shaped or molded by our cognitive or emotive faculties.[9] The laugh also bears relatively little sign of its concrete cause, for it indicates not mastery of a situation but a moment of crisis caused by the failure of our faculties. It is a sign, in fact, of our momentary disorientation that has to be overcome by spurring the body into action. Of course, the degree of this disorientation will vary from case to case, and this, in turn, may also be a reason for the various forms of comedy, depending on the function they are to fulfill. When comedy is subdivided into categories, such as wit, satire, irony, humor, the toppling process is geared to particular intentions, that is, its "collapsing positions" are subject to special, expectable regulations. The degree of strain exercised by comedy upon the spectator is thus reduced, for we know from psychoanalysis that forms generally have a channeling effect; they are a defensive structure that brings order into psychic turbulences. Hence the various categories or forms of comedy result in alleviating the overstrain of our cognitive and emotive faculties, thereby reducing the explosiveness of the laughter that is the spectator's physical reaction.

This is borne out by the types of laughter with which we are all familiar, ranging from the raucous down to the inward laugh and the smile. Indeed, with certain forms of humor, where the cognitive or emotive faculties are in complete command, there need be no laugh at all. Nietzsche said that laughter was a banishment of anxiety.[10] If we follow this idea through, we will see that the less mastery we have over situations (through the toppling process of comedy), the greater will be our anxiety, and so the more vehement will be our physical reactions, since we call upon our bodies as a last resort. The degree of the "emergency" is expressed by the intensity of the laugh, and its threatening quality is evidenced by the lack of pattern in our laughter. The smaller the emergency — thanks to the regulating function of comic forms — the more clearly patterned our response will be. There are certain kinds of smiles that may even convey the impression that our cognitive or emotive faculties are declaring themselves incapacitated just for fun and are in fact putting their own imprint on this playful enactment of their own failure.

If laughter, as the banishment of fear, is an answer by the body to a situation of crisis, the question naturally arises as to the effect of such a reaction. By laughing we free ourselves from entanglement in a situation that otherwise we could not cope with, and this fact is tantamount to saying that our very attitude turns an uncomfortable situation into one that is not to be taken seriously, thereby freeing us from an overstrain to which we have been subjected.[11] The urge to laugh becomes irresistible when the contrastive relationships of comedy keep collapsing. And when we speak of people shaking with laughter, or laughing themselves silly, or laughing their heads off, it is because these convulsive moments denote their reaction to a helplessness that the comedy has initially aroused in them.[12] This helplessness harbors a serious threat from which we liberate ourselves by laughing and so regaining the detachment necessary for a processing of the situation; indeed, this processing often takes place in the laughter itself.

However, it is possible to conceive of comic situations in which laughter as a precondition for processing is itself subjected to the toppling process. So far we have only talked of comedy that incapacitates the cognitive or emotive faculties, thus inducing laughter as a defensive last resort. This laughter releases us from entanglements by enabling us to declare that the toppling of positions in comic situations is something we are not going to take seriously. What happens if this attitude is also nudged and toppled? Supposing that, at the very moment when we have recognized nonseriousness as a means of self-liberation, it suddenly turns into seriousness again? In such cases, we can no longer escape from the tension, and, instead, our laughter dies on our lips. This is precisely what happens in the theater of Samuel Beckett.

THE QUESTION NOW arises as to what specific features of comedy bring about this self-frustrating laughter in the spectator. The two Beckett plays that form the basis of this analysis show a very definite stratification of comic elements, and we shall be studying these in sequence. *Waiting for Godot* seems to be the most approachable in terms of traditional comedy: the laughter is relatively frequent, and Beckett himself called the English version a tragicomedy. One can clearly trace the disintegration of comic representation in this play, as well as the processes initiated thereby. The play opens with a theme that renders virtually every subsequent action almost parenthetic:

> Estragon: Nothing to be done.
>
> Vladimir: I'm beginning to come round to that opinion. All my life I've tried to put it from me, saying, Vladimir, be reasonable, you haven't yet tried everything. And I resumed the struggle.[13]

Against the background of the "genre," this opening should mark the *end* of the play rather than the beginning, for action is the prime component of drama. "If the action of classical drama had a starting-point that needed no justification of itself and so had no past as such (its preliminary history also functioned as part of the action), then the beginning of *Godot* is identical to the structure of the end of a classical drama: it is the conclusion of an action—i.e., the result."[14] This opening typifies a stratagem that is integral to modern literature in general and to Beckett in particular: it is what Lotman calls "Minus-prijom"[15]—a minus function, indicating an omitted, though perhaps an expected, technique. This, briefly, signifies the nonfulfillment of what is expected. Literary texts nearly always presuppose particular expectations and reactions that are molded and stabilized in equal measure by social codes and literary conventions. Consequently, such texts reveal not only the prevailing conventions of their time but also the way in which these conventions are to be acted upon, with a resultant exposure of things that have been lost, never noticed, concealed, or even made a taboo. If an action begins with a statement that nothing can be done, this "minus function" clearly implies that of all the possibilities of doing something, only the possibility that nothing can be done remains unexplored. This as yet unexplored possibility of action is now put to the test, and this is the plot of *Godot*. Testing a possibility means having to do something. But how does one "do" the fact that nothing can be done? One can only rescind everything that one does. To accomplish this, one cannot merely do a single particular thing; one must go on "doing" things indefinitely, and so for the fulfillment of this last remaining condition of the classical drama there is in fact no end to the actions arising. In order to establish, or indeed to experience, the fact that nothing can be done, one must act not just continually but endlessly.

This process, already foreshadowed at the very beginning of the play, is built into the structure of a comic plot and could probably only be brought about through the structure of comedy. Testing the possibility of being unable to do anything could only take place through a series of failed actions, for any successful action would automatically disprove the result announced at the beginning. The characters *must* act, because otherwise their initial insight would only be a mere assumption; it cannot take on any reality until it is actually experienced. This is why Vladimir replies that he is "beginning to come round" to the view that nothing can be done; he is not yet certain, and certainty can only be gained by an endless succession of failed actions. Now failed action is a paradigmatic basis of comedy. "The semantic field of comedy generally has a binary structure, along the contrastive lines of Normality vs. Abnormality, Reason vs. Folly; a hero enters and crosses the border between Reason and Folly."[16] The failed action is potentially related to conflict, because the hero crosses a border and so violates a system of norms that can only be restored by the failure of action. In *Godot*, too, the failed action involves crossing a border, but not one of normative systems; here the border lies within that which, with regard to the action itself, appears impossible: namely, the demonstration by action that action is impossible. The comic paradigm of the failed action is thus turned over onto itself, thereby designating an almost insoluble moment of crisis in the comic paradigm itself, to which we shall return when focusing on its processing by the spectator.

Failed action in *Godot* can only take place as a continuous repetition that must be episodic in character, because otherwise the individual actions would begin to be marshaled into a teleological order. Repetition, then, is another comic paradigm that dominates the action of *Godot*. Comic repetition bears with it two implications (1) the comic hero learns nothing from his failures, because he is condemned by his own disposition to continual disaster—made permanent by the episodic repetition; and (2) the repetition of failure renders the action futile, because no meaningful event *could* be repeatable in this way. In the Aristotelian sense, the comic failure is therefore ridiculous but cannot hurt us as it causes no "serious damage either to the sufferer or to the world around him."[17] But the repetition of failed actions in *Godot* does not demonstrate the futility of failed actions so much as it uses actions to demonstrate that nothing can be done. Futility is therefore not a criterion for judging the nature of an action, but it is an instrument used in the testing of the nothing-to-be-done thesis. And so once again a comic paradigm is, so to speak, turned on its head.

We must consider one further aspect of the comic structure

through which the two upturned comic paradigms receive their dynamic force. They become comic only when they are related to an overall level of action that provides them with a syntagmatic articulation. This overall level, sometimes known to theorists as the "overall plot line,"[18] is incorporated in the title of the play: the characters are waiting for Godot. The function of this level is to initiate the comic action, to carry it along and to bring it to a conclusion. The two levels of overall plot line and comic paradigms, however, are merely the components of comedy, and it is their interaction that enables the comic effect to come into being and to be communicated. Consequently, comedy is not situated on either of the two levels but is generated by the relation between them. This relation normally stabilizes itself as one of theme and background, with the overall plot line constituting the background, and the comic paradigms the theme. The structure of theme and background is basic to the processes of perception and comprehension. But in *Godot* the relation remains highly unstable. Whenever the overall level functions as background, the characters appear to be inextricably entangled in a series of ridiculous blunders, whose ceaseless repetition renders all too obvious the futility of their actions. The failures are ridiculous because the characters are evidently incapable of learning from them; they are comic because the characters nevertheless prove to be indestructible.[19] In the conventional comic plot the pattern is one of restitution, with the turbulent stream of failed actions finally discharging itself into the calm waters of a stabilized resolution, usually brought about by the irrevocable failure of the actions.

The plot must "fashion this final calamity in such a way that the character who fails may nevertheless still be reintegrated."[20] But this is not the case in *Godot*. The second act repeats the patterns of the first act so faithfully that even the minimal differences only serve to highlight the repetition, which results in the impression that repetition of failed action becomes an end in itself. This, however, has repercussions on the overall plot line, which then makes the waiting for Godot appear to be a futile endeavor, merely funneling substance into the failed actions of the characters. Consequently, not only do the component parts of the comic plot continually break down, but the very structure of comprehension provided by the theme-and-background relationship is made to collapse continually; at one moment it induces a leveling-out of comic paradigm and overall plot line, and the next is itself drawn into the process of obliterating distinctions. This happens whenever the action of waiting for the unknown Godot loses its character of overall plot line and is reduced to the level of the comic paradigm of failed actions. Then, instead of the comic paradigms receiving a syntagmatic articulation, there arises an extraordinary equivalence of futility between the two levels of action, with even such opposition as yes and no rendered meaningless. This equivalence is remarkable because it is due not to the merging of opposites into unity but to the collapse of all the constituent parts into a nothingness that renders them all equally futile. Now, with this process, Beckett's play in fact reduces to a "minus function" the theme-and-background structure that underlies our relation to the world; thus a necessary prerequisite for our acts of comprehension is turned into a nonfulfilled expectation. In this way his play nullifies expectations that would hitherto have been taken for granted: in comedy we naturally expect the unexpected, but the surprises we anticipate are only related to that which we are given to observe and comprehend, and which is therefore related to subject matter; we do not expect surprises in relation to our own faculties of observation and comprehension (i.e., the very act of grasping subject matter).

Beckett's comedy, however, breaks up the whole structure of comprehension, not, as one might think, by invalidating the comedy but by radicalizing it in such a way that it violates our accustomed sense of what is comic. This process might perhaps best be described in terms of *carnival* and *nonsense*, which are closely akin to *vaudeville*—a word often applied to the humor of *Godot*.[21] It is a basic feature of the carnival that "elevation and debasement are inseparable—they merge into one another." Consequently there is always a "logic of misalliances," above all in the "build-up of plot and subject-matter."[22] Bakhtin writes that "a typical feature of carnival thinking is pairs of figures chosen according to the principle of contrast (tall and short, fat and thin) or that of identity (doppelgänger, twins). Another common trait is the inverted use of objects: clothes worn upside down, trousers or saucepans as head-coverings, kitchen utensils as weapons. This expresses the carnival principle of eccentricity. One departs from normal practice; life goes off the rails."[23]

This description, though not aimed at *Godot*, nevertheless fits in very well with what happens on Beckett's stage, and so long as the characters' actions signify this leaving of the rails they will elicit the laughter that encompasses "both poles of the change" and focuses on "the process of constant interchange of incompatibles," thus "building up a moment of crisis." "The act of carnival laughter unites death and rebirth, negation (scorn) and affirmation (triumph). The ambivalent laughter of the carnival is an ideological and universal laughter."[24] But it can only become so against the background of that from which it frees itself, and being thus freed, it naturally appears superior to that which had originally held it in check. This laughter is "ideological" to the extent that it brings out the characteristic tendencies of the object laughed at, and this object is generally in the form of institutions that are tendency-governed. The laughter is "universal" because the institutions it always aims to puncture more often than not lay claim themselves to universal validity.

"Tendency" is also the key word that Freud applies to the "pleasure-gain" that results from the joke and is discharged through laughter. Success very often depends far less on the technique of the joke than on the tendency revealed by it.[25] If the "pleasure-gain" derives from the neutralization of inhibitions arising from convention-bound cultural repressions—an idea that Freud extends, with certain variations, to all forms of comedy[26]—the discharging of the comic effect (i.e., the laughter) will always be at its most potent when the tendency of neutralization is at its most unequivocal.[27]

In Beckett's *Godot*, however prevalent may be the pleasure gained from its nonsense—with its continual dislocation of all logical and other expected connections—the neutralization clearly applies not to certain determinable inhibitions caused by civilization or the reality principle but to the primary tendency of comedy to bypass inhibitions; thus the very tendency itself is turned into a "minus function." But does this mean that the play presents us only with a technically comic situation that has lost its specific tendency of neutralizing inhibitions? Or does it perhaps mean that the anthropological conditions of comedy postulated by Freud, and the universal, historical conditions of comedy developed by Bakhtin, function here only as preconditions, comprising as they do the conventional expectations we bring to comedy—expectations that are then revealed as an institutionalized pattern of our social behavior, the exposure of which is the unformulated tendency of the Beckett comedy? If this latter were the case, then no matter how accurate the anthropological or historical explanations of comedy may have been when first developed, they would now be conditions—precisely *because* they are explanations—for the repression of that which comedy, as an aesthetic phenomenon, is able to achieve. Now if, conventionally, we expect to enjoy nonsense through the return of what has been displaced by civilization and the reality principle (for nonsense is excluded from the convention-bound relations of social communication), then comedy, in the Beckettian sense, could only fulfill itself through the frustration of this anticipated enjoyment, that is, it could only discharge itself under conditions of its own disintegration.[28] Freud was wise to confine his observations to the comedy of real life, as opposed to the comedy that represents reactions to real life.

A BASIC FEATURE of the technique we have so far noted in *Godot* is the unmistakable miscarriage of comedy. Perhaps we might remind ourselves once more of the individual structures so that we may then have a clearer view of the processes they initiate in the spectator. The failed action, as one comic paradigm, does not demonstrate the failure expected when borders are crossed in the semantic field of comedy; instead, it shows through action what is actually meant by "nothing to be done." Similarly, the repetition does not signify the futility of failed actions, but the fact that nothing can be learned from failed actions. Consequently, the link between comic paradigms and overall plot line is dislocated so that the latter completely loses its syntagmatic function and the only relation left between the two different levels is one of mutual toppling. This instability results in a breakdown of the basic structure of comprehension, as syntagmatic and paradigmatic levels are flattened to equality and the interchangeability of their contents serves to emphasize the apparent futility of those contents. This leveling-out, however, produces a carnival effect, manifested in enjoyment of the nonsense, even though the tendency has disappeared upon which the inversions of the carnival or the relieving devices of comic pleasure are based.

It goes without saying that such dislocated comedy is bound to mobilize the interpretative faculties; indeed, if one might anticipate the effects produced by these structures, one might say that, in the manner in which the failure is presented, the artistry lies in the manipulation of these mobilized faculties. The comic paradigms, the mutually upsetting levels of action, the carnival effect, the enjoyment of nonsense, and finally the basic theme-and-background structure of perception and comprehension all constitute "minus functions," and this means that, because of what they are, they always evoke that which they have excluded. Such a process continually compels the spectator to provide his own background, but at the same time it tells him nothing about why his expectations have been thwarted, or what sort of relationship exists between these thwarted expectations and what has actually been presented. He is therefore left with an array of empty spaces into which his mobilized interpretative faculties are relentlessly drawn as they attempt to fill the spaces with substance. For the purposes of laying bare the mechanics of this process, we will now try to give a schematized description of the interpretative activities triggered by the play; we may thereby understand the text-guided processes occurring in the spectator's mind, and these in turn will serve as an indication of the kind of aesthetic experience that is to be imparted.

Vladimir and Estragon, the two main characters, both seem to be tramps; we learn right at the beginning that Estragon spent the night in a ditch. But they also seem like clowns, as many critics have pointed out, although in fact neither "tramp" nor "clown" is ever mentioned in the text.[29] This clowning effect comes about through their constant failures and through their inability to learn from their failures, as evidenced by their endless repetitions. In Joachim Ritter's words:

> The clown is simply the outcast, the dropout, yet he proclaims this nonconformity not by the antithesis of meaning, but by an extreme distortion of it. His clothes are very different from normal clothes, but the long gloves, the countless jackets, the giant trousers represent a distortion, a perversion of ordinary dress. He carries around with him a meaningful piece of equipment, a garden-gate, but it is totally detached from its usual context, and so he uses it to keep entering the realm of nonsense, which becomes nonsense when set against sense, and thereby raises the liberating laughter that breaks down the barriers of seriousness and moderation.[30]

The laughter with which we greet the clown's actions is liberating because we perceive the naiveté in which he is trapped. Everything he does goes wrong, but he persists, as if the repetition denoted constant success. Such distortions are generally so absolute that the naiveté of failure is immediately apparent and so is greeted by immediate and spontaneous laughter. No mental activity is really required to put the distortion right, and the momentary perplexity can be relieved at once. The clown's naiveté places the spectator in a position of superiority which, as Freud observed, arises out of a comparison between the mental and intellectual qualities perceived in the comic character and the qualities that determine one's own situation. The comparison of intellectual qualities is comic "if the other person has made a greater expenditure than I thought I should need. In the case of a mental function, on the contrary, it becomes comic if the other person has spared himself expenditure which I regard as indispensable (for nonsense and stupidity are inefficiencies of function). In the former case I laugh because he has taken too much trouble, in the latter because he has taken too little."[31] The clown's "inefficiencies of function" signalize his being trapped in his naiveté, and it is precisely this impression that makes Vladimir and Estragon seem like clowns. People appear naive if they do not know the restraints imposed by civilization—restraints of which we ourselves are aware and which, in the given situation, we would also expect them to be aware of. We laugh at such people when, in their ignorance, they cross the borders of these restraints. In *Godot* these borders are set by the fact that the characters are waiting for Godot—a fact that seems to determine their whole lives, even though with their constant failures they behave as if the situation did not exist. Now if these characters seem to us like clowns, then we are already caught up in a process of interpretation, and in our efforts to find plausible reasons for the never-ending repetition of failed actions we ourselves become the prisoners of the play.

Viewing the characters as clowns, or making them into clowns, is an interpretation arising out of a process of comparison which is comforting insofar as it enables one to reduce the unfamiliar to terms of the familiar, the abstract to the concrete, and so to master a strange and puzzling world. So long as Vladimir and Estragon represent comic paradigms through their repeated failures, we are misled into such a comparison. This is encouraged at first by the level of the overall comic plot line. The characters are waiting for Godot, but they frequently behave as if they did not have any such purpose, and so we are constantly tempted to project into their conduct a certain naiveté: we begin to laugh because they always seem to bypass the restraints set by their overall purpose. Our laughter is evidence of our position of superiority, but this position depends upon conditions that we have produced for ourselves. For this reason our laughter does not make us happy; it has no cathartic effect because, at the very moment when we believe we can take the protagonists for clowns, this idea begins to fall apart owing to the increased indifference they show toward their avowed aim of waiting for Godot. Consequently our reaction is, in the last analysis, not to the clowning of the play but to our own interpretation of it as clowning, which manifests itself in the flaring up and the dying down of our laughter.

This cutoff reaction is not due solely to the fact that we make the protagonists into clowns; it results in an even greater measure from a preconceived pattern of audience response that is built into the structure of the play. Whenever the diverse and apparently nonsensical actions seem to converge unequivocally into clowning, the characters suddenly relate once more, with detailed and often weighty allusions, to the overall plot line of waiting for Godot. Biblical references to the crucified thieves,[32] an intricate casuistic debate, reminiscent of St. Augustine, as to which of the thieves was saved,[33] Estragon's comparison of himself with Jesus[34]—all permeate the play with a density of allusions that have, logically enough, led many to conclude that the two men might in fact be waiting for God. But there is nothing in the text to confirm this, and Beckett himself, when asked who Godot was, merely replied that he would have said so if he had known it himself.[35] But whatever the heart of the matter may be, it is clear that our mobilized interpretative endeavors are guided in a certain direction. If these characters are waiting for God or some such all-powerful figure, if their identities are somehow connected with the thieves on the cross, then clearly we can no longer regard them as clowns. This means that we have erected a concept of the characters—admittedly with the guidance of the text—and are then forced to dismantle this concept as soon as we are made to relate the comic paradigms to the overall action.

Now in conventional comedy the overall plot line provides the background for the humor of the comic paradigms. In *Godot*, however, the overall plot line seems to be the background against which the comic paradigms *lose* their humor. Naiveté as a source of comedy is not denied, but only when we ourselves deny its humor does it become possible for us to relate the two levels of action to one another. And even if we were to persist in viewing the characters as naive, this naiveté would be very dangerous in the light of their purpose, so that the situation would still take on a seriousness that would stifle our laughter. But whose is this seriousness? At times, it is true, the characters themselves cry out in despair, but we can never be sure of its extent or even its reality; at times we may project seriousness onto them without their knowing it; at times this projection of seriousness constitutes a perfectly natural and instinctive reaction akin to that of children at a pantomime, when they cry out to warn the unsuspecting hero that the villain is just behind him.

There is no need to go on illustrating these patterns of reaction, for one can already pinpoint the structure underlying and guiding the processing of such a text, as well as the function the structure is to perform. The play leads us into making a whole series of projections in order to provide some kind of overall background that will give coherence to the events we are witnessing. But, remarkably, our projections do not function as a substitute for canceled expectations at all; on the contrary, we find ourselves compelled to abandon them. We conceive of the protagonists as clowns, but this view is upset by the allusions that deepen and intensify the dialogue. However, the apparent depth provided by the overall plot line itself begins to topple when the characters fall back into the characteristic futility of their normal dialogue. The most striking features of this dialogue are its simplicity of syntax and vocabulary, the ease with which it can be understood, and above all the fact that it only describes what they do.[36] What is said means nothing but what in any case we can see—in other words, the language is purely denotative, so that we even begin to project intentions onto the absence of connotations. We feel ourselves being pushed into processes of interpretation because the actions denoted by the language seem to have no representative value, whereas the overall plot line leads us to believe that there must be a representative value hidden somewhere. But if we think we have found such a value, it is quickly invalidated by the characters themselves. Furthermore, we are tempted to project references onto the purely denotative language, but these are wiped out whenever the dialogue itself becomes allusive. If we sense a pattern through the reference to the crucified thieves, it is wiped out by the fact than no one can say which of the thieves was saved, since even the apostles disagree.[37] What cannot be decided cannot be significant, and so the overall action ceases to impart any syntagmatic articulation to the comic paradigms; once the two levels come into contact, the overall plot line is made trivial. The relation between the two levels is obviously such that whatever missing links the spectator may provide will at once begin to fall apart when they take on any degree of unequivocalness. Thus the view of the protagonists as clowns begins to topple when set against the Godot level, and the latter as a concept of possible salvation begins to topple when viewed against the protagonists' indifference.

This mutual destruction of interpretative concepts stimulated by the text does, however, constitute a "connection" between the two levels of action, even if this connection is far from that which one would expect from a comic plot. Thus, the process of overturning our concepts—whatever their substance may be—implies that we are incessantly forced to build up a concept at one moment and then to dismantle it the next. It follows that the aesthetic object of the drama, which the spectator is always bound to assemble for himself in realizing the intentions laid down for him, here comprises this very alternation of building and dismantling imaginary concepts. If one thinks back to the carnival effect, which permeates the whole atmosphere and construction of the play, the aesthetic object consists in the switching between extremes that, for the sake of brevity, one might classify as clowning and salvation — two concepts that so undermine one another that they both disintegrate. Now with the carnival effect, as with one's enjoyment of nonsense, these confusing switches normally stabilize themselves by way of one tendency or another, but in Beckett's play there is no tendency to latch onto because the two levels of theme and background, or comic paradigm and overall plot line, have been leveled out.

But it is this very absence of any tendency that acts as a goad to the spectator's interpretative faculties, for an aesthetic object that constitutes itself through dismantling constructed concepts can only consolidate itself by means of a tendency. Any tendency in *Godot*, however, can only be in the form of a projection, as is only too clear from the well-documented range of audience responses and interpretations since the play was first performed. Whatever the nature and substance of this projected tendency may be, it functions structurally as the syntagmatic articulation that balances out the "minus function" of the overall plot line (waiting for Godot), whose articulating force has become inoperative. It reestablishes the theme-and-background structure basic to comprehension, although it may remain completely open as to whether the comic paradigms are the background and waiting for Godot the theme, or vice versa. Our interpretation will vary according to which is which. When the prisoners of San Quentin recognized themselves in Vladimir and Estragon, the protagonists constituted the theme and their helpless waiting the background.[38] When the play is experienced as an existentialist apocalypse,[39] the helpless waiting is the theme, and the apathetic characters are the background. In both interpretations one can see the compulsion to impose on the play a tendency that will allow a syntagmatic organization of its paradigms.

Whatever the tendency projected onto the play, it is not an arbitrary act on the part of the spectator. It is the response to three central expectations relating to the carnival effect and enjoyment of nonsense, the theme-and-background structure of comprehension with its resultant organization of the levels of action, and the significance and precision necessary for each and every interpretation.

The first two points concern canceled expectations pertaining to genre and cognition within the structure of the drama; the last denotes a basic requirement of comprehension insofar as meaning is only meaningful in the degree to which its significance is precise. As we have seen, the text of *Godot* undermines this basic requirement of meaning, and it is this process that gives rise to the peculiarity of the aesthetic experience offered by the play. For the continual building and dismantling of concepts that brings about the aesthetic object not only compels the projection of tendencies but also challenges the unequivocalness essential to those tendencies. Thus the sense and the non-sense and the countersense of the play translate themselves into an experience for the spectator.

What *is* this countersense and what are the reactions that such an experience can bring about? Countersense—as Plessner has emphasized[40]—is the basis of the comic situation. The countersense of *Godot* consists in the fact that on the one side we have the characters' incessant repetition of failed actions, and on the other the hopeless wait for an unforeseeable change through an unknown being. The spectator will react to these divergent themes by seeking a point of intersection. He can find one only to the extent that the protagonists' behavior seems reduced to the level of clowning without actually *being* so, and the wait for salvation sinks into apathy without ever actually being lost from view. Thus the mutual distortion of the two "senses" brings out a common element that we become aware of when we recognize that the source of these distortions is our own interpretations. In trying to impose significance and unequivocalness on the countersense, we experience our own interpretations as that which has been excluded by the countersense. Now this is also a comic effect, albeit an insidious one. If comedy focuses on that which is excluded by prevailing norms, thereby subverting their claim to comprehensiveness,[41] the resultant countersense will, in Beckett's case, keep drawing our interpretations into the play in order either to exclude them again on account of their incompleteness or to unmask their distortive nature. In both cases the projected norms of the spectator become part of the play and there arises the effect that Beckett himself once described as his plays' "clawing" into the spectator.[42] For the spectator is no longer confronted with a comic conflict; instead, the comedy *happens* to him, because he experiences his own interpretations as that which is to be excluded. If the basic effect of comedy is to illuminate the whole of life[43] by showing the excluded striking back at the excluder (i.e., the norm), in Beckett this effect is inverted, as the spectator experiences the shortcomings of his interpretative norms just when he thinks they will enable him to grasp the whole.

This experience is conditioned by various factors connected with our own dispositions and, above all, with the expectations that we bring to art and that are deliberately exploited by Beckett's plays. The countersense in these plays does not come about by means of contrastive positions, such as one finds in traditional comedies. Instead, it is present to us as an experience because, to begin with, we must formulate the aesthetic object by continually building and dismantling concepts, and ultimately—through this very same inescapable process—we are forced to realize (in both senses of the term) the deficiencies of our interpretations. However, the countersense of comedy has always been accompanied by a pattern that, so to speak, holds in store an overall resolution. It is the constant availability of such a pattern that allows us to remain detached from the events depicted and, furthermore, to experience these events as fiction rather than fact. So long as we live through the play as a presentation and not a reality, the events—particularly when the situation threatens danger—will always allow for a degree of distance, thereby providing the relief necessary to enable us to disentangle ourselves. But if the countersense is our very own experience, from which we cannot detach ourselves (because the attempt to free ourselves and to understand the experience reveals that even such attempts are only partial and restricted), then the situation seems to us more real than fictional. Here we have a comic structure that denies us the relief normally inherent in such structures. Freud once wrote: "It is a necessary condition for generating the comic that we should be obliged, *simultaneously or in rapid succession*, to apply to one and the same act of ideation two different ideational methods, between which the 'comparison' is then made and the comic difference emerges."[44] But if this difference does not emerge, because the countersense is so total that any comparative operations will only succeed in uncovering their own inadequacies, then the comedy of the structurally comic situation will remain open-ended if not actually threatened with destruction. In conventional comedy, the differences resulting from the process of comparison point in the direction of a whole, albeit a whole that is signalized by way of bypassing the restraints that are caused by repression and by substitutions for taboos violated. But in Beckett's play the differences are wiped out by the continual overturning of the countersenses so that the whole can never be produced even though it is present in the toppling effect. This whole, evidenced

PARADIGMS

only by the toppling effect of the countersenses, might be described as the "human condition," which can only be perceived as such by warding off every individual interpretation in order that it should not become a mere token for something other than itself. It cannot be referentially subsumed, and it cannot be represented either; it can only be experienced as a reality.

A PRESENTATION OF the human condition through comedy seems in fact to be a logical continuation of the "genre"; the play evokes specific expectations that it then proceeds to juggle. The laughter that always greets the play might well be equated with the response expected in any comedy. But this laughter is of a very special kind. Ritter writes in his classic analysis of laughter:

> Laughter as a sound has its moment: namely, the precise moment at which comprehension has taken place, which is when the material has merged with the ideas already present in the listener or observer. However, this *ex*cludes the possibility that laughter should be attributed to particular layers of the inner being, particular moods, particular feelings during a particular "pleasure"; but at the same time it *in*cludes another implication: that laughter is only possible when an excluded and opposing idea can be grasped as an inalienable part of human existence; i.e., when it can be integrated as a meaningful component into this very existence.[45]

Now the laughter of Beckett's audiences does not seem to fit in with this definition at all. It has been noted time and again that the laughter that greets his plays is not contagious or communal. The latter category of mirth is confirmatory in its effect, for it communicates to others that "an opposing idea" has been "grasped as an inalienable part of human existence."[46] But laughter at Beckett's plays is always isolated, apparently robbed of its contagious qualities; indeed, in *Endgame* and *Happy Days* it is often accompanied by a sort of shock effect, as if the reaction were somehow inappropriate and must therefore be stifled.

The stifled burst of laughter is an individual reaction indicative of the breakdown of the liberating function of laughter. We normally laugh when our emotive or cognitive faculties have been overtaxed by a situation they can no longer cope with. "The disoriented body takes over the response from it (i.e., the mind), no longer as an instrument for action, speech, movement or gesture, but simply as a body. Having lost control of it, having renounced any relation to it, man still evinces a sovereign understanding of the incomprehensible, displaying his power in his impotency, his freedom and greatness in his restraint. He can even find an answer where an answer is no longer possible. He has, if not the last word, at least the last card in a game whose loss is his victory."[47] But in Beckett's theater, this victory out of defeat turns into defeat again. We have seen how in Beckett's play the different levels upset one another—an effect that becomes increasingly potent and virulent. The result of this mutual overturning is the collapse of the theme-and-background structure essential to comprehension. In attempting to stabilize this structure we are forced to dismantle the tendencies we have projected onto the play. This means that the comic action, the structure of comprehension, and the structure of participation all collapse the moment we try to stabilize them. This collapse involves the continual neutralization of contrastive differences, and as has been shown by de Saussure and his structural semantics, if not by others before him, contrastive opposition is the basic condition of meaning. The toppling effect consequently cancels out each meaning as soon as it seeks to establish itself. This is the reason for the isolation of the laughers in Beckett's audiences. The timing of the toppling effect will largely depend on the disposition of the individual spectator so that laughter as a reaction to and a relief from his entanglement is deprived of a collective confirmation at the very moment when it is most needed; the individual spectator then finds that he is laughing alone and is thus made conscious of his own loss of control. This can be highly embarrassing. It should be borne in mind that inherent in the sound of laughter, in Plessner's words, "is the power of self-affirmation: one hears oneself."[48] But supposing one also sees oneself, because others are silent?

This brings us to the special nature of the laugh that is elicited by the toppling effect. Freud made an interesting observation in his practice: "Many of my neurotic patients who are under psychoanalytic treatment are regularly in the habit of confirming the fact by a laugh when I have succeeded in giving a faithful picture of their hidden unconscious to their conscious perception; and they laugh even when the content of what is unveiled would by no means justify this. This is subject, of course, to their having arrived close enough to the unconscious material to grasp it after the doctor has detected it and presented it to them."[49] Now surprisingly enough, this observation coincides with a remark of Beckett's about laughter, which also sheds light on a strange feature of his plays: in *Godot*, *Endgame*, and *Happy Days* there are brief, violent bursts of laughter

from the characters that end as abruptly as they began. In Beckett's
Watt there is a short catalogue of laughs:

> Of all the laughs that strictly speaking are not laughs but modes of
> ululation, only three I think need detain us, I mean the bitter, the hollow
> and the mirthless. They correspond to successive, how shall I say suc-
> cessive . . . suc . . . successive excoriations of the understanding, and
> the passage from the one to the other is the passage from the lesser to
> the greater, from the lower to the higher, from the outer to the inner,
> from the gross to the fine, from the matter to the form. The laugh that
> now is mirthless once was hollow, the laugh that once was hollow once
> was bitter. And the laugh that once was bitter? . . . The bitter laugh
> laughs at that which is not good, it is the ethical laugh. The hollow
> laugh laughs at that which is not true, it is the intellectual laugh. Not
> good! Not true! Well well. But the mirthless laugh is the dianoetic laugh
> . . . It is the laugh of laughs, the *risus purus*, the laugh laughing at the
> laugh, the beholding, the saluting of the highest joke, in a word the
> laugh that laughs—silence please—at that which is unhappy.[50]

For Beckett, then, the real gradation of laughter begins where
the laughter of comedy normally ends: with derision of that which
is bad or malicious. But it is the mirthless "laugh of laughs," the
dianoetic mockery of unhappiness, that makes the latter transparent
and, interestingly enough, draws Freud and Beckett together. The
raising of what has been displaced to the threshold of its perception
allows one to face up to unhappiness, which in being faced is no
longer exclusively itself but appears in the perspective of its being
perceived.

Unhappiness raised to consciousness is the source of dianoetic
laughter. This observation would seem to explain the frequent,
apparently unmotivated, laughter of Beckett's characters. They
burst out laughing when they have interpreted their own situations.
Now, if hollow and mirthless laughs are a response to untruth and
unhappiness respectively, this means that the application of the
cognitive faculties can no longer cope with that untruth and unhappiness. For such an intervention would inevitably lead to interpretations through which the unhappiness would not be raised but
covered up, even displaced, and so in its ultimate effect intensified,
because interpretations are commitments with a presumption of
reality, whereas, when set against reality, their claims to authenticity
fall apart. Laughter as a physical response to such a precarious
situation is a last attempt to liberate oneself from a seemingly hopeless challenge; with our cognitive exertions stalled and our urge for

interpretation (as a means of warding off unhappiness) frustrated, laughter remains as the one reaction that can cut us off from unhappiness, thus banishing anxiety. It is true that Beckett's characters show, through their laughter, that they cannot avoid interpreting their situation, but at the same time they seem to know that clinging to such interpretations—even though these are doomed to eternal failure—embodies the source of untruth and unhappiness, the awareness of which announces itself through the physical reaction of laughter.

This laughter has no cathartic effect, but in its mirthlessness is still a response to the human condition, which is lit up by the laughter and is accepted as itself and not as an interpretation of itself. If unhappiness arises from our need to stabilize our situation, our ultimate liberation would be to escape from the norms we have chosen or adopted in our efforts at stabilization. And this is precisely what Beckett's characters are forever doing, which is why they seem so alien to us. This impression communicates itself through the extraordinary feeling that the characters, although they appear to behave like clowns, reveal a striking superiority that tends to efface the clowning element without removing it altogether. This is because they go the whole way in liberating themselves from the normally inescapable need to stabilize situations by means of interpretation, and their laughter marks the shattering of all self-imposed censorship. It has no healing power, for here the human condition presents itself not as something that can be contained within prevailing systems of norms, but as something that demands continual explanations only in order to appear as itself by dissociating itself from these explanations. Such laughter is physical, and so elemental that it has no definable content of its own; it lies beyond the scope of the defining intellect. In this respect it is an entirely appropriate expression of the human condition, which is equally beyond definition and reveals itself only through an irremediable insufficiency of interpretative frameworks that are molded not by reality but by man's need to explain reality.

The laughter and embarrassment with which Beckett's audiences react to a manifestation of the human condition indicate the fact not only that they are facing this condition but also that they cannot cope with it. Why not? The answer can only be hypothetical, for, as we have seen, the laughter defies ultimate definition. It produces a mixed reaction insofar as it registers the nonsensical conduct of the characters who constantly turn aside from their own opinions and intentions; at the same time, however, we are unable to fulfill our enjoyment of the nonsensical by laughter, as we realize that the abandonment of purpose has a liberating effect on the characters. We see the tendency of the nonsense, but we do not understand it. Clearly, the laughter of the characters themselves destroys their own interpretations of precarious situations, for they seem to know that their unhappiness will only increase if they continue to seek compensatory resolutions. We, however, are not able to free ourselves in the same way, for we cannot suddenly regard our interpretations and guiding norms as nonsense. Consequently, we are left dangling and our laughter dies. This position—being trapped halfway—is an almost insoluble paradox. Beckett's plays compel us to construct the aesthetic object by continually building up and dismantling concepts, and through this process we are inescapably drawn into the experience that whatever objects we construct can only be formulations of objects—in other words, reality is never reality as such, but can only be formulations of reality. And yet we generally act as if our formulations were identical to reality, that is, as if our realities were more than mere formulations. In fact they are simply pragmatic arrangements of reality through which we gain security. Beckett's plays force us to develop a sense of discernment so that we find ourselves playing off our need for security against our insight into the products of this need. Thus we come to the very borders of our own tolerance. But this is not the whole of the paradox. Beckett's plays seem to dissatisfy us because they make us block our own paths to possible solutions. It is, however, not the plays themselves that deny us solutions; we are left dangling so long as we continue to identify with the world of our own concepts. This is a problem revealing and relevant for modern consciousness: we always long to be free from constraints, repressions, and prefabricated solutions imposed upon us—and yet we are bewildered and shocked when such solutions are withheld from us in the theater. Could it be that the ultimate source of laughter at Beckett's plays is the fact that they confront us with this unpalatable contradiction within ourselves? And could it be that this very same fact is also the source of irritation? If we were able to laugh in spite of it all, then laughter might—at least momentarily—indicate our readiness to accept our buried life, thus liberating it from the displacement caused by social and cultural repression. But are we really able to free ourselves from unhappiness by facing up to it?

WHAT IS THE nature of the buried life that Beckett's plays bring to light? Such a question can only be tackled by delving into the function of art in our time—an art that could be said to fascinate us by its denial of immediate comprehension, although this denial cannot be the sole reason for the fascination. *Endgame* is a vivid example of this phenomenon, especially if we view it against the background of our discussion so far. Is it still a comedy, or is the tangle now so perplexing that laughter is no longer possible? When Beckett directed the play in Berlin, he said: "I want as much laughter as possible in this play. . . . It is a play."[51] The account of the rehearsals details these remarks as follows: "He means the laughter of his characters, not of the audience. It must sound convincing when Hamm says to Clov: 'Ah great fun, we had, the two of us, great fun!' "[52] And in fact the characters in *Endgame* do laugh rather more frequently than those in *Godot*, whereas the response of the audience is, according to reliable accounts, marked by a decrease in laughter. Thus we read in the same report quoted above: "Beckett only seems to think of the audience when he warns his actors not to make them accomplices in the play."[53] This remark is of prime importance to our understanding both of the processing of *Endgame* by the spectator and of the response pattern prestructured in the text. Beckett's words are to be taken literally and radically, for in this play the basic structures of comedy have become the subject matter of representation to such a degree that laughter as a reaction is no longer left to the spectator; instead, it forms an integral part of the action represented by the characters, thus robbing the audience of their own last resort (unless they can laugh at the laughter of the characters, which seems unlikely). Given the fact that laughter is a response to comedy, the laughter produced on stage shows that the play does not seek to unfold a comic situation but uses the representation of a comic reaction to signalize something different, the side effect of which is to deprive the spectator of his chance to liberate himself (through laughter) from the critical situation in which he finds himself.

This structure is already apparent at the very beginning of the play. Clov's mime exemplifies the comic paradigm of the failed action: he demonstrates the impossibility of coordinating action and experience by continually forgetting the ladder he needs to enable him to look out of each window. The repetition of this failed action remains strangely abstract, to the extent that Clov accompanies each failure with a short laugh, though this in no way indicates that he is now able to master the situation.[54] Thus the comic paradigm is robbed of its expected reference and consequence, and at the same time the audience is robbed of its chance to react to the failure. What normally makes a comic paradigm funny is its relation to an overall plot line and its ability to elicit the reaction of laughter from the audience. But when Clov himself "performs" the reaction to his own failure, without his laughter in any way meaning that a resolution is to be provided, the comic paradigm loses its representational function. Instead, what is represented is the actual absence of representation, since Clov's laughter indicates that the reason for his conduct escapes representation. The question therefore arises as to how far Clov's failed action can be called a comic paradigm at all. Normally such actions would be comic because the repetition would represent the inability to learn from one's mistakes, whereas here the comic paradigm serves to indicate that the mainspring of Clov's action defies representation. Thus, at the very beginning of the play a comic technique is used to throw into relief the borderlines of representation[55] in a literary genre that historically has always been defined by way of its representation of action. To mark the limits of representation by a comic paradigm is in itself a remarkable feat.

We know that the conventional comic effect always points the way toward a virtual wholeness, and this emerges partly through the reciprocal toppling of mutually negating positions, and partly through laughter as a signal that a crisis has been mastered. Comedy therefore holds in readiness the potential solvability of its conflicts, and in Beckett's play this potential—vestigial though it may be— serves to bring about the removal of representation through what appears to be an act of representation. This very paradox triggers the action and imbues the play with its dramatic character, because that which is unrepresented is offered to the audience as if it *could* be accessible, even though by its very nature it is unrepresentable. Thus, the play resists interpretation as the representation of an enigma, even though our habitual expectations of the theater will continually lead us to suppose that such an enigma exists. This focusing upon what is not there seems even more compulsive in *Endgame* than it was in *Godot*. In the latter, the comic paradigms and the overall action did continually topple one another, but the toppling effect was never taken to such lengths as it is with Clov, through whom it not only embraces the failed action but also the laughter that ought to indicate the correction of the failed action. In *Godot* the spectator still had the chance of reacting to the toppling effect, but in *Endgame* even this reaction has been toppled by the character himself. It is little wonder, therefore, that in this play—whose theme is already encapsulated in its opening sequence—we sense the presence of a profound mystery, for the overturning of the represented reaction seems to strip us of any possibility to react.

Does the fact that we sense the presence of a hidden mystery spring from our habitual expectation that a representation must represent *something*, or is it a defensive mechanism with which we seek to make the unrepresentable accessible by means of our own projections? If both explanations are true, we might assume that the denial of representation in *Endgame* does not serve to cloak some hidden mystery but constitutes a strategic ploy to bring the spectator into play. Beckett's own words seem to confirm this assumption. When asked, "Do you think *Endgame* sets the audience puzzles?," he answered: "*Endgame* is nothing but play. Nothing less. There's no question of puzzles and solutions."[56] The questioner clearly was dissatisfied and persisted: "Do you think the author should have a solution to the puzzles?" Beckett's reply was "Not the author of this play."[57]

But what is the nature of this play, or game, in which language is continually used though it never divulges the reason for its use? Toward the end of the play, Clov says "There is nothing to say," and then—almost as a kind of explanation—he adds a little later, "Then one day, suddenly, it ends, it changes, I don't understand, it dies, or it's me, I don't understand that either. I ask the words that remain—sleeping, waking, morning, evening. They have nothing to say."[58] The fact that words have nothing to say, and that there *is* nothing to say, remains the strategy of this dialogue, which is all the more unacceptable to the spectator as the characters themselves seem unable to stop talking, despite their apparent awareness that there is nothing to say. Nevertheless, Clov's words reveal that something is in him, and something is happening in him, although this something defies language and indeed becomes incomprehensible the moment it is translated into language. As Beckett's remarks bar the way to any mysterious explanation, clearly the "mysterious" language cannot lead in that direction. But if language is not used in the manner to which we are accustomed, and indeed rejects our conventional grasp of its functions, then it brings about a distinct schism between speaker and speech, thus dislocating the human self from its language.[59] Such a process cannot be represented by language, but can only be experienced through it, and so the language of *Endgame* serves "only" to structure such an experience for the spectator. The dialogue itself offers distinct indications of this function. Hamm and Clov seem to find it genuinely funny when their conversation begins to verge on the meaningful, and it is interesting to note that in such a situation—when meaning has to be warded off—their interchange suddenly gains an accord in distinct contrast to what they normally have to say to each other:

> Hamm: We're not beginning to . . . to . . . mean something?
>
> Clov: Mean something! You and I, mean something! [*Brief laugh.*] Ah that's a good one!
>
> Hamm: I wonder. [*Pause.*] Imagine if a rational being came back to earth, wouldn't he be liable to get ideas into his head if he observed us long enough.[60]

Getting into a situation in which they might mean something seems like a joke to these characters. For it is clear that a linguistic manifestation of that which they are could only be in the form of a comic distortion. And thus they actually unmask the true nature of meaning, which is nothing but a substitute for reality.[61]

It seems strange that the characters should continually be exposed to the risk of "meaning something" when they are apparently so well aware of what the mere use of language might lead them into. This constant threat, however, is brought about by the basic human situation, which is precarious insofar as we are, without knowing what it is to be.[62] Hence the human self can only strive to transmute itself through language into something that will represent it. Language thus becomes a kind of reflection that enables man to represent himself in order that he might thereby "have" himself. Such representations, however, must inevitably contain elements of fantasy which arise from his own wishes and desires, and these projections combine to form an image for the purpose of self-representation.[63] Thus Hamm continually returns to his narratives, drawn from the fragmented story of his life, for he wants to try and use these imaginary identities to bring himself before himself. Likewise, Clov projects specific desires of his own, aimed at the creation of orderliness and regularity.[64] But no sooner are these desires put into words than they lose their meaningfulness: Hamm's stories fizzle out; all the references to the end, to time, to the old questions and the old answers, appear only in order to disappear again without further ado. And so the imaginary projections of the speaker radiate forth into his speech only to lose themselves in that same speech. Language therefore reveals itself to be an event, in the course of which the speaker's projections, self-manifestations, and interpretations, and even his very awareness of all these things, are transcended (and so nullified) by himself. There is no other way to demonstrate the impossibility of translating the human self in its entirety into language; or to put it differently, language is only capable of representing the human self in the form of its alienation, cutting it off from the silent self and thus creating an oppressive fixation from which the characters seek to liberate themselves by means of an often convulsive laughter in which the verbalized self evaporates. Having a meaning is for them a substitution, insofar as language is used to bypass that which they really are. This is why they laugh when they have the feeling they might mean something. Forcing language to encounter the unconscious, which defies verbalization, and then using language to represent this self-defeating operation can only be conveyed by an incessant process of dislocating speaker from speech or self from language.[65]

This use of language impedes comprehension, because it no longer achieves its end by fulfilling the function of representation, and indeed, actually makes a game out of this conventional function in Beckett's play. If we are to assess the consequences of this fact, we must remind ourselves of the representational function of language. The basis of this lies in the capacity of language to symbolize: in the symbol "we think a meaning which is separate both from its medium, the language, and from its producer, the speaking subject."[66] Language, especially represented language, therefore has the structure of double meaning; we generally understand a literary text as an utterance "while signifying one thing at the same time signifies *another* thing without ceasing to signify the first."[67] Thus the manifest meaning of a work belongs "in its literalness . . . [to] the observable historical world,"[68] but through its "surplus of meaning"[69] points the way to a *latent* meaning that is expressed or, more often, represented by way of the manifest one. Through this dialectic of revealing and concealing there arises the double meaning of representative language, which is thus able to achieve its purpose of representation. If, through the manifest meaning, there is unfolded the historical individuality of a represented story—such as we also find in the dialogue of *Endgame*—then this individuality must in turn function as an indicator of something beyond itself, but this "something" can only take on its perceivable or experienceable existence through the concrete gestalt of the manifest meaning. The same structure is also to be found in everyday language, where whatever is said garners its full meaning from that which is implied.[70] Thus meaning can no longer stabilize itself if the intention of what is stated is to obliterate the indicative character of the statement. And it is this "minus function" that forms the basic pattern of language in *Endgame*.

The basic pattern itself was already visible in the split between the two levels of action in *Godot*. There the waiting and the characters' indifference toward their avowed aim formed the two dislocated levels, but in *Endgame* the split is far more radical; instead of having two dislocated levels of action represented, the dislocation now occurs between the levels of language: the manifest meaning is deprived of its indicative function. The confinement of language to its literalness removes both its semantic and its pragmatic relevance; this truncated form of language, however, is used as a means to represent the unrepresentable. Hence we perceive the conversations of these characters as a continual suppression of linguistic representation, which is all the more conspicuous as the subject matter concerns such existential topics as time, identity, role-playing, and personal history. The characters constantly change language back into raw material for their games, thus freeing themselves from the need to mean something through their words—for such a meaningful "something" would force them to be an indication of, if not actually an expression of, something other than themselves. By removing the double meaning from their language, the characters therefore counter the threat that they will be dispossessed of themselves by their linguistic self-manifestations. The reduction of language to raw material for games makes its application a matter of chance, not intention. And this is why it is also possible for those topics that have interested the human self to emerge and disappear again without trace, for they are no more than its miscarrying attempts to stabilize, if only temporarily, its precarious situation between being and knowing what it is to be. Such attempts are bound to break down—since the part can never encompass the whole—and so the withdrawal of the double meaning serves to articulate nothing more and nothing less than the basic dichotomy between the silent and the verbalized self, thus testifying to the precarious position of the self dangling between being and knowing itself.

It is therefore only natural that the characters should see their linguistic contact solely in terms of a game[71]—but not for the purpose of establishing pragmatic connections through such language games; the purpose here is to use language in such a way that it will wipe out the connections that begin to arise through their speech. From this situation of language play there arises the interminability of the dialogue, and herein lie both the happiness and the plight of the characters. The happiness consists in the fact that the game of using language to break down the representational claims of language can never have an end, for the structure of double meaning never ceases to bring about new references, and the removal of these can therefore continue ad infinitum. "Writing so as not to die . . . or perhaps even speaking so as not to die is a task undoubtedly as old as the word."[72] *Endgame* dramatizes this occupation. The plight of the characters consists in the fact that they are playing the "end." Instead of ending, they make ending into a game, but it is a game they are compelled to play if the end is to be prevented. By playing it, they bring out the limitless variations on the theme of ending, thus avoiding the necessity actually to end. This restoration of endlessness to the end is a sort of stratagem on the part of the characters. A stratagem, however, implies a motive, and so the characters' constant efforts to use language in order to expel story, history, semantics, and pragmatics from their own speeches are now seen in a different light. They strive to make their speech continuable, their horizons ever open, and the end deferrable, yet the very propellant of this activity draws its dynamic force from a negative quality the characters appear to be aware of: the finiteness of the body. The body is the last hold on the world, and upon it depends the happiness to be obtained from playing the endlessness of the end. Consequently both their happiness and their plight enter into a strange form of coexistence. They are both different states of consciousness, which usually negate and indeed exclude each other.[73] And yet the happiness of continuance feeds on the plight that the characters must keep playing with their illusory linguistic self-manifestations in order to gloss over the inevitability of their bodily end. In this way, the happiness and the plight can no longer be viewed as contrasting mirror images of each other; instead, they link up in a single complex of negativity that the conscious mind can no longer penetrate. And it is this very complex that actually makes it possible for the different states of consciousness to be explored. For negativity is not a manifestation of heightened consciousness; it is, at best, a provocation to the conscious mind to assert itself wherever the borders of comprehension are threatened with closure. Insights into states of consciousness are only possible against the background of their cancelation, which is why we read at the end of the play: "Old endgame lost of old, play and lose and have done with losing."[74] Only through the continual loss of the game does it become possible to experience the consciousness of the self as a sort of reification that is permeated by a massive proportion of imaginary projections, because the dangling of the self between being and knowing itself is hard to endure.

Herein lies the dramatic function of the game. The characters can only express the experience of their dangling by devaluating their linguistically manifested states of consciousness to the level of role-playing. This is their sole means of countering the basic tendency of each individual state to assume a universal character and to lay claim to the whole of the mind. This negativity, however, does not entail freeing the character from his states of consciousness, even though they are shown up in their partiality.[75] And so the characters can only "perform" their inescapable situation by means of role-playing. The mode of the game shows that the player is not identical to that which he "is" at any one time; the endlessness of the game shows that that which the player "is" can never be translated as a whole. Now this downgrading of linguistically manifested states of consciousness to the level of role-playing in turn leads to each individual state losing its claims to reality. But this constant loss of reality also constitutes a state of consciousness, and if the structure of the game were to remain unchanged, then the relation of the mind to its various individual states would also lay claim to universality and the role-playing would then be a representation of *this* state of consciousness.

Such a representation is not exposed by everything actually ending. If this were to happen, then something would have to change. The player would no longer be in his position of dangling, because he would forget his desire not merely to be but also to know that which he is. Without this desire he would also lose his feeling for being that which he is. Since an end is therefore out of the question, the only way in which roles can be unmasked as roles is through the characters' detaching themselves from those roles. Thus they can always draw away from those states in which they find themselves as a result of their dialogues with one another. This is why Hamm yawns right at the beginning of the play, when it is his turn,[76] and the awareness of what happens in the role-playing is constantly devaluated through the remainder of the play.[77] There is, therefore, a continual toppling effect between role-playing and detachment from the role, and this effect not only overturns the individual states of consciousness and the awareness of those states but also gives rise to the coexistence of mutually negating states (such as happiness and plight) which, because they have lost their exclusiveness, can no longer affirm their claims to being ultimate realities.

The territory we are exploring now may best be designated by the term *negativity*, but this is essentially a referential concept, and it cannot cover the *quality* of the ground. This stretches beyond the borders of consciousness and yet at the same time provides a base for the states of consciousness, none of which can ever be ultimate. And if this territory is to be opened up for conscious exploration, then it can only be through the playful devaluation of the individual states, and this devaluation must in turn lose its representational significance through the player's detachment from his role. This is a game in which the roles and the rules are continually overturned, and as such it would appear to offer one last chance to bring to light (through the coexistence of mutually negating states) that which constitutes the consciousness of the self and that which actually happens to the self through its consciousness.

Here we go way beyond the borders of semantics, for we are in a region that cannot be encompassed by meanings. We can only enter it by experiencing it, although this experience will in turn seek to stabilize itself by way of meaningful connections. The very variety of these connections is in itself sufficient indication that the ultimate dimension of the text—its aesthetic object—could not be semantic in nature. In *Endgame* this fact is made evident by a countersense that permeates all levels of the play. And in view of this all-pervasive countersense, it is questionable whether it can still be conceived in terms of what the traditional form of comedy gives us to expect. It might be said that the countersense of this play points, rather, to an overriding human condition that defies all such restrictive epithets as "comic" and "tragic." Comedy and tragedy as terms imply a restitution of unequivocal meaning to the apparent countersense of the dramatic action either by resolving the conflict (comedy) or by ending it in unavoidable catastrophe (tragedy). But the countersense of *Endgame* is as far removed from solution as it is from catastrophe, for both outcomes imply systems of reference which, whenever they are brought to bear, are bound to reduce countersense to a plausible set of alternatives. In *Endgame*, however, the countersense appears to be the only plausible feature. Consequently, comedy and tragedy as time-honored literary genres begin to assume an almost historical character because their pattern of restitution provides a defense against countersense that threatens to make nonsense of our everyday lives. But if comedy and tragedy are turned into "minus functions," then neither our laughter nor our horror can enable us to defend ourselves against the countersense we have to face up to. And it is this refusal of any means of defense that endows Beckett's play with its own special impact.

A COUNTERSENSE THAT invalidates both comic and tragic patterns of restitution can only serve to mark the end of representation. An observation of Foucault's is particularly relevant here: "Representation has lost the power to provide a foundation—with its own being, its own deployment and its power of doubling over on itself—for the links that can join its various elements together. No composition, no decomposition, no analysis into identities and differences can now justify the connection of representations one to another."[78] Thus the end of representation is manifested in the production of countersense, and in *Endgame* this comes about through the language that is deprived of its basic structure: the double meaning. This very deprivation, however, as a basic mode of representing countersense, is a process that in turn must be represented by means of language. And it is at this point that the act of representation switches over into an act of eliciting responses.

The way in which this process works can perhaps be grasped in terms of psycholinguistics: "Human nature abhors a semantic vacuum,"[79] says I. M. Schlesinger, and this most basic fact is tantamount to saying that the hearing or reading of sentences is always accompanied by the "expectation of meaningfulness"[80] which exerts a "guiding pull"[81] on listener or reader. This relation, which Hörmann calls "the meaning constant,"[82] "can best be described as an anthropological factor that determines the linguistic event, because this event takes place between people."[83] Whoever talks means something, and whoever listens understands something.[84] And so this "effort after meaning"[85] constitutes a basic element of cognitive activities, because every utterance arouses the feeling that it must have a specific meaning. This fact becomes most striking when we have difficulty in understanding an utterance, for we should not attempt to clarify its meaning if we did not presuppose a "meaning constant"—that is, if we did not expect utterances to have meaning. This is the principle underlying the attempts of psychoanalysis to interpret apparently random utterances, and it also underlies the linguistic experiments of nonsense poetry and Dada, which make their effects precisely because of our expectations that language aims at meaning.[86]

> Grasping an utterance as something meaningful is not . . . primarily the result of analyzing that utterance, but is the signpost on the way to such an analysis (namely, a signpost that always points the way to that which is meaningful). Meaningfulness, comprehensibleness—this does not come about gradually or laboriously, through the translation or interpretation of signs in accordance with a code; it is the assumed intention

which always precedes this process of interpretation. Comprehension—
generally speaking—is older than what is *linguistically* said. Linguistic
comprehension filters and concretizes in any given utterance the relationship it has to something general that already existed before the
utterance.[87]

And that is why one can only understand utterances if one understands more than what is uttered;[88] for comprehension only takes
place on the assumption that the utterance invokes and then influ-
ences the recipient's store of knowledge and experience. Consequently, it is inaccurate to say that an utterance conveys information; it is rather the recipient who creates the information by setting
the meaning of the utterance against the background of his own
knowledge and experience.[89] And so what "happens between
speaker and listener is an act of guidance, not so much of knowledge
. . . as of consciousness: the speaker changes that which the listener
is conscious of, and thereby changes that which, on the basis of his
consciousness, the listener can do, experience, and think."[90]

The psycholinguistic idea of the "meaning constant" runs parallel
to the hermeneutic observation that comprehension always contains
prethematic understanding, as it occurs whenever something happens to the prethematic understanding. If the "meaning constant"
embodies an anthropological expectation in regard to the meaningfulness of linguistic utterances, then it is only logical that the
countersense of *Endgame* should come to fruition as a dramatic
effect only in the minds of the audience. The effect is intensified by
the fact that the countersense cannot be equated, let alone identified,
with some overall representational function, but since the countersense emerges as the product of what language is meant to represent,
it must mean something and cannot be dismissed as meaningless.
But once our expectation of meaning has been thwarted without
our being able to see any reason for our disappointment, the countersense then appears in the form of a denial that can no longer be
explained in terms of the traditional alienation effect of literature.
And when linguistic expectations are wedded to literary expectations, the thwarting of both leads to an ever-increasing interpretative
activity on the part of the recipient. This activity, however much it
may vary from individual to individual, unfolds itself in a structured
process.

In *Endgame* the language is robbed of its double meaning and
so the existential themes of the dialogue lose their referential status.
While language generally provides an opportunity for the self to
depict itself in terms of its identity and history, in *Endgame* this

function is extinguished, for we are made aware that every translation of the self into words is a translation into something that the self is not. But if language uses its manifest meanings only in order to obliterate its latent meanings, this does not mean that it loses its referential qualities altogether; these remain present as a kind of blank space. It is scarcely surprising that the spectator struggles to fill in this blank[91] and to supply what is absent so that through his own projections he might restore what remains stubbornly and deliberately excluded from the speeches of the characters—namely, the supposed latent meaning of their utterances. The characters go on talking, and so the spectator goes on expecting a full meaning, and his disappointment can only be compensated by meanings projected out of his own imagination.

The urge to understand is geared to the deep-rooted expectation that meaning must exist, and generally we understand linguistic utterances by relating them to our own background of knowledge and experience. But if the linguistic utterance defies this internalized expectation, then we are liable to engage in an increasingly frantic activation of these background faculties. And this is precisely how the language of *Endgame* leads the spectator to integrate himself into the play. The constant obliteration of linguistic referents results in structured blanks, which would remain empty if the spectator did not feel the compulsion to fill them in, thus himself being turned into an actor of the play. And as such empty spaces exercise a kind of suction effect, there is in fact no way that the spectator can avoid being drawn into the proceedings by constantly supplying what appears to be missing. Through this process, the dramatic focus of the play is shifted away from the plot—and indeed many spectators have complained bitterly about the lack of action in Beckett's plays—and onto the spectator himself. The dramatic action, therefore, comes about through the projections of the spectator and occurs in the mind of the spectator, thus setting off a response pattern in which the spectator's projections are cast as an integral part of the dramatic performance. This rather strange integration is sparked off by the expectation that represented language on stage is bound to be meaningful.

Although each individual spectator will pursue his own path toward an expected solution, the process itself allows for schematization. The characters on stage cannot stop talking about such vital subjects as their identities, their lives, and their relations to one another, to the world, and to the end, but they do not seem to be in any way affected by these topics. The spectator's immediate reaction will be one of bewilderment. This in itself is structured to the extent that it bars the way to some possible reactions and opens up the way to others. For instance, it is no longer possible for the spectator to identify himself with the characters, for in his experience it is unimaginable that he should remain unaffected by what obsesses him. If he cannot identify with the characters, and so cannot relate the events on stage to events in his own real world of experience, he will nevertheless inevitably base his increasing attempts at interpretation on that same world of experience—not least because he will try to bridge the gap between himself and what is happening on stage. The spectator's bewilderment, therefore, separates him from the characters, and this separation drives him to make their behavior "meaningful." Here the existential themes of the dialogue begin to have a guiding effect, because they constantly invoke what the spectator himself understands by identity, human relations, the world, and so forth. The resultant concepts will vary from spectator to spectator, as each will draw on his own personal store of knowledge, experience, and competence, but the process that gives rise to these concepts is of an intersubjective nature, no matter how different the individual ideas may be. Whenever the spectator fills in the latent meaning so obviously left open by the manifest meaning, he begins to "perform" the play, producing his own concepts in order to explain if not remove altogether the characters' lack of concern about the matters so vital to their own existence. The spectator's ideas restore the lost reference to the manifest meaning of the dialogue, which thus regains the representative quality that seems to be necessary to our understanding of what the characters are doing. But herein lie the "difficulties in understanding the *Endgame*."[92] For there is an unceasing clash between the different meanings imposed upon the play. Thus the spectator himself produces the very failure of his interpretative endeavor; guided by his deep-rooted expectation of the meaningfulness of represented language, he cannot help supplying what obviously is not there. In doing so, however, he does not succeed in constituting the meaning of the play, but is made to subvert that which he intends to bring about through the self-produced conflict of the very meanings projected.[93] Such a conflict is unavoidable if the apparently missing representational quality of the play is to be restored, even though its acts of representation are aimed at eliminating representation in order to draw the spectator strategically into "acting" the play. Thus the meanings with which *Endgame* is endowed are not its meanings at all, but are simply the imaginary projections of the spectators, which

PARADIGMS

are revealed as projections through the conflict of meanings they produce.

The restoration to language of its double meaning therefore constitutes a failed action, which the spectator keeps repeating so long as he thinks that his projections are the latent meaning of the play. This process has all the structural features of a comic action, because constant repetition and the inability to learn from one's failures are comic paradigms. In *Godot* the comic paradigms were still components of the act of representation on stage, but in *Endgame* these paradigms have now shifted to the acts of interpretation (structured by the text) that take place in the spectator himself. He is no longer confronted by a play with a comic structure; instead, the absent double meaning of the dialogue leads him to load trivialities with meaning, only to withdraw that meaning himself. Alternatively, he imposes on the characters an awareness of their situation that they have long since transcended, whereupon he then projects onto them a naiveté that—as it is produced by himself and not by the characters—applies far less to them than to the ideas he has invented in order to understand them. His insistence on interpreting and so on repeating his failed actions makes the spectator's own activity comic; he is not only integrated into the play but actually becomes a comic figure himself. For like a clown, he acts out the failure of his endeavors as if it were a continual success. But when we are caught up in a comic action, we cannot laugh about it, because the compulsion to try again freezes all incipient laughter into the rigidity of comic entanglement. The fact that there is laughter at all only indicates that the body would like to react while the "mind" vainly struggles against the continued breakdown of its projections.

As the strategy of the play forces the spectator into a comic role, the distance between himself and the events represented on stage dwindles to nothing. In *Godot* at least the spectator was still confronted by two clearly separated levels of action—waiting for Godot as overall plot line, and the comic paradigms of repeated failures—and these separate levels demanded some kind of reconciliation through him. The establishment of links, and their subsequent invalidation, structured the spectator's activity and so brought him into the play. But in *Endgame* the absence of double meaning from the language induces the spectator to project a latent meaning and so to provide an overall plot level for himself if he is to articulate even the manifest meaning. And if the spectator is made to produce the background that is a prerequisite for deciphering the utterances, then we may truly say that the dramatic action takes place in himself.

This means the removal of the type of detachment we normally take for granted when we watch a performance, and if we are to regain that detachment we have to free ourselves from whatever it is in which we are entangled. And this is impossible, since we are in fact entangled in ourselves. We are trapped in our own projections of a latent meaning we have produced in order to clarify for ourselves the events on stage. And if we have brought about our own loss of detachment through our own projections, we cannot hope to regain detachment by means of further projections. Thus, the more the spectator struggles to free himself from the quicksands of his own projections, the deeper he will sink into them. The main cause of this extraordinary spiral of failed actions is the fact that the spectator always takes his projections for the representational intention of the dramatic action. And this is scarcely surprising, since we normally expect an act of representation to represent something. Indeed, it is neither surprising nor altogether misguided, for in principle this expectation is actually upheld in *Endgame*, though in a strikingly modified form. If our loss of detachment is produced by our projections, and our attempts to regain detachment only increase our entanglement, then whatever is represented must be present in our own failures. This of course is quite different from what we would expect of a theatrical performance. The thing represented is therefore the insight—produced by our failures—into the fictional character of our projections, which continually run up against the resistance of an incomprehensible "reality" and so break apart into their imaginary components before our very eyes. The loss of representation achieved in *Endgame* makes possible the representation of those imaginary elements that never cease to influence our acts of comprehension.

Now if the structure of *Endgame* casts the spectator in a comic role, this comedy would seem to indicate that the conflicts are potentially capable of solution. This would even be so of a comedy that prevents itself from effectively fulfilling its inherent promise of cure, as can be seen from the fact that the spectator still goes on trying to regain the detachment he lost through his projections by making still further projections. It is in this context that the laughter of the characters themselves takes on its dramatic function. They laugh frequently—considerably more than in Beckett's other plays;[94] at times their laughter is convulsive and occasionally even communal.[95] The laughter is a means by which they confirm for one another the onset of helplessness whenever their words or deeds threaten to mean something. And so when they are induced to restore the double meaning to their own linguistic actions, they escape through laughter from their imminent imprisonment in that which they represent (by means of language) and which consequently they "are" not.[96] This possibility of liberation is hard for the spectator to exploit, because the represented laughter of the characters unmasks the latent meaning as a cathectic object, and this unmasking represents the deconstruction of that which the spectator is constantly striving to restore to the play: the double meaning of the language. Thus he cannot laugh together with the characters, and he cannot feel their laughter as something contagious. He can only cut himself off from what they are doing, even though it could offer him guidance when he sees his interpretative work blocked by the constant failure of his own actions. Instead of being a safety valve of merriment, the sporadic laughter of Beckett's spectators is far more an expression of shock, which bears witness to the force of the self-inflicted compulsion to understand. The strategy of the play leads the spectator to deprive himself of his own chances of relief, and this self-imposed frustration brings out a basic mode of communication in the play: it reveals to us how difficult it is to stop identifying ourselves with the imaginary elements of our ideas, because we regard them as norms, and so we do not feel free to laugh at them since our laughter would mean that our own norms are not to be taken seriously.

As we have seen, the spectator is induced to act a comic role and so to experience the breakdown of his own projections, and this process ultimately reveals to us that we are incapable of getting along without the double meaning of language in spite of the fact that not everything we are can be translated into language. The comic role of failed action the spectator is given to perform makes it possible to experience the human condition precisely through a play that represents the breakdown of representation. For the fact that we may now see into the fictional character of our projections does not in any way imply that we can cast these aside and adopt new, hitherto inconceivable, methods of coming to grips with the world. We cannot escape from our projections, even when we know what they are. This fact is demonstrated both by the characters themselves and by the spectator's spiral of failed interpretations. But only the characters can actually laugh at this "unhappiness" of our existence, and this puts them one up, so to speak. It also places them far beyond our grasp. As our own laughter breaks off, our physical response to the crisis switches over into an awareness that our helplessness evinces traces of a life that is hidden away from us. It is a life that can only be experienced through the impossibility of its being processed, and it can only retain its authenticity if it is not translated and so neutralized by our conventional systems of reference. This hidden life becomes present through the helplessness of our reaction and becomes an aesthetic experience when we can see ourselves in the "endlessness" of our futile interpretations, which initially are forced out of us, but are then kept in production by our own inner compulsion. The experience is aesthetic because we can observe ourselves while we are performing an activity,[97] whereas in everyday life the activity is an end in itself. It is also an essential feature of the aesthetic experience here provided that the activity delegated to the spectator should remain without a final resolution, for only if he is induced to perform ultimately unresolvable operations will he be prepared to observe his own performance; such an attitude of observation could not be initiated if his interpretative endeavor, activated by the play, were to lead him in the direction of a concrete and indisputable meaning. *Endgame* puts the spectator in this position of detachment by giving him the chance to see himself in the role of a comic figure—a role he is compelled to play because of his own basic experiences. And yet although his own comicalness constantly tends to stifle his laugh, preventing him from obtaining relief, his detached self-observation turns out to be the last remnant of the humanizing force of comedy, which makes the human condition both experienceable and palatable.

As THE HUMAN condition can never be experienced as such, let alone as a whole, we must finally focus on its historic manifestation as revealed and mediated through the response pattern in Beckett's play. In doing so, we should also be able to spotlight a significant function of art in our time. A form of theater that makes the spectator into an integral character of the play can no longer perform *to* him, but only *with* him. The representation that he will have expected is blocked off by the peculiar structure of communication, which draws the spectator into the proceedings. The only representation possible is that which the spectator himself must achieve, but as his only point of reference is ultimately himself, it follows that he can only represent himself. He is forced into this position through the failure of his attempts at deciphering meanings he expects to be there. The frustration of his expectations of meaning therefore becomes the object of representation, which—if the attempts were successful—would not come to the fore. Thus the spectator himself is, at one and the same time, the producer and the addressee of what is represented. This process makes it possible for a decentered subjectivity to be communicated as an experience of self in the form of projections continually created and rejected by the spectator. Once this experience has "clawed" its way into the spectator, the frustration of his expectation of meaning begins to take on another shape. It gives rise to a new consciousness that every revelation coincides with a concealment, and that every awareness presupposes an unawareness to which it refers. This self-restricting consciousness arises from and points toward a hidden life, which the spectator can experience only because every concrete gestalt he forms turns out to be limited by the very meaning it entails. Dwarfing the significance of meaning is a method of enabling the buried life to signalize its presence. And as the gestalts of consciousness keep changing, so the conscious mind keeps linking up with the submerged realm to which it refers, but which now appears to be unfathomable in terms of semantics. But if, in this constant movement, the hidden life emerges into light, this does not mean that—as the reverse side of consciousness—it must now necessarily be cast in the form of some apocalyptic emptiness. The emptiness does not begin outside the walls of Hamm's home. It reaches right up to every single word of the dialogue. It is in fact nothing more and nothing less than an indication of our referential use of language, which is semantically so determinate that it must leave blank that which cannot be grasped semantically. The art of *Endgame* lies in its use of language to convey the necessity and the conditionality of language by way of that very realm of life language is incapable of grasping. It may well be that the spectator will see none of this and will turn his back on it, but if the process does strike home, then it will produce an experience that transcends the capabilities of language.

The traceable response pattern inscribed in *Endgame* permits an experience of the decentered self, which is a striking indication of Beckett's anti-Cartesian position,[98] and this in turn is a characteristic sign of our times. The identification of the self with its consciousness of itself means the eclipse of that which the self is so that it may be transmuted into that which, in such a restricted form, it cannot possibly be. Only when the self's consciousness of itself is marked by an awareness of its own limitations in the face of that which is unspeakable—that is, only when the conscious mind obliterates its own formulations in order to articulate a silence that is ungraspable through language—can the decentered self be turned into an experience, such as art alone is able to communicate.

PART III
AVENUES FOR EXPLORATION

NINE
CHANGING FUNCTIONS OF LITERATURE

he place of literature in modern society is something that can no longer be taken for granted. Once upon a time its significance was unquestioned, whereas now, paradoxically, the significance has been eroded in proportion to the increasing accessibility of books. Clearly it has lost certain functions that had formerly been so integral that they were taken for literature itself. This fact implies that ideas entertained about literature, but not literature itself, have come to an end. Thus, the repeated announcements of the death of literature which have punctuated the last hundred years from Lautréamont through the revolt of '68 have, rather, concerned the function attributed to it in bourgeois society. Instead of indicating something about literature per se, they are symptoms of a malaise that affects the conceptions, functions, and applications of literature.

Throughout its history, literature has always stood in need of being justified, and since Aristotle we have grown accustomed to a branch of criticism that strives to analyze just what literature should be or should achieve. This gives rise to the extraordinary fact that, while literature achieves its own effects through itself, it is accompanied by a critical activity in the form of poetics or aesthetic theory which constantly tries to translate it into other terms in order to make it accessible to the prevailing requirements of the day. And since these requirements change, the functional values of literature also change. Evidently literature has reached just such a turning point today.

Why has it been relegated to the fringes of modern society? Does this marginal position denote a complete loss of function, or merely the loss of those functions with which literature has hitherto been identified? If we are to answer these questions, we must look back into the recent past so that we can ascertain those potential functions that have *not* been fully exploited. Without this backward glance it will be impossible to see new possibilities for literature, since these can only come into being through what has been superseded: the negation of what literature *was* becomes the condition for what it can become.

Two outstanding twentieth-century "rebellions"—dadaism and the 1968 Paris revolt—point accusing fingers at the old bourgeois concept of literature, which was finally swamped by the upheavals that followed the two world wars. But precisely what were these rebellions directed against, and what lesson can be learned from them?

Tristan Tzara wrote, in his Dada manifesto *Pour faire un poème dadaiste*:

> Prenez un journal.
> Prenez des ciseaux.
> Choisissez dans ce journal un article ayant la longueur que vous comptez donner à votre poème.
> Découpez l'article.
> Découpez ensuite avec soin chacun des mots qui forment cet article et mettez-les dans un sac.
> Agitez doucement.
> Sortez ensuite chaque coupure l'une après l'autre.
> Copiez consciencieusement dans l'ordre où elles ont quitté le sac.
> Le poème vous ressemblera.[1]

Instructions of this kind are meant to dissolve the boundary between literature and reality. A good ten years later André Breton proclaimed that the poet of the future would overcome the depressingly unbridgeable gap between Action and Dream.[2] Dream becoming action, newspaper cuttings becoming poems—here we have the hitherto unquestioned distinction between literature and reality being paraded as a sort of period scandal.

The hectic aggression of the Dadaists and the deliberate provocations of the Surrealists show how deeply rooted in people's minds was the contrast between the dream of art and the prose of reality. It needed a course of shock therapy to drive this concept out of the collective unconscious of the bourgeoisie.

One can trace a direct link between Dada and the Surrealists on the one hand and the "cultural revolution" sparked off by the Paris student revolt in 1968. A placard at the Sorbonne proclaimed:

> The society of self-alienation must disappear from history. We shall discover a new and original world. Fantasy has come to power.[3]

What is meant by this can be gauged from statements like the following:

> It is not in the seminars of the German departments that the poems of Brecht and Mayakovsky should be interpreted, but in the meetings of

AVENUES FOR EXPLORATION

the workers' revolutionary councils. Let us chase painted desires out of the museums and on to the streets. Let us bring written dreams down from the overcrowded bookshelves of the libraries, and press a stone in their hands.[4]

These stones are to be thrown to the following effect:

> The Revolution: let us create conditions such that everyone can share in Picasso's work. The Cultural Revolution: let us create conditions such that everyone can become a Picasso and Picasso can become everyone.[5]

This proclaimed interchangeability between art and revolutionary practice is not far removed from the Dada revolt, although much more clearly expressed here. The interpenetration between aesthetic self-expression and political action is meant to herald the coming of a new reality that is to form the basis of a future society.

A clear and consistent thread running right through the proclamations of this cultural revolution is the violent need to merge literature and reality. But if literature becomes reality then the latter can only become a game, and so, freed from its governing codes, the 'real' game becomes anarchic. The anarchic game, then, is the price that has to be paid if literature changes into what it is not, and if reality is to change into that which in fact it can never be — namely, literature. In the anarchic game, literature and reality are forced by reciprocal negation into a symbiotic relationship.

Negating the fictional character of literature, so that it can make the leap into reality, is itself a piece of literature, which is reflected in the Dadaist manifesto and the writings of the Surrealists, just as it emerges from the pronouncements of the "Fantasy" that assumes power. In still more recent times the same line is to be observed in the various forms of drama, from the Happenings through to living theater and street theater, all of which negate the traditional structure of the drama, which is based on a representative function. This literature offers itself as a continuous event, its content being the artist himself, or the audience, or even — as in living theater — the intermingling of play and revolution.[6] Is this compulsive urge to make literature into reality more than just the wanton whim of impatient activists?

It is clear that what we have here is an aspect of literature which is concerned with destroying another aspect of itself. If literature is to dispose of distinctions by becoming reality, this can only be as a direct reaction to the tenet that there *is* a distinction between literature and reality — a belief that was produced and established by the aesthetic idealism of the nineteenth century. And if this reaction assumes the proportions of a revolution, then the violence can only be a sign of the extent to which that belief underpinned bourgeois culture. The upheaval required to destroy this existing concept acts as a sort of seismograph, indicating the reification of the bourgeois concept of literature—reified in the sense that a particular historical concept of literature was taken to be literature itself. In this respect the revolution offers us a key to the past. It does not, however, offer us a key to the future—it does not reveal to us *potential* aspects of literature. For all their claims to be "rebels of today" or "new mutants,"[7] the revolutionaries are still descended from the aesthetic idealists.

Literature has become reality in the form of the anarchic game, but it is a fallacy to believe that by negating something, you have already grasped its otherness. This is also the fallacy embraced by the "Fantasy" that has come to power. People take the announcement itself to be an indication that all things have changed for the better. "No-one thought it necessary to ask—and no-one would have been allowed to ask—what fantasy had to offer, and what it had ever offered."[8]

With pure negation, the revolution remains dependent upon that which it negates, and the more radical the destruction, the more inevitably it must lead to self-destruction. Thus, the tradition of the nineteenth century has prevailed over its would-be destroyers, because they could not free themselves from the contradiction that is inherent in that tradition and that prevented the revolution from becoming a starting point for a literature of the future. We must therefore take a closer look at this contradiction inherited from the nineteenth-century aesthetic tradition—not only because it blunted the knives raised against it, but also because the impasse that it created released new possibilities for literature.

GERMAN IDEALISM INVOLVED a significant reorientation of the age-old relationship between Art and Nature. As an imitation of Nature, Art had the task of making it accessible to man, and even of perfecting it where necessary. In classical antiquity this relationship derived its stability from the orderliness of the cosmos, and in its final stages, during the eighteenth century, from the belief in the perfectibility of the world. But with the erosion of this guaranteed stability came a complete change in the Nature-Art relationship, with Nature giving way to the subjective self, known to the Idealists as the genius.

AVENUES FOR EXPLORATION

Initially the genius was viewed as one favored by Nature, for he was able to create like Nature, though what he produced distinguished itself by rising above any practical use or application. Thus, the work of genius was considered to be quite different from what the craftsman produced; in its essence it was the embodiment of the creative process itself.[9] Art was no longer a matter of technical skill, but had become a realm for exercising individual freedom, and it was Schiller who, in his *Briefe über die ästhetische Erziehung*, radicalized this concept, which was drawn from Kant's *Critique of Judgment.*

Kant's theory of genius had shown the extent to which the beautiful in art is able to activate human faculties, causing an interplay between them as a necessary prerequisite for cognition. Schiller attributed the same function to the human disposition for play, but he saw the aim as being not cognition but training for freedom. For him the play-drive (*Spieltrieb*) provided a precise balance between the striving for form and for content,[10] which in terms of art gives rise to a realm of *der schöne Schein*, "beautiful semblance" — a realm that lies beyond the borders of the real. It is exactly this division — at the time heralded as a new humanistic ideal — from which a great many of the troubles began to ensue. If Art is now conceived as an exercise in human freedom, it is all too obvious that man's education *through* Art will lead ultimately to an education *to* Art.[11] In other words, Art not only freed itself from its traditional links with Nature, but it also set itself up in opposition to reality, since reality did not contain the freedom that was only possible by means of education through Art. And so, instead of Art and Nature complementing one another, they settled into opposing positions of Appearance and Reality, their paths so divergent that they could never come together again. Where Art ruled, reality was overstepped; and so the nineteenth-century concept of Art is that of "beautiful semblance" contrasted with prosaic reality.

The persuasiveness of this concept is to be inferred from the manner in which its influence spread even to such places as Britain, where the ground was originally far from fertile. Thomas Carlyle summed up the whole situation is his series of lectures *On Heroes, Hero-Worship, and the Heroic in History*: "Literature, so far as it is Literature, is 'an apocalypse of Nature', a revealing of the 'open secret.' "[12]

This view of literature as the apocalypse of Nature entails a radical revision of the old complementary relationship between Art and Nature; what literature reveals is a secret whose manifestation leads to the out-stripping of Nature. But if Nature is exceeded by literature, then reality itself can only be a collection of juggled appearances.[13] With this reorientation of the relationship, Carlyle completes the switch of ontological predicates initiated by Schiller.

Now, even if Art as beautiful semblance embodies a reality of its own, this in turn remains dependent on the given prosaic reality that it must transcend in order to set man free. This is the defect inherent in the humanistic concept, for Art draws its determination from what it sets out to remove. In other words, not only is it dependent on something outside itself, but it is also the very negation of this "something" that helps bring about the basic characteristic of Art as beautiful semblance. This paradox lies at the heart of an Art that has become autonomous. Its pervasiveness becomes clear from such traditional descriptions of Art as beautiful appearance, magic, transfiguration, illusion, and so forth, all of which show how impossible it is for an autonomous Art to break free from the reality it is supposed to annihilate. Evidently autonomous Art is not a transcendence of reality so much as a flight from it.

Since the middle of the nineteenth century, abundant support has been offered for this view. Matthew Arnold, who postulated norms of Art widely embraced throughout the century and who was as influential as Schiller had been earlier, wrote: "Criticism must maintain its independence of the practical spirit and its aims."[14] This meant that the critic must refrain from "immediate practice in the political, social, humanitarian sphere, if he wants to make a beginning for that more free speculative treatment of things."[15] Instead of linking Art with life, the critic must separate the two in order to give Art 'reality', which is liberation from the social and political world. But what it is that enables Art to achieve this, as well as what qualities the new sphere is to possess, remains uncertain, as is evinced by the biblical metaphor with which Arnold attempts to describe the critic's situation: "[T]here is the promised land, towards which criticism can only beckon. That promised land will not be ours to enter, and we shall die in the wilderness: but to have desired to enter it, to have saluted it from afar, is already, perhaps, the best distinction among contemporaries."[16] And so the promised land of Art is no more than a hope, whose religious overtones resound with the desire for deliverance. And as the century wore on, autonomous Art revealed itself more and more overtly to be nothing but a haven from the burdensome character of experience; it served to make people forget that world in which they were so inextricably entangled.

AVENUES FOR EXPLORATION

This function was acknowledged explicity at the end of the nine-teenth century, in the concept of art for art's sake. Walter Pater sums it all up:

> Well! We are all under sentence of death but with a sort of indefinite reprieve . . . we have an interval, and then our place knows us no more. Some spend this interval in listlessness, some in high passions, the wisest, at least among "the children of this world," in art and song. For our chance lies in expanding that interval, in getting as many pulsations as possible into the given time. Great passions may give us this quickened sense of life, ecstasy and sorrow of love . . . [O]nly be sure it is passion — that it does yield you this fruit of a quickened, multiplied consciousness. Of such wisdom, the poetic passion, the desire for beauty, the love of art for its own sake, has most. For art comes to you proposing frankly to give nothing but the highest quality to your moments as they pass, and simply for those moments' sake.[17]

Art, then, is simply a response to man's oppressive awareness of the temporal nature of his existence; by giving him moments of rapture, it can make him forget everyday life and its transitoriness. What at the start of the century was a promise of freedom became, by the end of the century, a stimulus to ecstasy. Little wonder, then, Art at this time hid itself away in its ivory tower, its refuge from the sordidness of life.

But this very retreat indicates that Art was not free from those practical functions it so vehemently disclaimed and whose very removal was supposed to give it its autonomy. For the flight from oppressive reality into the worlds of fantasy serves very real needs and shows very real practical purposes, the fulfillment of which inevitably involves an innate contradiction within the concept of autonomous Art.

AT THIS POINT we must note that autonomous Art constitutes a concept of art, and should by no means be taken to cover all the *products* of artists and writers throughout the nineteenth century. Even though it was a principle that was continually put into practice by those who considered romanticism as an ongoing process, a good deal of literature was written in opposition to this principle. But the very effectiveness of this literature depended in no small measure on the fact that it deliberately went against established expectations. While the aesthetic creed of the day was the liberation of Art from social reality, realistic and naturalistic literature gained its potency from its rebellion against such a creed.

At first, however, this opposition had no influence on the validity of the autonomy concept, and what has since been called the aesthetic consciousness drew its criteria for Art from the classical periods in literature, whose peak achievements gave rise in the nineteenth century to what Heine had called a Religion of Art. The ground had already been prepared by the fact that during this period social and philosophical systems, as well as religious and scientific world pictures, had been rivaling one another as attempts to penetrate the truth of reality. Art transcended all these various interpretations, not least because its very nature was to open up territories beyond those of the empirical world. This was the function that raised it to the status of religion, as can be seen from such contemporary critical terms as *Offenbarungsgeschehen* (revelatory event), signifying the superiority of Art over the various conflicting world views. But this claim of revelation was one that the religion of Art could never fulfill, for the intended transcendence of reality revealed itself as merely an escape, thus laying bare the needs it was meant to satisfy. Art had advanced to the level of a religion because after the period of the Enlightenment such an intramundane transcendence of reality *could* only come about through Art—but as a result Art was more dependent than ever upon the worldly reality that it was supposed to outstrip.

RIGHT FROM THE start this contradiction was aggravated by the need to provide a concrete idea of what autonomous Art meant. The mere impulse of abstracting Art from the given world was not enough to convey an image of its autonomy. After all, Art was claiming to be the realm of freedom in which lay man's only chance to ennoble himself; but if man was to be led to true humanity by way of Art, then this Art that was to underlie his education could scarcely remain an abstract idea. How, though, can one concretize something that only lives through the transcendence of its direct opposite?

The answer was: by collecting all the great artistic achievements of the past. Hence the emergence of that typically nineteenth century institution, the museum. Originally, collections had grown from the personal tastes of individuals; but now the multiplicity of tastes had to be unified into a single concept of taste which could take on normative authority. And so works of art were taken out of their sacred or profane settings and placed in the museum. It is this "abstraction," this uprooting of the work from its context, that underlies whatever we have now come to call a work of art. As a representative of a normative taste, it must exercise its effectiveness entirely through itself, and not through any purposes or functions. It is scarcely surprising that when Duchamp displayed a bottle rack in a museum, everyone was shocked. For the museum was the final triumph of autonomous Art, in that it took works of art out of their historical settings and endowed art of all periods with contemporaneity, so that from their various appearances there could be extrapolated a single, universally valid norm of Art.

Once again, however, there is no escaping the problem that the museum was in fact meant to dispose of. The museum is "a late stage of all the successful representations in the history of art, which are preserved by a present that simultaneously distances itself from them, in order to enjoy its own uniqueness."[18] This enjoyment, however, brings to light precisely the factor that the unified collection of works sought to cover up—namely, the historical relativity of taste, as evinced by the individual works and also by the historical functions, sacred or profane, that they had to fulfill in their original settings. Thus, the contemporaneity with which the museum endows the works actually causes stress to be laid on their historical *differences*, the concealment of which was supposed to underpin the claim of Art to be autonomous.

THE CONTRADICTION HAD even more drastic consequences for literature, which followed the same trend by replacing its "canonized texts" with an imaginary museum of literary masterpieces. From Saint-Beuve's *Temple du goût* to Walter Pater's *House Beautiful*, literary critics of the time strove to filter out the great works from the stream of history, in order to put them in a treasure house. It is this continual attempt to salvage artistic achievements from oblivion that made the treasure house into such a conspicuous ideal of the cultural attitude prevailing throughout the nineteenth century. As a place of detached enchantment, the imaginary museum of literature gave man the chance to gaze at himself in the mirror of his achievements made tangible in history.[19] Just as the museum enabled men to enjoy detachment from their preserved past, so too did the great literary and cultural achievements bring inspiration to the human mind. The meaning of the humanistic education beloved of the nineteenth century was precisely release from an oppressive present, and retrospective contemplation of the past, whose preserved contemporaneity in museum and treasure house drives out the threat of the real world and offers the constant ennobling of man to help him on the path to his own humanization.

The importance of the treasure house in the nineteenth century can be gauged most obviously from the various collections of quotations from world literature published at that time. In 1855 Bartlett's *Familiar Quotations* was published in England, with similar success to that of Georg Büchmann's *Geflügelte Worte* in Germany, which actually bore the subtitle *Zitatenschatz*, or "treasury of quotations." At the same time in Germany, Reclam brought out the first paperbacks, publishing cheap editions of the classics under the collective heading of *Universalbibliothek* (Universal Library) with the motto *Bildung macht frei* (Culture liberates).

The commercial success of these enterprises shows clearly that they must have fulfilled an existing need. It was as if the ideal of humanistic education was now available to all; for easy access to the treasure house was essential, since only a knowledge of the literary past was satisfactory evidence of culture. If one could lace one's conversation with quotations, one could pass for an educated being, thus gaining access to that elite group of persons who, regardless of class or profession, shared the same all-important status symbol of education. The fact that class and profession ceased to be social barriers for those in command of what culture had to offer, points up an important difference between *this* humanistic tradition and the original aims of autonomous Art. What initially was conceived as a haven from the burdensome pressure of social realities turned out to be a means of gaining social recognition.

The fossilized nature of this culture is unmistakable, for just as the work of art in the museum was removed from its functional setting, so too was the quotation wrenched out of its context and made to serve as a sort of password among the educated. And yet, despite this functional devaluation, such educational fossils still retain one subtle characteristic of their former selves: autonomous Art sought to release people from their webs of reality, so that they could enter into a higher realm—and precisely this was accomplished by the new opportunity to climb social barriers and enter the ranks of the initiated.

AUTONOMOUS ART DID not ennoble man, as is all too clear from the appalling slaughter that has taken place in this century. The humanistic ideology led instead to a whole fabric of delusions. Marcuse described this as follows:

> Culture means not so much a better as a nobler world: a world that is to be brought about not by overturning the material order of life, but

through an event within the soul of the individual. Humanity becomes an internal condition; freedom, goodness, beauty become spiritual qualities: understanding for all things human, knowledge of the great things of all times, appreciation of all things difficult and sublime, respect for history, in which all this has taken place . . . Culture should permeate and ennoble the given world, not replace it with a new one. In this way it raises the individual . . . The beauty of culture is, above all, an inner beauty . . . Its realm is essentially a realm of the soul.[20]

This basic disposition of humanistic culture, Marcuse concluded, lent itself readily to any kind of manipulation, as evinced by the political fate of Germany, from which this ideal originally arose.

The illusory nature of humanistic culture is further revealed by a remark of Freud's. The great unmasker himself seems to have fallen into the same self-deluding trap as so many of the educated elite of his time. When visiting Berlin in 1930, he was asked by the American ambassador what he thought were the chances of National Socialism succeeding. His answer was: "A nation that produced Goethe could not go to the bad."[21]

Humanization through culture has been proved by history—especially in Germany—to be an illusion, and this fact is responsible in no small measure for the loss of status suffered by culture in our time. Since the end of the Second World War, industrial societies have experienced a marked acceleration in the erosion of the one-time firmly entrenched class structure, with a resultant social mobility and a far-reaching change in the nature of its status symbols. Social recognition no longer depends on education, but on success in the professional world. Instead of asserting ourselves by quoting from world literature, we make our social mark with expensive cars, houses, holiday homes, and other luxuries of life.

In societies where social mobility has always prevailed—as in America, for instance—rank has never been linked to literary culture. Indeed, bringing quotations into conversation can often lead to the speaker being misunderstood or viewed as a sort of freak. Culture as such has become almost a fringe eccentricity, and the only time it arouses public admiration is when it features in TV quiz shows.

Furthermore, literary culture—the source of all the quotations—has had to face heavy competition. The surfeit of optical and acoustic appeals to the human mind has considerably reduced the significance of readings in our time. "I wonder," Marshall McLuhan once mused rhetorically, "whether the rebellion today in classrooms and against the book has anything to do with the new electronic age we live in."[22] He leaves no doubt as to his own answer to the question, for he attributes the decline of the culture of the written word to the fact that the media have enabled people to create new extensions of themselves.

WE HAVE SEEN that in the past, literature increased its status in accordance with its use; this was most evident in Dada and in the revolt of the Left, through which literature was meant to become reality itself. But it is an integral feature of literature that—apart from exclusively didactic writing—it is not *created* for any one specific use. Thus, all attempts to assign such a use to it can be taken as an indication of some historically conditioned need. This applies to humanization through literature as well as to fantasy's seizure of power, as demanded by the Paris revolutionaries. In fact, literature seems constantly to provoke translations of itself into terms of prevailing social situations, which in turn makes it into a sort of divining rod for those impulses that have given rise to whatever use has been attributed to it. Thus, any talk of "use" remains naive if the conditionality of this use is not taken into consideration. However, can this use still be effective if its underlying presuppositions are exposed?

As any use of literature implicitly entails the discourse of historically conditioned needs, a further dimension is revealed which remains hidden so long as utility constitutes the be-all and end-all of literature. Harnessing literature to practical purposes, or even equating it with them, appears to be a defense mechanism directed against the growing complexities of an open society. For literature confronts people with themselves—which might prove irritating for those who consider themselves firmly rooted in their social roles. As self-confrontation tends to shatter conventions, it remains questionable whether any use is to be derived from it. Practical use, more often than not, presupposes the stability of a given framework. For this reason, any talk of the practical use of literature is a thing of the past. In retrospect, use becomes an indicator of the secret longings prevalent in bourgeois society and of the anthropological necessity for people to reduce complexities in an expanding world.

THE IDENTIFICATION OF literature with its practical function seems outdated, not least because literature failed to bring the human being to full fruition. Nevertheless, this very failure does raise the question of what happens to us when we make ourselves available for the literary experience. In this respect the past concept of lit-

208   AVENUES FOR EXPLORATION

erature conditions a new question as to what it might be. Two answers can be excluded: it is neither an escape from reality nor a substitute for it. Instead, it reacts to reality, and in doing so interprets it.

Today we no longer cling exclusively to classical achievements in literature, nor do we select them as guides for our assessments, as was the case in bourgeois culture. We no longer focus on the pinnacles of classical periods, nor do we consider them as objects of contemplation in order to be lifted out of our pedestrian ordinariness. Such an attitude resulted from a restrictive view of literature as a model to help us in our lives—a view that was bound to assume normative validity at the expense of other views. This exclusion concealed the degree to which literature, as a reaction to reality, opened up this reality by interpreting it.

Today it is the multifarious need for interpretation prevalent in our lives that turns literature into a paradigm quite different from the contemplation of the aura emanating from the classical masterpiece. It has ceased to be an imaginary museum[23] such as served in nineteenth-century culture to underpin the aesthetic consciousness, which defined itself by exceeding empirical realities. Instead, it reveals the vast number of ways in which human faculties can be used to open up the world in which we live. What makes literature so fascinating and so relevant today is the discovery that all our activities are permeated by acts of interpretation—indeed, that we live *by* interpreting.

Through interpretation we establish something that will correspond to the needs of a particular situation without laying claim to any normative validity for other situations. Thus, interpretation entails an attempt to pin down meaning; but, through this very precision, it also makes such meaning strictly nontransferable. It is an attitude geared to the changeability of situations, with the objective of stabilizing them for our pragmatically oriented actions. Therefore it has to be determinate and open at the same time, since the managing of changing situations necessitates an awareness of what underlies and thus guides our acts of interpretation. Only if we catch sight of these presuppositions will comprehension ensue. Interpretation, then, is a never-ending process of directing ourselves in the world, and literature provides an exemplary form of this process in that it is a reaction to the world accompanying its ever-changing situations. Thus, it objectifies something inherent in our disposition, as the accommodation of ourselves in the world requires a constant editing of reality. Man is an interpreting animal, and in this respect literature is an integral feature of our makeup. It may be nothing but a game, yet as a game it allows us to simulate an inexhaustible variety of trial runs, far in excess of what life may demand of us.

SINCE LITERATURE ITSELF is a form of interpretation, it must be linked to the real world. Consequently, it cannot be abstracted from reality—the ideal of autonomous Art—and it cannot replace reality—the ideal of the Paris revolutionaries. Nor can it merely imitate reality, as was claimed by the concept of mimesis. What, then, *does* it do?

According to Dieter Wellershoff,

> Writing has increasingly assumed the character of a *Probierbewegung* [testing or experimental movement], which advances constantly from place to place, enthralled by the endeavour to communicate the unspeakable. Criticism will have to be geared to this endeavour; and, indeed, it is a supporting form of its articulation. It, too, has to become an act of surveying of what lies beyond the familiar and hence can no longer be guided by so-called eternally valid norms. It is as if fantasy had thrust itself into realms outside itself, in which our as yet unarticulated lives strive for cognizance of themselves.[24]

These "testing movements" of literature are directed to hidden and as yet unknown dimensions of our lives. The world we live in is always an interpreted world, and we are conditioned by world-pictures and organizations that, because of their successful operations, we take for reality itself. But all our organizations are in fact solutions to problems, and even if they are successful, these solutions will still bring about further problems, since they must exclude elements of reality in order to achieve their success. Literature is preoccupied with precisely these exclusions—those aspects that have been omitted, ignored, displaced, and the like in order that our world may be stabilized by its institutions. In this respect, literature certainly depends on given structures in the real world—but not in order to perfect or to imitate them; on the contrary, literature serves to bring to our attention the price we must always pay for the pragmatically oriented sense of security.

On the one hand, we cannot do without the institutions, organizations, and world-pictures that reduce the contingency of reality and enable us to come to terms with it. On the other hand, we cannot come to terms with the price that we must pay. Now, what happens if we want the security *and* the return of whatever had to be sacrificed to gain security? In terms of the function of literature, there are two possible answers to this question; but they are answers that appear irreconcilable.

THE FIRST ANSWER is the widely held view that literature is Utopian fantasy: it embodies that which does not yet exist but ought to exist. Adorno has put it succinctly: "[W]hat is not is nevertheless promised through the fact that it appears."[25]

The problem here is with the nature of Utopia itself. Literature would have to present the deficiencies of the present as if they were correctible; in other words, literature would have to incorporate into the present what is needed to make it perfect. But if literature embodied a counterbalance to existing conditions in order to repair their deficiencies, it would be nothing more than the extrapolation of a bad reality turned, as it were, upside down. And this would mean imposing specific aims upon literature, tying it inescapably to the conditions of a given society in order to make it serve the needs of that society. If this were so, the solutions provided would at best arouse a historical interest and would lose their immediacy of appeal for succeeding generations.

Furthermore, the Utopian concept would set literature and society in diametrically opposed positions: literature would then be reduced to acting as a contrast or counterbalance to reality, without the vast range of *different* reactions that in fact it does incorporate. Such a concept is an offshoot of logocentristic thinking—a category that applies least of all to literature. Furthermore, it would imply the demise of literature if, by some revolutionary event, the Utopian reflection were to become reality. We all know that Trotsky made this forecast, now hushed up in Marxist thinking in view of a flourishing Social Realism.

The Utopian concept fails to explain the special position that literature occupies in our culture, perhaps not least because such a concept is based on the now superseded idea that we are capable of perfecting ourselves. Finally the suspicion looms large that literature once again wants to turn itself into reality.

LITERATURE REFERS TO things that are suppressed, unconscious, inconceivable, and perhaps even incommensurable, but this does not mean that a view of the invisible must necessarily be Utopian. The urge to present whatever is beyond the range of conscious life has its roots in something other than a desire for completeness, let alone perfection. Nietzsche once said of Art that it is functionally allied to the predicaments of the human situation;[26] less dramatically, we could say that literature relates to what prevailing organizations of reality have made unavailable. These unavailable territories mark the boundaries beyond which the systems cannot work, and they are in themselves featureless. They resist conceptualization by the conscious mind and can only be conjured provisionally into shape through arrangements of language such as those found in literature. The arrangements can take the form of narratives, sequences of images, repetitions and contrasts of sound, or any of the other literary structures that help release the invisible self for the performing, responding self to view. Now, world-pictures and social and thought systems come into being as a means of tackling that which initially eludes our grasp; but they, in turn, cause other ungraspables to emerge, so that there can never be a complete coverage of all eventualities. Awareness of this fact is not implanted in the systems themselves; if it were, they would continually be forced to restructure themselves in order to counteract the blind spots they inevitably produce, thus rendering themselves incapable of fulfilling their objective of establishing order. Literature, in turn, deals with the inescapable residue that escapes the mastery of the systems concerned. The manner in which it does this is not featureless but conditioned by the achievements through which the various organizations of reality have coped with contingency.

These various ungraspables can be brought to the fore by being cast in imaginary shapes. Literature makes them conceivable, because the stories it tells and the images it features employ techniques of perceiving and imagining identical to those that operate in our daily activities. Thus, literature generates the illusion of a perception, so that the inconceivable may gain presence by being staged through a sequence of images.

Therefore, literature does not head toward a future Utopia so much as continue the process begun by myth. Like myth, it takes hold of the ungraspable, or rather *appears* to take hold of it. Yet it simultaneously discloses that the outcome is only to be taken *as if* it were real. From this results a close correspondence between literature and reality. It gives form to what the very success of the organizing systems leaves behind and makes it conceivable as the unconscious level of the world we live in.

It is in this respect that literature is a continuation of myth, whose main function consisted in allaying primeval terror through its images. It is different from myth in that it spotlights the unavailable, which it draws out into the open through its stories and images.

As such, it may even enable us to visualize what gave rise to the split between the available and the inaccessible; but as the latter will vary according to what our ways of worldmaking have made available, clearly the origin of the split will vary, too. Consequently, literature, like myth, can never be brought to an end, for every reality must perforce produce its own attendant irreality. The very attempt to bring literature to an end would itself have to be a piece of literature.

By highlighting simultaneously both the repressive impulse of our world-pictures and the displacement caused by them, literature allows the reader momentarily to bridge the difference through a process that does not otherwise occur in life. Because it conjures up an image of the origin out of which this split arose, literature makes perceivable what is otherwise sealed off from cognitive penetration. Yet picturing what eludes our grasp in the incessant effort to accommodate ourselves to the world serves only to indicate how we conceive the inconceivable and why we conceive of it in such kaleidoscopically changing imagery. Since the impenetrability of that origin inscribes itself insistently into all of literature's ideas, it turns them into pure semblance. At this point the question of why we should want to think the unthinkable at all arises.

Here we enter into the realms of cultural anthropology. The extraordinary duality of thinking the unthinkable, picturing the inaccessible, bridging the unbridgeable—all this has its roots in the decentered position of man: he is, but he does not have himself.[27] Wanting to have oneself as one is, means needing to know *what* one is. Thus, we ourselves are marked by a duality that constantly seeks to be reconciled but never can be. From this irreconcilable split arises the need for representation, the need for images that can bridge the unbridgeable. This is why literature can never be reality but remains a form of semblance that—for all our awareness of its fictionality—is nevertheless indispensable. We live, as it were, on the subsidies of fantasy, not because fantasy in this sense allows an escape or because it projects a realizable image of some future society. Instead, through the changing images of fantasy, which stage what we are, it enables us to overcome our own duality, according to the changing requirements of our social and historical situations.

The extent to which literature expresses our social and historical self-understanding is also the extent to which it helps us to gain insight into the nature of our imagination—that faculty that seeks to achieve what our nature forbids: namely, the state of being and, at the same time, of knowing what it is to be. Literature as a means of insight into the workings and functions of the imagination, and as a means of access to that uniquely human equipment that comes into operation when all our faculties have reached the limits of their capabilities—this is a subject with which literature itself is perennially concerned; and this no doubt is an area that the literary critic will also be bound to explore.

TEN
KEY CONCEPTS IN CURRENT LITERARY THEORY AND THE IMAGINARY (1978)

n the last ten years, literary theory has made a powerful impact on criticism, giving new direction to a discussion that was losing itself down a very blind alley. But despite this impact, it is still dogged by an unmistakable element of ingenuousness as evinced not least by its opalescent character. What exactly *is* literary theory? Does it mean theorizing about literature, or about possible means of access to literature? If the distinction between the two has not yet been adequately brought out, this is mainly because literary theory sprang not from any intensified study of literature so much as from the parlous state of literary criticism at the universities — a state that it was meant to remedy. Literature has, to a large extent, lost its social validity in contemporary society, and it was the attempt to counteract this erosion that led to the breakthrough of theory; but this, in turn, brought out into the open problems inherent in literary theory. As a reaction to the crisis in the humanities, literary theory became increasingly dependent on the relationship between literature and society—a relationship that stood in urgent need of clarification. In this sense, literary theory was certainly linked to literature, but only under conditions that were relevant to the current preoccupations of that society. Consequently the study of literature had to be channeled into this conditionality, with the result that the needs of the moment somehow became norms governing the assessment of literature. Thus literary theory swiftly fell under the influence of prevailing social objectives, which as commonplaces of the time scarcely needed literature as a medium through which to articulate themselves. The result was that in these early stages, literary theory was more or less in the nature of an apology, for it was attempting to explain the uses of literature to a society whose appreciation of learning was at best confined to applauding the winners of TV quiz shows.

The endeavor to salvage the traditional status of literature in the face of new social requirements has formed a basic impulse for a rapidly developing diversification of literary theory over the last ten years. Its vindication of literature, however, has tended to gloss over the question of what exactly *is* this "old status" that is to be preserved. If the value of literature was traditionally based upon its social function, then literary theory could scarcely preserve that value once social circumstances had changed. And so even if the attempt to vindicate literature was the driving force behind the rise of this new theoretical endeavor, it is clear that such a theory could only lead into a cul-de-sac, given the changes in the values that provide such vindication. In the nineteenth century, literature formed the keystone of education in middle-class society, enriching all who came to it, regardless of rank and profession.[1] In a socialist society, literature is the heritage that is cherished because it heralds the intellectual liberation that had been neither socially nor politically possible in the times preceding the revolution. But literature as the keystone of education can fulfill its social function in completely different ways; the college at American universities provides a case in point. The close connection between the college and the humanities is certainly a tradition stretching right through to the present, but the college is also a gateway through which different social and ethnic groups will have to pass on their way to leading positions in their society; thus the humanities are still endowed with a social value that—although not entirely immune to the perceptible erosion—enjoys a social function, in marked contrast with the arts scene in Western Europe.

If literature has assumed its importance in the past as a result of social needs, literary theory can neither generate nor restore the one-time social validity of literature for contemporary society, and therefore it is at times permeated by a nostalgic streak, testifying involuntarily to the erstwhile prominence of literature in bourgeois society.

Moreover, the development of literary theory in the 1960s had another root cause. It was an attempt to break free from the impressionistic approach to literature which had reached both its zenith and its nadir in the lecture halls of German universities. Even after 1945, "encounter with literature" was still regarded, to use a description of Anatole France, as the great adventure of the soul among masterpieces; the impressionistic approach to literature— always colored by a claim to elitism and appealing in its esotericism only to the initiated—continued right up until the time when the heavy enrollment of the postwar generation opened up a gulf between what was taught and what students wanted to learn. Hence the postwar generation of critics began to query the validity of such personalized adventures. The need then was to find intersubjective means of access to literature which would make it possible to separate comprehension from subjective taste and to objectify insights into literature. Such attempts entailed putting emergent theories into practice, and this very "practice" shows clearly that literary theory is concerned primarily with approaches to literature and not with literature itself. Consequently, literary criticism strove to become a "science of literature" as borne out by the unfolding of a broad spectrum of methods, which in turn were hotly debated as regards their criteria.

Although some methods won more general favor than others, methodology nevertheless aroused controversy. And as each method could only succeed at the cost of various exclusions, the evident relativity of such methods led to the advance of pluralism as a universal concept. "Synthetic interpretation" became the fashionable order of the day:

> [P]utting prejudice on one side, it is therefore not difficult to extrapolate from the word *relativism* a whole series of very useful elements. One positive gain from this kind of cognition would be the abandonment of fixed guiding images, for only in this way can one escape the continuing effects of views and perceptions left over from earlier centuries or decades. The mental image of the "classical," for instance, stretched out to cover innumerable other periods, thus making them inaccessible to scholarly observation. It took an unconscionable length of time for attention to be focused upon the Baroque, Romantic, and Biedermeier periods, and domestic Realism. Only through such "relativism" is it possible to free ourselves from that which more committed times have felt to be "inimitable." The word *relativism* might therefore be defined as "uncommittedness" or "freedom of one's own opinion."[2]

The attraction of the pluralism concept, which still has its fair share of followers, lies in its methodological tolerance. The validation of anything or everything within its framework of relativity seems to offer a vantage point from which the basic assumptions of the various methods may be put in perspective and evaluated according to the range of their efficacy. But what sort of vantage point is it that sets itself up as a means of evaluating without offering any concrete base of its own? A method only becomes a method by way of its assumptions, which must perforce favor specific aspects of the literary text, to the exclusion or relegation of others. Pluralism renounces any such methodologically essential preconceptions, and so it can never itself be accounted a method.

This would not matter if it were not for the fact that the concept of pluralism is related to the evaluation of individual methods and their results. Indeed, it is through this relation that pluralism stakes its claim to methodology, setting itself up as a frame of reference for prevailing methods precisely by renouncing the constitutive conditions that underlie both method and theory. Therefore, it is interesting to note that the champions of pluralism put forward various arguments comparable to methodological assumptions, which would—if developed to their logical conclusion—come into at least a latent conflict with the relativism they advocate. For instance:

> In the context of such observations, literary history could also teach us to view each individual work of art as a component part of an eternal reflection which never reaches its goal but is nevertheless moving in a specific direction or, at least, should be moving in that direction. For only in this way does each new style, each historical innovation take on its particular significance within the overall process of history, thus assuming—despite all relativity—some small "trait of eternity" as it takes its place in the apparently endless process of human self-realization.[3]

The "trait of eternity" behind the process of history shows itself at least structurally as a methodological assumption that would take on the character of a method to the degree in which the blurred connotations of the "trait of eternity" become clearer.

As methodology, pluralism is a sort of sterile hermeneutics, for it cannot even pinpoint the relation of one method to another, let alone theorize about them. If one defines methods as means of solving problems, one need only glance at the present-day mass of critical methods to see the extent to which solutions in turn produce new problems. The fact that methods prevail for a while and then lose their position of dominance shows that their very achievements are based on the exclusion of facets that gradually begin to demand attention, thus invalidating those methods. This reactive process highlights the limitations and the conditionality of each method— and it is inevitable that any solution should ultimately be pushed aside by the material it has failed to encompass. It follows, then, that whatever method is used will evince first and foremost a distinctive, individualized attitude toward the literary text, thus fanning out the plurality of methods into vantage points for reciprocal observation. The only way in which pluralism might lay claim to being a method in itself would be if it actually focused upon this reactive relationship between methods. But then its distinguishing feature would no longer be relativism; its concern would be to describe the range of individual methods and to define the limits of their application. This, however, would no longer correspond to the concept of pluralism as we understand it today; in actual fact, it would amount to self-liquidation. For the evaluation of efficiency and deficiency—which might even allow the critic to deduce the deficiencies from the achievements—necessitates a distinction not only between methods but also between method and theory.

Theories generally provide premises, which lay the foundation for the framework of categories, whereas methods provide the tools for processes of interpretation. Thus the phenomenological theory, for instance, explores the mode of existence of the artwork; the hermeneutic theory is concerned with the observer's understanding of himself when confronted with the work; the gestalt theory focuses upon the perceptive faculties of the observer as brought into play by the work. All three theories are based upon very different premises: ontological for the phenomenological theory, historical for the hermeneutic, and operational for the gestalt. Distinctive assumptions are made which reveal a particular mode of access to the work of art, although they do not represent a technique of interpretation. Theories must undergo a definite transformation if they are to function as interpretative techniques. Thus the bases laid down by the three theories above must be transformed into (1) the strata model, (2) question-and-answer logic, and (3) the concepts of schema and correction.

There is, in fact, a hermeneutic relationship between theory and method. Every theory embodies an abstraction of the material it is seeking to categorize. If the degree of abstraction is the precondition for the success of categorization, then, clearly, the theory tends to screen off the individuality of the material, whereas it is the central function of interpretative methods to bring out and elucidate this very individuality. Thus the theory provides a framework of categories, while the method, in turn, provides the conditions whereby the basic assumptions underlying the theory will be differentiated by the results emerging from individual analysis.

Theories generally assume plausibility through closure of the framework provided, but in the realm of art they often attain closure only through the introduction of metaphors. Polyphonic harmony (the strata of the work merging together) is the favorite metaphor of phenomenological theory; the fusion of horizons (between the past experience embodied in the text and the disposition of the recipient) is a metaphor basic to hermeneutics; and the interrelation between making and matching (adapting inherited schemata to the world perceived) is a metaphor favored by gestalt theory. The metaphor performs the necessary function of finishing off the system, for only if the system is closed can it put on the mantle of a theory. As methods need not trouble themselves with basic premises—for these are laid down by the theory—their proximity to the text serves to elucidate the concrete significance of polyphonic harmony, fused horizons, and inherited schemata to be transformed by a new reality. By translating the central metaphors of the theory into the concrete terms of various perceptions, the methods lend stability to the theories at precisely those points where their efficacy reaches its limits. This concrete processing of problems left open by the theory itself constitutes, in turn, a practical application of the possibilities inherent in the theory. In this sense, the method clears up the problems arising from the theory's basic attempt at abstraction from the individuality of the material, thereby utilizing the explanatory potential of the theory to chart the territory that the latter had already signposted.

So far we have simply indicated the tasks that pluralism ought to be setting itself. However, so long as a mere collection of assumptions and presuppositions masquerades one minute as theory and the next as method, and receives official blessing on both its assumed identities, literary criticism will continue to be in the state of confusion which the pluralists seek to preserve in the name of freedom. It must be pointed out, though, that pluralism is not a concept in itself. As eclectic syncretism, it is an implicit confession of indecision in the face of a multiplicity of competing theories and methods and the need to relate them to one another.

Now if we delve into the welter of theories and methods and try to ascertain the basic conditions of their respective frameworks, we will find that there are certain recurrent key terms (*structure, function, communication*) which are employed in textual analysis. The significance of these terms stretches way beyond the sphere of literary criticism, for they are indicators of the intellectual climate of our time. Although they vary as to their relative importance and interrelatedness within each of the critical concepts, they are nevertheless organizing features of almost all concepts advanced so far in literary criticism. For the investigation of literary texts, they offer an equal number of advantages and disadvantages. The advantages consist in the fact that the key terms in question not only govern literary analysis but enjoy an almost universal application in contemporary science; thus they function as codes, allowing us to translate the literary text into terms equally applicable to contemporary consciousness. Through this homology the disadvantages come to the fore, as the very translatability by way of the key terms tends to obscure and distort an important potential of the literary text.

If the key concepts of structure, function, and communication have such an all-pervading importance in present-day theoretical discourse—providing constitutive elements for theories and methods extant—then it is to them that we must turn our attention. Consequently, our task is not to focus primarily on structural poetics, aesthetics of reception and aesthetics of response, Marxism, analytical language theory, information theory, gestalt theory, phenomenology, hermeneutics, and psychoanalysis so much as on the efficacy and achievements of these concepts, which with varying degrees of emphasis shape the respective frameworks of contemporary theoretical reasoning.

Structure, function, and communication, as component parts of all literary theories and methods, reduce the literary text to the scale of their own dimensions. Obviously, structural, functional, and communication-oriented reductions will each give a different slant to the text, and so the question arises as to the conditions given in and by the text, which appear to provoke such a reduction of its potential. Each of the key concepts is bound to open up a different access to the text, thereby highlighting some aspects of it while pushing others into the background. The fact that this is possible cannot be explained simply by the assumptions of the respective theories and methods. The text itself must contain the preconditions that enable the different approaches to be effective. And this fact in turn cannot be grasped in terms of structure, function, or communication. But what cannot be grasped is always a challenge demanding attention.

One of the key concepts we have listed, that of structure, has become the scientific ideology of our century. It has proved indispensable in all walks of life, regardless of social and political systems. In view of the ever-mounting flood of information, it fulfills a typically modern need by enabling data to be arranged and related according to patterns that will classify, store, and retrieve information. The fact that structuralism has now assumed an ontological character in the eyes of its champions and its opponents is due to its concrete success in meeting a contemporary demand. And this success has given reality to the idea of structure itself, as is constantly hammered into us by studies ranging from the structure of archaic family relationships to that of the literary text.

The notion of structure appears to be firmly grounded in language itself, whose organization, in turn, is given a paradigmatic representation by this very notion. Its distinguishing features are "(1) the whole, (2) the differential relationships between the structural elements, (3) the immanence of structure."[4] As the literary text *is* language, the structure concept offers an obvious key for its decoding, since there will either be a repetition of the structures of language itself, or the text will be understood as a secondary system using language structures to form its own individual structure. The former concept corresponds to that developed by Barthes and the latter, to that of Lotman.

Ascertaining the structures of a literary text means classifying and listing its component parts in order to assemble the inventory of its structural features. In a novel, these would comprise structures of narration, time and space, descriptions, presentation of character, and so forth. Such classifications lead to a constant differentiation of the elements of the text, which in the end amount to no more than a carefully assembled catalogue. Propp, in his famous study of fairy tales, was therefore able to distinguish thirty-one different structural features of the genre, and in principle there would seem to be no limit to the number of structures and structural features that a basically taxonomy oriented structuralism might discover. Neither the compilation nor the fastidious discrimination of features listed, however, need to be arbitrary. Each is governed by the ontological assumption of an immanent structure whose hidden individuality is brought out in proportion to linguistic differentiation between its various features.

The ontological assumption that conditions our view of the text as an assembly of structures also leads us to see the different potential relations between elements as something structured. The binary opposition of these elements forms the basic structure of these relations. This opposition originally derived from the structural description of phonology, then realized its massive explanatory potential in Lévi-Strauss's description of archaic cultures, and has undergone innumerable mutations during its application to the analysis of literary texts. The relating of elements in the literary text reveals itself as the structure of applied techniques. Some structural analyses of texts actually describe the work of art as "a sum of techniques."[5] For it is only through the techniques that the separate elements can be combined to produce the subject matter of the text. Contrast, polarity, difference, repetition, parallelism, successiveness, concatenation, counterpoise, juxtaposition, progression— these are all techniques of relating elements which bring about the syntagmatic articulation of subject matter.

In this context it is of minor importance whether the techniques are seen as variations or violations of the binary system. In both cases, the binary system is the basis for the relating of the elements:

in the one, its potential is to be fully exploited, and in the other it is a "minus function" that is presupposed but not realized. However, as the "sum of techniques" a structural theory is also taxonomic as far as the relations of elements are concerned. For such a sum has no limits; it assumes its potential extension by way of the presupposed immanent structure, and the more concrete this becomes, the denser must be the techniques applied.

The combinations of textual patterns, just like the syntactic links between linguistic structures, serve to produce the semantic potential of the text—in other words, its meaning. The extent to which a description of meaning-production contains the idea of purpose (integral to the concept of structure) can clearly be seen from the dominance of the binary technique: meaning arises out of the opposition of two factors that are merged into a single gestalt, thus establishing the whole that typifies the structure concept.

Structural analysis of the literary text therefore makes possible an intersubjective and plausible description of the composition of the subject matter; it also facilitates description of the production of meaning. In this respect the model of language, which the structure concept seeks to copy, holds good. But this very achievement also reveals certain limitations of the structure concept, for structuralism favors the semantic dimension of the text, and indeed turns it into an end in itself. This would only make sense if the structure really were ultimate, but certain doubts arise here, which are nourished rather than diminished by the structuralists themselves.

If one surveys the different concepts that have been advanced by outstanding advocates of structuralism, one is struck by the variety of forms it may take. Lévi-Strauss, for instance, equated it with the binary system; Jakobson, on the other hand, linked it with symmetry.[6] Furthermore, if structuralism represents a system that is identical to that of language, one cannot help wondering why the system does not change when it is forced to absorb new elements. The system of language is a natural one, which changes the semantic fields of words when new elements come on the scene, for the whole system must adapt itself to new elements if it is to incorporate them.[7] This alone shows that the structure concept is an artificial system, whose mode of operation differs considerably from that of natural systems simply through the fact that its taxonomic classifications can be indefinitely extended without affecting the system, let alone changing it altogether. The question therefore arises as to whether the close connection between structuralism and language, and the homology claimed for the two systems, might not in fact only be metaphorical,[8] serving just to give the necessary legitimacy to the analytical operations of the structure concept. There is also the objection raised by Eco: "If there is such a thing as the *Ultimate Structure*, this must be indefinable: there is no metalanguage that could encompass it. If it is identified, then it is not the *ultimate*. The *ultimate* is that which—hidden and ungraspable and nonstructured—produces new phenomena."[9]

But these objections may still not invalidate the structural approach to describing the literary text. Jonathan Culler ends his account of structuralist poetics with the following observation: "Structuralism has succeeded in unmasking many signs; its task must now be to organize itself more coherently so as to explain how these signs work. It must try to formulate the rules of particular systems of convention rather than simply affirm their existence. The linguistic model, properly applied, may indicate how to proceed, but it can do little more than that."[10] Once the presence of structures has been established in the literary text, attention falls exclusively on factors given by the text itself. Even if the structuring of the text embraces such different elements as conventions, linguistic habits and attitudes, changing viewpoints and social roles, the basic tendency of a structuralist operation will nevertheless assert itself by relating them into an intratextual coherence that assumes a determinate form through the resultant semantic dimension of the text. It is here that we witness the reduction brought about by the structure concept. The inventory of its elements produces an order, the sum of its techniques relates the elements to one another, and there thus emerges a semantic dimension that constitutes the end product of the text—but all this sheds no light whatsoever on why such a product should emerge, how it functions, and who is to make use of it and to what end. These questions are not merely of a critical nature, for language—as the model that the structure concept seeks to emulate—offers us an insight that is both relevant and revealing: "One can only understand language if one understands more than language."[11]

The problems begin where the efficacy of the structure concept ends. The objections are therefore not to be taken as criticism but as indications of problems arising out of the explanatory potency of the structure concept itself. If we pursue the language parallel, we might say that the structure concept allows for a minute description of texts, but it cannot describe, let alone explain, more than texts. And just as language only becomes meaningful through its application, so the structures of the literary text only become relevant through the function of that text. Indeed it might be claimed that only through the success of the structure concept has the importance of function come to the fore. In this respect, the key concepts of function and communication are dependent on the structure concept, and in no way invalidate it. They build on it, and they seek to settle the problems that it has left in its wake—though in doing so they raise new problems, as far as the literary text is concerned.

Structuralism leaves behind a problem that cannot be satisfactorily solved even by the many variants that the concept had produced. The problem is the meaning of meaning. In describing the techniques of the literary text, we can show how their interplay leads to the assembly of meaning, but this meaning as an end in itself remains something unrelated and abstract. The structure concept actually prevents us from inquiring into the nature of the meaning, for such an inquiry would presuppose a frame of reference beyond the structure, so that the latter could no longer be regarded as "ultimate." Since meaning remains an abstract entity produced by the structure concept, and since the latter bars the way to any ontological definition, it is clear that one can only find the meaning of meaning by seeking the function of meaning. And this is the main reason why in literary theory the structure concept has given such stimulus to the function concept. For the meaning of meaning *is* its function.

The function concept has been given its solid foundation by General Systems Theory, which has reversed the priority between structure and function, whereby the unrelatedness of meaning—as an offshoot of the structure concept—is given its concrete significance through its application. Luhmann has some apposite comments to make on this subject:

> The deficiencies of the structural-functional General Systems Theory lie in its basic premise: namely, that the structure concept precedes the function concept. Because of this, the structural-function theory deprives itself of the chance to problematize structures and actually to seek the meaning of structure-building and system-building. This possibility does arise, however, if we reverse the order of these basic concepts: i.e., if the function concept precedes the structure concept. A functional-structural theory *can* seek the function of system structures without having to presuppose an all-embracing systems structure as point of reference for the search.[12]

These observations generally hold true of the literary text, where the order and the formation of structures depend on the function that the text has to fulfill. For literary texts represent intentional approaches to the world; as such they are, of course, structured, but the structuredness is governed entirely by the apparent intentionality. Thus it follows that "[f]unctional theory is System/Context theory."[13]

Literary texts are always related to contexts; it is this relation that endows them with the concrete meaning of their structures and application. The function concept focuses upon the context and elucidates the two-way relationship between text and world. Literary texts collect and store elements from many other texts, which may themselves be literary or may—as "contexts"—reflect social norms and conventions. The selection from texts and contexts lays down the direction from which the world is to be approached through the literary text in question. This basic two-way relationship between literary text and sociocultural context underlies the arrangement of textual structures, turning the encapsulated elements into signs showing how the text is meant to impinge on the social and literary systems from which selections have been made. This reciprocal relationship governs both the arrangement of textual structures and the meaningfulness of the structuring process. Thus we may say that the function concept designates the relationship between text and extratextual realities, and the meaning of the structures within the text is revealed through their intended application.

The interconnection described is guided and influenced by the historical needs and attitudes of the prevailing zeitgeist. The function concept therefore no longer has the systematic reference that the structure concept was still possessed of, but it is this very absence of sticking points that enables it to indicate the deficiencies or conspicuous needs of a given historical situation. The structure-formation of the text will vary according to the requirements of these situations—a fact that becomes clear if we compare, for instance, the Russian formalist view of the function of literary texts with that of the Marxist. For the Russian formalists, art has to de-automate perception, in order to "enforce a new vision of things and so correct one's own relation to the world."[14] For this purpose it was necessary for the structures in the literary text to be seen as running contrary to the workings of perception, so that the resultant alienation would draw attention to the automated modes we use in gaining access to the world. In certain pronouncements of Marxist aesthetics, on the other hand, the function concept is far less situation-oriented.

AVENUES FOR EXPLORATION

Art, according to Christian Enzensberger, must compensate for the deficiencies of meaning that arise out of the dehumanized process of industrial production in bourgeois society. The function of art /Marxist is to make possible that which has been excluded by the dehumanized process of industrial production—namely, fulfillment of meaning. This leads to a special organization of structures in the work of art, aimed at making the function of the meaning effective. Thus Enzensberger's basic thesis runs along the following lines:

> [T]he beauty of art is its Utopian order. It has the same structure as the factually realized meaningful relation between the individual and the society for which he produces: (a) as a productive and consistent reciprocal determination between the whole and its parts, with expansion on both sides through the necessary interrelation of all parts and their alignment to fulfill an overall meaningful aim; (b) as liberation of the individual from the oppression of his own interests and of direct business and consumer pressures as well as the gratification of his own fantasies. The work of art is the democracy of its parts and the last semantic symbol for the forgotten, generally social purpose of material production, and hence for Utopia.[15]

Such a function is almost diametrically opposed to that described by the Russian formalists. For them, the function consisted in undermining our automated, established modes of perception, which required a substantial degree of discontinuity in the organization of textual structure. But for the Marxists the function consists in compensating for deficiencies, so that the structural components of the text must join together in harmony; otherwise they would not be able to close the gaps of meaning arising out of the industrial production process in bourgeois society. Discord versus harmony—the structural organization will depend entirely on the function of the text in relation to the world.

The function need not be so extreme, however, as in the two examples cited. The history of literary functions shows clearly the different ways in which literature relates to extratextual systems and the extent to which its structures are regulated by the situation to which it represents a reaction. If the literary text represents an act of intentionality directed toward a given world, then the world it approaches will not simply be repeated in the text; it will undergo various adjustments and corrections, as testified by the examples cited. Hence the relationship between text and extratextual systems functions according to the principle of homeostasis, balancing out a reality that is problematic or is made problematic by the text itself.[16] Thus the text/context relation may result in the negation or affirmation of the social or aesthetic values called into question—the respective function in turn leading to different structure formations in the text.

There is no denying that the function concept also has limited scope as an explanatory model for literary texts. If these are defined according to their function, there are bound to be areas of doubt and indefinability. For the relation of text to world—incorporating literary allusions and social norms, together with the intentional approach to the world that they give rise to—is conditioned by historical situations and is therefore entirely pragmatic in character. Any functional definition of a text requires a far greater amount of interpretation than does an analysis of its structures. The latter can confine itself to classifying the structures used; the former deals with the far less tangible fields of relationships and "reality."

Just like the structure concept, the function concept reaches its own limits by way of its achievements. In elucidating the relation of text to extratextual realities, it also elucidates the problems that the text sought to settle. As a result of this, it is possible to reconstruct a past world and thus restore historical experience that can be grasped—even though it can never become a concrete reality—in the present. But in uncovering this dimension of the text, the function concept can only cope with its genesis; it has no answer to the question of that dimension's continued validity. The question of validity, however, is of vital importance to literary theory, for we need to know how it happens that a literary text born under the conditions of a specific historical situation can outlast that situation and maintain its freshness and its impact in different historical circumstances. Furthermore, the function concept remains an abstraction until its relations to extratextual systems are more closely defined by way of a potential recipient, who is called upon to concretize the very relations mapped out by the text. The function concept itself, however, provides no slot for the recipient, without whom the pragmatic application foreshadowed in the text/context relationship remains unactivated and thus nonexistent.

The gap created by the function concept can only be closed by a concept of communication. It is only recently that communication has taken up a central position in literary theory, but it has swiftly assumed an almost universal character. Unlike structural description and functional definition, the communication-oriented approach dispenses with all a priori premises. Its one concern is to clarify processes of transmission and reception, and its stunning success in literary theory is largely due to the fact that its operational nature is not hedged in by clearly defined or historically conditioned presuppositions — such as those under which the structure concept has to labor.

The model of text-reader interaction forms the basis of the communication concept. The reader "receives" the text, and guided by its structural organization, he fulfills its function by assembling its meaning. From a communications point of view, structures are in the nature of pointers or instructions, which arrange the way in which a text is transferred to the reader's mind to form the intended pattern. In literary theory, therefore, the communication concept incorporates those of structure and function, and indeed cannot do without them if it is to describe the processes of transmission and reception.

The communication concept allows for the fact that every literary text contains a certain potential for innovation. This potential may be of different kinds. A structural order that undermines our automated perception of the world may be as innovative as one that recodes literary allusions and social norms by placing them in a new context. Communication presupposes an initial nonalignment of or asymmetry between text and reader, for the latter is to be presented with information and experiences that do not form a part of his existing and stabilized repertoire of knowledge and experience.

The communication-oriented approach also allows the literary text to be grasped as a process. The nature of this process is determined by the interaction between text and reader. The innovations of a text arise principally from the recoding of selected literary allusions as well as social norms and values; the effectiveness of this recoding depends on the degree to which the reader's own codes and conventions are pushed into a background against which a new experience can be gained. At the same time, the reader's code guides the selections that make the text/world relation or the organization of intratextual structures concrete for him. For if the new experience can only be gained against the background of familiar experiences, clearly the selection principle behind the text/world relation and the rest must be governed in the first place by what is familiar to the reader. Thus text and reader act upon one another in a self-regulating process.[17] Viewed from this standpoint, the text itself is a kind of process, leading from interaction of structures to interaction with extratextual realities, and ultimately to interaction with the reader.

The question left unanswered by the function concept—namely, the continuing validity of the literary work—can now be approached in terms of the communication achieved by the work. The text's selective utilization of the reader's own faculties results in his having an aesthetic experience whose very structure enables him to obtain insight into experience acquisition; it also enables him to imagine a reality that is real as a process of experience, though it can never be real in a concrete sense.

The three key concepts of current literary theory—structure, function, and communication—have joined together through a sort of historical chain reaction. The dominance of the structure concept led to the emergence of the function concept, and this has led in turn to an ever-increasing interest in communication. The historical sequence of the respective booms enjoyed by each of the concepts has a certain element of inevitability, as the links in this chain are the deficiencies of each preceding concept. The structure concept allows a taxonomic arrangement of the textual components and a description of meaning-production through the structuring techniques. The meaning, however, remains an abstraction, and so the function concept gives concrete form to the abstraction. It is therefore not taxonomic, but concerns itself with the text/world relationship. It incorporates the structure concept, but in turn runs out of steam once it has pinpointed the pragmatic purpose of the text. The effect or implementation of this purpose remains, once again, an abstraction. And so this abstraction, in turn, is concretized by the communication concept, which shows how the pragmatic function becomes a reality by being conveyed to the recipient of the work. The pivot on which the whole reading experience turns is the interaction concept. Just as communication incorporates structure and function as its own preconditions, so too does the interaction concept incorporate both the taxonomic order of structures and the relation of text to world.

The importance of these concepts for literary theory lies in the fact that, while each represents a different mode of access to literature, they all enable us to discuss the fictional text in terms of referential discourse. It follows, then, that there must be a vital difference between fictional and theoretical discourse, if the one—for the purpose of our understanding—is to be translated into terms of the other. The difference between fictional discourse (the literary text) and theoretical or criteria-governed discourse provokes an intellectual activity, in the course of which the literary text tends to become equated with the criteria provided by whichever key concepts we use when seeking to grasp the "nature" of the literary text. The understanding that we are seeking has been described by Culler as "naturalization," which means that the gap between fictional and criteria-governed discourse is bridged by superimposing the rationality of existing frames of reference upon the literary text. "Naturalization proceeds on the assumption that action is intelligible, and cultural codes specify the forms of intelligibility."[18] The intentional acts of our comprehension are therefore always attempts to subjugate fictional discourse to existing theoretical frameworks. "Naturalization" requires a degree of adaptation, and structure, function, and communication simply represent means of adaptation. However, it is evident that such means involve processes of reduction, since each concept is incapable of embracing the whole of the literary text. The chain reaction we have spoken about is already an obvious indication of the reduction involved, since each succeeding concept tries to cover the ground laid and left bare by its predecessor. There is no escaping this reductive process, even when the concept is primarily of an operational nature, and it is no doubt this fact that has led to the demand by aesthetic theorists for open concepts. In elucidating fictional discourse, it is argued, such concepts would at least temper, if not eliminate, the reductive character of the closed concept.[19] However, open concepts create their own problems, for in seeking to restrict reduction, they inevitably restrict the explanatory scope of the concept.

Our intentional acts of understanding will always result in an unavoidable reduction of the potential contained in the literary text, and this holds true for one reason in particular: these very acts are semantically oriented. The structure concept describes the production of meaning, the function concept gives concrete definition to the meaning, and the communication concept elucidates the experience of the meaning. In all cases, then, meaning—in spite of the different facets illuminated—is seen as the be-all and the end-all of the literary text. But is the semantic dimension of the text indeed the ultimate dimension? The very fact that it can be viewed from different perspectives (production, function, experience) raises doubts. Are we not led to surmise that the different concepts discussed—which are basically intentional acts of understanding—simply extrapolate their own semantic intentionality as the ultimate and hence constitutive quality of the literary text?

The doubts increase when we consider the different historical interpretations of individual works. If one work can be interpreted in different ways, it must contain this variety of meanings within itself, and so it can hardly be reducible to one single meaning. It would therefore seem futile to try and use a semantic model in order to develop criteria that would define the one and only meaning intended by an author. Using semantics to determine the semantic must lead either to aporia or to metaphysics, which alone can cope with the essence of meaning.

In this respect the key concepts of current literary theory have destroyed a certain naiveté, which still lingers on in areas of criticism where the establishment of a single meaning appears to be the only worthwhile pursuit. Although the key concepts remain semantically oriented, they nevertheless provide perspective and hence divergent views of what the semantic dimension, as the supposedly ultimate one, is like. This very diversification of meaning makes dubious the assumption that meaning is the be-all and end-all of the literary text.

In view of this situation the following thesis could be advanced: meaning as such is not the ultimate dimension of the literary text, but of literary theory, whose discourse is aimed at making the text translatable into terms of understanding. Such a translation presupposes that there is a dimension in the text which both provokes and stands in need of a semantic transformation in order that it may be linked up with existing frames of reference. It follows, then, that the *ultimate* dimension of the text cannot be semantic. It is what we might call *imaginary*—a term that harks back to the very origins of fictional discourse.

The imaginary is not semantic, because it is by its very nature diffuse, whereas meaning becomes meaning through its precision. It is the diffuseness of the imaginary that enables it to be transformed into so many different gestalts, and this transformation is necessary whenever this potential is tapped for utilization. Indeed fiction, in the broadest sense of the term, is the pragmatically conditioned gestalt of the imaginary. Its determinate form enables the imaginary not only to be organized but also, through this organization, to be utilized within given contexts. As the gestalt of the imaginary, fiction cannot be defined as counterfactual to existing realities. Fiction reveals itself as a product of the imaginary insofar as it lays bare its fictionality, and yet it appears to be a halfway house between the imaginary and the real. It shares with the real the determinateness of its form, and with the imaginary its nature of an 'As If'. Thus features of the real and the imaginary become intertwined, and their linkup is such that it both demands and conditions a continuing process of interpretation. For fiction always contains a represen-

AVENUES FOR EXPLORATION

tation of something, but its very fictionality shows that what is represented is merely an "image," is put in parentheses and thus accorded the status of an 'As If'. And this is neither totally real nor totally imaginary; the gestalt is too real to be imaginary, but its substance is too imaginary to be real. Thus fiction can never be identified either with the real or with the imaginary, and if the two are bracketed together through that which fiction represents, this does not mean that what is represented is the object of the representation; the object is the possibility of formulating what is represented in a different way from that given by the linguistic formulation. So there is a split between what is represented and what the representation stands for, and interpretation is an attempt, as it were, to heal the split by translating it into a semantic whole. The structure involved here is that of double meaning (manifest and latent meaning). Fiction, as we have seen, does not "mean" that which it represents, and so the linguistic manifestation serves as a pointer to a latent or hidden meaning to be uncovered by interpretation, thus endowing the 'As If' with a specific reference. In this process, the dimension of the imaginary is translated into that of the semantic. It follows, then, that the imaginary dimension of the text not only precedes the semantic but is conditional for its existence, and the latter would not be possible if semantics already embodied the be-all and end-all. Every concept of meaning that interpretation postulates as ultimate in fact turns out to be a concept of communication, adaptation, and translation, allowing the imaginary dimension of the text to be linked up, through acts of comprehension, to existing frames of reference or individual dispositions of recipients, who thus take the imaginary experience over into their own lives.

The linking-up is performed in different ways by the different concepts of current literary theory, but they are all characterized by the structure of double meaning as a basic mode of interpretation.[20] This may well explain why semiotics has been elevated to a dominant model of interpretation. For if the sign is a signifier serving to guide the "interpretand" to the formulation of the signified, then clearly the semiotic model shows how the structure of double meaning may be transformed into a formal, operational model of interpretation. As signifier and signified are interdependent in sign usage, the sign becomes meaningful only by its reference, and the reference, in turn, is given existence by the sign. The key concepts of structure, function, and communication follow this same interrelation of double meaning, their starting point being the fact that fiction is not identical with that which it represents—a fact that, as we have seen, indicates the presence of the imaginary as the ultimate dimension of the text.

In this context, we can also differentiate between interpretation and reception. The aim of interpretation, with its structure of double meaning, is to assemble meaning. It invests the imaginary with semantic determinacy. But as the imaginary is capable of different semantic translations, in accordance with whatever assumptions underlie the interpretation, the individual work has its own history of interpretations, just as literary theory has its own history of sequent, interdependent concepts. Reception, on the other hand, is not primarily a semantic process. It is a process of experiencing the imaginary gestalt brought forth by the text. Reception is the recipient's production of the aesthetic object along structural and functional lines laid down in the text. This experience of the text is aesthetic insofar as the recipient produces the object under conditions that do not or need not correspond to his habitual disposition. The aesthetic object is produced in the recipient's mind as a correlate of the text, and as such it is open to inspection by acts of comprehension; hence the business of interpretation, which translates the aesthetic object into a concrete meaning. Reception is therefore one step closer to the imaginary than interpretation, which can only seek verbally to give a semantic determination to the imaginary. This is why it is even possible to make reception—the experience of the imaginary—an object of interpretation. The diffuseness of the imaginary is further evinced by the concepts of interpretation themselves, which if not always open are very often highly metaphorical. These metaphorical concepts are not, in the last analysis, signs of a missing but findable precision; they are an expression of the imaginary that a code-governed discourse can only bring to view by offering metaphorical approximations.

The imaginary is a field that is only just opening up to literary theory, and there is no doubt that it is dependent upon all the factors that we have discussed here. However, charting this field requires the development of cultural-anthropological frames of reference which will enable us to inspect the imaginary as well as its protean manifestations in our innumerable fictions, and which consequently will enable interpretation to reflect upon itself. Existing assumptions must be reduced to mere heuristic preconditions, for each interpretative step must be accompanied by an awareness of its own limited scope. Prospecting the regions of the imaginary entails conveying the experience of an intangible pot of gold which is always within our reach whenever we need it and which offers us such wealth that even the coveted treasure of meaning is devalued to the level of a mere pragmatic concept.

ELEVEN
REPRESENTATION:
A PERFORMATIVE ACT

he following is an attempt to develop an implication of my essay "Feigning in Fiction."[1] I shall try to give a rough outline of how representation in literature is to be conceived, but the ideas put forward are of a tentative nature and could at best be called work in progress. The presentation will therefore be rather abstract and at times foreshortened.

The English term *representation* causes problems because it is so loaded. It entails or at least suggests a given that the act of representation duplicates in one way or another. Representation and mimesis have therefore become interchangeable notions in literary criticism, thus concealing the performative qualities through which the act of representation brings about something that hitherto did not exist as a given object. For this reason I am tempted to replace the English term *representation* with the German *Darstellung*, which is more neutral and does not necessarily drag all the mimetic connotations in its wake. In order to avoid macaronic language, however, I shall retain *representation*, which should always be read in the sense of *Darstellung*, that is, as not referring to any object given prior to the act of representation.

To conceive of representation not in terms of mimesis but in terms of performance makes it necessary to dig into the structure of the literary text, laying bare the levels and conditions out of which the performative quality arises. This archaeology of the act of representation begins at a layer that I shall call the doubling structure of fictionality, produced by the fictionalizing acts of the literary text. This doubling is the implication of the essay mentioned above, and I shall take it as a point of departure. The argument to be developed, then, is not cast in current linguistic, tropological, or deconstructivist terms, but rather in terms of our anthropological makeup, aiming to answer the question: What does representation—arising out of the doubling structure of fictionality—tell us about ourselves? In view of the rather common practice of equating literature with fictionality, a caveat must be made right at the beginning. Fictionality is not to be identified with the literary text, although it is a basic constituent of it. For this reason I refrain from using the word 'fiction' whenever I can and speak instead of fictionalizing acts. These do not refer to an ontologically given, but to an operation, and therefore cannot be identical to what they produce. An archaeology of representation in literature could not dispense with these fictionalizing acts that, in turn, gain their objective in the performative quality of representation into which they merge.

THE ACT OF selection which is integral to fictionality is a form of doubling. Each text makes inroads into extratextual fields of reference and by disrupting them creates an eventful disorder, in consequence of which both the structure and semantics of these fields are subjected to certain deformations, and their respective constituents are differently weighted according to the various deletions and supplementations. Thus each one is being reshuffled in the text and takes on a new form—a form that nevertheless includes and indeed depends on the function of that field in our interpreted world.

This function now becomes virtual and provides a background against which the operation of restructuring may stand out in relief, thus featuring the intention underlying the "coherent deformation."[2] In addition the act of selection splits up each field of reference, since the chosen elements can only take on their significance through the exclusion of others—this being the precondition for the eventful disorder, the resolution of which demands the assembly of a new meaning.

The act of selection also culls elements from other texts, but the resultant intertextuality should not be thought of in terms of blurring distinctions, let alone transcending the text to which reference has been made. On the contrary, the doubling process becomes even more complex, for the texts alluded to and the segments quoted begin to unfold unforeseeably, shifting relationships both in respect to their own contexts and to the new ones into which they have been transplanted. Whatever the relationships may be like, two different types of discourse are ever-present, and their simultaneity triggers a mutual revealing and concealing of their respective contextual references. From this interplay there emerges semantic instability that is exacerbated by the fact that the two sets of discourse are also contexts for each other, so that each in turn is constantly switching from background to foreground. The one discourse becomes the theme viewed from the standpoint of the other, and vice versa. The resultant dynamic oscillation between the two ensures that their old meanings now become potential sources for new ones. It is such transformations that give rise to the aesthetic dimension of the text, for what had long seemed closed is now opened up again. The more one text incorporates other texts, the more intensified will be the process of doubling induced by the act of selection. The text itself becomes a kind of junction, where other texts, norms, and values meet and work upon each other; as a point of intersection its core is virtual, and only when actualized—by the potential recipient—does it explode into its plurivocity.

The structure pinpointed in the act of selection also underlies the act of combination. Here the boundaries that are crossed are intratextual, ranging from lexical meanings to the constellation of characters. Once again the process should not be mistaken for an act of transcendence, because the various clusters—be they words with outstripped meanings or semantic enclosures exceeded or infringed by the characters—are inseparably linked together and thus mutually inscribe themselves into one another. Every word becomes dialogic, and every semantic field is doubled by another. Through this double-voiced discourse every utterance carries something else in its wake, so that the act of combination gives rise to a duplication of what is present by that which is absent—a process that often results in the balance being reversed and the present serving only to spotlight the absent. Thus what is said ceases to mean itself, and instead enables what is not said to become present. The double meaning engendered by the act of combination opens up a multifariousness of interconnections within the text.

The act of selection brings about a network of relationships by invoking and simultaneously deforming extratextual fields of reference, thereby giving rise to the aesthetic quality, while the act of combination—by inscribing the absent into the present—becomes the matrix of that aesthetic quality.

A further and similar doubling effect comes about through the literary text's disclosure of itself as fiction. This takes place on two different levels: that of the attitude to be imposed on the reader, and that of what the text is meant to represent. If the literary text reveals itself to be a staged discourse, asking only that the world it represents should be taken *as if* it were a real world, then the recipient has to suspend his or her natural attitude to the thing represented (i.e., the real world). This does not mean that the natural attitude is transcended, for it is still present as a virtualized background against which comparisons may be made and new attitudes may take their shape.

If we regard the world of the text as being bracketed off from the world it represents, it follows that what is within the brackets is separated from the reality in which it is normally embedded. Thus the bracketed world of the novel is not only to be seen as if it were a world, but it is also to be seen as a world that does not exist empirically. Consequently there will be a continual oscillation between the bracketed world and that from which it has been separated. The former therefore becomes a medium for revealing what has remained concealed in the empirical world, and whatever may be the relation between the two, it is the 'As If' world that brings about the interplay between them. Thus self-disclosed fictionality as an act of boundary-crossing causes the recipient's natural attitude to be doubled by the new attitude demanded of him, and the world of the text to be doubled by the world from which it has been bracketed off and whose reverse side is thus brought to the fore.

THE VARIOUS ACTS of fictionalizing carry with them whatever has been outstripped, and the resultant doubleness might therefore be defined as the simultaneity of the mutually exclusive. This formula may help us to describe the structure of the fictional component of literature. It also allows for certain distinctions that are pertinent to the literary text. As the simultaneity of the mutually exclusive, the literary text can be clearly set off from structures that govern our everyday world but are left behind by the coexistence of what is mutually incompatible. Even more important, fictionality also exceeds what psychoanalysis has come to describe as the "ego-rhythm," by inscribing the latent into the manifest or absence into presence. Primary and secondary processes are not usually telescoped into each other as, in the words of A. Ehrenzweig, "structured focusing" and "oceanic undifferentiation" tend to interlink rhythmically, thereby establishing what he calls the "ego-rhythm."[3] It is therefore interesting to note that Ehrenzweig considers the coexistence of structured focusing and oceanic undifferentiation/dedifferentiation as a basic condition for art.

Furthermore, only in dreams does a coexistence between primary and secondary process occur, which poses the question of the extent to which fictionality as the simultaneity of the mutually exclusive has its anthropological roots in the dream pattern, and the extent to which its various manifestations can be conceived as a form of rehearsing such patterns. Fictionality, then, might be viewed as a staging of what only dreaming normally allows.

If fictionality in literature exceeds both the structures of our everyday reality and our psychic patterning, it produces a specifically aesthetic quality. The coexistence of the mutually exclusive gives rise to a dynamic oscillation resulting in a constant interpenetration of things that are set off from one another without ever losing their difference. This tension ensuing from the attempt to resolve this ineradicable difference creates an aesthetic potential that, as a source of meaning, can never be adequately replaced by anything else. This does not imply that the fictional component of literature is the actual work of art; it implies that the fictional component is what makes the work of art possible.

Besides allowing us to pinpoint the aesthetic nature of fictionality in literature in its contrast to empirical reality, the simultaneity formula also enables us to distinguish literary fiction from that concept of fiction that has arisen from a logocentric way of thinking. Vaihinger defined fiction as a contradiction, because in order to represent reality it posits something that does not exist. He introduced into the discussion of fiction what he termed the law of "shift of ideas," implying that according to its use fiction assumes three different shapes: (1) if equated with what it is meant to represent, fiction turns into dogmatism; (2) if used in order to investigate given realities, it turns into a hypothesis; and (3) if its true nature is laid bare, it turns into a way of positing something that in itself is totally unreal yet serves as a means of ordering, measuring, and computing things that *are* real.[4] Therefore, Vaihinger maintains that all assumptions and presuppositions put forward in the history of epistemology are nothing but useful fictions that posit something as real in order to constitute reality or make given realities manageable. Whatever use fictions are put to, basically they are "consciously false"[5] and hence have to be unmasked. But if fiction is understood as a posited reality—no matter how necessary such a positing may be—in philosophical discourse it will lose the all-important qualities that characterize it in literature: its self-disclosure, its doubleness, and its simultaneity of the mutually exclusive.

When these features of fictionality are eclipsed in philosophical discourse, an irreconcilable dichotomy is bound to open up: what appears to be useful is something in disguise. The necessary unmasking, however, so painstakingly executed by Vaihinger, puts the usefulness into jeopardy. If this is to be preserved, epistemology, then, has to turn a blind eye to what it has seen through. Thus in philosophical discourse—particularly that of the empiricists—at one moment fiction is being unmasked as an invention, and the next it is being elevated to the status of a necessity. Small wonder that it turned into a burden for epistemology, which could not come to grips with the dual nature of the fact that make-believe is indispensable for organizing that which appears to be given.

So long as the vision of duality remains blinkered in this way, the particularity of literary fiction will remain hidden from view. What distinguishes fiction in philosophical discourse from fiction in literary discourse is the fact that in the former it remains veiled whereas in the latter it discloses its own fictional nature; therefore it is not discourse, but staged discourse, which, unlike fiction in philosophical discourse, cannot be falsified. It is not subject to any rules of practical application, as it is not designed for any specific use but is basically an enabling structure generating an aesthetic potential.

The doubling effect as the hallmark of literary fictionality comes about because the mutually exclusive realms that are bracketed together nevertheless retain their difference. If they did not, that which appears as doubled would instead merge into one. But while difference is a precondition for doubling, it is also the driving force behind its own removal. From this countermovement arises the act of representation (*Darstellung*), for whatever is opened up by the simultaneity of the mutually exclusive demands to be closed again, so that representation might be described as the third dimension, in which whatever emerges from the doubling effect seeks to be united in a meaningful form.

Elementary operations of representation are inevitable simply because of the fact that boundary-crossing accentuates difference, and difference requires reconciliation of what now appears separated. Since every representation is to be conceived as a bridging of what has been split apart by difference, the question arises as to whether difference can ever be removed. It cannot, for the removal of difference that is the origin of representation is always visible in the product.

WE SHALL NOW try to pinpoint the modes of interrelation. The fictionalizing acts simultaneously separate and encompass the extratextual fields and their intratextual deformation (selection), the intratextual semantic enclosures and their mutual telescoping (combination), and finally a bracketed world and its suspension of the empirical world; the difference is bridged by such modes of connection as overlap, condensation, disfigurement, displacement, mirroring, and dramatization. In all cases, the fields, positions, and worlds marked in the text undergo a change. However, all the modes of difference-removal bear the mark of their origin, out of which arise forms of representation articulating both the connection and the separation of the elements they encompass. The difference simultaneously appears to be overcome and present. Again a close resemblance suggests itself between these basic forms of representation and the world of dreams, in which occurs an interpenetration of what defies combination according to the terms set by the "symbolic order" of our conscious life.

It is the versatility of this structure that gives rise to the variety of representational forms. The presence of difference within the modes of its removal can be intensified through duality, subversion, or negation of the interlinked though mutually exclusive positions. It can also be weakened through correspondence, equivalence, affirmation, confirmation, or reconciliation, though even at this end of the scale the apparent absence of difference cannot be absolute, because otherwise correspondence, affirmation, and the rest could not signal anything. If difference is removed, representation appears only to be serving pragmatic ends, with a resultant loss of aesthetic tension, and indeed of truthfulness, as evinced in a good deal of light literature. The elimination of difference therefore makes representation seem deficient, so that even the attempt at total removal of difference spotlights the impossibility of such an endeavor. But perhaps the most interesting points on the scale are those in the middle, especially where difference is present as ambivalence or duplicity in the forms of its removal.

Representation, then, might be classified as "fact from fiction,"[6] in that it arises out of the difference characteristic of fictionality in literature which, as a form of boundary-crossing, leads to the simultaneity of mutually exclusive positions. It is the elucidation of difference that makes representation necessary, but the elementary forms of representation already show clearly that in the last analysis difference can never be eradicated, because as the origin of representation it can never be pinpointed by or equated with its product. Thus difference defies determination by any form of representation. As representation, however, arises out of the attempt to remove difference, what is to be removed appears to be something that does not have the nature of an object and cannot be qualified as actually 'being' in the Heideggerian sense of the term 'seiend'. It is intangible, and this fact cannot be concealed by any forms of representation — on the contrary, this intangibility inscribes itself into every form of representation, thus suffusing all of them with aesthetic semblance.

Semblance, then, appears to be a basic ingredient of representation, as it gives form to the otherwise inaccessible, for although difference (or the attempt to remove it) is the driving force behind representation, it is so only because it perpetually defers its own removal. The semblance is therefore the result of the resistance put up by difference against any form of mediation, and in turn this resistance ensures that no conceptualization of the inaccessible can ever be authentic. This apparent lack of authenticity, however, makes the semblance into a critical instrument to be applied against all explanations that claim to have fathomed origins, and so we may say that difference is present in the aesthetic semblance as a simultaneous conceptualization and inaccessibility of origins. But although difference downgrades representation to the level of semblance, it also needs this semblance in order to manifest itself.

The semblance is aesthetic insofar as something is represented that has no given reality of its own, and is therefore only the condition for the production of an imaginary object. Representation can only unfold itself in the recipient's mind, and it is through his active imaginings alone that the intangible can become an image. It follows, then, that representation, by bridging difference and thus making the intangible conceivable, is an act of performing and not— as Western tradition has repeated time and again—an act of mimesis, since mimesis presupposes a given reality that is to be portrayed in one way or another.

Similarly, this performative element distinguishes the aesthetic semblance from Schiller's "beautiful semblance" and from Hegel's "sensuous appearance of the idea." The beautiful semblance always presupposes a reality on which it depends, but which it was meant to transcend. The sensual appearance of the idea presupposes the existence of a truth, with an inseparable unity between its abstract notion and its tangible manifestation; thus "the idea is not only true but also beautiful."[7] Aesthetic semblance, on the other hand, neither transcends a given reality nor mediates between idea and manifestation; it is an indication that the inaccessible can only be approached by being staged. Representation is therefore both performance and semblance. It conjures up an image of the unseeable, but being a semblance, it also denies it the status of a copy of reality. The aesthetic semblance can only take on its form by way of the recipient's ideational, performative activity, and so representation can only come to full fruition in the recipient's imagination; it is the recipient's performance that endows the semblance with its sense of reality. And so representation causes the recipient to repeat the very same performance out of which it arose, and it is the repeat of this performance that initiates and ensures the transfer from text to reader of what is to be represented. Now the fact that the aesthetic semblance brings about this transfer from text to reader does not mean that the recipient's status advances to that of "a sovereign of understanding" or "the hero of the text."[8] If the aesthetic semblance is to take on its tone of reality, we must place our own thoughts and feelings at the disposal of what representation seeks to make present in us.

In this respect the required activity of the recipient resembles that of an actor, who in order to perform his role must use his thoughts, his feelings, and even his body as an analogue for representing something he is not. In order to produce the determinate form of an unreal character, the actor must allow his own reality to fade out. At the same time, however, he does not know precisely who, say, Hamlet is, for one cannot properly identify a character who has never existed. Thus role-playing endows a figment with a sense of reality in spite of its impenetrability which defies total determination. The reader finds himself in much the same situation. To imagine what has been stimulated by aesthetic semblance entails placing our thoughts and feelings at the disposal of an unreality, bestowing on it a semblance of reality in proportion to a reducing of our own reality. For the duration of the performance we are both ourselves and someone else. Staging oneself as someone else is a source of aesthetic pleasure; it is also the means whereby representation is transferred from text to reader.

REPRESENTATION AS AESTHETIC semblance indicates the presence of the inaccessible. Literature reflects life under conditions that are either not available in the empirical world or are denied by it. Consequently literature turns life into a storehouse from which it draws its material in order to stage what in life appeared to have been sealed off from access. The need for such a staging arises out of man's decentered position: we are, but do not have ourselves.[9] Wanting to have what we are, that is, to step out of ourselves in order to grasp our own identity, would entail having final assurances as to our origins, but as these underlie what we are, we cannot 'have' them. Beckett follows similar lines when he says that "live and invent" appears to be the alternative;[10] we know that we live, but we don't know what living is, and if we want to know, we have to invent what is denied us. Our unwillingness to accept this state of affairs is evinced by the multiplicity of our attempts to conceptualize life. Anthropologically speaking, these conceptualizations are motivated by our inherent drive to make accessible the inaccessible, and this holds true even of the pragmatic solutions offered by our many ideologies, which in the final analysis are meant to determine what eludes our grasp. It is therefore little wonder that one set of concepts is frequently rejected and subsequently replaced by another, which in turn has to be exposed as a fiction merely designed to compensate for what has been withheld from us. Whatever shape or form these various conceptualizations may have, their common denominator is the attempt to explain origins. In this respect they close off those very potentialities that literature holds open. Of course literature also springs from the same anthropological need, since it stages what is inaccessible, thus compensating for the impossibility of knowing what it is to be. But literature is not an explanation of origins; it is a staging of the constant deferment of explanation, which makes the origin explode into its multifariousness.

It is at this point that aesthetic semblance makes its full impact. Representation arises out of and thus entails the removal of difference, whose irremovability transforms representation into a performative act of staging something. This staging is almost infinitely variable, for in contrast to explanations, no single staging could ever remove difference and so explain origin. On the contrary, its very multiplicity facilitates an unending mirroring of what man is, because no mirrored manifestation can ever coincide with our actual being. This may be viewed as a drawback for literature, in comparison with the temporary comfort provided by conceptualizations of life as an explanation of origins; but it is also an advantage—indeed a unique advantage, insofar as knowledge of what man is can only come about in the form of play. Play, however, is something that the global conceptualizations of life cannot afford to incorporate into their explanatory patterns; they have to be one-dimensional in view of the finality of the explanation to be achieved and the certainties to be provided by them. The ludic nature of literature is basically unlimited, and as the different moves in the game attempt to stage the inaccessible, so they simultaneously present an illusion of origin and defer explanation of it.

It is the play element in the removal of difference which distinguishes literature as a form of staging from all conceptualizations of life as forms of explanation, but even this infinite variety does not fully explain the fascination of the aesthetic semblance. Staging presupposes a given something that is to appear on stage. But this 'something' cannot be totally incorporated into the process of staging, since this would make the staging its own given something. In other words, staging is an activity propelled by something other than itself. Whatever takes place on the stage is in the service of something absent which makes itself felt through what is present. Staging is therefore a basic form of doubling, not least because it entails an awareness of the ineradicability of its own doubling. Out of this doubleness of staging arises its aesthetic character as opposed to the conceptualizations of life as explanations of origins which seek to exercise an interest-oriented and hence a pragmatic control over what cannot be known. The determinacy of all the global conceptualizations make the unknowable disappear, whereas staging enables us both to register and even experience it. This makes the aesthetic semblance into a source of satisfaction, but also endows it with an ineluctable sense of duplicity. Perhaps this form of doubling—having the unavailable through an image of make-believe—may help us to explore given items in our anthropological makeup.

WHAT IS MEANT by this exploration can be briefly illustrated by having a look at two of Shakespeare's greatest tragedies. In *King Lear* we have the co-presence of two mutually exclusive facts of life. On the one hand there is Lear's insight into the inevitability of endings, and on the other is his experience that things go on. Ending and continuing are basic forms of life, but when they are both present simultaneously in one man's consciousness, they begin to invalidate each other. Continuing robs the end of its uniqueness, which would otherwise be a consolation. But from the standpoint of a finite individual, endless continuation is both aimless and beyond his control. Thus at the beginning of the tragedy, Lear acts as if the end were unique. He is set to glorify this event by trading his kingdom for deliberately solicited flattery. But after a while he realizes that things go on, and so the end is robbed of its consoling pathos, and Lear is 'left darkling' in the co-presence of ending and continuing.

There is a similar problem in *Macbeth*. Macbeth wishes that his blow might be the be-all and the end-all—in other words, that being and the ending of being should coincide. Once again a co-presence of the mutually exclusive looms large in the play, although Macbeth's impossible desire seems quite plausible from a human point of view.[11]

The simultaneity of the mutually exclusive, as it variously appears in Lear and Macbeth, is not even to be viewed in terms of a conflict, as the co-presence allows neither a real conflict nor an imaginable solution. Such basic facts of life as ending/continuing, or being/simultaneously ending, are clearly beyond conflict, as there is no direction for unfolding this mutual cancellation. Thus we are given the impression that great literature is characterized by its presentation of insoluble human predicaments. If this is indeed so, then the decentered position of man, as staged by literature, appears in a somewhat unexpected light. Given our deep-rooted desire to be and at the same time to have ourselves in order that we might know what it is to be, literature—as the staging of this inaccessibility—would seem to offer two ways of meeting that need: either it can fulfill the desire by providing an image of having the unavailable, or it can stage the desire itself, and so raise the question of the origin and nature of that desire—though the question, of course, is unanswerable. In the first instance, by staging the fulfillment of it, literature will come close to what conceptualizations of life intend to achieve, and consequently historical necessities will condition the form of this desired fulfillment. The greater the emphasis on compensation, the more dated will the solution appear to future generations of readers. In the second instance, the inversion or nonfulfillment of the deeply entrenched desire to be and simultaneously to have oneself will, paradoxically, endow this kind of literature with far greater longevity and even enduring fascination, since what it stages is not an ephemeral compensation but a deferment of compensation. This enacted deferment is indeed a reason for literature's surviving beyond the context of its genesis, and from this fact we might draw two possible conclusions: (1) the staging of what eludes our grasp due to man's decentered position exercises greater impact if, instead of an illusory wish-fulfillment, it spotlights the illusory nature of wished-for compensations; and (2) such a staging will lead not to a flight from what is inaccessible but to an awareness of the fact that we can never be identical to the countless possibilities we produce in our attempts to grasp the ungraspable.

It is precisely because we are the source of all these possibilities that we cannot be identical to any of them, but can only hang suspended, as it were, amid our own products. The kind of literature that exceeds its period of genesis by exercising an undiminished appeal stages this 'hanging between', whose depicting no longer compensates for anything. Yet the image it offers of this precarious state makes us realize that knowledge of our origin is withheld from us. Perhaps ultimately the fascination of the aesthetic quality in literature originates in providing an experience of what it is to hang between our achievements and our possibilities. It is a state of unending oscillation by means of which closed positions are opened up again and apparent finalities are outstripped. To provide conditions for this state to be imagined, its staging must simultaneously deprive these conditions of any claim to authenticity. Otherwise we would get a frozen image of the ever-oscillating state, thereby turning it into an untruth. If this state, however, can never take on the character of an authenticated object, its presence is always an aesthetic semblance, and representation is first and foremost an act of performance, bringing forth in the mode of staging something that in itself is not given.

TWELVE

THE PLAY OF THE TEXT

he traditional notion of representation assumes that mimesis entails reference to a pre-given 'reality' that is meant to be represented in a text. A quite different, conflicting view is possible, however, if author, text, and reader are thought of as interconnected in a relationship that is the ongoing process of producing something that did not previously exist. In the Aristotelian sense, the function of representation is twofold: (1) to render the constitutive forms of nature perceivable; and (2) to complete what nature has left incomplete. In either case mimesis, though of paramount importance, cannot be confined to mere imitation of what is, since the processes of elucidation and of completion both require a performative activity if apparent absences are to be moved into presence. Since the advent of the modern world there has been a clearly discernible tendency toward privileging the performative aspect of the author-text-reader relationship, whereby the pre-given is no longer viewed as an object of representation but rather as material from which something new is fashioned. The new product, however, is not predetermined by the features, functions, and structures of the material referred to and encapsulated in the text.

There are historical reasons for the shift in focus. Closed systems, such as the cosmos of Greek thought or of the medieval world-picture, gave priority to representation as mimesis because of their overriding concern that whatever existed—even if it eluded perception—should be translated into something tangible. When the closed system, however, is punctured and replaced by open-endedness, the mimetic component of representation declines and the performative one comes to the fore. The process then no longer entails reaching behind appearances in order to grasp an intelligible world in the Platonic sense, but turns into a "way of worldmaking." If what the text brings about were to be equated with worldmaking, the question would arise as to whether one could continue to speak of "representation" at all. The concept could be retained only if the "ways of worldmaking" themselves became the referential object for representation. In this case, the performative component would have to be conceived as the pre-given of the performative act. Irrespective of whether this might or might not be considered tautological, the fact remains that it would lead to a host of problems that are not within the scope of this essay. There is, however, one inference that is highly relevant to our discussion: what has been called the "end of representation"[1] may, in the final analysis, be less a description of the historical state of the arts than the articulation of misgivings relating to the ability of representation as a concept to capture what actually happens in art or literature.

This is not to deny that the author-text-reader relationship contains a vast number of extratextual elements that undergo processing, but these are only material components of what happens in the text and are not represented by it one-to-one. It therefore seems fair to say that representation in the sense in which we have come to understand it cannot embrace the performative operation of the text as a form of happening. Indeed, it is striking to note that there are hardly any clear-cut theories of representation that actually set out the workings necessary to bring about mimesis.

Among the rare exceptions is Gombrich's idea of representation: he broke up the received notion into clearly distinguishable phases of a process, starting out from the interaction between painter and inherited schemata, followed by the correction of the latter in the painting, and eventually by the deciphering activity of the beholder, whose reading of the corrected schemata brings the object of representation to fruition.[2]

THE FOLLOWING ESSAY is an attempt to raise play above representation as an umbrella concept to cover all the ongoing operations of the textual process. It has two heuristic advantages: (1) play does not have to concern itself with what it might stand for, and (2) play does not have to picture anything outside itself. It allows author-text-reader to be conceived as a dynamic interrelationship that moves toward a final result.

Authors play games with readers,[3] and the text is the playground. The text itself is the outcome of an intentional act whereby an author refers to and intervenes in an existing world, but though the act is intentional, it aims at something that is not as yet accessible to consciousness. Thus the text is made up of a world that is yet to be identified and is adumbrated in such a way as to invite picturing and eventual interpretation by the reader. This double operation of imagining and interpreting engages the reader in the task of visualizing the many possible shapes of the identifiable world, so that inevitably the world repeated in the text begins to undergo changes. For no matter which new shapes the reader brings to life, they are all certain to encroach on—and hence to change—the referential world contained in the text. Now since the latter is fictional, it automatically invokes a convention-governed contract between author and reader indicating that the textual world is to be viewed not as reality but as if it *were* reality. And so whatever is repeated in the text is not meant to denote the world, but merely a world enacted. This may well repeat an identifiable reality, but it contains one all-important difference: what happens within it is relieved of the consequences inherent in the real world referred to. Hence in disclosing itself, fictionality signalizes that everything is only to be taken *as if* it were what it seems to be, to be taken—in other words— as play.

The world repeated in the text is obviously different from the one it refers to, if only because, as a repetition, it must differ from its extratextual existence, and this holds equally true of all types of discourse, textual or otherwise, since no rendering can *be* that which it renders. There are therefore various levels of difference that occur simultaneously in the text.

1. Extratextually:
   a. between the author and the world in which he or she intervenes;
   b. between the text and an extratextual world as well as between the text and other texts.
2. Intratextually:
   a. between the items selected from extratextual systems;
   b. between semantic enclosures built up in the text.
3. Between text and reader:
   a. between the reader's natural attitudes (now bracketed off) and those he or she is called upon to assume;
   b. between what is denoted by the world repeated in the text, and what this denotation—now serving as a guiding analogue—is meant to adumbrate.

The levels of difference are quite distinct, but all of them constitute the basic blank of the text which sets the game in motion.

The movement is one of play in three different respects:

1. On each level distinguishable positions are confronted with one another.
2. The confrontation triggers a to-and-fro movement that is basic to play, and the ensuing difference has to be eradicated in order to achieve a result.
3. The continual movement between the positions reveal their

many different aspects, and as one encroaches on the other, so the various positions themselves are eventually transformed. Every one of these differences opens up space for play, and hence for transformation, which even at this early stage of our argument would appear to discredit the traditional notion of representation.

Games head toward results, and when the differences are either bridged or even removed, play comes to an end. The result of the textual game, however, must be highly reductive, since the moves of the games split positions up into multifarious aspects. If we take the result of the textual game to be meaning, then this can only arise out of arresting the play-movement that, more often than not, will entail decision-making. But any decision will eclipse countless aspects brought to view by the constantly shifting, constantly interacting and hence kaleidoscopically iterating positions of the game, so that the game itself runs counter to its being brought to an end.

Thus the duality of play comes to the fore. It is directed toward winning something, thereby ending itself at the same time as it removes difference. But it also refutes any such removal of difference, and outstrips its achievements in order to reestablish its own freedom as an ever-decentering movement. In short, it upholds the difference it seeks to eradicate.

These mutually exclusive features inscribe themselves into one another and so turn the meaning of the text into something of a 'supplement'. The multiplicity of differences that give rise to play and also result from it can never be totally removed but may in fact increase with attempts at eradication. Consequently the 'supplement' arises not only out of the winning of the game (i.e., establishing meaning) but also, and at the same time, out of freeplay— not least because freeplay itself would remain ungraspable if it did not have some form of manifestation. If the 'supplement' is the product of these two countervailing features, we may draw two conclusions:

1. The 'supplement' as the meaning of the text is generated through play, and so there is no meaning prior to play.
2. The generation of the 'supplement' through play allows for different reenactments by different readers in the act of reception—even to the extent that it can be played either as achieving victory (establishing meaning) or as maintaining freeplay (keeping meaning open-ended).

This duality of play—removing and maintaining difference—defies further conceptualization. It cannot be reduced phenomenologically by tracing it back to an underlying cause. Even such one-sided theories as that of Huizinga assert that play precedes all its possible explanations.[4] Therefore, the play of the text can only be assessed in terms of its possibilities, by way of the strategies of playing and the games actually played in the text.

As a playground between author and reader, the literary text can be described on three different levels: (1) structural, (2) functional, and (3) interpretive. A structural description will aim to map out the playground, a functional one will try to explain the goal, and an interpretive one will ask why we play and why we need to play. An answer to this last question can only be interpretive, since play is apparently built into our anthropological makeup and may indeed help us to grasp what we are.

WE MUST NOW look in more detail at the three different levels. The focus at the structural level is on countermovement as the basic feature of play. The operational mode of the countermovement converts the text from a mimetic to a performative act. It manifests itself by creating what we might call the play-spaces of the text that, it must be remembered, both repeats and encapsulates extratextual worlds whose return is indicative of a difference. In Gregory Bateson's words, it is "a difference which makes a difference"[5]—for a great many differences arise out of the initial one between the components of the text. The difference, as we have seen, triggers the to-and-fro movement, which opens up play-spaces between the positions it separates.

The smallest play-space is produced by the split signifier, which is stripped of its designating function so that it may be used figuratively, thanks to the text's fictional indication that what is said is only to be taken *as if* it meant what it said. The signifier therefore denotes something, but at the same time negates its denotative use without abandoning what it has designated in the first instance. If the signifier means something and simultaneously indicates that it does not mean that something, it functions as an analogue for figuring something else that it helps to adumbrate. If what is denoted is transformed into an analogue both triggering and shaping a picturing activity, then something absent is endowed with presence, though that which is absent cannot be identical to the analogue that facilitated its conceivability. Thus the split signifier—which is simultaneously denotative and figurative—invokes something that is not a pre-given for the text, but is generated by the text, which enables the reader to endow it with a tangible shape.

Thus the play-movement turns the split signifier into a matrix for double meaning, which manifests itself in the analogue as the mutual interpenetration of the denotative and the figurative functions. In terms of the text, the analogue is a 'supplement'; in terms of the recipient, it is the guideline enabling him to conceive what the text adumbrates. But the moment this becomes conceivable, the recipient will try to ascribe significance to the 'supplement', and whenever this happens, the text is translated into the dispositional terms of the individual reader, who ends the play of the split signifier by blocking it off with a meaning. If the meaning of a text, however, is not inherent but is ascribed and only achieved through play-movement, then meaning is a metastatement about statements, or even a metacommunication about what is supposed to be communicated (i.e., experience by means of the text).

Another basic play-space in the text is opened up by the schema. A schema, so Piaget maintains in his play theory, is the outcome of our constant endeavor to adapt to the world we are in.[6] In this respect it is not dissimilar to imitation, since it is motivated by the desire to overcome the difference that marks our relation to the world. First and foremost, it is perception that has to work out these schemata of adaptation.

Once these schemata have been formed, the first vital step is for them to be internalized, so that they may function subconsciously. This means that they tend to become ritualized in one way or another, and when this happens, they become separable from the very objects that initially gave rise to their formation. The conventions of art are nothing but sets of such schemata, which lend themselves very easily to new uses, especially when they have been separated from the world of objects.

Instead of facilitating adaptation to the physical world, the schemata may be used to pattern things that are otherwise ungraspable or that we want to bring within reach on our own conditions. Just as schemata enable us to adapt ourselves to objects, so too do they allow us to assimilate objects into our own disposition. When this reversal occurs, it opens up the play-space. The schema is dissociated from its accommodating function and, in becoming subservient to the assimilative function, permits whatever is withheld from us to be staged as both present and manageable. This process is immediately evident in child's play. The play-movement takes place when the schema ceases to function as a form of accommodation, and instead of taking its shape from the object to be imitated, now imposes a shape on what is absent. In other words, the schema of accommodation copies the object, whereas the schema of assimilation shapes the object in accordance with the needs of the individual. Play therefore begins (1) when assimilation displaces accommodation in the use of schemata, and (2) when the schema is turned into a projection in order to incorporate the world in a book and to chart it according to human conditions.

A striking feature of the assimilative use of schemata is that they become subject to disfigurement. This highlights the switch in their function, and also the difference in their application. It is a duality inherent in all textual schemata where the original function of the schema is backgrounded, though retaining its shape, and now instead of imitating something it serves to represent the unrepresentable.

In this respect, the inverted schema bears a close resemblance to the split signifier. Both form basic play-spaces of the text, and set the game in motion. And in both cases, a basic function is transformed into a medium for something else: with the signifier the denotative function becomes the medium for figuration, and with the schema, the accommodating function becomes the medium for shaping the featureless. The original functions, however, are never totally suspended, and so there is a continual oscillation between denotation and figuration, and between accommodation and assimilation. This oscillation, or to-and-fro movement, is basic to play, and it permits the coexistence of the mutually exclusive. It also turns the text into a generative matrix for the production of something new. It invites and enables the reader to play the games of the text, and to finish playing by coming up with what he or she considers to be its meaning. In the final analysis, oscillation is a patterning of freeplay—which may be a feature of nature or even of human nature, but is not one of the text. Oscillation, however, can also restrain freeplay. This is evident when we see how the strategies of the text restructure the manner in which the respective duality of the split signifier and the inverted schema is played out.

There are four main strategies, each of which allows for a different type of game. They are *agon, alea, mimicry*, and *ilinx*. The mixture of Greek and Latin terms may be jarring, but the expressions have become standard terms in game theory since Caillois,[7] although he himself did not relate them to texts as verbal structures.

Let me first explain the terms and the types of games they cover, in order to ascertain the patterns of gaming which they organize:

1. *Agon* is a fight or contest, and is a common pattern of play when the text centers on conflicting norms and values. The contest involves a decision to be made by the reader in relation to these opposing values, which are in collision with one another.
2. *Alea* is a pattern of play based on change and the unforeseeable. Its basic thrust is defamiliarization, which it achieves through storing and telescoping different texts, thus outstripping what their respective identifiable segments were meant to mean. By overturning familiar semantics, it reaches out into the hitherto inconceivable, and frustrates the reader's convention-governed expectations.
3. *Mimicry* is a play pattern designed to generate illusion. Whatever is denoted by the signifier or foreshadowed by the schemata should be taken as if it were what it says. There are two different reasons for this:
   a. The more perfect the illusion, the more real will seem the world it depicts.
   b. If the illusion, however, is punctured and so revealed as what it is, the world it depicts turns into a looking glass enabling the referential world outside the text to be observed.
4. *Ilinx* is a play pattern in which the various positions are subverted, undercut, canceled, or even carnivalized as they are played off against one another. It aims at bringing out the rear view of the positions yoked together in the game.

Although these play strategies allow for different games to be played, more often than not they link up as mixed modes. For instance, if *ilinx* plays against or is combined with *agon*, there may be two possible types of game: *ilinx* gains the upper hand, in which case the contest between norms and values becomes illusory, or *agon* dominates, and then the contest becomes more differentiated. These strategies can even be inverted, playing against their own underlying intentions. For example, *agon* appears to be directed toward winning the game, but in postmodern literature it is frequently used to play a losing game. This may entail all conflicts of norms and values being deliberately marked as things of the past, thus exposing the closed nature of the systems that gave them their function and validity. It may also show that all forms of meaning are nothing but defense mechanisms designed to achieve closure in a world where open-endedness reigns.

These four strategies of play can be combined in a great number of ways, and whenever they *are* combined, each of them takes on a particular role. All roles—as we have to remind ourselves—are characterized by an intrinsic doubleness: they represent something they aim to project, and yet simultaneously they lack total control over the intended achievement, so that there is always an element in role-playing that eludes the grasp of the player.[8] This applies equally to the play patterns outlined above when they become roles, and so the game to be played may either enhance or restrict the degree of uncontrollability.

Now no matter what type of game ensues from indulging in the doubleness of role-playing, it is always governed by one of two different sets of rules. In game theory these are called 'conservative' and 'dissipative' rules.[9] With regard to the text, they may be called regulative (which function according to stabilized conventions), and aleatory (which set free whatever has been restrained by the conventions). Aleatory rules apply to what cannot be controlled by the role in question, whereas regulatory rules organize what the role represents in terms of hierarchical, causal, subservient, or supportive relationships. Aleatory rules unleash what regulative rules have tied up, and thus they allow for freeplay within an otherwise restricted game.

LET US NOW summarize our structural description so far: the split signifier and the inverted schemata open up the play-space of the text. The resultant to-and-fro movement is patterned by four basic strategies of play: *agon*, *alea*, *mimicry*, and *ilinx*. These in turn may undergo innumerable combinations, thereby turning into roles. Roles are double-faced, with representation inevitably shading off into uncontrollable adumbrations. The games ensuing from roles may be acted out in accordance with regulative rules, which make the game basically conservative, or aleatory rules, which make it basically innovative.

All of these structural features provide a framework for the game. They mark off both the limits and the free areas of play, and so represent the preconditions for 'supplements'—in the form of meaning—as well as for the playful undoing of these 'supplements'. Thus there is a countervailing movement in which play strives for a result and freeplay breaks up any result achieved.

The structural features, however, assume significance only in relation to the function meant to be performed by the play of the text. Since play strives for something but also undoes what it achieves, it continually acts out difference. Difference, in turn, can be manifested only through play, because only play can make conceivable the absent otherness that lies on the reverse side of all positions. Thus the play of the text is neither winning nor losing, but is a process of transforming positions, thereby giving dynamic presence to the absence and otherness of difference. Consequently, what the text achieves is not featuring a pre-given, but a transformation of the pre-given material that it encapsulates. If the text highlights transformation, it is bound to have a play-structure; otherwise transformation would have to be subsumed under a cognitive framework, thus obliterating its very nature. Should the notion of representation be retained at all, one would have to say that the text 'represents' play, insofar as it spells out the individual process of transformation as it is happening in the text.

This process of transformation is common to the literary text, and it unfolds through all the various interconnected phases that we have outlined so far—from split signifier through inverted schemata and strategic roles of *agon*, *alea*, *mimicry*, and *ilinx*, to the mutual interference of regulative and aleatory rules. Although we have separated these phases for analytical purposes, they in fact overlap and interlink, but through them we may observe transformation in slow motion, as it were, thereby rendering this otherwise intangible process perceivable.

Transformation, however, comes to full fruition through the recipient's imaginative participation in the games played, for it is only a means to an end, and not an end in itself. The more the reader is drawn into the proceedings by playing the game of the text, the more he or she is also played *by* the text. And so new features of play emerge. It assigns certain roles to the reader, and in order to do this, it must clearly have the potential presence of the recipient as one of its component parts. The play of the text is therefore a performance for an assumed audience, and as such it is not just a game as played in ordinary life, but it is actually a staged play enacted for the reader, who is given a role enabling him or her to act out the scenario presented.

The staged play of the text does not, then, unfold as a pageant that the reader merely watches, but is both an ongoing event and a happening for the reader, enabling and encouraging direct involvement in the proceedings and indeed in the staging. For the play of the text can be acted out individually by each reader, who by playing it in his or her own way, produces an individual 'supplement' considered to be the meaning of the text. The meaning is a 'supplement' because it arrests the ongoing process of transformation, and is additional to the text without ever being authenticated by it.

In this respect something important is to be revealed by the textual play. As a means of transformation, play does not only undercut the position presented in the text; it also undercuts the status of what transformation has moved from absence into presence, that is, the 'supplement' that the reader has added onto the text. But the undercutting, even if it may seem negative, in fact is highly productive, because it brings about transformation and generates 'supplements'. Hence this operation is driven by negativity, which is basically an enabling structure. Negativity is therefore far from negative in its effects, for it lures absence into presence, but by continually subverting that presence, turns it into a carrier for absence of which we would otherwise not know anything. Through these constant shifts, the play of the text uses negativity in a manner that epitomizes the interrelation between absence and presence. And herein lies the uniqueness of play: it produces, and at the same time allows the process of production to be observed. The reader is therefore caught up in ineluctable doubleness by being involved in an illusion and aware that it *is* an illusion. It is through this incessant hovering between the closed and the punctured illusion that the transformation effected by the play of the text makes itself felt to the reader.

Transformation, in turn, appears to head toward some aim that must be realized by the reader, and so the play of the text can be ended in various ways, one of which is in terms of semantics. In this case what is paramount is our need for understanding and our urge to appropriate the experiences given to us. This might even indicate a defense mechanism operating within ourselves, as the search for meaning may be our means of warding off the unfamiliar.

Another way in which we may play the text is by obtaining experience. Then we open ourselves up to the unfamiliar and are prepared to let our own values be influenced or even changed by it.

A third mode of play is that of pleasure. Then we give precedence to the enjoyment derived from an unusual exercise of our faculties which enables us to become present to ourselves. Each of these options represents a tendency according to which the play of the text can be acted out.

WE NOW COME to the final point: What is play, and why do we play? Any answer to this fundamental question can only be in the nature of tentative interpretation. In phylogenetic terms, play in the animal kingdom begins when the space of the habitat expands. Initially it appears to be an activity for its own sake, exploring the bounds of the possible, in view of the fact that everything is now possible. But we may also see it as a would-be action, or a trial run that trains the animal to cope with the unforeseeable that is to come. The more the animal's territory expands, the more important and sometimes the more elaborate play becomes as a means of preparing for survival.

In ontogenetic terms, there is a distinction to be observed in child's play between perception and meaning. When a child rides a hobbyhorse, that is, a riding-stick, he or she is engaged in a mental action that is quite distinct from what he or she actually perceives. Since the child does not, of course, perceive a real horse, the play consists in splitting the object (horse) and the meaning of that object in the real world. Its play is therefore an action in which a defamiliarized meaning is acted out in a real situation.

What these two instances of playing have in common is a form of staging. But in neither case is the staging carried out for its own sake. In the animal kingdom, it serves as preparation for future actions; in child's play, it permits real limitations to be overstepped. Staging, then, is basically a means of crossing boundaries, and this holds for the play of the text as well, which stages transformation and at the same time reveals how the staging is done. This duality arises largely from the fact that transformation here has no pragmatic outcome: it does not change one thing into another. It is, rather, a purpose that can be properly fulfilled only if its own procedural workings are exhibited.

What is the nature of this purpose? Transformation is an access road to the inaccessible, but staged transformation does not only make available the unavailable. Its achievement is perhaps even more gratifying. It allows us to have things both ways, by making what is inaccessible both present and absent. Presence comes about by means of the staged transformation, and absence by means of the fact that the staged transformation is only play. Hence every presented absence is qualified by the caveat that it is only staged in the form of make-believe, through which we can conceive what would otherwise elude our grasp. Herein lies the extraordinary achievement of play, for it appears to satisfy both epistemological and anthropological needs. Epistemologically speaking, it imbues presence with adumbrated absence by denying any authenticity to the possible results of play. Anthropologically speaking, it allows us to conceive what is withheld from us. Interestingly enough, the epistemological and anthropological perspectives do not conflict, even though they may appear to run counter to each other. If there were a clash, it would undo the play, but as there is not, the cognitive irreconcilability in fact reveals something of our own human makeup. By allowing us to have absence as presence, play turns out to be a means whereby we may extend ourselves. This extension is a basic and ever-fascinating feature of literature, and the question inevitably arises as to why we need it. The answer to that question could be the starting point for a literary anthropology.

THIRTEEN
TOWARD A LITERARY ANTHROPOLOGY

urveying the current state of literary theory in the space of a single essay can only be like taking a snapshot, and hence a great deal is liable to be left out. But perhaps it is best to begin with the fact that, for all the current discontent regarding theory, there is still much interest in methods of interpretation. From New Criticism right through to Deconstruction, this interest remains comparatively constant in spite of shifting preferences. Some methods find favor relatively swiftly, but this does not save them from an equally swift waning of their attraction, as is the case with Deconstruction, whose dominance is already fading in America. Its importance is due not least to its emphasis on textuality—a commitment firmly established by the New Critical practice of interpretation. Herein lies its structural kinship to New Criticism, for both approaches stress close reading—and indeed prominent advocates of Deconstruction have actually described it as the closest of close reading. Scrutinizing the text, then, is their common feature—irrespective of noticeable differences in execution—and so they take the text as something given, to be focused upon from different angles. These, in turn, are conditioned by cultural requirements and hence are subject to change.

One wonders, however, whether this is the only reason for the relegation of once prominent modes of interpretation, in the course of which process literary theory itself has become a tarnished endeavor. Literary theory—at least in the past—was conceived as providing the framework for methods of interpretation, which implies that its prime concern was model-building. It is, however, this constriction to model-building that has caused present-day literary theory to come under increasing fire. The criticism leveled against theory cannot be met either through the innovative claims of the individual methods or through their occasional pretensions to universality, for no matter how new or how comprehensive they may be, or purport to be, they all depend ultimately on the existing text for confirmation of their claims.

It is therefore scarcely surprising that talk is now of pluralism or even a new pragmatism. Such talk is based on the conviction that perhaps after Deconstruction there can be no more generally acceptable concepts, so that all different approaches must be allowed free rein, and the text—as something naturally given—must be continually related to situational requirements.

THERE ARE ALSO trends toward breaking the confines of the literary text and extending insights gained from literature and art to the media at large. Behind this movement is the more or less conscious idea that literature and art are no longer the cultural paradigms that they were, as their function has shifted to the mass media that now truly represent our civilization. Without doubt this is a highly significant change of direction, for it touches on something that the merry-go-round of changing approaches has always left unquestioned—namely, the assumed validity of the literary text as a cultural paradigm. But what at present casts certain doubts on this trend toward expansion is the negative motivation behind its overstepping the old limits. Dissatisfaction is a good driving force, but it cannot provide a foundation for a theory to embrace the heterogeneity of the media in terms of what they signify. Thus it is not enough to make an eclectic transference of literary and artistic methods of criticism to the exploration of the media, but what does make the movement noteworthy is the fact that paradigms turn into such by virtue of their signification.

The body of literary texts is also a sign, the significance of which remains obscured as long as the canonized status of the text is left unquestioned. To mediate between the canonized text and the respective present is no longer the exclusive business of interpretation, in view of the fact that literature as a medium is also indicative of the needs to which it responds. In addressing itself to this issue, literary theory is bound to change direction. Instead of providing a matrix for model-building, it has to explore the sign-function of the medium, thus turning the text into a reflection of the needs in question.

Literature as a mirror, though, is by no means a new discovery, and we are well acquainted with the multifarious types of subservience to which literature has been subjected down through the ages. The question, however, which now arises is whether literature—in relation to history or society—reflects something special that neither philosophies of history nor sociological theories are able to capture. No one will deny the indexical value of literature both for history and society, but what emerges almost incidentally from this fact is the question of *why* such a mirror as literature should exist and how it enables us to find things out. Since literature as a medium has been with us more or less since the beginning of recorded time, its presence must presumably meet certain anthropological needs. What are these needs, and what does this medium reveal to us about our own anthropological makeup? These are the questions that would lead to the development of an anthropology of literature. Literary theory would thus take on a new function, for it must be remembered that its now disputed status came about largely through its attempts to establish frameworks in order to counter a merely taste oriented, impressionistic type of interpretation, and to provide models as a much needed impulse to legitimize literary criticism itself.

In so doing, it was exposed on two flanks to attacks that ultimately undermined its initial success. Insofar as it served to structure frameworks of interpretation, it became more and more an institution for model-building; insofar as it served to legitimize criticism, it tended more and more to draw on other disciplines, thus imposing alien orientations on literature, very often to its disadvantage. This applied above all to frameworks taken from psychoanalysis, Marxism, and social theory in the broader sense. Instead of subjugating the medium to theories successful in other realms of thought or social practice, we must make the medium the starting point if we are to pinpoint the indexical value it appears to possess. A literary theory with this aim will cease merely to provide models of interpretation, and instead will enable us to ask and perhaps to understand why we have this medium, and why we continually renew it. We may be able to draw our answer from studying the anthropological implications of texts, or in other words by developing literary anthropology as a paradigm for research. By using the special nature of this medium to open up insights into our human equipment, we shall make literature an instrument of exploration. Such an approach may even reveal what literature is and does, and at the same time it will automatically rid us of the thorny problem of having to examine what is literary in literature, or what is poetic in poetry.

Current structuralism still torments itself with the unwieldy concepts of 'literariness' or 'poeticity', without seeming to realize that this is simply the same old problem that plagued classical aesthetics. Our awareness that literature cannot be ontologically defined is a direct offshoot of the problems bequeathed to us by Classicism. And so terms like 'literary' and 'poetic' merely disguise what in fact is the continuation of autonomous art in an age when art can no longer find its own justification within itself. Literature is not self-sufficient, so it could hardly bear its own origin within itself. What it is, is the result of its function. This was already apparent to Edmund Burke, who, in 1756, while Classicism still flourished—although he was by no means a radical—traced the Sublime and Beautiful back to their anthropological roots, thus impugning the 'auratic' character of the work of art rather than confirming its classical attributes.[1]

Burke, however, can also be regarded as an exemplary warning against an anthropologically oriented literary theory, for he considered what he had exposed as the conditionality of classical attributes to be constants of human nature. A literary anthropology faces the same danger. The moment it passes off its findings as anthropological constants, or draws its heuristics directly from other anthropologically oriented disciplines—especially psychoanalysis—it will obscure, if not eclipse, the state of affairs to be investigated.

If there were really anthropological constants—and many people believe that there are—then history would be nothing but an illustration of them. Instead, historical situations continually activate human potentials, which issue forth into a history of their own variegated patternings. These cannot be exclusively attributed either to anthropological dispositions or to given circumstances, but they are products of an interaction, have a touch of singularity, and always exceed the conditions from which they emerge. The result of such interactions sheds retrospective light on potentials and on the necessity of their historically conditioned actualizations. Literature appears to modify anthropological dispositions to the extent that their otherwise hidden peculiarities come to light. For this reason it is not sufficient to subject it to received notions of cultural anthropology, devoted to investigating the structures of archaic civilizations. It requires instead a heuristics of its own which will enable us to answer questions such as: Why do we need fiction?

FICTIONS ARE INVENTIONS enabling humankind to extend itself—a state of affairs which can be studied from various angles. If we ask about the point of these inventions, we are confronted with the different uses to which they have been put and have to distinguish between the many fictions that pervade our everyday life and the fictionality of literature. Clearly they are not the same, but take on different forms according to their function, thereby implicitly revealing the different needs that they satisfy. The link between fiction and function is not, of course, a new discovery. It has always been in the forefront whenever attempts have been made to purge fiction of the taint of deception. As deception is generally for a specific purpose, even this negative charge is evidence that fiction is defined according to its use. The latter will determine whether judgment is positive or negative, but whichever is the case, it is clear that intention governs function and therefore form.

The process emerges vividly from two significant attempts made in the nineteenth century by Bentham and by Vaihinger to rehabilitate fiction. Bentham *thematized* it by introducing "fictitious entities" into epistemology as the unalterable modality for the given nature of all reality. Vaihinger *systematized* it by extolling fiction as the basis for the constitution of all reality. Bentham believed that he could distinguish between "fictitious entities" and "real entities" on the ground that "real entities" are given, though perceivable only through their mode of existence,[2] which, in turn, is a "fictitious entity" because there can be no factual correspondence to it *in re*. Vaihinger believed that fiction was the "consciously false" that constituted realities but then had to be abstracted from them in order to allow what has been constituted to perform its function.[3] Thus for Vaihinger, virtually everything was fiction, apart from human emotions, which were ultimately necessary as realities in order to prevent the whole world from being hollowed out into a fiction.

What is important for the present context, however, is not the individual statements of Bentham and Vaihinger concerning the use of fiction, but the fact that their respective concepts of its function led to very precise definitions. Historically, this precision is easy to explain, for fiction could only be rehabilitated in opposition to a tradition that left no doubt as to its negative nature (this was particularly true of the empirical tradition), and indeed Vaihinger actually felt it necessary to hold his work back for several decades because he did not think the time was ripe for his particular insights.[4]

Bentham's and Vaihinger's certainty over the use of fiction was conditioned by their attempts to counter the then current trends of thought, and if such certainty has vanished today, we are, as a result, much freer to perceive the variety of fiction's uses. It is no longer restricted to the epistemological confines to which Bentham and Vaihinger had to refer in their effort to rehabilitate it. At that time it could only justify itself as a mode of explanation in epistemological terms, as epistemology held sway in nineteenth-century philosophy.

But if fiction is seen as a means of explaining, or even as positing, realities, then it relapses into what it had already been in many of its historical and mythological guises—namely, "concord-fiction,"[5] a phenomenon that Bacon regarded as the psychological satisfaction of the human mind in creating certainty where "the nature of things doth deny it."[6] Viewing fiction as "concord-fiction" means identifying it exclusively with its explanatory function, which not only restricts it to a single use but also entails making it into the very object that in fact it is meant to explain. Thus fiction for Bentham is the mode of existence of all reality, while for Vaihinger it is the basis for constituting reality. Even if we do not regard these definitions as "concord-fiction" in the sense of what Kermode calls "complementarities,"[7] fiction—against the background of its philosophical revaluation—still remains a basis for something outside itself, which it is bound to be if its function is to explain. Indirectly, this means that the nature of the use decides what fiction is, and between fiction and its uses there is an interaction of reciprocal differentiation.

Explanation is therefore no more than a single, though classic, instance, which was regarded as being *the* function of fiction, because it initiated a debate that had developed a history of its own.

THE MORE FICTION eludes an ontological definition, the more unmistakably it presents itself in terms of its use. If it is no longer confined to an explanatory function, its impact becomes its prominent feature. Impacts, however, can only be made on or within given contexts, which, in turn, condition the respective use fiction is meant to achieve. Thus the field of application is responsible for the differentiation of fiction. No matter what its constitutive presuppositions may be, fiction will always be a mode of exercising an impact, and what is effected will vary according to requirements necessitated by the context in question. As long as fiction was restricted to explanation it functioned as "concord-fiction," which had to incorporate the inaccessible into otherwise familiar realities. If fiction, however, is conceived as a mode of impacting, the indefinability of our world is inscribed into it, and hence qualifies all its restriction-breaking as pragmatic necessity. Impacting as the pragmatics of fiction never loses sight of its situational function, whereas explanation as the semantics of fiction aims precisely to make its situational necessity disappear. Thus the pragmatic function unfolds the special use of fiction, and the special use determines the individual nature of fiction.

It has always been assumed that fiction can produce realities. For Vaihinger this was an incontrovertible truth, which led to his formulating the law of "shift of ideas."[8] Ideas, he assumed, pass through a transformation of their inherent potential. At first they are realities, because they are taken for the thing itself, though they were originally only devised in order to explain the thing. Once this latter fact is accepted, they change into hypotheses, but still with the insinuation that there is a certain reality that corresponds to them. Finally, these hypotheses reveal themselves to be fictions that—precisely because there is nothing that corresponds to them—condition the constitution of realities. In 'truth', however, all realities for Vaihinger are just such fictions, even if their operational success makes them appear to be a reality and may therefore prevent us from realizing that they are fictitious. Wherever and whenever realities are produced, there are fictions involved.

The law of shift of ideas is in fact a continual rearrangement of the attributes of reality, and ultimately such a process can only function on the basis of an assumed distinction between fiction and reality. But discussing fiction on such a basis means taking up what one might call metastandpoints, which presuppose knowledge of this distinction. This tacitly assumed 'knowledge' may, in turn, be a fiction, dictated by pragmatic needs, much as one finds in politics. The reality of politics is a striking example of fiction performing a double function. It is at one and the same time something masked and something unmasking: in the former case its claims to reality are challenged, and in the latter it gains reality by its critique, that is, through what it unmasks. Its reality then consists in its operative function, which therefore means that it cannot be identical to what it produces. Consequently it is different from what it does and what it brings about, and so a clear-cut distinction between fiction and reality is hardly to be upheld. For there is no transcendental stance that would allow us to distribute the predicates of fiction and reality according to a preordained frame of reference. To maintain such a distinction can only be an *asylum ignorantiae*, and therefore the solution that offers itself is to discard the time-honored, but by now frozen, opposition of 'fiction vs. reality' altogether in view of their interpenetration. Instead, we may perhaps conceive the fictive as a means of overstepping the given, which is bound to cause a transformation of what is.

Whatever the use of fiction may be, everything fictitious is something made, and making entails determinate intentions. Fiction is thus produced under certain conditions that demand consistency and that denote its referential nature. The referentiality is bound up with a discernible objective that fiction is designed to fulfill, and herein lies a major distinction between fiction on the one hand and

AVENUES FOR EXPLORATION

illusion and convention on the other. Fiction is neither totally deceptive nor totally dependable. It is an 'As If' indicating hypothetical presuppositions, which cannot be eclipsed no matter what disguise the fiction may adopt. The 'As If' always aims at overshooting what is, and for this reason it has to have a certain direction, adumbrating by its referentiality the function it is meant to fulfill—a function that is conditioned by the context upon which the impact is to be made.

THE ABILITY TO cause an impact is not totally derived from the use to which fiction is put, so that the question arises concerning the extent to which fiction is actually capable of truth. To say that it is truthful would imply that all traditional definitions must either be totally changed or at least so modified that their status is altered. Previous definitions vary according to the nature of the use, and irrespective of whether they are stretched to generalizations or narrowed down to individual cases, in none of its many applications does fiction depart so far from its function that it can be contained within the confines of a single definition—not least because its referentiality will decide on its use and on its form.

In Kantian philosophy the 'As If' figures as the quintessence of everything thinkable, and therefore fiction is something to which there is no alternative. This is what makes it feasible for fiction to appear in an infinite variety of contexts, but especially where boundaries have been drawn and need to be crossed. Thus fiction is never more than the thinkable, and so is more comprehensive than any of the contexts that give rise to its function. In this way, and perhaps only in this way, is fiction a truth in our experiential world. It is a truth, however, not to be substantiated by any manner of proof, as its only backing lies in the fact that there is no alternative to fiction; out of this arises its potency.

It is clear from this glimpse of fiction's 'truth' that fiction can be viewed from different perspectives that may relate to its function or to its necessity. The more pragmatic the viewpoint, the more differentiated will be the various uses: but if the focus falls on the necessity, then the clearer will be the nature of the 'truth' that there is no alternative for fiction. Both the pragmatic and the necessary aspect are closely linked. The lack of alternative, however, sheds no light on the multiplicity of uses, just as this multiplicity prevents the extrapolation of any generalized pattern of usage. Through the concurrence of functional use and capability of truth, fiction continually opens up the unforeseeable, and as such it offers a standpoint from which to investigate the anthropological makeup of humankind.

From all this we may draw a conclusion concerning the way in which fiction is classified. Many current definitions testify to a myopic view imposed not only by tradition and convention but also by the various pragmatic functions. The idea that it is a deliberate falsehood, as Vaihinger believed, is just one particularly vivid form of identification which is not fundamentally different from those advanced today by cognitively oriented linguistics.[9] But such reifications of its use do not in fact define fiction. If it allows us to penetrate the impenetrable to which it alone holds the key, then the lack of any alternative to it—as well as the impossibility of deriving its nature solely from its function—should be reflected in all the various attempts to describe it. It is true that fiction largely coincides with its use, but that is only a half-truth, for fiction itself does not arise out of the context of its use.

As human beings' extensions of themselves, fictions are "ways of worldmaking",[10] and literature figures as a paradigmatic instance of this process because it is relieved of the pragmatic dimension so essential to real-life situations. The fictionality of literature is not identical to the result it creates, but is rather a modus operandi that manifests itself in distinguishable acts.

THESE ACTS ARE marked by the fact that they are boundary-crossings, the concerted action of which sets literature apart from other types of fiction already described.*

There are three basic acts: selection, combination, and self-disclosure, which for analytical purposes may be distinguished from one another, but which interact and so compose the underlying pattern of fictionality operative in the literary text. The act of selection makes inroads into extratextual fields of reference, and by disrupting them creates an eventful disorder, in consequence of which both the structure and the semantics of these fields are subjected to certain deformations, with their respective constituents being differently weighted according to the various deletions and additions. Thus each field is reorganized in the text, but its new form includes and indeed depends on its function in our interpreted world. This function now becomes virtual and provides a back-

---

*The following passage is virtually the same as one in a previous essay; I had, however, to reproduce it in order to make understandable the different inferences to be drawn from it.

AVENUES FOR EXPLORATION

ground against which the new structure may stand out in relief, thus giving focus to an intention underlying the "coherent deformation."[11] Furthermore, the act of selection splits up each field of reference, since the chosen elements can only assume significance through the exclusion of others—this being the precondition for the eventful disorder, the resolution of which demands the assembly of a new meaning.

The act of selection also culls elements from other texts, but the resultant intertextuality should not be thought of merely in terms of blurring distinctions, or simply transcending the text to which reference has been made. The segments alluded to in the passages quoted begin to unfold unforeseeably shifting relationships both with their own context and with the new one into which they have been transplanted. Whatever form these relationships may take, two different types of discourse are always present, and their simultaneity triggers a reciprocal revealing and concealing of their respective contextual references. From this interplay there emerges a semantic instability that is exacerbated by the fact that the two sets of discourse are also contexts for each other, so that each in turn constantly switches from background to foreground, becoming a theme viewed from the standpoint of the other and vice versa. The resultant dynamic oscillation between the two ensures that their old meanings now become potential sources for new ones. The text itself becomes a kind of junction where other texts, norms, and values meet and work upon each other; as a point of intersection its core is virtual, and only when actualized—by the potential recipient—does it explode into its plurivocity.

The structure pinpointed in the act of selection also underlies the act of combination. Here the boundaries that are crossed are intratextual, ranging from lexical meanings to the constellation of characters. Once again the process should not be mistaken for a mere act of transcendence, because the various clusters—whether they be words with outstripped meanings or semantic enclosures broken open by the characters—are inseparably linked together and thus inscribe themselves into one another. Every word becomes dialogic, and every semantic field is doubled by another.

Through this double-voiced discourse every utterance carries something else in its wake, with the act of combination duplicating what is present by that which is absent—a process that often results in the balance being reversed, the present serving only to spotlight the absent. Thus what is said ceases to mean itself, but instead enables what it is not said to become present. The double meaning engendered by the act of combination thereby opens up multifarious connections within the text.

A similar doubling effect comes about through the literary text's disclosure of itself as fiction. This occurs on two different levels: that of the attitude to be imposed on the reader, and that of what the text is meant to represent. If the literary text reveals itself not as discourse, but as 'staged discourse', asking only that the world it represents should be taken as if it were a real world, then the recipient must suspend his or her natural attitudes to the thing represented (i.e., the real world). This does not mean that the natural attitude is transcended, for it is still present as a virtualized background against which comparisons may be made and new attitudes may take their shape. If we regard the world of the text as being bracketed off from the world it represents, it follows that that which is within the bracket is separated from the reality in which it is usually embedded. Consequently there will be a continual oscillation between the bracketed world and that from which it has been separated. The former therefore becomes a medium for revealing what has remained concealed in the empirical world, and whatever may be the relation between the two, it is the 'As If world' that brings about the interplay between them.

Thus self-disclosed fictionality as an act of boundary-crossing causes the recipient's natural attitude to be doubled by a new one that is demanded of him or her, while the world of the text is doubled by that from which it has been bracketed off, and whose reverse side is thereby brought to the fore.

The various acts of fictionalizing carry with them whatever has been outstripped, and the resultant doubleness might therefore be defined as the simultaneity of the mutually exclusive. This formula may help us to describe the structure of the fictional component of literature. It also allows for certain distinctions that are pertinent to the literary text—for example, setting it off from structures that govern our everyday world but are outstripped by the coexistence of what is mutually incompatible. The coexistence of the mutually exclusive gives rise to a dynamic oscillation resulting in a constant interpenetration of things that are set off from one another without ever losing their difference. The tension ensuing from the attempt to resolve this ineradicable difference creates an aesthetic potential that, as a source of meaning, can never have a substitute. This does not imply that the fictional component of literature is the actual work of art. What it does imply is that the fictional component makes the work of art possible.

YET FICTIONALITY IS only an instrument that channels the necessary flow of fantasy into our everyday world. As an activity of consciousness it taps our imaginary resources, simultaneously shaping them for their employment, and so the interplay between the fictional and the imaginary turns out to be basic to the heuristics of literary anthropology.

But what *is* imaginary? This has always been a thorny problem, even for those philosophers who were traditionally regarded as skeptics and of whom it has been said that their skepticism generally helped to eliminate unanswerable questions as pseudoquestions. What David Hume called synonymously "fancy" and "imagination" he saw as "a kind of magical faculty in the soul, which, tho' it be always most perfect in the greatest geniuses, and is properly what we call a genius, is however inexplicable by the utmost efforts of human understanding."[12] The imaginary defies discursive definition not least because it cannot be isolated but only exists in connection with something else, forming an indivisible alloy.

This can be borne out by important examples. As Hume, Kant, and Wittgenstein demonstrated in their different ways, perception cannot take place without a proportion of imagination. Perception functions neither as factual recording nor as pure concoction. Above all it is the continuity and the identity of the object perceived that can only be established by way of an imaginary ingredient, for the actual impression of perception can only come about in relation to nonactual perception. This process has been summed up as follows by P. F. Strawson, referring to Kant: "Insofar as we have supplied anything like an explanation or justification of Kant's apparently technical use of 'imagination,' we have done so by suggesting that recognition of an enduring object of a certain kind *as* an object of that kind, or as a certain particular object of that kind, involves a certain sort of connection with other nonactual perceptions. It involves other past (and hence nonactual) perceptions, or the thought of other possible (and hence nonactual) perceptions, of the *same* object being somehow alive in the present perception."[13]

There is a similar argument in Wittgenstein. If seeing functions primarily as "seeing as," then the object is identified with the aspect under which it is perceived. Mary Warnock interprets this as follows:

In concentrating on the particular kind of seeing which he (i.e. Wittgenstein) calls seeing an aspect he has done two things. First he has linked at least *this* kind of seeing (or hearing) with knowing or having concepts; and in some cases he has linked it as well with the use of the imagination. Secondly, he has connected the actual use of images with some cases of aspect-seeing and has strongly suggested their use in cases of recognition . . . [W]e may therefore quite legitimately argue that he has raised again the question raised by Hume and Kant as to the role in *all* perception (not just aspect-seeing) of the imagination; and that the connexion between perception and imagination is through the image itself (for the notion of aspects and that of images are, as he says, akin). Whenever seeing and hearing seems to take us beyond the actual immediate object of the senses . . . there it looks as if Wittgenstein . . . has left room for the imagination.[14]

These arguments, advanced in the analytical tradition, counter the suspicion that the imaginary is nothing but a problem of discourse, or that it is simply a prerequisite for a heuristics necessary to literary anthropology. Instead it is evident from both Kant's and Wittgenstein's assessments that the imagination is not a separable faculty but exists in combination with other faculties and indeed can only operate in conjunction with them if they are to function adequately. This, of course, does not tell us anything about the nature of the interplay, or why the imaginary portion is necessary for the production of a stable perception or impression of the object. It only tells us that these nonactual or aspectual 'images' have to precede objects in order for us to perceive them as such.

A quite different philosophical approach leads to a similar conclusion. Sartre considered the imaginary as an ideational activity, the unfolding of which is due to its being governed by consciousness. This holds true even for the dream, where consciousness is frozen as pure ideation and consequently deprived of its intentionality. Thus for Sartre the dream is the complete realization of a self-contained imaginary, as he puts it, whose total dominance removes all freedom from us.[15]

The same applies to madness and hallucination, but even here a preliminary ideation process is involved during which consciousness loses its freedom, although such images could not exist if consciousness were not present, albeit in a state of paralysis. Madness, hallucination, and dream feature a certain tangibility of the imaginary by swamping the intentionality of consciousness, thus indicating a tilt in the balance between conscious and imaginary components.

In daydreaming the slant given to the interpenetration of the conscious and the imaginary is again different. What we sense as diffuse, discontinuous, or associative strands are qualifying features of an ideational activity in which intentional directions have paled to insignificance. In all these cases, the kaleidoscopically changing relationships between the conscious and the imaginary condition the shifting patterns into which our ideational activity is cast. In fact the latter arises out of the intimate permeation of the conscious and the imaginary, just as the continuity and identity of the perceived object issue from the interpenetration of actual and imagined non-actual perceptions.

It is evident from the experiences described above that the imaginary cannot possibly be regarded as a *materia prima* that merely has to be processed. On the contrary, it only exists in combinations, that is, with sight, with consciousness, and hence in forms through which we establish contact with the world. But it is precisely because the imaginary can only be grasped by way of its contextualization that we are tempted to try and define it by isolating it.

IF WE LOOK at the most significant of these definitions that have sought to capture the imaginary in its history, we will be struck by a phenomenon that has already emerged from the Kant, Wittgenstein, and Sartre examples. The imaginary has long been considered as a tangible manifestation of perfection, and it was assumed that only art allowed man's participation in it. This concept was virulent up to Nietzsche, who regarded art as an urge to transform our phenomenal world to the pitch of perfection. Such ideas radiate a knowledge as to what the imaginary is, but they mark it off in contradistinction to reality, whereas in fact it counters and compensates for reality, thus being conditioned by what it is supposed to transcend. The contrast that is integral to the definition completely ignores the dependence.

The same is true of those concepts that view the imaginary as 'otherness'. In the traditional invocation of the Muses, this otherness can be grasped as inspiration and invention. It enables something to come into the world that had previously not existed, and so its appearance is able to bring about an impact that could not be deduced from what already is. In relation to the empirical world, the imaginary as otherness is a sort of holy madness that does not turn away from the world but intervenes in it.

But even when definitions are more rational or analytical, their referentiality remains integral. If the imagination is seen as a faculty, which is the case from Kant to Coleridge, it assumes its shape by presenting itself either as the organizer of interacting conditions of cognition, or as the unending repetition of nature in the human mind.

If the imaginary is equated with the unconscious, then there has to be consciousness so that the errant offshoots of fantasy can be experienced. And, finally, if the imaginary is desire, then there has to be what Lacan calls the 'mirror-stage', which the self projects of itself, because the imaginary is the reverse side of the self which can only be made palpable through a mirror image.

Whether the imaginary potential is viewed as perfection, otherness, the organizing faculty of cognition, unconscious fantasy, or desire, every one of these ontologically oriented definitions shows that it can only be grasped by way of its function and so in relation to contexts. These may be a counterimage to existing realities, a world shaken by inspiration, an organized interplay of cognitive faculties, an explanatory schema for the interpenetration of the conscious and the unconscious, or a deprivation that cries out for expression. None of these historical concepts makes the imaginary into *materia prima* that merely has to be processed, and although all the definitions, being discursive, aim primarily to capture the imaginary as a determinate phenomenon, they also demonstrate clearly that it is viewed in the contexts that enable it to take effect. For in all the definitions mentioned it has something of the character of an event: it acts as a counter to imperfection; it changes the world in which it appears; it combines the cognitive faculties by interrelating their functions; it wanders fantastically through the conscious mind; and it overturns the barriers to desire by way of a mirror image. In its eventfulness, the imaginary reveals itself only as a function and never as a substance. It precedes what is, even if it can only show itself through what is.

From this roughly sketched history of the various notions designed to capture the imaginary, there emerges the fact that the latter will take on different forms according to its varied performances in different contexts, and so it may reasonably be assumed that the literary context will again give rise to a different type of manifestation. Hence we may rule out the idea that the imaginary is nothing but a heuristic construct, concocted for the purpose of making a theory of fictionality work. On the contrary, here as elsewhere there is indisputable evidence that such a potential exists.

THE HISTORY OF the concept reveals to what extent the imaginary is given a perspective slant by the contexts within which it manifests itself. It may seem therefore as if the latter were nothing but a setting subservient to the appearance of the imaginary, whereas this supposed subservience in fact conditions the precise manifestation of

AVENUES FOR EXPLORATION

the imaginary and shapes the *form* of its presence. This holds equally true for the interplay between the imaginary and the fictional, the latter providing the medium for the imaginary to assume a tangible gestalt. It is inherent in the nature of all media that they point to what they themselves are not. The fictional—as I have outlined elsewhere[16]—is an 'As If' construction, which goes beyond itself in order to act as bearer for something else. In so doing, it imposes a perspective upon what it is not but which it bears. Therefore the imaginary, which is manifested through the medium of fictionality, also has a form that reveals the perspective imposed upon it by the medium. The fictional and the imaginary thus interpenetrate, with the medium giving form to what is not, and at the same time ensuring the manifestation of what it is not by imposing a perspective on it.

We have seen that fictionalizing acts as boundary-crossings should not be taken as a process of transcending, but, rather, of doubling, because whatever has been left behind is carried along in the wake of the individual acts and remains a potential presence. This is what constitutes the basic doubling structure of fictionality in literature. Moreover, this doubling structure is of a more comprehensive nature, for it always repeats an extratextual world within the text, thus establishing a simultaneity between the repeated world and the reason for its repetition, or sometimes even presenting two worlds in coexistence, as evinced by the fifteen-hundred-year-old tradition of pastoralism.

There is a striking similarity between the doubling structure of fictionality in literature and those phenomena of perception described by Strawson with reference to Kant. The continuity and identity of the perceived object are established by the doubling of actual perception by nonactual perception, the combination of which generates evidence that the individual object has been properly perceived. On the basis of this experience, literary fictionality appears to be a paradigmatic manifestation of the imaginary. For if the imaginary must always be bound up with something else (e.g., sight and consciousness) in order to be revealed, then its ideal manifestation is in the doubling structure of literary fictionality. If the imaginary can only be presented by way of a medium, then obviously it cannot be totally equated with that medium. It will always be something 'other'. And if the medium itself is a doubling structure, not only will it link the imaginary to something determinate which it cannot itself be, but at the same time it will reveal that the positions that have been doubled are bound, through this very doubling, to be changed. The positions cease to represent something determinate, and instead they begin to adumbrate something that they themselves are not. In this way both their status and their function undergo a change, simultaneously featuring both their structure and its undoing. In this manner they become a matrix for what might be termed the interplay of constantly shifting 'figurations'.

It must be pointed out, however, that the fictional dominates the imaginary in a manner distinctly different from the situation in acts of perception and consciousness, in which the imaginary is functionally related to and therefore absorbed by the respective pragmatic use. The doubling structure of literary fictionality gives presence to the imaginary in a diversified play of transformation which liberates it from all directly pragmatic links. In acts of perception and ideation, sight and awareness must be doubled by the imaginary, while the doubling of literary fictionality is the distinctive medium for the imaginary, whose presence consists precisely in the fact that it enables us to view things differently from what they seem to be.

THE QUESTION CONCERNING how we can ultimately distinguish the one from the other naturally arises. Certainly the medium gives a particular perspective to the mode of manifestation, but the latter could not be described if medium and mediated were identical. If we define fictionality as a doubling that conditions the presence of the imaginary, the doubling itself can only come about because there is a difference between the things doubled. Indeed this difference is the very origin of the doubling, and whatever may be the individual nature of the double state of affairs in literature, the difference itself remains both intangible and ungraspable. It is the hollow space between the world repeated in the text and those fields of reference from which that world is extracted; it is also the space between the discourses, semantic enclosures, and lexical connotations of the text, and finally it is the space between the world represented by the 'As If' mode and that for which the 'As If' mode acts as an analogue enabling conception. Fictionality gives presence to the simultaneity of the mutually exclusive, thus becoming the medium for the imaginary, but the imaginary, as we have seen, cannot be fully equated with the perspective imposed on it by the medium. It manifests itself, rather, as a difference that cannot be deduced from the medium itself. This difference spotlights the imaginary as resistance to conceptualization.

As literature does not allow the imaginary to be absorbed into the pragmatic applications of the real world, it enables us to concentrate our attentions on the nature of our human resources. It is

AVENUES FOR EXPLORATION

not subjected to any premature definition but is simply present in all its multifarious forms, the exploration of which is a basic objective of literary anthropology. Relieved of all practical constraints, literary fictionality can exploit the imaginary in any number of ways. It can allow its inherent consciousness to be swamped by the imaginary, or it can freeze the imaginary into a purely cerebral configuration. Between these two extremes are innumerable possibilities, and indeed this very freedom of play turns out to be a basic category for capturing the protean potential of the imaginary. Play also structures the interpenetration of the fictional and the imaginary, without determining the relationship, which unfolds itself in a veritable welter of games. It simultaneously allows us to reverse the games we play, and thus erase the definite imprint made on the relationship in order to manifest the imaginary differently. As play precedes any control exercised by thinking, the interplay between the conscious and the imaginary highlights the fact that neither exists independently of the other. There are no formal boundaries to this interplay, even though every literary work plays the game in its own particular way. Indeed, the game itself becomes a means of making present that which defies definition, while those elements of the imaginary which are to be observed through the literary work can only be mirrored forth by way of the game.

IF THE INTERPLAY between the fictional and the imaginary forms the heuristics of a literary anthropology, the question of the objectives of such an anthropology arises. That question might be tackled from pragmatic, systematic, and historical points of view.

Pragmatically such an approach would seek to diagnose the human condition. The text as a cultural object would then become a sign for the mastery of a situation and hence for the clarification of those potentials that must be mobilized if mastery is to be achieved. From this would emerge a physiognomy of history that would detach itself from its political, economic, and social features. As elements of the prevailing culture, these provide only the conditions for the necessary funneling of fantasy into that culture, thereby revealing the reverse side of what thought and social systems claim to be their overriding validity in the respective cultural context. This uncovering need not be confined to stressing deficiencies; it may also bring out desires, needs, and necessities which may now take their rightful place through fantasy.

In systematic terms, a literary anthropology would allow a reappraisal or even a reopening of an issue apparently long since decided on by the Aristotelian tradition concerning the nature of human faculties. The assumed clear distinction between imagination, reason, and the senses, as settled by faculty psychology, crumbles when applied to literature. Literature draws its life from interaction between imaginary, conscious, and perceptual activities, and appears to have no clear basis or origin in any of these 'faculties'. If one takes the clear-cut distinctions of faculty psychology as a framework, literature appears to merge them in a protean coalescence. Imaginary, conscious, and perceptual activities constantly inscribe themselves into one another, in consequence of which the 'faculties' appear condensed or distorted, transfigured or mirrored, dramatized or subverted.

This implies a certain "family likeness" between literature and dream, which gives rise to the question of why basic dream structures recur so insistently in literature. What is repeated, however, never remains precisely the same in the repetition, and literature is not merely a copy of the dream but, rather, facilitates something that is not possible through the dream itself: anxiety-free access to the inaccessible.

The "family likeness" may also suggest that dream and literature are not dependent on each other so much as they are different manifestations of a common stock. Such a suggestion is supported by the fact that literature reverses the retrograde movement of the dream into one that is progradient: instead of repeating archaic conflicts, it opens up new possibilities. Literature appears to entertain a transgressive relationship to the dream pattern in the sense that it steps out of what it repeats. Repetition comes to full fruition by exceeding the repeated; otherwise it remains lifeless and sterile. If literature repeats the dream, a doubling is bound to occur, resulting in a change of perception; we are caught up in the dream, and what we live through is made by the repetition into an object of observation. But what can be observed can also be changed, and indeed *is* changed by the very process of observation.

Finally, there is also a historical objective for literary anthropology. Research devoted to literature and the arts in the broadest sense was, as long as bourgeois culture held sway, closely associated with the formation of personality. In the latter half of our century the erosion of the idea of education as well as that of the significance of the individual has had far-reaching repercussions on the inherited canon, whose validity was challenged to such a degree that a total abolition of disciplines concerned with interpreting literature and the arts was considered to be in accordance with current social interest.[17] The study of literature as practiced by the various academic disciplines had its justification in opening up the treasures of a book culture whose benefits they were meant to spread. For the disciplines were committed to developing humanity, and to training human faculties in order to promote the ennobling of humankind.[18] In view of the fact that these ideas no longer apply, the question arises concerning the ability of an anthropologically oriented study of literature to regain some of the importance of literature for our lives in the manner taken for granted by past scholars.

Clearly, the goal of literary anthropology is not to provide that kind of education once promised by the study of literature. It might instead contribute to a different kind of self-enlightenment of the human being, one that is not to be brought about by the encyclopedic accumulation of knowledge formerly considered to be a prerequisite for education. It would do so by elucidating our unconscious guidelines in order to trigger a chronic process of self-reflection that would no longer seek its fulfillment in some kind of ideal. Rather, this process would enable us to see through the attitudes offered to us, if not imposed on us, by our everyday world. Even if at first its character were predominantly critical, it would still constantly bring to light our own situational premises in order to expose what constitutes our outlook.

This sketch is a very cautious answer to the question of how literary anthropology might legitimize itself. It is cautious because it conforms to the social and cultural code of our time, which is predominantly critical. This is very evident today in America, where the trend is toward criticism of institutions and of power monopolies. It is to be hoped that there will not be a repetition of the process that took place in Europe in the late sixties and early seventies when literary studies—because they were regarded as a medium for revolutionary institutional change—ceased to be important subject matter altogether. After this historical experience, the heirs of bourgeois culture must now see that the desire to change institutions through literature is nothing but a delusion.

Can literary anthropology ever be more than just another way of transposing the current critical code into an interpretative practice? Perhaps it may form the starting point for a task to be shared by all the interpreting disciplines in the humanities—namely, to work out a theory of culture. In view of the heterogeneity of cultures that the twentieth century has opened up to us, the need for such a theory seems to be particularly impelling. The task would not only endow the interpreting disciplines with a new goal, but would also restore to them the legitimacy that they have lost. Certainly such a theory could not be achieved by literary theory alone, but the study of literature can contribute to an interdisciplinary discussion both by stating problems and by identifying issues. As the product of a particular culture, literature draws life from tensions with and impacts on the cultural context from which it has emerged. It intervenes in its real environment and establishes its uniqueness not least by highlighting its otherness in relation to the situations that have conditioned it. In this manner it adumbrates new regions that it inscribes into the already charted topography of culture. For if what is, is not everything, then what is must be changeable.[19] It is this function of literature in the context of culture that moves the overriding objective of literary anthropology into focus.

LITERATURE IS NOT only the continual recurrence of the world in which we live, but it is also the reflection of what we are. For this reason it has been primarily conceived as mimesis. But no matter what definitions this term has been given in history, mimesis is always a repetition that produces something. Initially mimesis was thought to be the representation of the constituent forms of nature or the perfection of what nature had left imperfect. Thus mimesis as a repetition is also an overstepping of limits. How are we to understand this 'overstepping'? The Aristotelian tradition claimed that art imitates the constitutive forms of nature, which are perfect, and also perfects the imperfections of nature, and so the two original impulses of the mimetic tradition implied the at least temporary absence of what was to be represented. From the very beginning, therefore, the inherent tendency underlying the repetitions of art and literature was toward making the absent present. It can be said, then, that the recurrence of particular worlds in the literary text has always taken place on the prior understanding that it is a mode of enacting what is not there.

Why have we created this mode of staging, and why has it accompanied us throughout our history? The answer must certainly be the desire, not to repeat what is, but to gain access to what we otherwise cannot have. We have no access, for example, to the beginning, the end, or the 'ground' out of which we are. The beginning and the end are paradigms of realities that we can neither experience nor know. But there are also experiences, such as identity and love, whose reality is just as incontestable as the fact that we can never know precisely what they are. Evidently, however, we are not prepared to accept the limits of cognition, and so we need

AVENUES FOR EXPLORATION

images to mirror forth the unknowable. These images are nourished by the ideas and desires that hold us in thrall, but they can have neither permanence nor enduring validity. As a consequence, their content, which gives shape to those inaccessible phenomena arising from and fashioned by the cultural context of the day, will be changeable. The images of what is withheld from us thus reflect the potential range of the respective cultural reality. This is doubled by what we might call its reverse side.

The doubling brought about by literature in turn produces what is characteristic of all doubling: a change of perception. This does not mean that the cultural context changes; it is, however, translated into the dimension of its perceivability. The doubling, therefore, allows us to see ourselves as that within which we are entangled, and in this respect literature is a decisive means of shaping cultural reality. It must be stressed again that literature does not reflect this reality, but mirrors its reverse side, which would otherwise remain hidden by the cultural context itself. It is only this mirroring that—in Kosík's words—brings the reality of a historical period to full fruition.[20] By throwing into relief the uncharted regions of the prevailing culture, it changes the map, which is overlaid by the imagery of what remains cognitively unfathomable.

The interplay between the fictional and the imaginary provides the necessary heuristics for such an exploration. In its boundary-crossing capacity fictionality is first and foremost an extension of humankind which, like all operations of consciousness, is nothing but a pointer toward something other than itself. Basically it is void of any content and hence cries out to be filled.

Into this structured void the imaginary potential flows, because what is unavailable both to cognition and perception can only be given presence by way of ideation. Without the imaginary, fictionality remains empty, and without fictionality, the imaginary would remain diffuse. Out of their interplay emerges the staging of what is unavailable to us.

If this staging is indeed a necessary alternative to what we are, the investigation of it would endow literary anthropology with an irrefutable legitimacy. Simultaneously a more far-reaching question would be posed concerning why we cannot cease to create such images, even though we are aware of their illusory character and know that they cannot supply the answers we are so anxious to learn. Historical experience shows that the validity of these imaginary worlds becomes increasingly short-lived if the staging merely features compensation for what has been withheld from us. Clearly the staging itself must not lead to closure, but must remain open-ended, if its spell is not to be broken. This historic observation testifies to the fact that we ourselves are the end and the beginning of these stagings, each of which is nothing but a possibility. In light of that insistent fact, a central task of literary anthropology would be to explain why we find an insatiable pleasure in making ourselves into our own possibilities and why we cannot—in spite of knowing what it is—cease to play the game of our potentials.

Notes

One. Indeterminacy and the Reader's Response in Prose Fiction

1. Susan Sontag, *Against Interpretation and Other Essays* (New York, 1966), p. 14.

2. Ibid., pp. 6f.

3. Lowry Nelson, Jr., "The Fictive Reader and Literary Self-Reflexiveness," in *The Disciplines of Criticism: Essays in Literary Theory, Interpretation, and History, Honoring René Wellek on the Occasion of his Sixty-fifth Birthday*, ed. Peter Demetz, Thomas Greene, and Lowry Nelson, Jr. (New Haven, 1968), p. 174.

4. J. L. Austin, *How to Do Things with Words*, ed. J. O. Urmson (Cambridge, Mass., 1962), pp. 1ff.

5. This matter is also treated in Susanne K. Langer's *Feeling and Form* (New York, 1953), p. 59: "The solution of the difficulty lies, I think, in the recognition that what art expresses is *not* actual feeling, but ideas of feeling; as language does not express actual things and events but ideas of them."

6. E. H. Gombrich, *Art and Illusion* (London, 1962), p. 76.

7. See Roman Ingarden, *The Literary Work of Art*, trans. George G. Grabowicz (Evanston, Ill. 1973), pp. 262ff.

8. At this point there ought to follow a critical discussion of the term *Unbestimmtheitsstellen* (places of indeterminacy), which Ingarden sometimes uses in his writings about the work of art, in order to differentiate clearly the concept of this essay from an apparently related posing of the problem. Such a discussion would, however, exceed the limits of an essay and would certainly upset its balance. It will be dealt with later in a more detailed presentation. However, a few important differences might be stated here. Ingarden employs the concept of *Unbestimmtheitsstellen* to indicate, above all, the distinction between literary objects and real ones. Hence the *Unbestimmtheitsstellen* reveal what the subject of literature or the literary object respectively lacks in comparison with the total definitiveness of real things. Accordingly, one of the main operations going on in a literary work is the constant removal of *Unbestimmtheitsstellen* in the act of composition, thus diminishing their occurrence as far as possible. Thereby the latent deficiency adhering to them can clearly be seen. Yet the gaps of indeterminacy are vital for eliciting the reader's response and are consequently an important factor for the effect exercised by a work of art.

For Ingarden, however, this function plays hardly any role at all, as can be seen in his book *The Cognition of the Literary Work of Art* (trans. Ruth

Ann Crowley and Kenneth R. Olson [Evanston, Ill. 1973]), in which the conditions of the literary response are analyzed. Communication occurs, in Ingarden's terms, whenever the reader feels the impact of the *Ursprungsemotion* (original emotion) radiating from the literary text, so that the explanation of responses is nothing but a rehearsal of the well-known argument of empathy. Consequently, the *Unbestimmtheitsstellen* are defined as the omission of the unimportant, mostly supplementary, details, for which Ingarden often gives quite trivial examples (see p. 50). In his opinion there is no compelling necessity for filling in the *Unbestimmtheitsstellen*. Occasionally, they may disturb the artistic worth or value—even destroy or annihilate—the work of art when, as in modern texts, they increase. Thus for Ingarden the *Unbestimmtheitsstellen* demand only a single activity from the reader—that of completion. This means that the filling of the *Unbestimmtheitsstellen* contributes toward a completion of the polyphonic harmony, which, for Ingarden, embodies the basic quality of a work of art. If the completion is specified as a supplementation of what is omitted, the undynamic quality becomes visible. Moreover, the ideal of polyphonic harmony which Ingarden sets up as a yardstick for judging a work of art lends itself as a means to separate true from false supplementations, and thereby confirms or corrects, respectively, the supplementation the reader is supposed to provide. Behind such a concept there looms the classical conception of a work of art, so that consequently for Ingarden there are true and false realizations of a literary text.

9. See Kathleen Tillotson, *Novels of the Eighteen-Forties* (Oxford, 1962), pp. 28ff., 33, and George H. Ford, *Dickens and His Readers* (Princeton, 1955), p. 6.

10. See Tillotson, *Novels of the Eighteen-Forties*, pp. 34f., 36f.

11. When Dickens published the first cheap edition of his novels, its success could hardly be compared with that which the later editions achieved. The first edition of 1846–47 occurred at a time when Dickens still published in serial form; see John Forster, *The Life of Charles Dickens*, ed. A. J. Hoppé (London, 1966), 1:448. In this connection two further examples are instructive. *Martin Chuzzlewit*, designated by Dickens himself as one of his most important novels, proved a flop on its first publication. Forster (*Life* 1:285) and Ford (*Dickens and His Readers*, p. 43) are of the opinion that this failure resulted from the manner of the publication; instead of following the previous method of weekly installments, this novel appeared at monthly intervals. The intermissions proved too long. We know that Crabb Robinson found the serial publication of Dickens's novels so disturbing that he occasionally decided he would sooner wait for the book form than endure the anxiety that the still unforeseeable action produced in him (see Ford, pp. 41f.) Furthermore, the week-to-week chapters themselves indicate how tightly they were organized as regards effect. In book form this manner of composition became so obvious that it led to critical evaluations by readers (see Ford, pp. 123f.) On the specific contact between

author and reader in the serialized novel, see also Tillotson, *Novels of the Eighteen-Forties*, pp. 26ff., 33. Trollope was of the opinion that the serialized novel avoided the "long succession of dull pages" which in book form could not be completely bypassed (Tillotson, p. 40).

12. See Tillotson, *Novels of the Eighteen-Forties*, pp. 25f.

13. Wayne C. Booth, *The Rhetoric of Fiction* (Chicago, 1961), pp. 211f., differentiates between a "reliable" and an "unreliable narrator," without, however, evaluating this fact for the communication process. The "unreliable narrator" naturally constitutes the more interesting type for the communication process, because his "unreliability" possesses a strategic intention, which relates to the steering of the reader in the text.

14. See Charles Dickens, *Oliver Twist*, New Oxford Illustrated Dickens (Oxford, 1959), pp. 12f.

15. Ibid., pp. 14f.

16. Northrop Frye, *Anatomy of Criticism* (New York, 1967), p. 73.

17. Henry Fielding, *Joseph Andrews*, Author's Preface, Everyman's Library (London, 1948), p. xxxi: "From the discovery of this affectation arises the Ridiculous, which always strikes the reader with surprise and pleasure; and that in a higher and stronger degree when the affectation arises from hypocrisy, than when from vanity; for to discover any one to be the exact reverse of what he affects, is more surprising, and consequently more ridiculous, than to find him a little deficient in the quality he desires the reputation of." Compare this with the similar comment in *The History of Tom Jones*, Everyman's Library (London, 1962), vol. 1, bk. 1., chap. 1, p. 12.

18. Fielding, *Tom Jones*, vol. 1, bk. 2, chap. 1, p. 39.

19. James Joyce, *A Portrait of the Artist as a Young Man* (London, 1966), p. 219.

20. W. M. Thackeray, *Vanity Fair*, Centenary Biographical Edition, ed. Lady Ritchie, (London, 1910), 1: liii. Hereafter, volume and page references to *Vanity Fair* are given parenthetically in the text.

21. W. J. Harvey, *Character and the Novel* (London, 1965), p. 147.

22. W. M. Thackeray, *The Letters and Private Papers*, ed. Gordon N. Ray (London, 1945), 3:391.

23. For details see "Patterns of Communication in Joyce's *Ulysses*," in my book *The Implied Reader: Patterns of Communication in Prose Fiction from Bunyan to Beckett* (Baltimore, 1987), pp. 196–233.

24. B. Ritchie, "The Formal Structure of the Aesthetic Object," in *The Problem of Aesthetics*, ed. E. Vivas and M. Krieger (New York, 1965), pp. 230f.

25. See James Joyce, *Ulysses* (London, 1937), p. 118.

26. Gombrich, *Art and Illusion*, p. 278. Although this quotation is related to a discussion of Constable, it nonetheless presents a point of view which is central in the thesis developed by Gombrich, a thesis whose validity is not limited to painting.

27. M. Merleau-Ponty, *Phenomenology of Perception*, trans. Colin Smith (New York, 1962), pp. 219, 221.

28. See Reinhard Baumgart, *Aussichten des Romans oder Hat Literatur Zukunft?* (Neuwied, 1968), p. 79.

29. For a more detailed discussion see "When Is the End Not the End? The Idea of Fiction in Beckett," in *The Implied Reader*, pp. 257–73.

30. Sir Philip Sidney, *The Defence of Poesie*, vol. 3 of *The Prose Works*, ed. Albert Feuillerat (Cambridge, 1962), p. 29.

Two.   Interaction between Text and Reader

This essay contains a few ideas that are dealt with more comprehensively in my book *The Act of Reading: A Theory of Aesthetic Response* (Baltimore, 1978).

1. See Roman Ingarden, *The Literary Work of Art*, trans. George G. Grabowicz (Evanston, Ill., 1973), pp. 276ff.

2. R. D. Laing, H. Phillipson, and A. R. Lee, *Interpersonal Perception: A Theory and a Method of Research* (New York, 1966).

3. Ibid., p. 4.

4. R. D. Laing, *The Politics of Experience* (Harmondsworth, Eng., 1968), p. 16, Laing's italics.

5. Ibid., p. 34.

6. Ibid.

7. See also E. Goffman, *Interaction Ritual: Essays on Face-to-Face Behavior* (New York, 1967).

8. Virginia Woolf, *The Common Reader: First Series* (London, 1957), p. 174. In this context, it is well worth considering Virginia Woolf's comments on the composition of her own fictional characters. She remarks in her diary: "I'm thinking furiously about Reading and Writing. I have no time to describe my plans. I should say a good deal about *The Hours* and my discovery: how I dig out beautiful caves behind my characters: I think that gives exactly what I want; humanity, humour, depth. The idea is that the caves shall connect and each comes to daylight at the present moment." (*A Writer's Diary: Being Extracts from the Diary of Virginia Woolf*, ed. Leonard Woolf [London, 1953], p. 60). The suggestive effect of the "beautiful caves" is continued in her work through what she leaves out. On this subject, T. S. Eliot once observed: "Her observation, which operates in a continuous way, implies a vast and sustained work of organization. She does not illumine with sudden bright flashes but diffuses a soft and placid light. Instead of looking for the primitive, she looks rather for the civilized, the highly civilized, where nevertheless something is found to be *left out*. And this something is deliberately left out, by what could be called a moral effort of the will. And, being left out, this something is, in a sense, in a

melancholy sense, present." ("T. S. Eliot 'Places' Virginia Woolf for French Readers," in *Virginia Woolf: The Critical Heritage*, ed. Robin Majumdar and Allen McLaurin [London, 1975], p. 192).

9. See Aron Gurwitsch, *The Field of Consciousness* (Pittsburgh, 1964), pp. 309–75.

10. Rudolf Arnheim, *Toward a Psychology of Art* (Berkeley and Los Angeles, 1967), p. 239.

11. For a discussion of the problem of changing relevance and abandoned thematic relevance, see Alfred Schütz, *Das Problem der Relevanz*, trans. A. von Baeyer (Frankfurt am Main, 1970), pp. 104ff., 145ff.

12. See Henry Fielding, *The History of Tom Jones*, Everyman's Library (London, 1962), vol. 1, bk. 3, chap. 7, p. 92, and vol. 2, bk. 18, Chapter the Last, p. 427.

13. Jean Piaget, *Der Strukturalismus*, trans. L. Häfliger (Olten, 1973), p. 134.

Three. Interview

1. Norman N. Holland, *The Dynamics of Literary Response*, 1st and 2d eds. (New York, 1968, 1975).

2. Norman N. Holland, *Poems in Persons* (New York, 1973).

3. Norman N. Holland, *5 Readers Reading* (New Haven, 1975).

4. Wolfgang Iser, *The Act of Reading: A Theory of Aesthetic Response* (Baltimore, 1978), originally published as *Der Akt des Lesens: Theorie ästhetischer Wirkung* (Munich, 1976). Page references to *The Act of Reading* are given parenthetically in the text.

5. English 692, "Poem Opening," *College English* 40 (1978): 2–16.

6. Holland and Sherman, "Virtualités du gothique," in *Romantisme noir*, eds. L. Abensour and F. Charras (Paris, 1978), pp. 234–43.

7. Norman N. Holland, "Transactive Teaching," *College English* 39 (1977): 276–85.

8. Wolfgang Iser, *The Implied Reader: Patterns of Communication in Prose Fiction from Bunyan to Beckett* (Baltimore, 1974), originally published as *Der Implizite Leser: Kommunikationsformen des Romans von Bunyan bis Beckett* (Munich, 1972).

9. Holland, *Dynamics* (1968), pp. 34–36.

10. Ibid., Preface (1975).

11. English 692, "Poem Opening."

12. See, for example, Ulric Neisser, *Cognitive Psychology* (Englewood Cliffs, N.J., 1967).

13. Norman N. Holland, "Identity: An Interrogation at the Border of Psychology," *Language and Style* 10 (1977): 199–209; idem, "What Can a Concept of Identity Add to Psycholinguistics?" in *Psychoanalysis and*

Language, ed. Joseph H. Smith (New Haven, 1976), pp. 171–234.

14. Kenneth Burke, "Literature as Equipment for Living," in Burke, *The Philosophy of Literary Form* (Baton Rouge, La., 1941).

Four. Spenser's Arcadia

This essay was first published by the Center of Hellenistic and Hermeneutical Studies, Pacific School of Religion, Berkeley, California, and is reprinted here with the kind permission of the Center.

1. For different historical assessments of pastoral literature, see Werner Krauss, "Über die Stellung der Bukolik in der ästhetischen Theorie des Humanismus," in *Gesammelte Aufsätze zur Literatur und Sprachwissenschaft* (Frankfurt, 1949), pp. 68–94. For views of pastoral literature since the eighteenth century, see in particular pp. 90ff.

2. See Bruno Snell, "Arkadien: Die Entdeckung einer geistigen Landschaft," in *Die Entdeckung des Geistes: Studien zur Entdeckung des europäischen Denkens bei den Griechen* (Hamburg, 1948), pp. 268–93, esp. pp. 275ff.

3. Snell, "Arkadien," pp. 277f.

4. Ibid., p. 269.

5. Daniel Defoe, "Serious Reflections during the Life and Surprising Adventures of Robinson Crusoe, with His Vision of the Angelic World," in *Romances and Narratives*, ed. George A. Aitken (London, 1895), 3:13.

6. Snell, "Arkadien," p. 269.

7. See Frank Kermode, Introduction to *English Pastoral Poetry: From the Beginnings to Marvell* (London, 1952), p. 41.

8. See Paul E. McLane, *Spenser's Shepheardes Calender: A Study in Elizabethan Allegory* (Notre Dame, Ind., 1961). He interprets the whole work as an allegory of England's political situation in the context of this event. Such an interpretation leads to a combination of interesting insights with a good deal of hairsplitting. This study does not explain why the *Shepheardes Calender* survived the event that it was meant to allegorize.

9. See ibid., pp. 112ff.

10. See, among others, E. M. W. Tillyard, *The Elizabethan World Picture* (New York, n.d.), pp. 16f.

11. See Douglas Bush, *Mythology and the Renaissance Tradition in English Poetry*, New Revised Edition (New York, 1963), p. 114; see also Jean M. Edwards, "Spenser and his Philosophy," *Cambridge Journal* 4 (1950/51): 622.

12. For details, see Herbert Schöffler, *Die Anfänge des Puritanismus: Versuch einer Deutung der englischen Reformation* (Leipzig, 1932), pp. 77f., 95ff., 108ff., 162, 165f.

13. Edmund Spenser, *The Faerie Queene: Books Six and Seven, The Works*, Variorum Edition (Baltimore, 1938), p. 152.

14. Ibid., p. 153; on the relation between *Natura* and *Mutability* see William Blissett, "Spenser's Mutabilitie," in *Essays in English Literature from the Renaissance to the Victorian Age, Presented to A. S. P. Woodhouse*, ed. M. MacLure and F. W. Watt (Toronto, 1965), pp. 26–42.

15. Spenser, *The Faerie Queene*, p. 180.

16. George Puttenham, *The Arte of English Poesie (English Linguistics, 1500–1800)*, ed. R. C. Alston (Menston, Eng., 1968), p. 30.

17. Edmund Spenser, *The Minor Poems*, vol. 1 of *The Works*, Variorum Edition (Baltimore, 1943), p. 10; gloss 1 of the January eclogue, p. 17; glosses 10 and 21 of the April eclogue, pp. 41–42; and, above all, Colin's role in the November eclogue. See also McLane, *Spenser's Shepheardes Calender*, p. 300.

18. Spenser, *Minor Poems*, p. 17, January eclogue; pp. 36ff., April eclogue; pp. 61ff. June eclogue; and pp. 104ff., November eclogue.

19. Ibid., gloss 50 of the April eclogue, pp. 42f.; glosses 54, 111 of the May eclogue, pp. 55f. Unless otherwise specified, page references to *The Minor Poems* are hereafter given parenthetically in the text.

20. Richard Cody, *The Landscape of the Mind: Pastoralism and Platonic Theory in Tasso's Aminta and Shakespeare's Early Comedies* (Oxford, 1969), p. 11.

21. See W. L. Renwick, *Edmund Spenser: An Essay on Renaissance Poetry*, University Paperbacks (London, 1964), p. 35.

22. On this controversial issue see, among others, Agnes Duncan Kuersteiner, "E.K. is Spenser," *PMLA* 50 (1935): 140–55; D. T. Starnes, "Spenser and E.K.," *Studies in Philology* 39 (1942): 181–200; and Robert W. Mitchner, "Spenser and E.K.: An Answer," *Studies in Philology* 42 (1945): 183–90. See also Spenser, *Minor Poems*, pp. 645–50, where there is a summary of the discussion.

23. See also Puttenham's similar description of the eclogue as genre (note 16 above).

24. Mary Parmenter, "Spenser: Twelve Aeglogues Proportionable to the Twelve Monethes," *ELH* 3 (1936): 195; see also S. K. Heninger, Jr., "The Implications of Form for *The Shepheardes Calender*," *Studies in the Renaissance* 9 (1962): 309–21. His main concern is with the function of the calendar in Neoplatonism.

25. This is a typically Spenserian procedure, strikingly summed up by Frank Kermode. *Spenser and the Allegorists*, Proceedings of the British Academy, no. 48 (Oxford, 1963), p. 270: "He does not convert event into myth, but myth into event."

26. See H. Walther, *Das Streitgedicht in der lateinischen Literatur des Mittelalters*, Quellen und Untersuchungen zur lateinischen Philologie des Mittelalters 5 Heft 2 (Munich, 1920), p. 45; on the "topos" of youth and age, see E. R. Curtius, *Europäische Literatur und lateinisches Mittelalter* (Bern, 1954), p. 180ff. The similarities between this theme and Mantuan's sixth eclogue, cited in Spenser, *Minor Poems*, pp. 256f., are only peripheral.

Krauss, "Über die Stellung der Bukolik," p. 74, points out that Mantuan's eclogues fluctuate between virtually every possible style. The fusion of medieval debate and eclogue is occasionally to be found even in the Middle Ages. In such cases, however, the pastoral element is reduced to a mere decorative background for the dispute itself. In Spenser's eclogues, on the other hand, the interlinked genres are far easier to distinguish, especially as the eclogue is joined by the fable as a further element in the combination.

27. Wylie Sypher, *Four Stages of Renaissance Style*, Anchor Books (Garden City, N.Y., 1956), p. 9, regards this as characteristic of Renaissance style: "Renaissance art and literature are filled with intersecting techniques." Wolfgang Clemen also stresses this feature as typical of Spenser's poetry. In *Spensers Epithalamion: Zum Problem künstlerischer Wertmassstäbe*, Sitzungsberichte der Bayerischen Akademie der Wissenschaften Phil.-Hist. Klasse 1964, Heft 8 (Munich, 1964), p. 29, he writes: "Very frequently the art of *Epithalamion* presents itself to us as a unification of the most diverse and indeed contradictory elements."

28. See also the commentator's remarks about the emblem, p. 45.

29. Colin Clout says to Hobbinoll: "That Paradise hast found, which *Adam* lost" (p. 60).

30. See also gloss 50, pp. 42f.

31. See also gloss, p. 68.

32. Menalcas is described in the gloss as "a person vnkowne and secrete" (p. 65); McLane, *Spenser's Shepheardes Calender*, p. 38, sees Menalcas as an anagram for Alençon.

33. There are some revealing observations on this general paradox to be found in Gilbert Ryle's *The Concept of the Mind* (Harmondsworth, Eng., 1969)—especially in the chapter dealing with the imagination. Concluding a discussion on seeing and imagining, Ryle says:

> Seeing Helvellyn [a mountain that Ryle uses as an illustration] in one's mind's eye does not entail, what seeing Helvellyn and seeing snapshots of Helvellyn entail, the having of visual sensations. It does involve the thought of having a view of Helvellyn and it is therefore a more sophisticated operation than that of having a view of Helvellyn. It is one utilization among others of the knowledge of how Helvellyn should look, or, in one sense of the verb, it is thinking how it should look. The expectations which are fulfilled in the recognition at sight of Helvellyn are not indeed fulfilled in picturing it, but the picturing of it is something like a rehearsal of getting them fulfilled. So far from picturing involving the having of faint sensations, or wraiths of sensations, it involves missing just what one would be due to get, if one were seeing the mountain." (p. 255)

34. See E.K. in "Dedicatory Epistle," Spenser, *Minor Poems*, p. 11.

35. Cody, *Landscape of the Mind*, p. 161.

36. Krauss, "Über die Stellung der Bukolik," p. 73, quotes a suggestion by Manitius that eclogue-type poems of the Middle Ages may have played a part in the development of the drama; see also the reference on p. 81 to Scaliger's opinion on the connection between pastoral literature and drama.

37. See Snell, "Arkadien," p. 286.

38. Erich Köhler, "Wandlungen Arkadiens: Die Marcela-Episode des 'Don Quijote' (1, 11–14)," in *Literaturgeschichte als geschichtlicher Auftrag: Werner Krauss zum 60. Geburtstag*, ed. Werner Bahner (Leipzig, 1960), p. 57.

Five. The Dramatization of Double Meaning

1. All quotations from *As You Like It* are from the Arden Shakespeare, ed. Agnes Latham (London, 1975). Parenthetical text references are to act, scene, and line.

2. For the terminology and its application, see M. M. Bakhtin, *The Dialogic Imagination: Four Essays*, Slavic Series 1, ed. Michael Holquist and trans. Caryl Emerson and Michael Holquist (Austin, Tex., 1981), pp. 324ff.

3. Bakhtin, *Dialogic Imagination*, p. 361.

4. Hans-Georg Gadamer, *Truth and Method*, trans. Garrett Barden and John Cumming (New York, 1975), p. 124.

5. Bakhtin, *Dialogic Imagination*, p. 60.

6. This is a point developed by Nina Schwartz in her paper "As It Likens You: The Metamorphosis of Consciousness in the Fictional Order," submitted in my seminar in the winter quarter 1980 at the University of California, Irvine.

7. See Hans Blumenberg, *Wirklichkeiten in denen wir leben* (Stuttgart, 1981), pp. 112f.

8. For reference see the German translation of Bakhtin: Michael M. Bachtin, *Literatur und Karneval: Zur Romantheorie und Lachkultur*, trans. Alexander Kaempfe (Munich, 1969), pp. 47–60.

9. See Dieter Henrich, "Freie Komik," in *Das Komische*, Poetik und Hermeneutik 7, ed. Wolfgang Preisendanz and Rainer Warning (Munich, 1976), pp. 385ff.

10. See also Agnes Latham, Introduction to *As You Like It*, p. xxii.

11. Paul Ricoeur, *Hermeneutik und Strukturalismus: Der Konflikt der Interpretationen I*, trans. Johannes Rütsche (Munich, 1973), pp. 82f.

12. For the individual speech functions, see Felix Martínez-Bonati, *Fictive Discourse and the Structures of Literature: A Phenomenological Approach*, trans. Philip W. Silver (Ithaca, 1981), pp. 87f.

13. Bakhtin, *Dialogic Imagination*, p. 405, maintains, however: "To a certain extent comedy is an exception to this."

14. The plot of the play sheds revealing light on this assumption. Those characters in the political world who suppress their doubles as well as the double meaning in their own speech, are never in a position to change into their own otherness. But at the end they are totally transformed. Duke Frederick and Oliver cease completely to be what they were before. In the

political world they constantly invoked—though always violated—the codes of government and family, and so they gave the impression that their conduct was regulated by these codes. However, they were not aware of the degree to which their conduct was in fact regulated by the breaking of these codes. Thus they have long since distanced themselves, unconsciously, from the selves associated with such codes, as a result of which they are now able to break radically with what they hitherto always claimed to be their guiding principles.

Duke Frederick comes to the forest, undergoes a religious conversion, and resolves to lead a monastic life. Oliver leaves the political world and takes on a new identity in the pastoral world. And so the characters who banished their doubles now change identities because they have never known what it was to play their own otherness.

Such a total transformation is fairy-tale in character, because what happens to Duke Frederick and Oliver is miraculous and unforeseen. In fairy tales the miraculous is commonplace, since it offers "the only possible guarantee that the unmorality of reality has ceased to be" (André Jolles, *Einfache Formen* [Tübingen, 1956], p. 203). But even this fairy-tale transformation is marked by the simultaneity of the mutually exclusive. The miracle is miraculous because it is shot through with failure. In the fairy tale, however, such a difference is bridged by miraculous transformations.

15. On the problem of multiple attention, see Anton Ehrenzweig, *The Hidden Order of Art* (Berkeley and Los Angeles, 1971), pp. 22f.

Six. Ulysses and the Reader

1. See Juri M. Lotman, *Struktura Khudozhestvennogo Teksta* (Providence, R. I., 1971), pp. 121ff.

2. See Stuart Gilbert, *James Joyce's Ulysses: A Study* (New York, 1960).

3. See Hermann Broch, *Dichten und Erkennen, Essays I*, (Zurich, 1955), pp. 187f.

Seven. The Pattern of Negativity in Beckett's Prose

1. See Jean-Paul Sartre, *Was ist Literatur*, rde. 65, trans. Hans Georg Brenner (Hamburg, 1958), pp. 52, 64, 82, 94, 98, 138.

2. Ibid, p. 45.

3. See Kenneth Burke, *Language as Symbolic Action* (Berkeley and Los Angeles, 1966), pp. 421ff.

4. For details see Wolfgang Iser, *The Implied Reader: Patterns of Communication from Bunyan to Beckett* (Baltimore, 1987), pp. 164ff.

5. Georg Lukács, *Wider den missverstandenen Realismus* (Hamburg, 1958), p. 31.

6. Maurice Merleau-Ponty, *Das Auge und der Geist: Philosophische Essays*, trans. Hans Werner Arndt (Reinbek, 1967), p. 40.

7. See R. D. Laing, *The Politics of Experience* (Harmondsworth, Eng., 1968), p. 16.

8. See R. D. Laing, H. Phillipson, and A. R. Lee, *Interpersonal Perception: A Theory and a Method of Research* (London, 1966), pp. 49ff.

9. Hans Vaihinger, *Die Philosophie des Als-Ob* (Leipzig, 1922), p. xii.

10. According to Ihab Hassan, (*The Dismemberment of Orpheus: Toward a Postmodern Literature* [New York, 1971], p. 224): "The trilogy . . . marks the highest achievment of Beckett in fiction."

11. For details see Iser, *The Implied Reader*, pp. 164ff. 261ff.

12. Maurice Merleau-Ponty, *Phenomenology of Perception*, trans. Colin Smith (New York, 1962), p. 295.

13. Samuel Beckett, *Malone Dies* (New York, 1965), p. 18.

14. Samuel Beckett, *The Unnamable* (New York, 1958), p. 84.

15. See Beckett, *Malone Dies*, pp. 51, 107; see also Samuel Beckett, *Molloy* (New York, 7 n.d.), p. 118f.

16. See Beckett, *Unnamable*, pp. 37f.

17. Ibid., p. 123.

18. See ibid., pp. 124ff.

19. See Samuel Beckett, *Endgame* (London, 1958), p. 27.

20. Stanley Cavell, *Must We Mean What We Say? A Book of Essays* (New York, 1969), p. 120.

21. For this remark see Hugh Kenner, *Samuel Beckett: A Critical Study* (New York, 1961), p. 165.

22. For psychological aesthetics see I. A. Richards, *Principles of Literary Criticism* (London, 1926).

23. For details see Iser, *The Implied Reader*, pp. 257–73.

24. Frank Kermode, in his *The Sense of an Ending* (New York, 1967), has given an illuminating assessment of this aspect.

25. Merleau-Ponty, *Das Auge und der Geist*, p.80.

26. Cavell, *Must We Mean What We Say?*, p. 149.

27. William York Tindall, (*Samuel Beckett*, Columbia Essays on Modern Writers, no. 4 [New York, 1964], p. 7), attributes this statement to Beckett. The sentence in Tindall reads: "In *Proust*, Beckett says that art, an arrangement of the inexplicable, never explains." Although the passage does not occur verbatim in Beckett's *Proust*, what comes closest is the following: "In this connection Proust can be related to Dostoievsky, who states his characters without explaining them. It may be objected that Proust does little else but explain his characters. But his explanations are experimental and not demonstrative. He explains them in order that they may appear as they are—inexplicable. He explains them away" (Samuel Beckett, *Proust* [New York, 1957], pp. 66f.).

Eight. The Art of Failure

1. Helmuth Plessner, *Lachen und Weinen: Eine Untersuchung nach den Grenzen menschlichen Verhaltens* (Berne, 1950), p. 211.

2. I first noticed this at one of Beckett's own productions in Berlin in 1967. I later compared notes with others who had attended the same performances and productions, and we found that this phenomenon was common to all. The same reaction was to be observed during Beckett's productions in 1973. Newspaper reviews shed little light on the subject, as the laughter of the audience is scarcely described in terms of a reaction but is most frequently and in actual fact mistakenly considered as an integral feature of the play itself. Heinz Ritter's review of 26 February 1965 in *Der Abend* talks of *Godot* as "enigmatic farce"; the two main characters of *Endgame* "actually turn out to be two right cheerful chappies" according to Horst Windelboth in the *Berliner Morgenpost* of 29 September 1967; " 'End of the codswallop,' cried a healthy male voice in relief from the stalls," says a review of *Happy Days* that appeared in the 7 *Uhr-Blatt* of 10 January 1961. Further examples may be found in Ruby Cohn, ed., *Casebook on "Waiting for Godot"* (New York, 1967). This supplements the Berlin reactions quoted with others from Paris, London, Dublin, Miami, and New York. For the connections between absurdity and laughter, see Karl Günter Simon, *Das Absurde lacht sich tot: Kleine Vorschule des modernen Humors* (Munich, 1958), though the comments here remain very generalized.

3. Regarding characteristics and consequences of communal laughter, see Plessner, *Lachen und Weinen*, pp. 195ff.; see also Michail Bachtin, *Literatur und Karneval: Zur Romantheorie und Lachkultur*, trans. Alexander Kaempfe (Munich, 1969), pp. 32–60.

4. See Georg Hensel, "Erfahrungen mit Beckett-Aufführungen," in *Das Werk von Samuel Beckett: Berliner Colloquium*, ed. Hans Mayer and Uwe Johnson (Frankfurt, 1975), p. 208; see also the remarks of the actor Rudi Schmitt, ibid., p. 226.

5. See Jean-Jacques Mayoux, "Beckett und der Humor," in *Beckett: Staatliche Schauspielbühnen Berlins* 25 (1973–74); see also the review by Armin Borski of 20 September 1971, ibid., concerning the Beckett productions; and see, too, the observations of Ruby Cohn, *Back to Beckett* (Princeton, 1973), p. 141.

6. Quotation from Cohn, *Back to Beckett*, p. 152.

7. Ibid., p. 154; also *Materialien zu Becketts "Endspiel": Berichte und Aufsätze* (Frankfurt, 1976), p. 50.

8. Plessner, *Lachen und Weinen*, pp. 14, 43, 87, 89, 149, 155, 198, 203ff.; see also Dieter Wellershoff, "Infantilismus als Revolte oder das ausgeschlagene Erbe—Zur Theorie des Blödelns," in *Das Komische*, ed. Wolfgang Preisendanz and Rainer Warning (Munich, 1976), p. 336.

9. Plessner, *Lachen und Weinen*, pp. 93, 198.

10. Friedrich Nietzsche, *Menschliches, Allzumenschliches*, ed. K. Schlechta (Munich, 1966), 1:558ff.; see also Bachtin, *Literatur und Karneval*, p. 35.

11. Plessner, *Lachen und Weinen*, pp. 189ff.; see also 100ff., where this idea is developed by way of the connections between laughter and play. Regarding the relation between play and seriousness in this context, see also Ludwig Giesz, *Phänomenologie des Kitsches* (Heidelberg, 1960), pp. 97–114.

12. See Harald Weinrich, "Was heisst: 'Lachen ist gesund'?" in *Das Komische*, ed. Preisendanz and Warning, p. 407.

13. Samuel Beckett, *Waiting for Godot* (London, 1959), p. 9.

14. Thomas Metscher, "Geschichte und Mythos bei Beckett," in *Materialien zu Samuel Becketts "Warten auf Godot,"* ed. Ursula Dreysse (Frankfurt, 1973), pp. 54ff.

15. See Juri M. Lotman, *Struktura Khudozhestvennogo Teksta* (Providence, R.I., 1971), pp. 121ff.

16. Rainer Warning, "Elemente einer Pragmasemiotik der Komödie," *Das Komische*, ed. Preisendanz and Warning, p. 284. This essay offers some basic insights into the plot structure of comedy.

17. Ibid., p. 285.

18. See ibid., pp. 296ff., where Warning elaborates on this concept, originally devised by Eduard von Hartmann, in relation to its communicatory function in comedy.

19. The effect of this comic phenomenon is described in more detail by Stanley Cavell, "More of the World Viewed," *Georgia Review* 28 (1974): 579.

20. Warning, "Elemente einer Pragmasemiotik der Komödie," p. 291.

21. Jean-Jacques Mayoux, *Über Beckett*, trans. Ursula Dreysse (Frankfurt, 1966), p. 57; Ruby Cohn, *Samuel Beckett: The Comic Gamut* (New Brunswick, N.J., 1962), pp. 5, 211; Cohn, *Back to Beckett*, p. 130; Renée Riese Hubert, "The Paradox of Silence: Samuel Beckett's Plays," *Mundus Artium: A Journal of International Literature and the Arts* 2 (1968): 85; Hensel, "Erfahrungen mit Beckett-Aufführungen," p. 207. Martin Esslin, *The Theatre of the Absurd* (New York, 1961), pp. 235–37, shows the close relation between vaudeville and the theater of the absurd.

22. Bachtin, *Literatur und Karneval*, pp. 52, 50.

23. Ibid., p. 53.

24. Ibid., p. 54.

25. Sigmund Freud, *Jokes and Their Relation to the Unconscious*, trans. James Strachey (Harmondsworth, Eng., 1976), pp. 146, 188.

26. Ibid., pp. 301ff.

27. See ibid., pp. 173ff., 202ff.; see also the critical comments and the distinctions drawn by Wolfgang Preisendanz, *Über den Witz* (Constance, 1970), pp. 24ff.

28. There is a very illuminating description of the strange mode of

communication that results from this disintegration in Wolfgang Preisendanz, "Zum Vorrang des Komischen bei der Darstellung von Geschichtserfahrung in deutschen Romanen unserer Zeit," *Das Komishe*, ed. Preisendanz and Warning, pp. 160ff.

29. See Cohn, *Back to Beckett*, p. 130; Cohn, *Samuel Beckett: The Comic Gamut*, p. 211; Beryl S. Fletcher et al., *A Student's Guide to the Plays of Samuel Beckett* (London, 1978), pp. 38, 45; Geneviève Serreau, "Beckett's Clowns," in Cohn, ed., *Casebook on "Waiting for Godot,"* pp. 171–75.

30. Joachim Ritter, "Über das Lachen," *Blätter für deutsche Philosophie* 14 (1940–41): 14.

31. Freud, *Jokes*, p. 255.

32. Beckett, *Godot*, p. 12.

33. Ibid., pp. 12ff.

34. Ibid., p. 52.

35. See Esslin, *Theatre of the Absurd*, p. 12, where he quotes Beckett's reply to a question asked by the American director Alan Schneider.

36. For a more detailed discussion, see my essay "Samuel Beckett's Dramatic Language," *Modern Drama* 9 (1966): 251–59.

37. Beckett, *Godot*, p. 13

38. See Martin Esslin, "*Godot* at San Quentin," in Cohn, ed., *Casebook on "Waiting for Godot,"* pp. 83–85.

39. See the material collected in *Casebook on "Waiting for Godot,"* as well as "They Also Serve," *Times Literary Supplement* (London), 10 February 1956, p. 84, and readers' letters from J. M. S. Tompkins, 24 February, p. 117; Katherine M. Wilson, 2 March, p. 133; J. S. Walsh, 9 March, p. 149; Philip H. Bagby, 23 March, p. 181; William Empson, 30 March, p. 195; John J. O'Meara, 6 April, p. 207, and the leading article of 13 April, p. 221. See also Friedrich Hansen-Löves's essay "Samuel Beckett oder die Einübung ins Nichts," *Hochland* 50 (1957–58): 36ff. Günther Anders, *Die Antiquiertheit des Menschen* (Munich, 1956), p. 213, was one of the first to express basic doubts concerning any religious interpretations of this play shortly after its first publication.

40. Plessner, *Lachen und Weinen*, pp. 111ff., 121.

41. One of Ritter's fundamental definitions of comedy; see "Über das Lachen," pp. 9ff.

42. See Hugh Kenner, *Samuel Beckett: A Critical Study* (New York, 1961), p. 165.

43. The degree to which the comic is always directed toward the totality of existence is dealt with most thoroughly by Ritter, "Über das Lachen," pp. 7, 9.

44. Freud, *Jokes*, p. 300.

45. Ritter, "Über das Lachen," p. 15.

46. Ibid.

47. Plessner, *Lachen und Weinen*, p. 89.

48. Ibid., p. 90.

49. Freud, *Jokes*, p.228, n.1.

50. Samuel Beckett, *Watt* (New York, 1959), p. 48. Regarding the conception of comic characters and their roles as clowns in Beckett's novels, see Yasunari Takahashi, "Fool's Progress," *in Samuel Beckett: A Collection of Criticism*, ed. Ruby Cohn (New York, 1975), pp. 33–40.

51. *Materialien zu Becketts "Endspiel,"* p. 65. The actors also have the impression that the play is "continually comic" (p. 29).

52. Ibid., p. 65.

53. Ibid., pp. 67ff.

54. Samuel Beckett, *Endgame* (London, 1958), pp. 11ff.

55. Jacques Derrida, *Die Schrift und die Differenz.* trans Ulrich Köppen (Frankfurt, 1972), gives in this collection of essays an analysis of Artaud entitled "Das Theater der Grausamkeit und die Geschlossenheit der Repräsentation," pp. 351–79, where he develops the idea of the end of representation as a predominant feature of modern drama.

56. *Materialien zu Becketts "Endspiel,"* p. 6.

57. Ibid.

58. Beckett, *Endgame*, pp. 50ff.

59. Gabriele Schwab analyzes this problem in depth and pursues its consequences in *Samuel Becketts Endspiel mit der Subjektivität: Entwurf einer Psychoästhetik des modernen Theaters* (Stuttgart, 1981).

60. Beckett, *Endgame*, p. 27.

61. Substitute is, for Freud, "the core of the technique of verbal jokes" and "the joke-work makes use of deviations from normal thinking—of displacement and absurdity—as technical methods for producing a joking form of expression" (*Jokes*, pp. 130, 97). However, here displacement and absurdity are applied not to a particular social code that is to be affected by the joke, but to "normal thinking" itself.

62. Helmuth Plessner summarizes this basic condition of the self as follows: "I am, but I do not have myself." See "Die anthropologische Dimension der Geschichtlichkeit," in *Sozialer Wandel: Zivilisation und Fortschritt als Kategorien der soziologischen Theorie*, ed. Hans Peter Dreitzel (Neuwied, 1972), p. 160.

63. See the detailed discussion in Schwab, *Endspiel mit der Subjektivität*, the chapter entitled "Projektion und Dezentrierung des Subjekts," pp. 54–62.

64. See Beckett, *Endgame*, p.39 and elsewhere.

65. For further details and the resultant demands made on modern literature, see Michel Foucault, *The Order of Things* (New York, 1970), pp. 382f.; see also Derrida, *Die Schrift und die Differenz*, pp. 17f.

66. Schwab, *Endspiel mit der Subjektivität*, p. 27.

67. Paul Ricoeur, *The Conflict of Interpretations: Essays in Hermeneutics*, ed. Don Ihde (Evanston, Ill., 1974), pp. 63, 69ff. The term *double meaning* is used here in accordance with Ricoeur's use of it.

68. Ibid., p. 66.

69. Ibid.

70. See Stanley Cavell, *Must We Mean What We Say?* (New York, 1969), pp. 12, 32ff.

71. "Me—(*he yawns*)—to play" is Hamm's first utterance in *Endgame* (p. 12), and this is echoed at the end: "Since that's the way we're playing it . . . let's play it that way" (p. 52).

72. Michel Foucault, *Language, Counter-Memory, Practice: Selected Essays and Interviews*, trans. Donald F. Bouchard and Sherry Simon (Oxford, 1977), p. 53.

73. On this relationship between happiness and plight, and their mutually exclusive presence in the real world, see Dieter Henrich, "Glück und Not," in *Positionen der Negativität*, ed. Harald Weinrich (Munich, 1975), pp. 512–18.

74. Beckett, *Endgame*, p. 51.

75. Henrich (*Positionen der Negativität*, ed. Weinrich, p. 515) suggests that "the knowledge of plight and the knowledge of happiness are related to each other in a figure and ground pattern."

76. Beckett, *Endgame*, p. 12.

77. Ibid., p. 51.

78. Foucault, *The Order of Things*, pp. 238ff.

79. I. M. Schlesinger, "Production of Utterance and Language Acquisition," in *The Ontogenesis of Grammar*, ed. Dan I. Slobin (New York, 1971), p. 68, quoted by Hans Hörmann, *Meinen und Verstehen: Grundzüge einer psychologischen Semantik* (Frankfurt, 1976), p. 201.

80. Hörmann, *Meinen und Verstehen*, p. 187.

81. Ibid.

82. See ibid., pp. 187, 192–96, 198, 207, 241, 253, 403ff., 500.

83. Ibid., p. 214.

84. See ibid., p. 198.

85. F. C. Bartlett, *Remembering* (Cambridge, 1932), quoted by Hörmann, *Meinen und Verstehen*, p. 196.

86. It is therefore impossible for a grammar based on the sentence as the ultimate unit to grasp such a fact. The famous example given by generative grammarians—"Colourless green ideas sleep furiously"—meets the criterion of syntactic correctness but fails to meet that of connectability of different semantic units; however, this in no way excludes the possibility that such a sentence might, in the right context, take on a specific meaning. One could conceive of a context that would endow this sentence with a comparatively rich meaning. For example, if it occurred during the description of a dream, the mutually exclusive qualifications of the "ideas" might indicate the change in the colors of the dream—a change that would then take on a particular dramatic quality through the adverb "furiously." Indeed, one can imagine contexts in which this sentence would assume a poetic quality if, for instance, it were to evoke a de-automatization of our relations to the world. This is why we in fact find such "semantically

irreconcilable word combinations" so frequently in nonsense poetry and Dada.

> The decision as to whether two units of meaning are reconcilable or not clearly does *not* depend automatically on any criterion inherent and hence firmly rooted in these units; the decision is taken by a speaker or listener who stands in a particular situation, knows something about it, expects something, and tends to understand heard sentences even if perhaps they do not contain normal combinations of words; the "language" gives him the chance to follow this tendency for given periods, so long as "experience and imagination" allow him to. The criterion for what is permissible or normal therefore shifts from language in itself to the person who uses language for himself. (Hörmann, *Meinen und Verstehen*, pp. 182ff.)

87. Ibid., p. 500.

88. Ibid., p. 210.

89. Ibid., p. 506.

90. Ibid., p. 500.

91. On the function of the blank in relation to the act of communication, see my book *The Act of Reading: A Theory of Aesthetic Response* (Baltimore, 1978), pp. 180–203.

92. Theodor W. Adorno's essay "Versuch, das *Endspiel* zu verstehen," in *Noten zur Literatur II* (Frankfurt, 1961), pp. 188–236, is in many respects a typical example. The "difficulties" are shown, for instance, as follows: "Interpretation of *Endgame* cannot therefore go off on the wild goose chase of seeking to convey its meaning philosophically. Understanding it can only mean understanding its incomprehensibility and concretely reconstructing the one coherent meaning, which is that there is no coherent meaning" (p. 190). But the limits of representability need not be meaninglessness; it is only that so long as the double meaning embodies the be-all and the end-all which appears to be such an inalienable pattern of language use that its artistic disintegration defies comprehension. If one clings to the classical ideal of representation, one must come up with such judgments as "While Kafka beheaded or confused meanings, Beckett calls a halt to the bad infinity of intentions: their sense is senselessness. That is objectively, without any polemic intention, his answer to the philosophy of existence, which declares meaninglessness itself—under the name of 'thrownness' and later absurdity—to equal meaning, under the protection of the equivocations brought about by the concept of meaning. Beckett draws no contrasting world view, but simply takes it literally" (pp. 202ff.). "Meaning nothing becomes the only meaning" (p. 216). These and similar statements evince norms of a specific paradigm of interpretation, whose validity is simply taken for granted here. But it is the unquestionable acceptance of classical norms of interpretation that provides the presupposed attitude on which Beckett's plays depend for their effectiveness. Adorno's essay provides clear, though certainly involuntary, evidence of this fact.

93. The clash of meanings is variously prestructured in the text. Like

Godot, Endgame is shot through with allusions to biblical events and theological arguments:

> The last move of Hamm's game is to cover his face with the blood-stained handkerchief of the opening tableau. The recollection is of St. Veronica's handkerchief stamped with Christ's features (already used in earlier Beckett works). The suggestion is that Hamm's life is a Passion, also consummated at Golgotha, the place of a skull. But if Hamm's death closes the play, is there a resurrection? Perhaps *Endgame*, with characteristic Beckett ambivalence, implies two resurrections—one occurring just after the curtain rises, and one just after it finally falls. As has been mentioned, the opening action, silent except for five brief laughs (possibly recalling Christ's five wounds?), is performed like a mock-ritual. (Cohn, *Samuel Beckett: The Comic Gamut*, p. 239)

As Cohn's reaction shows, such allusions lead one to expand on the reference, but in doing so one only produces an insoluble ambivalence. And so the realization of the suggested "meaning" does not result in its assumed fulfillment, but rather in a subversion of the very meaning arrived at. This is ensured by the context within which the realized reference has to be accommodated. Either the context trivializes the reference, or the reference begins to permeate the context with increasing obfuscation. The resultant network of connections continually demands semantic expansions or, alternatively, semantic reductions, thus giving rise to an unending sense of mutually destructive meaning. Another strategy is developed through the names in *Endgame*:

> In *Endgame*, there are apparently no believers—neither those who see (however dimly) nor blind Hamm. The onstage prayer, which Beckett refused to change upon request of the London censor, goes unanswered. The nails leave no print, or their print is perhaps no longer evidence for belief. Several critics have pointed out that Clov is *clou*, "nail," that Nell and Nagg derive from Germanic *naegel*, meaning "nail." To these might be added the offstage Mother Pegg, for a "peg" is also a nail. Latin *hamus* is hook, a kind of crooked nail, so that Hamm may be viewed as another nail. In this sense, every proper name in *Endgame* is a nail, and "nailhood" seems sardonically to symbolize humanity, whose role is to nail Christ to the Cross. All the characters are thus instruments working towards the play's paradoxical opening word, "Finished." But Hamm is also contained in "hammer," which strikes at nails, and is thus an even more active agent in the crucifying. If Hamm is a Christ figure, he is also a crucifier. Hamm as biblical *Ham*, as Latin *hamus*, as contained in "hammer," indicates a revival of Beckett's early taste for puns. The twisted quotation of *Murphy*, "In the beginning was the pun," parodies the opening sentence of the Gospel of St. John: "In the beginning was the Word, and the Word was with God, and the Word was God." In *Endgame*, words serve to form not only puns but jokes, prayers, proverbs, prophecies, maledictions, chronicles, poems, and, of course, the dialogue of the play. (Joyce called words "quashed quotatoes, messes of mottage.") Clov accuses Hamm, the wielder of words, "I use the words you taught me. If they don't mean anything any more, teach me others." Near the end, Clov complains, "They [the words that remain] have nothing to say.' " (Cohn, *Samuel Beckett: the Comic Gamut*, p. 233; cf. pp. 230ff.)

NOTES TO PAGE 188

The network of connections woven by the connatations of the individual names may be regarded as a paradigm for the variety of possible interpretations of *Endgame*. The variety, however, does not mean that every connection can be woven at the same time as all the others; at any one moment, there will be one set of connections that excludes or cancels out another. Every interpretation aims at establishing a fixed meaning, because meaning only *becomes* meaning through its own precision, and so each interpretation gains its validity at the cost of those that it excludes. The necessary precision of each interpretation requires a selection from the variety of options contained in the network of connections and therefore can only establish itself by ruling others out. Thus, any attempt at exhausting the possibilities of meanings potentially contained in the network would inevitably result in a clash; it is this continual clash of meaning—brought about by the required precision—that provides the basis for the impact the play is able to exercise. In this context, Stanley Cavell's comment on *Endgame*, on p. 117 of *Must We Mean What We Say?*, takes on its full significance: "The discovery of *Endgame*, both in topic and technique, is not the failure of meaning (if that means the lack of meaning) but its total, even totalitarian, success—our inability *not* to mean what we are given to mean." And this leads to the consequence Cavell expresses most succinctly: "Art begins where explanations leave off, or before they start. Not everything has an explanation, and people will give themselves *some* consolation. The imagination must have something to contain it—to drip into, as it were—or we must be mad. Hamm is in both positions" (p. 143).

94. See Ruby Cohn, "The Laughter of Sad Sam Beckett," in *Samuel Beckett Now: Critical Approaches to His Novels, Poetry, and Plays*, ed. Melvin J. Friedman (Chicago, 1975), p. 189. The frequency with which the characters laugh in *Endgame* is exactly twice that of the characters in *Godot*: the ratio is 16:8.

95. See Beckett, *Endgame*, pp. 35, 40. When Clov looks through his telescope at the audience, he says: "I see . . . a . . . multitude . . . in transports . . . of joy" (p. 25; the ellipsis points are in the text). But this must be the exact opposite of the audience's visible reactions.

96. In this context there is an apt remark by Cohn, *Samuel Beckett: The Comic Gamut*, p. 7: "Commitment is comic, but it is also compulsive for the Beckett hero." On the one hand we have the awareness that, in the last analysis, all actions and attitudes are commitments that prove to be of an inevitably restricted nature, because they depend on certain preconditions. But on the other hand, we can only have this experience through a series of commitments. As the characters talk, these commitments occur by way of the spoken word. Awareness of this unavoidable state of affairs comes about through the comic devaluation of the commitments, and this comic devaluation takes place in the continued failure of the spoken word.

97. See John Dewey, *Art as Experience* (New York, 1959), pp. 56ff.,

272; see also the development of this argument in my book *The Act of Reading*, pp. 132ff.

98. Beckett's relation to Cartesian positions is discussed in detail by Raymond Federman, *Journey to Chaos: Samuel Beckett's Early Fiction* (Berkeley and Los Angeles, 1965), as well as by Kenner, *Samuel Beckett*.

Nine. Changing Functions of Literature

This chapter was first given as a public lecture in winter 1980/81 at the Hochschule für Wirtschafts- und Sozialwissenschaften St. Gallen as part of the program "History and Future," and subsequently published in the series *Aulavorträge*.

1. Tristan Tzara, *Lampisteries précédées des sept manifestes dada* (Paris, 1963), p. 64.

2. See Maurice Nadeau, *The History of Surrealism*, trans. Richard Howard (New York, 1965), p. 304. The quotation from Breton is in "Les Vases Communicants" (1932).

3. Quoted by Peter Schneider, "Die Phantasie im Spätkapitalismus und die Kulturrevolution," *Kursbuch* 16 (March 1969): 1.

4. Ibid., p. 31.

5. Ibid., p. 4.

6. See Kurt Batt, *Revolte Intern: Betrachtungen zur Literatur in der BRD* (Leipzig, 1974), p. 51. On the wider significance of revolution in the twentieth century, see Karel Teige, *Liquidierung der "Kunst": Analysen, Manifeste* (Frankfurt am Main, 1968).

7. See Batt, *Revolte Intern*, p. 27.

8. Hans Blumenberg, *Arbeit am Mythos* (Frankfurt am Main, 1979), p. 179 (my translation). This statement refers explicitly to the proclamation made during the Paris revolt of May 1968 that fantasy had come to power.

9. See Hans Georg Gadamer, "Zur Fragwürdigkeit des ästhetischen Bewusstseins," *Rivista di Estetica* 3, no. 3 (1958): 378.

10. E. M. Wilkinson and L. A. Willoughby, eds., *Friedrich Schiller: On the Aesthetic Education of Man* (Oxford, 1967), have proposed "play-drive" as a translation for *Spieltrieb*, "formal drive" for *Formtrieb*, and "sensuous drive" for *Stofftrieb*. For reference see Hazard Adams, ed., *Critical Theory since Plato* (New York, 1971), p. 417. Thomas Carlyle, *Critical and Miscellaneous Essays*, Centenary Edition (London, 1899), 2: 201, suggests "sport-impulse" as a rendering for *Spieltrieb*.

11. See Hans Georg Gadamer, *Wahrheit und Methode: Grundzüge einer philosophischen Hermeneutik* (Tübingen, 1960), p. 78. He supplies a detailed explanation of the nineteenth-century ideal of art.

12. Thomas Carlyle, *On Heroes, Hero-Worship, and the Heroic in History*, Everyman's Library (London, 1948), p. 391.

13. See ibid., p. 385.

14. Matthew Arnold, *Lectures and Essays in Criticism*, vol. 3 of *The Complete Prose Works*, ed. R. H. Super (Ann Arbor, Mich., 1962), p. 280.

15. Ibid., p. 275.

16. Ibid., p. 285.

17. Walter Pater, *The Renaissance: Studies in Art and Poetry* (London, 1919), pp. 238–39.

18. Blumenberg, *Arbeit am Mythos*, p. 382 (my translation).

19. See Walter Pater, *Appreciations: With an Essay on Style* (London, 1920), p. 241.

20. Herbert Marcuse, *Kultur und Gesellschaft 1* (Frankfurt am Main, 1968), p. 71 (my translation).

21. Ernest Jones, *The Life and Work of Sigmund Freud*, edited and abridged in one volume by Lionel Trilling and Steven Marcus (New York, 1961), p. 480. Freud made this remark to U.S. ambassador Bullitt, who recounted it in English.

22. *McLuhan: Hot and Cool. A Primer for the Understanding of and a Critical Symposium with a Rebuttal by McLuhan*, ed. Gerald E. Stearn (New York, 1967), p. 143.

23. The idea of the imaginary museum was devised and developed by André Malraux in "Museum Without Walls," pt. 1 of *The Voices of Silence*, trans. Stuart Gilbert (New York, 1953) from *Les Voix du Silence* (Paris, 1951).

24. Dieter Wellershoff, *Literatur und Lustprinzip* (Cologne, 1973), p. 12 (my translation).

25. Theodor W. Adorno, *Ästhetische Theorie, Gesammelte Schriften* (Frankfurt am Main, 1970), 7:347 (my translation).

26. See Friedrich Nietzsche, *Die Geburt der Tragödie*, vol. 2 of *Werke*, ed. Karl Schlechta (Munich, 1977), pp. 98, 108. See also Blumenberg, *Arbeit am Mythos*, p. 369.

27. See Helmuth Plessner, "Die anthropologische Dimension der Geschichtlichkeit," in *Sozialer Wandel: Zivilisation und Fortschritt als Kategorien der soziologischen Theorie*, ed. Hans Peter Dreitzel (Neuwied, 1972), p. 160. He describes the human situation as "I am, but I do not have myself" (my translation).

Ten.   Key Concepts in Current Literary Theory

1. For a more detailed account, see my essay "Literaturwissenschaft in Konstanz," in *Gebremste Reform: Ein Kapitel deutscher Hochschulgeschichte. Universität Konstanz 1966–1976*, ed. Hans Robert Jauss and Herbert Nesselhauf (Constance, 1977), pp. 181–200.

2. Jost Hermand, *Synthetisches Interpretieren: Zur Methodik der Literaturwissenschaft* (Munich, 1968), pp. 231ff.

3. Ibid., p. 239.

4. Wolf-Dieter Stempel, *Gestalt, Ganzheit, Struktur: Aus der Vor- und Frühgeschichte des Strukturalismus in Deutschland* (Göttingen, 1978), p. 2.

5. Jurij Striedter, "Zur formalistischen Theorie der Prosa und der literarischen Evolution," in *Texte der russischen Formalisten I*, Theorie und Geschichte der Literatur und der Schönen Künste no. 6, ed. Jurij Striedter (Munich, 1969), p. xxvii.

6. See Jonathan Culler, *Structuralist Poetics: Structuralism, Linguistics and the Study of Literature* (Ithaca, 1975), pp. 32–109.

7. See the revealing example given by Harald Weinrich, "Interferenz bei Farbnamen: das Farbwort *bleu*," in *Sprachliche Interferenz: Festschrift für Werner Betz*, ed. Herbert Kolb and Hartmut Lauffer (Tübingen, 1977), pp. 267–77.

8. Culler gives voice to a similar suspicion in *Structuralist Poetics*, pp. 96–109.

9. Umberto Eco, *Einführung in die Semiotik*, UTB 105, trans. Jürgen Trabant (Munich, 1972), p. 411.

10. Culler, *Structuralist Poetics*, p. 265.

11. Hans Hörmann, *Meinen und Verstehen: Grundzüge einer psychologischen Semantik* (Frankfurt, 1976), p. 210.

12. Niklas Luhmann, *Soziologische Aufklärung: Aufsätze zur Theorie der sozialen Systeme* (Opladen, 1971), p. 114.

13. Ibid., p. 39.

14. Striedter, "Zur formalistischen Theorie der Prosa," p. xxiii.

15. Christian Enzensberger, *Literatur und Interesse I: Eine politische Ästhetik mit zwei Beispielen aus der englischen Literatur* (Munich, 1977), p. 141.

16. I have tried to devise a model in my book *The Act of Reading: A Theory of Aesthetic Response* (Baltimore, 1978), pp. 51–103, in order to assess this function.

17. See ibid., pp. 160–231.

18. Culler, *Structuralist Poetics*, p. 143.

19. See Morris Weitz, "The Role of Theory in Aesthetics," in *Philosophy Looks at the Arts*, ed. Joseph Margolis (New York, 1962), pp. 48–59.

20. On the structure of double meaning, see Paul Ricoeur, *Hermeneutik und Strukturalismus: Der Konflikt der Interpretationen I*, trans. Johannes Rütsche (Munich, 1973), pp. 81–100.

Eleven. Representation

1. "Feigning in Fiction," in *The Identity of the Literary Text*, ed. Mario J. Valdés and Owen Miller (Toronto, 1985), pp. 204–28.

2. For the significance of that concept see Maurice Merleau-Ponty, *Das*

Auge und der Geist, trans. Hans Werner Arndt (Hamburg, 1967), p. 84.

3. Anton Ehrenzweig, *The Hidden Order of Art* (Berkeley and Los Angeles, 1967), pp. 120f.

4. See Hans Vaihinger, *Die Philosophie des Als-Ob* (Leipzig, 1922), pp. 219–30.

5. Ibid., pp. xii, 290ff.

6. Nelson Goodman, *Ways of Worldmaking* (Hassocks, 1978), p. 102.

7. G. W. F. Hegel, *Ästhetik,* ed. Friedrich Bassenge (Berlin, 1955), p. 146.

8. As has been suggested by Odo Marquard, "Das Fiktive als Ens Realissimum," in *Funktionen des Fiktiven,* Poetik und Hermeneutik, 10, ed. Dieter Henrich and Wolfgang Iser (Munich, 1983), p. 491.

9. See Helmuth Plessner, "Die anthropologische Dimension der Geschichtlichkeit," in *Sozialer Wandel: Zivilisation und Fortschritt als Kategorien der soziologischen Theorie,* ed. Hans Peter Dreitzel (Neuwied, 1972), p. 160.

10. See Samuel Beckett, *Malone Dies* (New York, 1956), pp. 18f.

11. Cf. Frank Kermode, *The Sense of an Ending* (New York, 1967), pp. 82ff.

Twelve. The Play of the Text

1. See Michel Foucault, *The Order of Things* (New York, 1970), pp. 217–49, and Jacques Derrida, *Writing and Difference,* trans. Alan Bass (London, 1978), especially the essay on Artaud. For a detailed exploration of that issue see Gabriele Schwab, *Samuel Becketts Endspiel mit der Subjektivität: Entwurf einer Psychoästhetik des modernen Theaters* (Stuttgart, 1981), pp. 14–34.

2. See E. H. Gombrich, *Art and Illusion: A Study in the Psychology of Pictorial Representation* (London, 1962), especially pp. 154–244.

3. Peter Hutchinson, *Games Authors Play* (London, 1983), provides a catalogue of the various games played in literary texts.

4. See Johan Huizinga, *Homo Ludens: Vom Ursprung der Kultur im Spiel,* rowohlts deutsche enzyklopädie (Hamburg, 1956), pp. 9–14.

5. Gregory Bateson, *Steps to an Ecology of the Mind* (New York, 1972), p. 315.

6. See Jean Piaget, *Nachahmung, Spiel und Traum,* Gesammelte Werke 5, trans. Leo Montada (Stuttgart, 1975), pp. 178–216.

7. Roger Caillois, *Man, Play, and Games,* trans. Meyer Barash (Glencoe N.Y., 1961), p. viii.

8. See Erving Goffman, *The Presentation of Self in Everyday Life* (Garden City, N.Y., 1959), pp. 8f., 141–66.

9. See Manfred Eigen and Ruthhild Winkler, *Das Spiel: Naturgesetze steuern den Zufall* (Munich, 1985), pp. 87–121.

Thirteen. Toward a Literary Anthropology

1. See Edmund Burke, *A Philosophical Inquiry into the Origin of our Ideas of the Sublime and the Beautiful*, vol. 1 of *The Works* (London, 1899), pp. 110, 130, 140, 164, 192, 218, 233.

2. See *Bentham's Theory of Fictions*, ed. C. K. Ogden, (Paterson, N. J., 1959), pp. 30, 49ff, 154.

3. See Hans Vaihinger, *Die Philosophie des Als-Ob* (Leipzig, 1922), pp. xii, 194–219.

4. Ibid., p. iv.

5. Frank Kermode has advanced this concept in his important book *The Sense of an Ending: Studies in the Theory of Fiction* (New York, 1967) and has also given a very illuminating account of its history.

6. Francis Bacon, *The Advancement of Learning and New Atlantis*, ed. Thomas Case (London, 1974), p. 96.

7. Kermode, *The Sense of an Ending*, p. 64.

8. See Vaihinger, *Die Philosophie des Als-Ob*, pp. 219–30.

9. Compare for instance the essays devoted to the study of fiction in issues 1 and 2 of *Poetics* 8 (1979).

10. For detail see Nelson Goodman, *Ways of Worldmaking* (Hassocks, 1978), esp. pp. 10–17, 101f.

11. Maurice Merleau-Ponty, *Das Auge und der Geist: Philosophische Essays*, trans. H. W. Arndt (Reinbek, 1967), p. 84. Merleau-Ponty considers this a basic criterion for an art work.

12. David Hume, *A Treatise of Human Nature*, ed. L. A. Selby-Bigge, (Oxford, 1968), p. 24.

13. P. F. Strawson, "Imagination and Perception," in *Experience and Theory*, ed. Lawrence Foster and J. W. Swanson (Amherst, Mass., 1970), p. 43.

14. Mary Warnock, *Imagination* (Berkeley and Los Angeles, 1978), p. 192.

15. See Jean-Paul Sartre, *Das Imaginäre: Phänomenologische Psychologie der Einbeldungskraft*, trans. Hans Schöneberg (Hamburg, 1971), pp. 263ff.

16. Wolfgang Iser, "Feigning in Fiction," in *Identity of the Literary Text*, ed. Mario J. Valdés and Owen Miller (Toronto, 1985), pp. 204–28.

17. I have dealt with that issue in "Changing Functions of Literature," chapter 9 in this volume.

18. Ibid., pp. 205ff.

19. See Theodor W. Adorno, *Negative Dialektik* (Frankfurt, 1966), p. 389.

20. This idea has been given very strong support by the Czech Marxist Karel Kosík, *Die Dialektik des Konkreten: Eine Studie zur Problematik des Menschen und der Welt*, trans. Marianne Hoffmann (Frankfurt, 1967), esp. pp. 123ff.

Index of Names

Index of Subjects

Act of reading, 4, 7, 8, 16, 288, 289, 301, 306

Aesthetic, 127, 131, 132, 148, 152, 162, 164, 197, 200, 204, 209, 231, 237, 241, 247, 272; character, 246; consciousness, 204, 209; education, 304; effect, 19, 20, 51, 62; experience, 24, 138, 139, 169, 192, 230; expression, 199; function, 139, 153; object, 37, 38, 40, 45, 47, 53, 55, 56, 65, 132, 168, 169, 170, 175, 184, 234; pleasure, 244; response, 9, 133, 288, 289, 301, 306; structure, 5; tension, 242; value, 228

Aesthetics, 264; Marxist, 226; of reception, 221; of response, 221

Agon, 255, 256, 257, 258

Alea, 255, 256, 257, 258

Allegory, 19, 20, 27, 28, 79, 80, 124

Anthropological, 162, 186, 244; factor, 185, 186; framework, 152; makeup, VII, 126, 246, 253, 264, 270; need, 245, 264; root, 239, 265

Anthropology, 37; cultural, 213, 234, 265; literary, VII, VIII, 261, 264, 273, 274, 278, 279, 280, 281, 282, 283, 284

Arcadia, 73–75, 78–80, 90, 94–96, 104, 107, 128, 290

Art, 74, 90, 91, 131, 132, 148, 151, 170, 176, 193, 211, 216, 218, 219, 226, 227, 239, 250, 275, 285, 286, 287, 288, 294, 295, 303; for art's sake, 203; autonomous, 202–6, 210, 264; as beautiful semblance, 201, 202; erotics of, 3; function of, 90, 92, 93, 152, 176, 192; and literature, 132, 280, 282; and nature, 199, 200; and reality, 91, 98, 133, 200; religion of, 204; as response, 92

Beauty/beautiful, 47, 203, 227, 243, 265

Beckett, S.: All That Fall, 143; End-game, 143, 146, 150, 152, 153, 171, 172, 176–78, 180–82, 184–90, 192, 193, 295, 296, 299, 300, 302, 303; Happy Days, 143, 152, 153, 171, 172, 296; Imagination Dead Imagine, 141; Malone Dies, 143, 295, 307; Molloy, 143, 146, 295; Murphy, 144, 302; Proust, 295; The Unnamable, 143, 146, 295; Waiting for Godot, 143, 152, 153, 157–60, 162, 165, 166, 168, 169, 172, 176, 177, 181, 189, 296–98, 302; Watt, 173, 299

Blank, See Gap/Blank

Breton, A., Les vases communicants, 304

Carnivalization, 115, 126, 161, 162, 163, 168, 256, 293, 296, 297

Cervantes, M., Don Quixote, 96

Combination, 10, 80, 238, 241, 242, 257, 270, 271, 277, 291, 301

Communication, 151, 155, 163, 192, 220, 221, 230, 231, 286, 287, 289, 294, 297; act of, 12, 68, 301; artistic, 4; concept, 228, 229, 233; literary, 46, 61, 84; mode of, 146; and negativity, 141–44; process, 15, 31, 33, 34, 135, 287

Concord-fiction, 266, 267

Consistency, 27, 47, 53–56, 62, 147

Contingency, 210, 212

Countersense, 184, 185, 186

Dada/Dadaism, 185, 198, 199, 208, 301

Decentered, 120, 130, 252; position, 213, 244, 247; subjectivity, 193

Defoe, D., Serious Reflections, 74, 290

Dickens, C.: Martin Chuzzlewit, 286; Oliver Twist, 14, 287

Difference, 75, 76, 79, 98, 101, 104, 107, 108, 111, 112, 115, 116, 118, 120, 122, 126, 127, 130, 170, 172, 185, 213, 222, 241–43, 245, 251–53, 255, 257, 272, 278, 299

Discourse, 5, 139, 274, 278, 293;

Malraux, A., *Museum without Walls*, 305

Marxism, 221, 227, 264

Marxist mirror-reflection theory, 136

Meaning-constant, 185–86

Meaning of meaning, 225

Metaphor, 66, 67, 89, 219–20, 223

Mimesis, 127, 236, 243, 249–50, 282

Mimicry, 255, 256, 258

Minus function, 133, 158, 161–63, 168, 181, 184, 223

Mirror/mirroring, 5, 7, 18, 79, 80, 87, 96, 104, 105, 107, 109, 112, 122, 125, 136, 182, 241, 245, 263, 275, 276, 279, 280, 282, 283

Multiple attention, 128–30, 294

Myth, 73, 151, 212, 213, 266

Negation, 34, 93, 101–2, 140, 141, 143, 149, 155, 162, 200, 202, 242

Negativity, 140–44, 182–84, 259, 294, 300

Oscillation, 8, 138, 237, 239, 240, 247, 248, 255, 271, 272

Pastoral poetry, 73–75, 76–80, 81, 82, 83, 89, 94, 120, 290

Perception, 4, 24, 25, 31, 47, 48, 51, 56, 128, 129, 132, 133, 137, 160, 163, 173, 212, 220, 226, 227, 229, 249, 260, 273, 274, 278, 280, 283, 288, 295, 308

Performance, 6, 15, 18, 19, 21, 127, 130, 180, 191, 192, 236, 243, 244, 248, 258

Perspective, 7, 12, 21, 25, 80, 89, 90, 137, 149, 155, 173, 277; abundance of, 26; central, 133; changing of, 55, 87, 135, 136; of indeterminacy, 28; reader-oriented, 13, 57; status of, 87; textual, 34, 35, 37, 39, 54

Phenomenological theory, 68, 219, 221

Play, 105, 117, 176, 178, 201, 250, 251, 252, 255, 261, 279, 294, 297; acting, 20, 187, 188; duality of, 253; form of, 245; language, 181; movement, 254; within the play, 125–27; role playing, 64, 122, 183, 244, 257; staged, 258; strategies of, 256; of the text, 258–

60; of transformation, 278; on words, 99, 100; world, 107, 109

Poetic passion, 203

Polyphonic harmony, 219, 220, 286

Projection, 9, 10, 27, 28, 30, 34, 36, 134, 142, 143, 146, 147, 166, 187, 189, 190, 191, 193, 255

Psychoanalysis, 49, 68, 221, 239, 264, 265

Reader-in-the-text, 3, 63, 137, 140, 146–48, 287

Reader response, VII, VIII, 7, 12, 14, 42, 43, 47, 49, 50, 132, 135, 148, 285

Realistic novel, 17, 27, 135, 203

Representation, VIII, 8, 38, 74, 98, 111–12, 116, 118–20, 125–27, 130, 133, 134, 136, 157, 176–81, 183, 185, 186, 188, 189, 190, 192, 205, 213, 221, 232, 236, 237, 241–44, 248–50, 252, 257, 258, 282, 307; function of, 137, 180, 186, 199; self-representation, 179

Response, 5, 45, 50, 51, 56, 58, 128, 148, 171, 173, 174, 185, 191; act of, 135–36; aesthetic, VII, 9, 133, 221; affective, 58; audience, 166, 168, 176; crisis, 156; literary, 4, 5, 46, 48, 50, 286; pattern, 187, 192, 193; subjective, 68; theory of, 43, 50

Richardson, S., *Pamela*, 15

Russian Formalists, 226, 227

Saint-Beuve, Ch., *Temple du Goût*, 205

Satire, 17, 148, 156

Schemata, 9, 34, 35, 45, 46, 48, 51, 52, 65, 85, 128, 135, 137, 138, 187, 219, 220, 250, 254, 255, 256, 257, 258, 276

Schiller, F., *On the Aesthetic Education of Man*, 201, 304

Selection, 23, 25, 82, 102, 226, 229, 237, 238, 241, 270, 271

Semblance, 242; aesthetic, 243, 244, 245, 246, 248

Serial story, 10, 11, 286, 287

Shakespeare, W.: *As You Like It*, 98, 293; *The Comedy of Errors*, 48; *Hamlet*, 60; *Macbeth*, 246

Sign, 193, 224, 226, 233, 263, 279

Social theory, 264

Designed by Chris L. Smith
Composed by Capitol Communications, Inc., in Sabon text and display
Printed by Thomson-Shore, Inc. on 50-lb. Warren's Sebago Eggshell Cream Offset
paper and bound in Holliston's Roxite A